Conversions

Conversions

GENDER AND RELIGIOUS CHANGE IN EARLY MODERN EUROPE

Edited by Simon Ditchfield and Helen Smith

MANCHESTER UNIVERSITY PRESS

Copyright © Manchester University Press 2017

While copyright in the volume as a whole is vested in Manchester University Press, copyright in individual chapters belongs to their respective authors, and no chapter may be reproduced wholly or in part without the express permission in writing of both author and publisher.

Published by Manchester University Press
Altrincham Street, Manchester M1 7JA

www.manchesteruniversitypress.co.uk

British Library Cataloguing-in-Publication Data
A catalogue record for this book is available from the British Library

ISBN 978 0719 09915 1 hardback
ISBN 978 1 5261 4355 6 paperback

First published by Manchester University Press in hardback 2017
This edition first published 2019

The publisher has no responsibility for the persistence or accuracy of URLs for any external or third-party internet websites referred to in this book, and does not guarantee that any content on such websites is, or will remain, accurate or appropriate.

Typeset by
Servis Filmsetting Ltd, Stockport, Cheshire

Contents

~

Lists of figures and tables   vii
Notes on contributors   ix
Acknowledgements   xv

Introduction – *Simon Ditchfield and Helen Smith*   1

Part I: Gendering conversion

1   To piety or conversion more prone? Gender and conversion in the early modern Mediterranean – *Eric Dursteler*   21

2   The quiet conversion of a 'Jewish' woman in eighteenth-century Spain – *David Graizbord*   41

3   'A father to the soul and a son to the body': gender and generation in Robert Southwell's *Epistle to his father* – *Hannah Crawforth*   61

4   Gender and reproduction in the *Spirituall experiences* – *Abigail Shinn*   81

Part II: Material conversions

5   'The needle may convert more than the pen': women and the work of conversion in early modern England – *Claire Canavan and Helen Smith*   105

6   Uneven conversions: how did laywomen become nuns in the early modern world?– *Elizabeth A. Lehfeldt*   127

7 Domus humilis: the conversion of Venetian convent architecture and identity – *Saundra Weddle* — 144

8 Converting the soundscape of women's rituals, 1470–1560: purification, candles, and the *Inviolata* as music for churching – *Jane D. Hatter* — 169

Part III: Travel, race, and conversion

9 Narrating women's Catholic conversions in seventeenth-century Vietnam – *Keith P. Luria* — 195

10 'I wish to be no other but as he': Persia, masculinity, and conversion in early seventeenth-century travel writing and drama – *Chloë Houston* — 216

11 Turning tricks: erotic commodification, cross-cultural conversion, and the bed-trick on the English stage, 1580–1630 – *Daniel Vitkus* — 236

12 Whatever happened to Dinah the Black? And other questions about gender, race, and the visibility of Protestant saints – *Kathleen Lynch* — 258

Afterword – *Matthew Dimmock* — 281

Bibliography — 290
Index — 326

Figures

5.1 Dorothy Selby, 'The defeat of the Armada and the Gunpowder Plot', needlework picture. Courtesy of *Country Life*. Every reasonable effort has been made to contact the copyright holder. 115
5.2 WA 1947.191.316 Anonymous British, book cover with biblical scenes, mid-seventeenth century. © Ashmolean Museum, University of Oxford. 118
7.1 Map of Venetian convents showing parish boundaries. © Saundra Weddle. 145
7.2 Façade of the convent of Santa Maria dei Miracoli, Venice. © Saundra Weddle. 150
7.3 Detail of bird's eye view of Venice from the south, woodcut by Jacopo de'Barbari, c.1500. Courtesy of the Rijksmuseum, Amsterdam. 152
7.4 Bas-relief originally at the convent of Santa Marta, now at the church of Angelo San Raffaele, Venice. Didier Descouens/Wikimedia/CC BY-SA 4.0. 156
7.5 Sketched plan of the convent of Santa Maria delle Vergini, Venice, after 1519, Archivio di Stato di Venezia, Santa Maria delle Vergini, b. 38. © Archivio di Stato di Venezia. 160
8.1 Marian sequence *Inviolata, integra et casta* from the *Liber usualis* (1961), 1861–62. 178
8.2 Distribution of one hundred sources of polyphonic pieces based on the *Inviolata* chant. 180
8.3 Generic division of *Inviolata* settings. 182

FIGURES

8.4 *Inviolata* in the soprano part from an anonymous setting in Petrucci's *Motetti C* (Venice, 1504). Courtesy of the Bavarian State Library (http://www.digitale-sammlungen.de) / CC BY-NC-SA 4.0.   184

8.5 Josquin's *Inviolata a 5*, Tenor from Berg & Neuber, *Novum et insigne opus musicum* (1558–59). Courtesy of the Bavarian State Library (http://www.digitale-sammlungen.de) / CC BY-NC-SA 4.0.   185

12.1 Wenceslaus Hollar (1607–77). Portrait of a young African woman (1645). Folger Shakespeare Library Shelfmark: Art vol. b. 35 no. 46. Courtesy of the Folger Shakespeare Library / CC BY-SA 4.0.   260

TABLES

8.1 Sources with more than one *Inviolata* setting.   181

8.2 Settings of the *Inviolata* featuring the tune in a high register.   185

Notes on contributors

Claire Canavan is a doctoral student at the University of York, funded by a Wolfson Foundation Postgraduate Scholarship. Her thesis, entitled '"Various pleasant fiction": textiles and texts in early modern England', considers the material, practical, and conceptual intersections between needlework and practices of reading, writing, and devotion. Her publications include an article 'Textual and textile literacies in early modern braids' (*Renaissance Studies*) and an object lesson '"[A]ll sorts of stiches": looking at detail in a Proclamation of Solomon embroidery' (*Textile History*).

Hannah Crawforth is Senior Lecturer in Early Modern Literature at King's College, London, where she is also a founding member of the London Shakespeare Centre. She is the author of *Etymology and the invention of English in early modern literature* (2013) and co-author, with Sarah Dustagheer and Jennifer Young, of *Shakespeare in London* (2015). She is also co-editor, with Sarah Lewis, of *Family politics in early modern literature* (2016). With Elizabeth Scott-Baumann she has co-edited *On Shakespeare's sonnets: a poets' celebration* (2016), a collection of contemporary poetic responses to Shakespeare's verse.

Matthew Dimmock (Professor of Early Modern Studies (English), University of Sussex) is author of *Mythologies of the Prophet Muhammad in early modern English culture* (2013) and *New Turkes: dramatizing Islam and the Ottomans in early modern England* (2005). He has published widely on cultural, racial, and religious difference in the early modern period, and is part of the editorial team for the Oxford Hakluyt and the Oxford Nashe projects. He is currently writing a book about 'otherness' in the early modern period, provisionally titled *Reorientating the English Renaissance*.

Simon Ditchfield (Professor of History, University of York) has published widely on hagiography, history-writing, and identity-formation in early modern Roman Catholicism. He was co-director – with Helen Smith – of the AHRC-funded project *Conversion narratives in early modern Europe* (2010–13). Recent publications include 'Catholic Reformation and renewal' in *The Oxford illustrated history of the Reformation*, edited by Peter Marshall (2015) and 'Thinking with saints: sanctity and society in the early modern world', *Critical Inquiry* (2009). He is editor of the *Journal of Early Modern History* and advisory editor of the *Catholic Historical Review* and *Church History*. His book *Papacy and peoples: the making of Roman Catholicism as a world religion 1500–1700* is forthcoming from Oxford University Press.

Eric Dursteler (Professor of History, Brigham Young University) has published extensively on identity formation in the early modern Mediterranean. His books include *Venetians in Constantinople: nation, identity and coexistence in the early modern Mediterranean* (2006), *Renegade women: gender and boundaries in the early modern Mediterranean* (2011), and *The Mediterranean world: from the fall of Rome to the rise of Napoleon* (2016), all published by Johns Hopkins University Press. He also edited *The Brill Companion to Venetian History, 1400–1797* (2013). Eric is editor of the online newsletter for Venetianists, *News on the Rialto*, and book review editor of the *Journal of Early Modern History*.

David Graizbord (Associate Professor in Judaic Studies, University of Arizona) researches the Western Sephardi Diaspora of the seventeenth century. In particular, he has focused on the questions of religious, social, and political identity which shaped the lives of so-called 'New Christians', or 'conversos', from the Iberian peninsula who became Jews in exile. His well-received monograph, *Souls in dispute: converso identities in Iberia and the Jewish Diaspora, 1580–1700* (2004), offers an in-depth analysis of those 'renegades' who, having been compelled to leave the Iberian realms, adopted Judaism elsewhere, but then returned to Iberia and to Catholicism.

NOTES ON CONTRIBUTORS

Jane Hatter (Assistant Professor in Musicology, University of Utah) is a cultural musicologist who researches the contexts that generated and promoted musical knowledge and practice in the fifteenth and sixteenth centuries. She has published on musical time in early-sixteenth-century Italian paintings (*Early Music*, 2011) and also on intersections between popular devotions and ecclesiastical liturgy in Renaissance motets that include or quote the 'Ave Maria' prayer, in *The motet around 1500*, edited by Thomas Schmidt-Beste (2012). She is currently working on a book on compositions, especially motets and abstract Mass settings, that foreground music and musicians in the late fifteenth and early sixteenth centuries, exploring how this repertoire contributed to the development of the professional composer.

Chloë Houston (Lecturer in Early Modern Drama, University of Reading) works on utopias, travel and travel writing, and representations of cultural and religious difference in early modern literature. She is editor of *New worlds reflected: travel and utopia in the early modern period* (2010) and her article 'Persia and kingship in William Cartwright's *The Royall Slave* (1636)' was published in *Studies in English Literature* in 2014. Her monograph *Renaissance utopia: dialogue, travel and the ideal society* was published by Ashgate, also in 2014.

Elizabeth A. Lehfeldt (Professor of History and Dean of Jack, Joseph and Morton Mandel Honors College, Cleveland State University) is author of the monograph *Religious women in Golden Age Spain: the permeable cloister* (2005) together with several articles and chapters on related subjects including 'Ideal men: masculinity and decline in seventeenth-century Spain', *Renaissance Quarterly* (2008) and, most recently, 'Baby Jesus in a box: commerce and enclosure in an early modern convent', in Merry Wiesner-Hanks (ed.), *Mapping gendered routes and spaces in the early modern world* (2015). In 2013–14 she was President of the Sixteenth Century Society and Conference.

Keith P. Luria (Professor of History, North Carolina State University) is author of two monographs: *Territories of grace: cultural change in the seventeenth-century Diocese of Grenoble* (1991) and *Sacred boundaries: religious coexistence and conflict in early modern France* (2005). He has also published numerous articles on early modern religion and identity, most recently: 'Conversion and coercion: personal conscience and political conformity in early modern France', *The Medieval History Journal* (2009) and 'The power of conscience? Coexistence and confessional boundary building in early-modern France' in *Living with religious diversity in early-modern Europe*, edited by C. Scott Dixon, Dagmar Freist, and Mark Greengrass (2009). One of his current projects is the monograph *Conversion and cultural boundaries: seventeenth-century Vietnam in a global religious community*.

Kathleen Lynch (Executive Director of the Folger Institute, Washington DC) has written extensively on the religious literature of the seventeenth century from the perspectives of material culture and the book trade. Her *Protestant autobiography in the seventeenth-century Anglophone world* (2012) was awarded the Richard L. Greaves prize by the International John Bunyan Society, and she curated the summer 2012 Folger exhibition, *Open City: London, 1500–1700*. Recent publications include 'Inscribing the early modern self', a chapter for *A history of English autobiography*, edited by Adam Smyth (2016), and '"Letting a room in London-house": a place for dissent in Civil War London' in *Church life in seventeenth-century England*, edited by Michael Davies, Ann Dunan-Page, and Joel Halcomb (forthcoming).

Abigail Shinn (Teaching Fellow in Renaissance Literature, University of St Andrews) has co-edited, with Matthew Dimmock and Andrew Hadfield, *The Ashgate research companion to popular culture in early modern England* (2014); with Angus Vine, a special issue of *Renaissance Studies*: 'The copious text: encyclopaedic books in the Renaissance' (also 2014); and, with Peter Mazur, a special issue of the *Journal of Early Modern History* on 'Narrating conversion in the early modern world' (2013). Her current monograph project is *Tales of turning: conversion narratives in early modern England*.

Helen Smith (Reader in Renaissance Literature, University of York) is co-editor of *The Oxford handbook of the Bible in early modern England* (2015), and *Renaissance paratexts* (2011). Her monograph, *'Grossly material things': women and book production in early modern England* (2012), was awarded the SHARP DeLong Prize for Book History and the Roland H. Bainton Literature Prize. Helen has published widely on material texts, the history of reading, and conversion. She was co-director of the AHRC-funded project *Conversion narratives in early modern*

Europe (2010–13), and is Principal Investigator of the AHRC-funded network *Imagining Jerusalem: 1066 to the Present Day*.

Daniel Vitkus (Rebeca Hickel Chair in Early Modern Literature, University of California, San Diego) specialises in cross-cultural texts, travel literature, and Renaissance drama. He is editor of *Three Turk plays from early modern England* (2000) and *Piracy, slavery and redemption: Barbary captivity narratives from early modern England* (2001), and author of the monograph *Turning Turk: English theater and the multicultural Mediterranean, 1570–1630* (2003). He is currently co-editing the Bedford Texts and Contexts edition of Shakespeare's *Antony and Cleopatra* and working on a study titled *Early modern England and the origins of globalization: a cross-cultural history*.

Saundra Weddle (Professor of Architecture, Drury University, Missouri). Saundra's research focuses on the form and function of Florentine and Venetian Renaissance convents. She has edited, translated, and annotated *The chronicle of the Florentine convent of Le Murate, written by Suora Giustina Niccolini, 1598* (2010). Related publications include 'Identity and alliance: urban presence, spatial privilege and Florentine Renaissance convents', in *Renaissance Florence a social history*, edited by Roger J. Crum and John T. Paoletti (2006); 'Suspect Places in Venetian Convents', in *Encountering the Renaissance: Festschrift for Gary Radke*, edited by Molly Bourne and Victor Coonin (2016); and 'Tis better to give than to receive: client-patronage exchange and its architectural implications at Florentine convents', in *'A paradise where devils dwell': studies on Florence and the Italian Renaissance in honour of F. W. Kent*, edited by Cecilia Hewlett and Peter Howard (2016). Her research has been supported by a J. William Fulbright Grant, a National Endowment for the Humanities Summer Stipend, a Graham Foundation Grant, a Gladys Krieble Delmas Grant for Venetian Research, and a Samuel H. Kress Foundation Renaissance Society of America Grant. She currently serves on the editorial boards of *Architectural Histories* – the journal of the European Architectural History Network – and *The Journal of Architectural Education*.

Acknowledgements

~

The editors wish to thank, first and foremost, our contributors, whose patience, enthusiasm, and expertise have contributed in equal parts to the joys of bringing together this volume. Manchester University Press have been exemplary in their support and attention to detail. Many of the authors whose chapters are collected here came together in York for a 2012 symposium on 'Gender and Conversion in Early Modern Europe'; we wish to thank the Centre for Renaissance and Early Modern Studies and the Humanities Research Centre at York for their support of that event. Thanks, too, to Mark Jenner and Robin McDonald, whose insightful comments and queries did much to shape our thinking. The editors are also grateful for the hospitality of staff at the Folger Shakespeare Library, Washington DC, and the enthusiasm of participants in our Faculty Weekend Seminar on 'Narratives of Conversion in Reformation Europe, ca. 1550–1700' in September 2014. Though not tied directly to this volume, those conversations helped to shape and finesse our thinking on questions of conversion, narrative, and identity.

We also wish to thank the Arts and Humanities Research Council, whose generous funding of the three-year project 'Conversion Narratives in Early Modern Europe: A Comparative and Cross-Confessional Study' (2010–13) provided the occasion not only for this book but for a host of opportunities for scholarly exchange, research, and collaboration. Though there is not room here to thank all of those colleagues and scholars with whom we have enjoyed stimulating conversion conversations across and beyond the life of the project, we can at least acknowledge how much we have benefited from the inspiration – and the friendship – of our two postdoctoral colleagues Peter Mazur and Abigail Shinn, who readily converted us to the delights of collaborative research.

Introduction

Simon Ditchfield and Helen Smith

∽

'The first Nouell' of Boccaccio's *Decameron*, translated into English in 1620, takes as its theme the problem 'that virginity is very hardly to be kept, in all places'. Addressing an audience of 'Most woorthy Ladies', the narrator declares that 'there wantes no store of men and women, that are so simple, as to credit for a certainty, that so soon as a yong virgin hath the veile put on hir head (after it is once shorn and filletted) & the blacke Cowle giuen to couer her withall: shee is no longer a woman, nor more sensible of feminine affections, then as if in turning Nun, shee became conuerted to a stone'.[1] Boccaccio suggests that in the popular imagination the formal conversion of the maiden to a nun (her entry into conventual life) sets her outside the categories of both sex and gender. No longer 'a woman', she is also no longer subject to 'affections' stereotyped and construed as feminine. In this brief, satirical assertion, Boccaccio encapsulates the twin concerns of this volume: the shifts in social, professional, and personal identity that accompanied changes in religious affiliation, and the ways in which those changes were not simply refracted through but reshaped gendered experiences and ideologies.

In post-Reformation Europe (*c*.1550–1700), religious conversion took place on a scale that had not been seen since the official Christianisation of the Roman Empire in the fourth century. Under the combined effects of the Protestant and Catholic Reformations within and pressure from the Ottoman Empire without, early modern Europe became a site in which an unprecedented number of people were confronted by new beliefs, and collective and individual religious identities were broken down and reconfigured. Rival churches, supported by secular rulers, attempted to raise the bar regarding what it meant to be a practising Christian (of either Catholic or reformed persuasions), using the tools of social and ecclesiastical discipline to create distinct confessional identities. Even in the Protestant church, conversion continued to be used in the (traditional) *intra*-faith sense to refer to an intensification of religious life as much or more than in the *inter*-faith sense of a change from one creed to another. The renewed evangelical vigour of the Counter-Reformation Catholic church, observed and vigorously emulated by Protestant governments, ensured that questions of conversion, and of the nature of the true convert, occupied both church authorities and the popular imagination.

The experience of taking Christianity to the New World, Africa, South-East Asia, China, and Japan not only forced missionaries to reflect on how conversion could be best achieved, but also – thanks to the tsunami of written and printed reports that flooded west European libraries and the book market, providing edifying tales of derring-do to encourage generous donations to the missions or prayers for their success – stimulated Europeans into recalibrating what it meant to be a Christian. Central to this process was the 'invention of the indigenous', to borrow the phrase of the historian of science, Alix Cooper, who describes the role of New World flora and fauna in sensitising Old World observers to the unique 'indigeneity' of their own local natural world.[2] Realisation that 'what these New World barbarians now are, we once were' reverberated throughout the Old World, since tales of the missions crossed confessional lines and were read out in Protestant taverns as well as monastery refectories.[3] The Jesuit missionary to Peru, José de Acosta (1540–1600), told readers of his influential manual *On procuring the salvation of the Indians* (1588) that if they thought the Indians whose customs he was describing were wild, they should go and read Bede's account of the conversion of the Anglo-Saxons in his eighth-century *Ecclesiastical history*![4]

The effects of these religious changes on women have been widely debated. In 1989, Lyndal Roper reframed Joan Kelly-Gadol's famous question 'Did women have a Renaissance?' to ask whether women had a Reformation.[5] Like Kelly-Gadol, Roper concluded that the social and political changes seen by historians to constitute one of the major events of European history served to exclude women from religious and political life.[6] Luther's advocacy of the closing of convents and the marriage of priests, advice he himself took up with enthusiasm by marrying the former Benedictine nun, Katharina von Bora, led to the re-creation of 'the Holy Household' in which patriarchy was reinforced and women's already restricted options were limited still further. Roper's vision of a narrowing female sphere in Protestant Europe has been paralleled by research into the life of Roman Catholic religious women after the reaffirmation of monastic enclosure at the Council of Trent (1545–63). Yet our understanding of the early modern saying 'aut murus, aut maritus' (either enclosure in a nunnery or subjection in marriage) has been nuanced to the extent that we can now appreciate that, for some, convents provided a space for social action, if not self-determination.[7] Recent work on early modern women's writing has similarly contested the view that religion was an uncontroversial and limiting space for women, insisting upon the urgency of devotional, meditative, and polemical writing within a charged confessional economy, and arguing that 'the history of the Christian West is replete with stories of women who combined an exploitation of the liberating texts already available in the scripture with an imaginative response to potentially oppressive traditions'.[8]

The study of conversion lends an added urgency to the question of how women negotiated and responded to shifts in religious doctrine and practice. Eric Dursteler has suggested that for some women conversion provided a means to address or escape their existing social, political, and economic situation. In 'manipulating the [Mediterranean] regions' intertwined geographical, political, and cultural boundaries', Dursteler argues, 'women on the margin exerted "shaping power" over their own lives'.[9] Kim Siebenhüner, too, in a detailed case study of Mariana di Fiori, a Polish Jewish woman who emigrated to Italy, converted to Christianity, and was subsequently denounced to the Holy Office in Rome by her husband, who suspected her of apostasy, notes that both men and women crossed cultural and religious borders during their travels, and that, 'with the advent of the Reformation, a wholly new problem emerged within Catholic Europe, for now migrants traversed territories belonging to different confessions'.[10] Siebenhüner demonstrates how differences in faith disrupted the gendered order of the household, and (especially for a Jewish woman) raised unsettling questions about the religious complexion of children; Mariana's religious decisions and identity, she concludes, 'were strongly influenced by her personal relationships and her identity as a woman'.[11]

Such a conclusion, whilst insightful, might seem to take the category of 'womanhood' for granted. Recent work on the ways in which religious difference was imagined in gendered and sexualised terms, and in which sexual 'deviancy' was tied to ideas of erring or heretical religion, however, has shed new light on how religious belief and community shaped not only ideas about but the experience of sex and gender. Frances Dolan, for example, has shown how English Catholic priests were stereotyped by Protestant polemicists as both effeminate and sexually predatory, whilst recent work on the English vogue for 'Turk plays' has increasingly paid attention to what Jane Hwang Degenhardt describes as 'the stage's unique tendency to link Christian-Muslim conversion to interfaith sexual attraction and intercourse',[12] leading, as Chloë Houston points out in Chapter 10, to a pervasive 'association between religious conversion and unstable gender identity'. The process of 'Turning Turk' was associated not only with lust but with sodomy: in Robert Daborne's *A christian turn'd Turk* (1612), discussed by Daniel Vitkus in Chapter 11, Ward (a fictionalised version of the real-life pirate and convert John Ward), is mocked by the Jewish Rabshake after his conversion, prompted by his passion for the Ottoman princess Voada: 'You Turke, I haue nothing to say to you: Ha, ha, ha, poore fellow, how hee lookes since *Mahomet* had the handling of him? hee hath had a sore night at *Whose that Knockes at the backe-doore?*'[13] In a study of how 'eros and ethnos intersected during the sixteenth and seventeenth centuries', Carmen Nocentelli argues that the European–Asian encounter (and, by extension, cultural encounters across the Mediterranean and in the New World), 'inflected the ways in which the West came to define what was acceptable in matters of eros', as particular forms of domestic and sexual activity became identified with racial – and religious – otherness.[14] Missionaries and settlers sought to regulate domestic and erotic practices as part of the process of religious conversion.

The study of the relationship between gender, sex, and conversion thus takes in not only the question of women's religious experience, but the gendered identity of men, and both the fantasy and the reality of sexed encounters across domains ranging from the household to the inquisitorial court, the local parish to the far-flung mission. Recent work on early modern masculinity has highlighted the limited and frequently restrictive extension of patriarchal privilege across the social and economic order. As Alexandra Shepard points out: 'To discern the full complexity of the workings of gender in any society we need to be as aware of the gender differences *within* each sex as of those *between* them. Gender means different things for different men and women, and different things during the different stages of the life course.'[15] The chapters in this volume reveal the complex variety of ways in which men and women expressed and negotiated gendered identity in a range of settings and forms, from published narratives to domestic practice, legal testimony to devotional poetry. Our contributors are alert not only to the shifting and constantly re-determined relationships between men and women, but to the modes of masculinity and femininity produced and performed in religious contexts. In the case of 'the maiden who was made nun' (Lehfeldt, Chapter 6), or the Catholic son who rebuked his Protestant father (Crawforth, Chapter 3), we can see the extent to which religious belief and gendered identity intertwined. Crawforth's example of Robert Southwell in particular reminds us of the complex ways in which religious faith drew upon and remade gendered categories, not least in the performance of a tearful and affective masculine piety, and the repeated feminisation of the Christ figure.[16] Men and women did not simply bring an existing sexed self to the transformations of religion; they interacted with complexly gendered models which offered both patterns of piety and objects of devotion.

Both conversion and gender raise questions of performance and repetition. Recent work on conversion has emphasised its pragmatic and often prosaic nature, with converts changing faith rather for social, financial, or familial reasons than because of divine inspiration. Natalie Rothman, for example, narrates the case of Abdone, son of Giovanni of Aleppo, who changed faith on multiple occasions: 'When being Christian was inconvenient, he practiced Islam: when it became convenient again, he reembraced Christianity. By his own admission, he switched his allegiance at least five times, always due to contingent and pragmatic considerations.'[17] Arguing that questions of sincerity and motivation are not only necessarily evasive but 'embedded ... in specifically modern Christian understandings of intentionality, interiority, and authenticity', Rothman suggests that scholars need to turn their attention from the question of *why* people converted to the question of *how*.[18] A separate strand of scholarship has traced how conversion was staged, not only in playhouses but in churches, streets, and other public and devotional spaces.[19] That challenge is taken up by the chapters in this volume, which variously consider how the performance of conversion – whether in the elaborate ritual of a public change of faith, entry into monastic life, or the mundane repetitions of daily religious practice – might not simply reflect or announce a conversion (whether sincere or not), but inculcate changes in affect, social bonds, bodily experience, and belief.

Questions of the performativity of conversion align with influential arguments relating to gender-as-performance, not least in the work of Judith Butler. Celebrating the ability of drag artists to expose and trouble the artificiality of the apparently natural binary between the sexes, Butler argues that, through the excesses of a caricatured performance, drag reveals 'a dissonance not only between sex and performance, but sex and gender, and gender and performance', revealing the imitative and repetitive performances that constitute both gender and sex.[20] Offering a powerful critique of the sex/gender distinction, Butler argues that this division is predicated upon a body imagined as existing outside of culture and discourse, upon which sexed significance can be inscribed. In contrast, Butler urges us to 'consider that a sedimentation of gender norms produces the peculiar phenomenon of a "natural sex" or a "real woman" or any number of prevalent and compelling social fictions'.[21] Sex, in other words, is as much a product of culture as is gender, brought into being by the inescapable repetition of gendered behaviours and discourse.

The work of Thomas Laqueur, though subject to extensive revision and critique, has been influential in demonstrating that early modern concepts – and hence experiences – of the sexed body were very different from our own. Concentrating upon the Galenic tradition, Laqueur argues that early moderns subscribed to a one-sex model, according to which male and female bodies were understood to be inherently similar. Women, colder and wetter in constitution, had their genital organs inside; hotter, dryer men had the same organs on the outside of their bodies. The difference between sexes was, then, a difference 'of degree and not of kind'.[22]

Butler's work is powerful in revealing the formative force of both speech acts and repetition. In the context of early modern conversion, her insights ask us not only to consider how religious beliefs, ideologies, and debates contributed to the performance and internalisation of gendered models, but also to extend our analysis and ask how the rituals and repetitions of religious practice formed the basis of deeply-felt, faith-based identities and experiences, and produced effects of inwardness as well as social bonds.[23] Building on Butler's insights, Elizabeth Grosz goes so far as to argue that: 'Sex is no longer the label of both sexes in their difference . . . it is now the label and terrain of the production and enactment of sexual difference.'[24] In parallel terms, we might argue that early modern conversion – along with the numerous textual, musical, artistic, and other forms in which conversion was described and debated – was concerned precisely with the production and enactment of religious difference, working not simply as a means of moving between confessions but as the ground upon which the differences between faiths were repeatedly redrawn, and hence brought into being.

For Butler, drawing on the speech-act theory of J. L. Austin and John Searle, linguistic constructions are central to the construction both of gender and of subjectivity. Questions of the relationship between language and conversion have also recently come into view, not least in the work of Molly Murray, who argues, in her study of the 'poetics of conversion', that the ostentatious stylishness and 'dense "literariness"' of devotional, metaphysical poetry is deeply engaged with questions of religious affiliation and change.[25] The relationship between conversion and narrative has become the subject of particular scrutiny in recent years, as scholars move away from the paradigm of the 'conversion narrative' as a fixed genre, emerging from the gathered churches of the mid-seventeenth century, and towards a flexible sense of the various ways in which conversion is plotted, rhetorically performed, and built on (as well as able to reshape) powerful existing narrative models.[26] As the editors of a recent special issue on 'Conversion Narratives in the Early Modern World' point out, 'the retelling of the conversion experience was in many ways as important as the religious change itself'.[27] Narratives crossed linguistic and national borders, in spoken, printed, and manuscript forms, and their persuasive effects ranged from the stated desire for further conversions to the confirmation and assurance of believers already securely within the faith.

Narrative, of course, is not simply subsequent to conversion, a retelling of past events. Existing narrative models exerted a shaping force upon gendered and religious identity. The conversions of Saints Paul and Augustine were the dominant archetypes for Christian conversions, and numerous converts situated their own religious revelations as the result of reading, and reflecting upon, accounts of prior conversions.[28] Jeffrey Shoulson has recently argued that the figure of the converted or converting Jew was central to numerous narratives of conversion and cultural change.[29] Equally, the contributors to this volume recognise that narratives are brought into being as a result of institutional and bureaucratic, as well as generic, forms. As Natalie Zemon Davis influentially argues, historical subjects were alert to the 'shaping choices of language, detail, and order . . . needed to present an account that seems to both writer and reader true, real, meaningful, and/or explanatory'.[30] Thus we can ask how people told stories, 'what they thought a good story was, how they accounted for motive, and how through narrative they made sense of the unexpected and built coherence into immediate experience'.[31] In various ways, the chapters in this volume reflect upon the constraints which shaped narrative, as well as the ways in which language shaped both religious and gendered experience – forming, asserting, and confirming the gendered convert. David Graizbord (Chapter 2), for example, explores the ways in which one convert shaped her story in an attempt to negotiate the demands of the Spanish Inquisition, whilst Keith Luria (Chapter 9) brings into view the formal and polemical requirements of missionary reports. Kathleen Lynch (Chapter 12) reflects upon narrative absences within the archives, as well as the power of naming in the process of conversion.

Recent scholarship on religion and material culture has also begun to reflect on how belief and religious identity are shaped by the physical environment, by personal relationships with objects of devotion, by clothing and posture, and by the daily repetitions of prayer and devotional gestures. For Boccaccio, in the quotation with which we opened this introduction, it was the act of having 'the veile put on hir head . . . & the blacke Cowle giuen to couer her withall' that both marked and effected a virgin's conversion into a nun. Against the dominant paradigm of seeing religion as a series of propositions to which the believer assents, David Morgan asserts that we should instead consider belief as 'a shared imaginary, a communal set of practices that structure life in powerfully aesthetic terms'.[32] Religion is something heard, felt, tasted, smelt, and seen, a set of repeated practices which shape both body and mind.

In an influential recent study of *The Senses in Religious Communities* during the seventeenth and eighteenth centuries, Nicky Hallett explores the relationship between sensory experience and both gendered and religious identities, emphasising the range of sexed positions a nun might adopt and experience: 'Are nuns' sensory reactions cultural manifestations, overlaid (or not) by devotional? Might they (also or instead) be giving a response based on gendered reception; idealising their expressiveness to fit the expectations of a (particular kind of) woman, of a nun, of a Carmelite? Which came first in their self-perception, and does this perception coincide with their self-presentation?'[33] Men and women encountered their environments through perceptive faculties already mediated by the ideals of sex and religion; in turn, material encounters disciplined and directed the senses and the body, creating new forms and experiences of gender and faith.

Embodied belief, Morgan argues, takes place 'not *in* spaces and performances as indifferent containers, but *as* them, carved out of, overlaid, or running against prevailing modes of place and time'.[34] The same is true of gendered identity, produced as much through habits, patterns, and material practices as through assent (willing or otherwise) to stereotypes of gendered behaviour. As Sara Ahmed argues in *Queer Phenomenology*, that gender 'is an effect of how bodies take up objects, which involves how they occupy space by being occupied in one way or another'.[35] In recent scholarship, conventual space has become a crucial locus for the study of the mutual influence of materiality, gender, and religious identity. Offering a compelling study of seventeenth-century Neapolitan convents, Helen Hills urges scholars to bring together questions of belief, gender, and architecture, insisting that 'space does not merely provide the locus for social relations; it is primary to the construction of gendered and social identity'.[36] Architecture does not simply reflect but produces sexual, social, and religious difference or identity (in the sense of sameness, as well as of identification).[37] Questions of materiality and the environment are taken up in different ways in several of the chapters which follow. Claire Canavan and Helen Smith (Chapter 5) reflect upon women's needlework and domestic furnishings as agents of conversion, whilst Elizabeth Lehfeldt (Chapter 6) further advances our understanding of 'habit' (both repeated practice and clothing) in the process of personal and social identity-formation in Italian convents. Saundra Weddle and Jane Hatter (Chapter 7 and Chapter 8, respectively) extend further our sense of the effects of material 'conversions', reminding us of Boccaccio's blurring of spiritual and physical transformations in the imagined 'conversion' of the young woman to a stone. Where Weddle examines the transformations and permutations of the convent fabric, Hatter asks how the Catholic soundscape of women's churching rituals – crucial occasions for the expression of women's social and maternal identity – was 'converted' in the post-Reformation church.

In various ways, then, the chapters in this volume provide the reader with provocations for rethinking how gender and conversion interacted in this vital period for the history of religious identity in western Europe. Eric Dursteler's observation, in the opening chapter, that 'conversion was never merely a religious act' is a reminder that it was a process through which one could claim a new social self (or even reassert one's former identity). It was also a process in which it is clear that men and women's religious experiences must not be differentiated according to simplistic binaries that posit that either sex was necessarily 'to piety more prone'. Further comparative work on male and female narratives of conversion on (not only) the Mediterranean borderlands of the Christian world would further nuance this picture.

David Graizbord's chapter nicely complements Dursteler's in its insistence that we need to be alive to the degree to which 'cultural commuters' sought to meet the expectations of their audience. In Graizbord's case, this audience was the tribunals of the Spanish Inquisition, who even in their late-eighteenth-century dotage could elicit consciously 'scripted' performances from those under scrutiny. The socially marginal Carlota Liot used her alleged adoption of Jewish identity to claim the material rewards of conversion to the True Faith. Despite the 'vague quality' of her testimony she was ultimately believed by her questioners and so received no different a treatment from that meted out to the more culturally confident journeyman carpenter Salomón Bergom. The similar outcomes of these contrasting cases should make us more fully alive to the importance of the role played by the questioners not only in shaping conversion narratives but also in determining whether or not they were to be considered credible.

Hannah Crawforth (Chapter 3) treats of the connections between generation, gender, and genre in the writings of the Catholic poet and martyr, Robert Southwell. In tracing the complex and varied masculine positions exploited by Southwell, Crawforth's chapter points to the urgent need for further scholarship on the effects of confessional difference upon family relationships, and the modes of manhood both adopted by and attributed to fervent and suffering believers. Noting the preponderance of women's voices in the *Spirituall experiences, of sundry beleevers* (1653), a mammoth collection of conversion narratives, Abigail Shinn (Chapter 4) examines the interplay between the anonymity created by the use of believer's initials rather than full names, and the kinds of feminised, Christian experience created through repeated references to gendered histories and devotional acts. In exploring how the printed book creates a distinctive voice and gendered identity to be replicated across the gathered churches, Shinn's chapter poses provocative questions about the ways in which both gender and religious identity are (re)produced in print, and how acts of textual generation might themselves be gendered.

Both Shinn and Crawforth point to the generative logic of conversion, the declared impulse of the convert to effect more conversions, and of the conversion narrative to engender narrative imitation. The question must remain open how far these texts sought to promote conversion, and how far they sought to confirm existing believers in their own faith, through the figure of the errant, and often tormented, would-be convert. Claire Canavan and Helen Smith also take up the theme of the convert who, 'being conuerted her selfe [endeavours] the conuersion of others'. By taking seriously numerous accounts of women's evangelical activity, they reopen the question of women's religious agency, seeing accounts of women's exemplary behaviour not simply as techniques of commoditisation and silencing but as indices of the affective and public nature of women's piety.

Elizabeth Lehfeldt's insistence that nuns' habits inhabited a 'habitus' that was both more malleable and flexible than surface impressions might suggest is an important reminder that material culture is to be regarded not simply as a product to be described but also as a process to be interpreted in all its nuance and specificity. That this was precisely the age in which all religious – not only nuns, monks, friars, and clerks regular (such as the newly founded Jesuits who lived simultaneously in community and in the world) but also the 'seculars' (those religious who did not live according to a rule in community) – took on the appearance that they still largely exhibit today has not been remarked upon enough. Future research would do well to engage more thoroughly with this sartorial reformation.[38]

Attention to the material reality within which conversion was framed, expressed, lived, and staged – this time of stone and bricks and mortar, rather than fabric and leather – is also a preoccupation of Saundra Weddle's chapter. However, the close attention Weddle pays to the circumstances of the foundation and subsequent development of individual convents serves to remind us not only of the necessarily contingent and reciprocal nature of the relationship between buildings and their environment, but also that we must not overlook the ways in which the spaces within convents encouraged certain movements and discouraged others. In such a context 'enclosure' was necessarily something which also disclosed certain kinetic proclivities. Future research into the different ways in which male and female religious orders made use of similar spaces – which were sometimes the same spaces, inhabited sequentially – is sorely needed.

Jane Hatter invites us to consider the devotional and domestic soundscapes that surrounded women's churching rituals, identifying new evidence for the particular compositions that accompanied and shaped these important occasions. Her chapter allows us a rare glimpse into lay women's engagement with sacred music, and encourages us to consider not only how music and ritual might be 'converted' to reformed ends in the nascent Protestant church, but also how women might 'convert' public and festive occasions to meet their own needs, even as they were shaped and scripted by the requirements of performance and piety.

Keith Luria makes the important point that missionaries accommodated their conversion strategies not only to local circumstances but also to their audiences at home. Both missionaries and their readers in the Old World were busy and confident interpreters of signs of spiritual possession. In other words, spiritual possession was not only a shared, common language by means of which Old World Roman Catholics consoled, edified, and even entertained themselves with tales of missionary derring-do, but also a way of convincing themselves of the ultimate effectiveness of the Christian conversion of the New World by the Old. Luria's detailed study of the reception of Vietnamese women's conversions suggests the need for further studies of the ways in which such cultural encounters were 'translated' for their Old World audiences.

Chloë Houston explores English authors' efforts to establish early modern Persia as a site ripe for conversion both to Protestant Christianity and to modes of English masculinity, imaginatively countering the lure of Islam and the possibility of English travellers' conversions. Her chapter asks us to consider how tropes of masculinity and effeminacy were used to respond to and negotiate religious difference, and how the comforting fictions of the stage sought to establish both gendered and religious identity as tied to nationality, and as staunchly immutable. In its closing account of women's perceived religious fickleness, Houston's chapter suggests the need for further study of the ways in which relations between men, and between divergent religious traditions, were negotiated and explored through the figure of the female convert.[39]

Daniel Vitkus also asks us to consider the status of woman as commodity, this time in relation to the bed-trick, a fiction of substitution that became increasingly popular on the early Stuart stage. In a provocative account, Vitkus aligns three forms of trickery, exploring the imaginative and practical ties between economic, erotic, and religious deceit. Concluding with a series of plays in which a Moorish character is substituted for an English bed-fellow, Vitkus explores how, at these moments, fears of racial, commercial, and erotic difference converged on the English stage.

Like Shinn, Kathleen Lynch turns her attention to the gathered churches that constituted such a significant part of Anglo-American religious life in the mid-seventeenth century and have frequently been identified as the site from which the conversion narrative emerged as a specific genre.[40] Exploring Henry Jessey's *Exceeding riches of grace* (1647), an account of the illness and divine inspiration of Sarah Wight, Lynch demonstrates how a young girl, described as an 'empty nothing creature', could become a vehicle for divine grace, widely studied both in person and in print as a model for Christian inspiration. Lynch's focus is on a fleeting moment within Jessey's text: the mention of 'Dinah the Black' in a list of credible witnesses. Lynch tests the relationship between exemplarity and the exceptional, between the apparently ordinary inclusion of a black woman in Jessey's account and her possible role as a trophy convert. This chapter reminds us of the need for further research into not only the identities and experiences of individual converts, but the kinds of work – both in terms of religion and of gender – carried out through rituals of naming, renaming, and textual (including biblical) reproduction.

Taken together, these varied chapters pay sustained attention to how discourses and manifestations of gendered identity shaped the experience and actions of the convert. At the same time, they ask how religious change both manifested and reshaped the ideals and realities of sexed identity and behaviour. They demonstrate the intricate and overlapping performances of religious and gendered selfhood, and the difficulties as well as opportunities that this rocky terrain offered not only to converts but to their audiences, readers, and narrators. Shaped by the material environment, by practice and habit, by a host of texts and representations, and by particular contexts, the identity of the convert was at once persistent and malleable, intertwining with the multiple gendered – or de- or re-gendered – positions made available through the negotiation of the post-Reformation landscape.

INTRODUCTION

NOTES

1 Giovanni Boccaccio, *The decameron containing an hundred pleasant nouels* (London, 1620), P1ᵛ. This is a relatively faithful translation of the first novel but from the third day, as can be seen by looking at the most literal modern one by J. M. Rigg of 1903: 'Fairest ladies, not a few there are both of men and of women, who are so foolish as blindly to believe that, so soon as a young woman has been veiled in white and cowled in black, she ceases to be a woman, and is no more subject to the cravings proper to her sex, than if, in assuming the garb and profession of a nun, she had put on the nature of a stone'. Cfʳ. 'Bellissime donne, assai sono di quegli uomini e di quelle femine che sí sono stolti, che credono troppo bene che, come ad una giovane è sopra il capo posta la benda bianca e indosso messale la nera cocolla, che ella piú non sia femina né piú senta de' feminili appetiti se non come se di pietra l'avesse fatta divenire il farla monaca' (*Terza giornata, novella prima*). Both texts, with the Italian prepared by Vittore Branca (Turin: Einaudi, 1992), may be easily consulted via Decameron Web at: http://www.brown.edu/Departments/Italian_Studies/dweb/texts/.

2 Alix Cooper, *Inventing the indigenous: local knowledge and natural history in early modern Europe* (Cambridge: Cambridge University Press, 2007).

3 Book I of the Jesuit missionary Nicolas Trigault's edition of Matteo Ricci's *De Christiana expeditione apud Sinas suscepta ab Societate Iesu ex Mattaei Riccii eiusdem societatis commentariis libri V* (Augsburg, 1615) was translated into English and included in Samuel Purchas' massive five-volume, 4262-folio page *Hakluytus posthumus* (*Purchas his pilgrimes . . . The Second Part* (London, 1625), Ccccccc3ʳ–Ccccccc4ʳ). For an example of the way Jesuit missionary accounts were followed with interest beyond refectory walls of convents and monasteries see the manuscript writings of the Luzern chronicler and apothecary, Renward Cysat (1545?–1614) as discussed in Dominik Sieber, *Jesuitische Missionierung, priesterliche Liebe, sakramentale magie: Volkskulturen in Luzern, 1563–1614* (Schwabe: Basel, 2005), p. 28 n. 79.

4 'Legat qui volet antiquos anglorum mores, duriores nostris indis inveniet'; J. De Acosta, *De procuranda indorum salute*, ed. L. Pareña, 2 vols (Madrid: CSIC, 1984–87), II.40.

5 Joan Kelly-Gadol, 'Did women have a Renaissance?' in Renate Bridenthal and Claudia Koon (eds), *Becoming visible: women in European history* (Boston: Houghton Mifflin, 1987), pp. 137–64.

6 Lyndal Roper, *Holy household: women and morals in Renaissance Augsburg* (Oxford: Oxford University Press, 1989).

7 See Elizabeth Lehfeldt, *Religious women in Golden Age Spain: the permeable cloister* (Farnham: Ashgate, 2005); Silvia Evangelisti, *Nuns: a history*

of convent life, 1450–1700 (Oxford: Oxford University Press, 2007) and Cordula van Wyhe (ed.), *Female monasticism in early modern Europe: an interdisciplinary view* (Farnham & Burlington, VT: Ashgate, 2008). Ulrike Strasser, *State of virginity: gender, religion and politics in an early modern Catholic state* (Ann Arbor: University of Michigan Press, 2004) offers a less optimistic take on the position of women religious post-Trent.

8 Erica Longfellow, *Women and religious writing in early modern England* (Cambridge: Cambridge University Press, 2004), p. 13.

9 Eric Dursteler, *Renegade women: gender, identity, and boundaries in the early modern Mediterranean* (Baltimore: Johns Hopkins University Press, 2011), p. 118.

10 Kim Siebenhüner, 'Conversion, mobility and the Roman Inquisition in Italy around 1600', *Past and Present*, 200 (2008), 6.

11 Siebenhüner, 'Conversion', 29.

12 Frances E. Dolan, *Whores of Babylon: gender and seventeenth-century print culture* (Ithaca, NY: Cornell University Press, 1999); Jane Hwang Degenhardt, *Islamic conversion and Christian resistance on the early modern stage* (Edinburgh: Edinburgh University Press, 2010), p. 15. Such a connection was far from being unique to the stage; it was repeated in pamphlets, polemic, ballads, and numerous other genres.

13 Robert Daborne, *A Christian turn'd Turke: or, the tragical liues and deaths of the two famous pyrates, Ward and Dansiker* (London, 1612), G2^v–G3^r.

14 Carmen Nocentelli, *Empires of love: Europe, Asia, and the making of early modern identity* (Philadelphia: University of Pennsylvania Press, 2013), p. 5.

15 Alexandra Shepard, *Meanings of manhood in early modern England* (Oxford: Oxford University Press, 2003), p. 2.

16 Writing of the cross-confessional figure of mystical marriage, Longfellow argues that 'the confusions between male and female, the believer and the Church, open up possibilities for early modern writers to negotiate gendered power relations, whether real or metaphorical' (Longfellow, *Women and religious writing*, p. 3).

17 Natalie Rothman, *Brokering empire: trans-imperial subjects between Venice and Istanbul* (Ithaca, NY: Cornell University Press, 2011), p. 99. See also the cases of itinerant soldiers and mercenaries discussed in Peter Mazur, *Improbable lives: conversion to Catholicism in early modern Italy* (London and New York: Routledge, 2016), pp. 98–115; Brian Pullan, 'A ship with two rudders: Righetto Marrano and the Venetian Inquisition', *The Historical Journal*, 20 (1977), 25–58.

18 Rothman, *Brokering empire*, 88.

19 See, for example, Louise M. Burkhart, 'The destruction of Jerusalem as colonial Nahuatl historical drama', in Susan Schroeder (ed.), *The conquest all over again: Nahuas and Zapotecs thinking, writing, and painting Spanish*

colonialism (Eastbourne: Sussex Academic Press, 2010), pp. 74–100; Viviana Díaz Balsera, 'Celebrating the rise of a new sun: the Tlaxcalans conquer Jerusalem in 1539', *Estudios de cultura Náhuatl*, 39 (2008), 311–30; Matthew Dimmock, 'Converting and not converting "strangers" in early modern London', *Journal of Early Modern History*, special issue, 'Conversion Narratives in the Early Modern World', ed. Peter Mazur and Abigail Shinn, 17 (2013), 457–78.

20 Judith Butler, *Gender trouble: feminism and the subversion of identity* (London: Routledge, 1990), p. 137. For a discussion of Butler's work in the context of early modern theatricality, see Will Fisher, *Materializing gender in early modern English literature and culture* (Cambridge: Cambridge University Press, 2006).

21 Butler, *Gender trouble*, pp. 139–40.

22 Thomas Laqueur, *Making sex: the body and gender from the Greeks to Freud* (Cambridge, MA: Harvard University Press, 1990), p. 25. For subsequent critiques, see especially Joan Cadden, *Meanings of sex difference in the Middle Ages: medicine, science, and culture* (Cambridge: Cambridge University Press, 1993); Helen King, 'The mathematics of sex: one to two, or two to one?', *Studies in Medieval and Renaissance History*, special issue on 'Sexuality and Culture in Medieval and Renaissance Europe', 3rd series, II (2005), 47–58.

23 Older paradigms established a direct link between Protestant habits of self-scrutiny, autobiographical writing, and the development of a modern sense of self. See Leopold Damrosch, *God's plot and man's stories* (Chicago and London: University of Chicago Press, 1985); Karl Mannheim, *Ideology and utopia: an introduction to the sociology of knowledge*, trans. Louis Wirth and Eward Shils (New York: Harcourt, Brace & World, 1936). In *Renaissance self-fashioning: from More to Shakespeare* (Chicago: University of Chicago Press, 1980), Stephen Greenblatt argues that the early sixteenth century constituted 'a crucial moment of passage from one mode of interiority to another' (p. 85). This narrative of Protestant interiority has been challenged from several directions.

24 Elizabeth Grosz, *Space, time, and perversion: essays on the politics of bodies* (London: Routledge, 2005), p. 213.

25 Molly Murray, *The poetics of conversion in early modern English literature: verse and change from Donne to Dryden* (Cambridge: Cambridge University Press, 2009), p. 4.

26 On the seventeenth-century conversion narrative, see especially Patricia Caldwell, *The Puritan conversion narrative: the beginnings of American expression* (Cambridge: Cambridge University Press, 1983); D. Bruce Hindmarsh, *The evangelical conversion narrative: spiritual autobiography in early modern England* (Oxford: Oxford University Press, 2005);

and Kathleen Lynch, *Protestant autobiography in the seventeenth-century Anglophone world* (Oxford: Oxford University Press, 2012).
27 Peter Mazur and Abigail Shinn (eds), 'Introduction: conversion narratives in the early modern world', *Journal of Early Modern History*, 17 (2013), 428.
28 See Helen Smith, '"Wilt thou not read me, Atheist?": the Bible and conversion', in Kevin Killeen, Smith, and Rachel Willie (eds), *The Oxford Handbook of the Bible in Early Modern England* (Oxford: Oxford University Press, 2015), pp. 350–64.
29 Jeffrey S. Shoulson, *Fictions of conversion: Jews, Christians, and cultures of change in early modern England* (Philadelphia: University of Pennsylvania Press, 2013), esp. chapters 1 and 2.
30 Natalie Zemon Davis, *Fiction in the archives: pardon tales and their tellers in sixteenth-century France* (Stanford: Stanford University Press, 1987), p. 3.
31 *Ibid.*, p. 4.
32 David Morgan, 'Introduction', to Morgan (ed.), *Religion and material culture: the matter of belief* (London: Routledge, 2010), pp. 1, 7.
33 Nicky Hallett, *The senses in religious communities, 1600–1800: early modern 'Convents of Pleasure'* (Farnham: Ashgate, 2013), p. 21.
34 Morgan, 'Introduction', p. 8.
35 Sara Ahmed, *Queer phenomenology: orientations, objects, others* (Durham, NC and London: Duke University Press, 2006), p. 59.
36 Helen Hills, *Invisible city: the architecture of devotion in seventeenth century Neapolitan convents* (Oxford: Oxford University Press, 2004), p. 161.
37 For stimulating explorations of this idea, see Helen Hills (ed.), *Architecture and the politics of gender in early modern Europe* (Aldershot: Ashgate, 2003).
38 For a richly suggestive guide to the potential of such a field of enquiry see the exhibition catalogue, Giancarlo Rocca (ed.), *La sostanza dell'effimero: gli abiti degli ordini religiosi in Occidente* (Rome: Edizioni Paoline, 2000).
39 On women as tokens of homosocial exchange, see Gayle Rubin, 'The traffic in women: notes on the "political economy" of sex', in Rayna Reiter (ed.), *Toward an anthropology of women* (New York: Monthly Review Press, 1975), pp. 157–210. Rubin's account informs Eve Kosofky Sedgwick's influential *Between men: English literature and male homosocial desire* (New York: Columbia University Press, 1985).
40 See especially Hindmarsh, *Evangelical conversion narrative*.

Part I: Gendering conversion

1

To piety or conversion more prone? Gender and conversion in the early modern Mediterranean

Eric Dursteler

In 1592, Francesco Mosca, an inhabitant of the Venetian town of Sebenico (modern-day Šibenik, Croatia) on the north-eastern Adriatic coast, converted to Islam, or in the parlance of the day, 'turned Turk'. He had long had a disreputable reputation throughout the region: this was certainly due, in no small part, to his 'profession' of 'killing every type of man and merchant at sea, depriving them of both their goods and their lives'.[1] The previous year, however, Mosca had carried out a particularly violent robbery, and fearing that he would finally be captured and punished for his life of crime, he fled south across the Veneto-Ottoman frontier to Castelnovo (Herceg Novi, Montenegro), lifted his finger, and recited the *shahada*, or declaration of faith, in front of two Muslim witnesses. With this simple act, Mosca became a 'Turk', or from the Ottoman perspective, was 'honored by the glory of Islam'.[2] Though he had declared his conviction that 'there is no god but God, and Muhammad is the messenger of God', according to a Ragusan diplomat familiar with the case, Mosca's motivation in this dramatic act was 'not due to any devotion he had for the Turkish faith', but rather was done to save his skin so that he could continue his life of piracy. And, in partnership with several Ottomans from Castelnovo, he had a new boat constructed post-haste to support his larcenous activities.

At the time of his flight and conversion, Mosca left behind a son and a wife in Sebenico, the names of whom are not given in the sources. He appears to have attempted to convince his wife to join him in his new life in Ottoman lands, even to the point of enlisting official sources to inquire into her disposition. She refused his overtures, however, in part

21

because she felt that her husband 'had abandoned her'. For Mosca's wife, her husband's conversion definitively signalled the end of their relationship: she took possession of a small boat and all the merchandise he had left behind in Sebenico as payment towards her dowry, which she clearly doubted would be returned to her.[3] And, indeed, while canon law decreed that a woman's dowry be returned if her husband deserted her, according to Islamic law, conversion of one partner in a marriage annulled the relationship and all associated legal and economic responsibilities.[4]

In an early modern Mediterranean that scholars from Fernand Braudel onwards have depicted as being characterised by 'the ceaseless circulation' of people, stories such as that of Francesco Mosca and his family were commonplace.[5] This was the age of the renegade, a term applied specifically to Christians who 'rebelled against the faith' by converting to Islam, though many Muslims and Jews also breached the sea's religious boundaries and can thus also be classed as renegades.[6] In the sixteenth century alone, the number of renegades across the breadth of the Mediterranean is estimated to have reached into the hundreds of thousands.[7] They were so numerous, and those who achieved great wealth and influence were so widely known, that renegades became 'a sensational subject', subject to widespread curiosity and 'anxious fascination' in the literature of the day.[8]

In its broad outlines, Mosca's case follows a familiar script that was regularly repeated: a man seamlessly and seemingly without hesitation renounces a superficially held and often barely understood faith in order to advance his personal affairs, while his faithful wife refuses to follow, and is thus abandoned and left in dire circumstances. The region's archives are replete with similar tales, such as the papal military official from Calabria, Hettor Salem, who deserted his wife, Dorotea, in Venice and headed to Istanbul to seek his fortune,[9] or the Dalmatian Michiel Marghetich, who was described as having 'always been fickle and not very trustworthy', evidenced by his repeated see-saw conversions between Christianity and Islam; the third, and apparently final time, he left behind a pregnant wife.[10]

These cases suggest a gendered model of Mediterranean conversion that is buttressed by certain contemporary accounts and has been embraced by modern scholars. In 1630, for instance, the French Trinitarian François Dan, who dedicated his life to redeeming slaves in North Africa, estimated that in Algiers there were 8000 men and

1200 women renegades, and in Tunis 3000–4000 and 600–700, respectively.[11] These numbers are broadly in line with Anton Minkov's findings for the Balkans, where 80 per cent of all converts in his sample were men.[12] In their path-breaking study of renegades, *Les chrétiens d'Allah*, Bartolomé and Lucille Bennassar examined 1550 individual cases of conversion, of which only a minuscule 59, or under 4 per cent, were women.[13] Despite the statistical variation, these numbers clearly indicate that in the early modern Mediterranean, conversion was primarily a man's game.

And in a certain sense it was a game: as was the case with Francesco Mosca, whose conversion was 'not due to any devotion he had for the Turkish faith', the motives behind these acts of apostasy do not easily fit the traditional Christian paradigm. The archetype of Christian conversion was St Paul – a sudden, dramatic, and all-encompassing transformation resulting from a numinous encounter with the divine that mystically generated a new person who thereafter lived a transformed life. While other Christian models exist, such as St Augustine's experience of conversion as a process over time, or the mass conversions of the late classical and early medieval eras, the Pauline paradigm of conversion as a 'totalizing enterprise', a 'process of changing a sense of root reality', a 'radical reorganization' of 'identity, imagination, and consciousness', has been enshrined in the Christian world.[14] True conversion, when it occurred, was interior and initiated a 'mutation of the heart'.[15] Indeed, this model has been projected onto non-Christian contexts, including Islam, and in the process has masked or distorted very different notions of conversion.[16]

Unlike Paul or Augustine, however, the conversions of Mediterranean renegade men seem rarely to have been all-encompassing, transformative metamorphoses; rather, they were often acts of desperation or aspiration, religious indifference, or ignorance. Indeed, the term conversion may obfuscate more than illuminate their experiences. The motivations behind this common act of boundary transgression are summarised by the seventeenth-century English traveller Henry Blount: 'Many who professe themselves *Christians*, scarce know what they meane by being so; Finally, perceiving themselves poore, wretched, taxed, disgraced, deprived of their children, and subject to the insolence of every Raskall, they begin to consider, and preferre this present World, before that other which they so little understand.'[17] A limited understanding of their birth faith, oppression, poverty, and the hope of better socio-economic conditions in the more fluid Ottoman society were all motivating factors behind Mediterranean conversions.[18]

It is not surprising, then, that these were almost unanimously perceived by contemporaries as conversions of convenience, and the men who played the chief roles came in for heavy criticism. One traveller in the region wrote that renegades were 'for the most part Roagues, and the skum of the people, which being villaines and Atheists, unable to live in Christendome, are fled to the Turkes for succour, and releefe'.[19] Analogous views were widely shared by Ottomans; as one official observed, 'a pig remains a pig, even if they do cut off its tail'.[20] Such views should not obscure the fact that conversions of religious conviction certainly occurred,[21] particularly when conversion is considered as a dynamic social process playing out over time, rather than a singular event experienced internally and in isolation.[22] Indeed, some scholars reject outright attempts to assess the 'motivation and sincerity' of conversions, which are 'extremely hard to gauge from available documentation', and are 'embedded' in 'modern Christian understandings of intentionality, interiority, and authenticity'.[23] Whatever their intent and however they evolved, these seem for the most part to have been, as Jocelyne Dakhlia has labelled them, 'opportunistic conversions' with 'little place for religious conviction', and in the Mediterranean, those most likely to enact such a questionable religious metamorphosis were men.[24]

The other side of the equation in a conversion experience such as Francesco Mosca's, which the extant documents unfortunately treat only in passing and is just as often glossed over in contemporary scholarship, is that of his wife, who rejected the siren call of conversion and retained her birth faith at a not unsubstantial cost to herself. While we have little insight into her motivations, just as was the case with her husband, her own actions fit a familiar script that aligns with what we instinctively expect of an early modern woman. This widely shared view was articulated most memorably by the Earl of Stirling, who described women as being by nature 'to piety more prone'.[25]

The notion that women are more religiously committed than men, and therefore less susceptible to conversion, is deeply rooted. In modern western societies, sociologists of religion have found that 'women are more religious than men on every measure of religiosity', this despite the historical misogyny of Christianity and the fact that women continue to be systematically excluded from most positions of ecclesiastical authority. Women's heightened religiosity has been attributed to, among other factors, their 'social, economic and physical vulnerability', 'different structural locations in society', and differences in socialisation between men and women. Whatever the cause, popular and scholarly literature still axiomatically posits 'a strong link between being female and being religious'.[26]

Historical evidence supporting this view abounds, from the unyielding fidelity demonstrated by early Christian martyrs such as Saints Perpetua, Felicitas, and Thecla,[27] to the firm commitment to a religious life of medieval women and girls, often in the face of violent parental and spousal opposition, exemplified by St Catherine of Siena or the mystic Angela of Foligno.[28] In the early modern Mediterranean, scholars have argued that, in comparison to men, Coptic women in Egypt were more likely to resist conversion to Islam,[29] and Tijana Krstić has shown that, in contrast to narratives about male martyrs in the Ottoman Empire, Christian women who withstand the temptation to convert to Islam are depicted as 'virtuous . . . [and] steadfast in their religion'.[30] In seventeenth-century England, Catholic mothers were considered 'dangerously influential in preserving the faith through their control of the household and their role in educating their children',[31] and similar arguments have been made about women among France's Huguenots, Scotland's Roman Catholics, and Crete's crypto-Christian communities.[32]

And it was not just Christian women who were depicted as playing the determining role in the preservation of faith; as David Graizbord discusses in this volume, Jewish women in Iberia were considered by contemporaries as the 'de facto custodians and principal transmitters' of Jewish culture, which largely occurred within the domestic sphere. This view has generally been embraced by modern scholars, who have portrayed Jewish women as more resistant to conversion because of their 'maternal role' in perpetuating tradition and 'socializing their children'.[33] The same has been argued for women in the ghetto of Turin and in Egypt.[34] Ahmed Bouchareb has contended that Muslim women in Portugal resisted 'apostasy much longer than their male consorts', and women who did convert were more likely to be recidivists than men. Many 'secretly gave their children Islamic names and taught them Arabic and the precepts of Islam, hoping that one day they would escape back to Dar al-Islam'. Indeed, some went so far as to kill living or abort unborn children to avoid their baptism.[35]

The unique mode of women's resistance to religious change has been studied in greatest detail among early modern Spain's Moriscos. Though they had been forcibly converted in the first decades of the sixteenth century, the Moriscos continued to be viewed with suspicion as 'false Christians' who secretly and deceptively practised Islam, and were thus seen as a potential threat to the social and political order.[36] The growing tension between the crown and its Morisco subjects produced a stand-off in which royal and religious institutions tried to impose Christian cultural norms on the Moriscos, and were met in turn by varying degrees of compliance and resistance. For over a century, until their expulsion in 1609, the crown pursued a strategy that aimed at effacing all Morisco practices that were rooted in the culture of Muslim al-Andalus; these included foodways, dress, music, dance, and language.[37]

As Mary Elizabeth Perry has convincingly demonstrated, the role of Morisco women, or Moriscas, was central to this face-off. The chief arena of their defence was not the battlefield, the royal court, or the Inquisition, it was rather the 'Morisco home', which functioned as 'a bastion of cultural resistance'. Women were considered especially zealous in preserving Muslim religious practices; Morisco society assigned them the role of 'guardian of the Islamic tradition'. Though they often lived 'in domestic seclusion', this did not disempower Moriscas; on the contrary, they utilised 'weapons of the weak' to turn their homes into 'cells of resistance'.[38] Their homegrown opposition included refusing to learn Spanish and holding onto Arabic longer than men, producing copies of the Qur'an and other holy writings that they sometimes smuggled in their skirts, and preserving Islamic rituals of ablution and donning clean clothing on Fridays. Morisca mothers washed the chrism off of their babies after baptism, 'hid their children from Christian teachers', and taught them Arabic. In this way they transmitted the ritual practices of the community across generations to their children and grandchildren.[39] These efforts seem to have been effective, as inquisitors repeatedly heard confessions of individuals who reported that they had been instructed in the beliefs and rituals of Islam by 'mothers, grandmothers, or mothers-in-law'. Indeed some churchmen considered Moriscas 'their greatest rivals for the souls of Morisco children'.[40]

While the commitment of Moriscas and other women to their birth faiths, and their attendant resistance to conversion, was a common trope of the day, there was a pronouncedly schizophrenic quality to contemporary views of early modern women's religiosity. On the one hand, as we have seen, women were believed to be by nature more inclined to piety and committed religious practice. On the other, they were almost universally perceived as 'the weaker sex', and as such more likely to be disorderly, unbridled, unreliable, intellectually weak, and irrational.[41] These liabilities, it was generally believed, made women vulnerable to both heretical and infidel beliefs and practices.[42] In short, according to this view, early modern women were to conversion more prone. As a result, European rulers tried to prohibit women, as well as youths and children, from travelling in the treacherous Levant, a position mirrored by Muslim fears of the dangers that the *Dar al-Harb* represented to what was perceived as their own women's weak faith.[43]

There is an extensive body of contemporary scholarship that supports this vision of women's religiosity. Sociologists of religion, for example, have found that women have often been disproportionately attracted to new religious movements such as Mormonism, Christian Science, and the Unification Church, and thus seemingly more willing to abandon the mainline religions in which they were raised.[44] In the same vein, scholars working in a variety of historical contexts have shown that, in contrast to the figure of the naturally pious woman who devoutly and unwaveringly resisted conversion, women often proved to be quite open to religious change, often even more so than men. In early Christianity, for instance, there was a 'substantial sex bias in conversion': women significantly outnumbered men as primary converts, including 'an unusual number of high-status women'. Christianity proved so attractive that, in 370, Emperor Valentinian I ordered Christian missionaries to cease proselytising among pagan women.[45] The same was true in the early years of Islam, when many 'distinguished women' converted in advance of their more reticent husbands and other family men.[46] In the Middle Ages, it has been argued that women were disproportionately drawn to the era's numerous heretical movements.[47] In Reformation England scholars have found women were both 'enthusiastic and staunch supporters of Catholicism', but were also drawn, in significant numbers, to Protestantism,[48] while in France no clear pattern has been identified for women's response to religious reform.[49]

Paralleling these findings, in the early modern Mediterranean there is growing evidence of women who crossed religious boundaries in many different contexts. Marc Baer, studying Istanbul, found that in the years 1650–1700, 'hundreds of free and slave Christian and Jewish women converted' to Islam. These conversions were often pursued to obtain 'freedom from slavery, to escape bad marriages or to gain custody of their children'.[50] One study of Balkan conversion identified 94 adult female converts who petitioned the sultan for some degree of support, 80 per cent of whom were widows and divorced women. These women were often in exposed and tenuous personal circumstances, and by converting were seeking support that would normally have been provided by their husbands or perhaps their families.[51] There is also extensive evidence of non-Muslim Ottoman women, whose traditions did not normally permit divorce, converting to Islam as a way to be freed from an unwanted spouse or to gain legal control over their children.[52] Historians have also approached women's religiosity on a micro-historical scale, with detailed narratives of the motives and experiences of teenaged Muslim girls on the Balkan frontier fleeing undesired marriages,[53] a Venetian citizen woman who converted to escape a financially grasping husband,[54] and a Jewish woman whose conversion to Catholicism resulted not 'in a clear, new religious identity, but in ambivalence and tension' as she attempted to straddle both religious worlds.[55]

As this rapid survey suggests, many women converted in response to domestic and familial situations. Indeed, Natalie Rothman has argued that women often believed that 'the continuity of their social role as care givers (domestic slaves, concubines, wives) justified the discontinuity of their religious affiliation'.[56] Just as marital and parental ties might bind women to their birth faiths, these same factors could also provide the impetus for conversion. For example, 15-year-old Angela de Nicolo of Prevesa refused a match with a Greek Christian that her mother had arranged and instead converted to Islam (though this was not obligatory) in order to marry a Muslim 'who suited her more'. Another woman from Tinos wed a Muslim 'who fell in love with her' and then converted to Islam under the influence of several other women from the island. Nineteen years later, however, she ran away with a Greek Christian whom she married in an Orthodox church.[57]

Like Francesco Mosca, women also converted and abandoned their children in pursuit of financial and social advancement. This was the case with Anna Maria Micheli, a Jew from Ancona who converted to Christianity in order to dissolve her marriage to a Jewish goldsmith and to marry a wealthy, socially prestigious nobleman, and in doing so effectively renounced several children from her first marriage.[58] Similar cases of religious ambiguity and easy variability abound from Counter-Reformation Rome to the Venetian lagoon and the Jewish ghetto of Turin.[59]

In underlining the domestic component that was common to many of these conversion narratives, we should avoid the simplistic dichotomy between the public and the private sphere.⁶⁰ While many Mediterranean women's conversions played out against a familial backdrop, and domestic issues often occupied a central position in their experiences, they also frequently had a very public component to them. This is most evident in the cases of women converts within the imperial harem, who, Leslie Peirce has shown, exercised significant political, social, economic, and cultural power because of their cloistering within a seemingly quintessential domestic space.⁶¹ On a smaller scale, the conversion of a family of Muslim women in the Aegean Sea, while motivated by domestic concerns, was intentionally executed in a very public fashion which guaranteed the engagement of public officials in ways that ensured that the women were not forced to return to Islam.⁶²

These examples also suggest the need to reconsider the notion that the renegade phenomenon was primarily male, and that women's conversions were statistically insignificant. While no definitive census is possible, it seems clear that men represented the majority of renegades in the early modern Mediterranean. There is a growing body of impressionistic evidence, however, suggesting that the number of women renegades was much larger than has been assumed. In the valleys of Piedmont, in 1676–77, for example, one-third of the total number of converts were women, while in the catechumen house of Turin, Calvinist and Waldensian converts were evenly divided by gender, except among Jewish converts, where men outnumbered women.⁶³ A study of Venice's Pia Casa dei Catecumeni shows that women comprised 28 per cent of all neophytes in the period 1630 to 1670.⁶⁴ A late-seventeenth-century document from the Balkans suggests a conversion ratio of 45 per cent female to 55 per cent male,⁶⁵ and Bernard Heyberger has shown that Syrian Christians converted to Roman Catholicism in the late eighteenth century in nearly identical numbers.⁶⁶

Part of the challenge in measuring women's conversions in the Mediterranean is that many, perhaps most, resulted from the region's endemic slave trade. There is significant debate about the number of slaves in the Mediterranean, with the most recent estimates suggesting between 3 million and 5 million slaves were taken from 1500 to 1800, or an average of 300,000 per year, with a three to one Christian to Muslim ratio.⁶⁷ The orthodox view has been that the bulk of these slaves were men; while men certainly outnumbered women, scholars now contend that women represented a much larger percentage of all slaves. Because slavery was an important vector for conversion, particularly of women placed in certain relatively common domestic situations, we can reasonably conclude that these impressionistic numbers of renegade women represent only the tip of the iceberg. There is, in fact, some evidence that slave women were likely to convert in numbers that approach those of men. When the Canary island of Lanzarote was attacked by 36 corsair ships from Algiers in 1618, 900 captives were taken. Of these, 107 converted to Islam, divided almost equally between men and women.[68] Research on Cordova has shown analogous conversion rates among male and female Muslim slaves.[69]

In reconsidering women's conversion in the Mediterranean, we should not fail to re-examine men's experiences in a more nuanced light as well. As Joan Scott notes, 'information about women is necessarily information about men'.[70] The case of Francesco Civalelli provides a telling counterpoint to that of Francesco Mosca, and suggests a more complex picture of conversion for both men and women. Civalelli was descended from an ancient noble family in the Venetian city of Zara (Zadar, Croatia) on the north-eastern Adriatic coast. In 1584 he married a certain Donna Isabetta, and over the next six years the couple had three daughters. In response to Dalmatia's deteriorating economic situation and at the invitation of his wife's brother, an influential renegade eunuch in the imperial palace, Francesco and his wife joined the stream of Balkan migrants headed for Istanbul. Very soon after their arrival, alternately bribed and threatened by her brother and their mother, who had also recently converted to Islam, Isabetta 'turned Turk'. Whereas the women were described as converting with seemingly little compunction, despite being forcibly retained by his brother-in-law, aggressively pressured to convert, and terribly beaten, Francesco refused to follow suit. He was eventually released from detention, but was by then a broken man, 'stripped, all lacerated, and despoiled, and bearing the face of death'. He spent the next year struggling to regain his health, haunted by the loss of his wife, fearful for the safety of the children he had left behind in Zara, and traumatised by the collapse of his fragile finances. In the summer of 1591, faced with the harsh realities of his situation, and realising that conversion was the only way he could prevent the dissolution of his marriage and avoid losing his wife permanently, and hoping that he might also be reunited with his daughters, he finally followed Isabetta's lead and converted. Francesco's hopes of reuniting his family were fulfilled and his financial concerns resolved through the awarding of several benefices, but as with so many such conversions, little but surface practices seems to have changed in terms of his religious world view.[71]

While the traditional narrative is one of easy and instrumental male conversion because of any number of self-interested motivations, the reality, as Civalelli's case suggests, was significantly more nuanced. There are numerous examples of men, just as women, who actively resisted conversion. Tijana Krstić has identified almost 170 cases of male martyrs among the Orthodox Ottoman community, compared to only six women.[72] There are also numerous instances of women converting in kadı courts throughout the Ottoman Empire, while their husbands refused to follow.[73] And as Bennassar has pointed out, cases in which men followed the religious choices initiated by their wives were 'not necessarily rare'.[74]

By the same token, as Civalelli's experience also shows, we must acknowledge the central place that 'the homespace' could occupy in men's lives, and the ways in which their conversions might also play out along the public–private continuum.[75] For instance, one common experience that transcended religious communities was that of men who converted after establishing intimate relationships with women outside their faith.[76] Men might also function as custodians of the religious identity of their families in ways that have traditionally been codified as female, as was the case when a seventeenth-century crypto-Muslim father in France married a Christian woman and gave his many children Christian names, 'all the while instructing his family in the tenets of Islam'.[77]

As the stories of the Civalelli and Mosca families illustrate, the intersection of gender and conversion in the early modern Mediterranean was a decidedly more nuanced affair than is often depicted. While there may be a need for a 'feminist study of conversion' that queries women's motivations and experiences,[78] it is imperative to avoid essentialist notions of gender and facile generalisations about innate or socially constructed religiosity and instead to acknowledge that there is not a normative religious or conversion experience for either women or men, but rather a complex spectrum of possibilities.[79] Women were probably no more or less inclined to conversion than men: it was something they voluntarily embraced or rejected, or were compelled to perform, depending on individual circumstances and inclinations. The contemporary notion that women possessed an inherently deeper religious conviction – that they were 'to piety more prone' – was not an expression of some innate, unwavering predisposition toward faith, but rather one of widespread social and cultural assumptions and expectations.[80] Indeed, in the Mediterranean the motivation for 'turning Turk' for both men and women was inspired by a complex spectrum of socio-economic factors, though matters of faith may also have at times played a role. Conversion was never solely a religious act; rather, it occurred within a specific social context which had as great or greater a bearing as did issues of theology or praxis. Feminist scholarship has argued compellingly for the need 'to challenge the binarized nature of gender categories' and to adopt a more 'gender-critical' approach that moves beyond essentialist, dualist categories of man and woman and draws 'a sharp distinction' between their respective religious lives and identities.[81] The inclination to posit a single 'set of assumed commonalities' in women's and men's religiosity effaces the breadth and intricacy of both women's and men's religious experiences, which is evident in the lives of the renegade men and women of the early modern Mediterranean.

NOTES

1 Državni Arhiv u Dubrovniku, *Lettere di Levante* b. 38, 5 February 1593, cc. 42ᵛ–44ᵛ.
2 Marc Baer, *Honored by the glory of Islam: conversion and conquest in Ottoman Europe* (Oxford: Oxford University Press, 2008), p. 5; Tijana Krstić, *Contested conversions to Islam: narratives of religious change in the early modern Ottoman Empire* (Stanford: Stanford University Press, 2011), p. 22.
3 Državni Arhiv u Dubrovniku, *Lettere di Levante* b. 38, 5 February 1593, cc. 42ᵛ–44ᵛ.
4 Sophia Laiou, 'Christian women in an Ottoman world: interpersonal and family cases brought before the Shari'a courts during the seventeenth and eighteenth centuries (cases involving the Greek community)', in Amila Buturović and İrvin Cemil Schick (eds), *Women in the Ottoman Balkans: gender, culture, and history* (London: I. B.Tauris, 2007), p. 247; Ahmad ibn Naqib Al-Misri, *Reliance of the traveller*, ed. and trans. Nuh Ha Mim Keller (Evanston, IL: Sunna Books, 1994), pp. 532, 595–6; Maya Shatzmiller, 'Marriage, family, and the faith: women's conversion to Islam', *Journal of Family History*, 21 (1996), 242–3.
5 Fernand Braudel, *La Méditerranée et le Monde Méditerranéen à l'epoque de Philipe II*, 3 vols (Paris: Armand Colin, 1949); Sanjay Subrahmanyam, *Mughals and Franks* (Oxford: Oxford University Press, 2005), p. 213; Anthony Molho, 'Review of *The corrupting sea*', *Journal of World History*, 13 (2002), p. 490; Nicholas Purcell, 'The boundless sea of unlikeness? On defining the Mediterranean', *Mediterranean Historical Review*, 18 (2003), 20–1.

6 Adriano Politi, *Dittionario toscano: compendio del vocabolario della Crusca* (Rome: Gio. Angelo Ruffinelli, 1614), p. 667; *Le dictionnaire de l'Académie françoise, dédié au Roy* (Paris: Veuve de Jean Baptiste Coignard, 1694), 2.122; Guy Miège, *A new dictionary French and English, with another English and French* (London: Thomas Dawks for Thomas Basset, 1677), Zzz4.

7 Bartolomé Bennassar, 'Conversion ou reniement? Modalitiés d'une adhésion ambigué des chrétiens à l'Islam (XVIe–XVIIe siècles)', *Annales, ESC*, 6 (1988), 1349-50; Mercedes García-Arenal, 'Les conversions d'Européens à l'Islam dans l'histoire: esquisse générale', *Social Compass*, 46 (1999), 276-7.

8 Daniel J. Vitkus, 'Early modern orientalism: representations of Islam in sixteenth- and seventeenth-century Europe', in David R. Blanks and Michael Frassetto (eds), *Western views of Islam in medieval and early modern Europe: perception of other* (New York: St. Martin's Press, 1999), p. 215; Shatzmiller, 'Marriage, family, and the faith', pp. 235, 260.

9 Horatio Forbes Brown, *Studies in the history of Venice*, 2 vols (London: John Murray, 1907), vol. 2, pp. 146-58; Archivio di stato di Venezia, *Senato deliberazioni Costantinopoli*, b. 6, passim. See also, *V Savii alla mercanzia, Risposte*, reg. 142, cc. 9^v–10^r, 25 March 1607.

10 Archivio di stato di Venezia, *Capi del consiglio di X, lettere di rettori*, b. 281, #198, 8 October 1572.

11 See Bartolomé and Lucile Bennassar, *Les chrétiens d'Allah: l'histoire extraordinaire des renégats, XVIe–XVIIe siècles* (Paris: Perrin, 1989), p. 289; Stephen Clissold, 'Christian renegades and Barbary Corsairs', *History Today*, 26 (1976), 509. Dan's figures are supported by other sources, Mercedes García-Arenal and Miguel Ángel de Bunes, *Los españoles y el Norte de África. Siglos XV–XVIII* (Madrid: Editorial MAPFRE, 1992), p. 244.

12 Anton Minkov, *Conversion to Islam in the Balkans: Kisve Bahası petitions and Ottoman social life, 1670–1730* (Leiden: Brill, 2004), pp. 169-70.

13 Bennassar and Bennassar, *Les chrétiens d'Allah*, p. 291.

14 Simon Coleman, 'Continuous conversion? The rhetoric, practice, and rhetorical practice of charismatic Protestant conversion', in Andrew Buckser and Stephen D. Glazier (eds), *The anthropology of religious conversion* (Lanham, MD: Rowman and Littlefield, 2003), pp. 17-18; John Lofland and Norman Skonovd, 'Conversion motifs', *Journal for the Scientific Study of Religion*, 20 (1981), 375-7; Kenneth Mills and Anthony Grafton, 'Introduction', in Kenneth Mills and Anthony Grafton (eds), *Conversions: old worlds and new* (Rochester: University of Rochester Press, 2003), p. ix.

15 Massimo Leone, *Saints and signs: a semiotic reading of conversion in early modern Catholicism* (Berlin: Walter de Gruyter, 2010), pp. 48-50.

16 Tijana Krstić, 'Illuminated by the light of Islam and the glory of the Ottoman sultanate: self-narratives of conversion to Islam in the age of confessionalization', *Comparative Studies in Society and History*, 51 (2009), 44-5;

J. Dudley Woodberry, 'Conversion in Islam', in H. Newton Malony and Samuel Southard (eds), *Handbook of religious conversion* (Birmingham, AL: Religious Education Press, 1992), pp. 22–40.

17 Henry Blount, *A Voyage into the Levant* ... *The second edition* (London, 1636), O4ᵛ.

18 Lucetta Scaraffia, *Rinnegati: per una storia dell'identità occidentale* (Rome-Bari: Laterza, 1993), pp. 4–5; Bennassar and Bennassar, *Les chrétiens d'Allah*, pp. 228–50; Bennassar, 'Conversion ou reniement?', pp. 1363–4; Salvatore Bono, 'Pascià e Raìs algerini di origine italiana', in R. H. Raniero (ed.), *Algeria e Italia* (Milan: Marzorati, 1982), pp. 200–1.

19 Anthony Nixon, *The three English brothers* (London, 1607), H4ᵛ; repr. Amsterdam: Theatrum Orbis Terrarvm, 1970).

20 Clissold, 'Christian renegades', p. 515.

21 Gilles Veinstein, 'Sur les conversions à l'Islam dans les Balkans ottomans avant le XIXᵉ siecle', *Dimensioni e problemi della ricerca storica* 2 (1996), 165; Bennassar, 'Conversion ou reniement?', p. 1361; Norman Daniel, *Islam and the West: the making of an image*, rev. edn (Oxford: Oneworld, 1993), p. 308.

22 Lewis R. Rambo, *Understanding religious conversion* (New Haven, CT: Yale University Press, 1993), pp. 3–7.

23 E. Natalie Rothman, 'Becoming Venetian: conversion and transformation in the seventeenth-century Mediterranean', *Mediterranean Historical Review*, 21 (2006), 40.

24 Jocelyne Dakhlia, 'Turcs de profession? Réinscriptions lignagères et redéfinitions sexuelles des convertis dans les cours maghrébines (XVIᵉ–XIXᵉ siècles)', in Mercedes García-Arenal (ed.), *Conversion islamiques: Identités religieuses en Islam méditerranéen?* (Paris: Maisonneuve et Larose, 2001), p. 151.

25 Kenneth Charlton, *Women, religion and education in early modern England* (London: Routledge, 1999), pp. 57–8; Christine Peters, *Patterns of piety: women, gender and religion in late medieval and Reformation England* (Cambridge: Cambridge University Press, 2003), pp. 7, 154.

26 Tony Walter and Grace Davie, 'The religiosity of women in the modern West', *British Journal of Sociology*, 49 (1998), 640–41, 648; Edward H. Thompson, Jr., 'Beneath the status characteristic: gender variations in religiousness', *Journal for the Scientific Study of Religion*, 30 (1991), 381–2. See also David de Vaus and Ian McAllister, 'Gender differences in religion: a test of the structural location theory', *American Sociological Review*, 52 (1987), 472; Alan S. Miller and John P. Hoffman, 'Risk and religion: an explanation of gender differences in religiosity', *Journal for the Scientific Study of Religion*, 34 (1995), 63–4.

27 Gail Corrington Streete, *Redeemed bodies: women martyrs in early Christianity* (Louisville, KY: Westminster John Knox press, 2009); Joyce

E. Salisbury, *Perpetua's passion: the death and memory of a young Roman woman* (New York: Routledge, 1997).

28 Caroline Walker Bynum, *Holy fast and holy feast: the religious significance of food to medieval women* (Berkeley: University of California Press, 1987).

29 Shatzmiller, 'Marriage, family, and the faith', pp. 236-7.

30 Krstić, *Contested conversions*, pp. 156-7.

31 Patricia Crawford, *Women and religion in England: 1500-1750* (London: Routledge, 1993), pp. 60-2; Frances Dolan, *Whores of Babylon: Catholicism, gender, and seventeenth-century print culture* (Ithaca, NY: Cornell University Press, 1999), p. 136.

32 Marcel Bernos, 'Conversion ou apostasie? Comment les chrétiens voyaient ceux qui quittaient leur eglise pour l' "eglise adverse"', *Seventeenth-Century French Studies*, 18 (1996), 41; Christine Peters, *Women in early modern Britain, 1450-1640* (New York: Palgrave Macmillan, 2004), pp. 139-40; Stavro Skendi, 'Crypto-Christianity in the Balkan area under the Ottomans', *Slavic Review*, 26 (1967), 232.

33 Mark D. Meyerson, 'Aragonese and Catalan Jewish converts at the time of the expulsion', *Jewish History*, 6 (1992), 138; Renée Levine Melammed, 'Crypto-Jewish women facing the Spanish Inquisition: transmitting religious practices, beliefs, and attitudes', in Mark D. Meyerson and Edward D. English (eds), *Christians, Muslims, and Jews in medieval and early modern Spain: interaction and cultural change* (Notre Dame, IN: University of Notre Dame Press, 2000), pp. 199-200, 208-9. Also Anna Foa, 'The Marrano's kitchen: external stimuli, internal response, and the formation of the Marrano persona', in Elliott Horowitz and Moises Orfali (eds), *The Mediterranean and the Jews: society, culture, and economy in early modern times* (Ramat Gan: Bar-Ilan University Press, 2002), pp. 14-15.

34 Luciano Allegra, 'Conversioni dal ghetto di Torino', *Dimensioni e problemi della ricerca storica* 2 (1996), 189-90, 194-5; Luciano Allegra, 'All'origini del mito della Jewish momie. Ruoli economici e ideali domestici delle ebree italiane nell'età moderna', in Claire E. Honess and Verina R. Jones (eds), *Donne delle minoranze. Le ebree e le protestanti d'Italia* (Turin: Claudiana, 1999), p. 215.

35 Khalid Bekkaoui, *White women captives in North Africa: narratives of enslavement, 1735-1830* (London: Palgrave Macmillan, 2011), p. 11. The original Arabic source is Ahmed Bouchareb, *Al-Maghariba fi al-Burtugal khilala al-Qarn as-Sadis Ashar* (Rabat: Manshurat Kulliyat al-Adab, 1996), pp. 107, 121.

36 James B. Tueller, 'The assimilating Morisco: four families in Valladolid', *Mediterranean Studies*, 7 (1998), 168; Mary Elizabeth Perry, 'Behind the veil: Moriscas and the politics of resistance and survival', in Magdalena S. Sanchez and Alain Saint-Saens (eds), *Spanish women in the*

Golden Age: images and realities (Westport, CT: Greenwood Press, 1996), pp. 39–40.

37 Mary Elizabeth Perry, 'Moriscas and the limits of assimilation', in Meyerson and English (eds), *Christians, Muslims, and Jews*, p. 278.

38 Perry, 'Behind the veil', pp. 39–40; Jacqueline Fournel-Guérin, 'La femme morisque en Aragon', in Louis Cardillac (ed.), *Les morisques et leur temps* (Paris: Éditions du Centre national de la recherche scientifique, 1983), pp. 533–4. The term 'weapons of the weak' was coined by James C. Scott, *Weapons of the weak: everyday forms of peasant resistance* (New Haven, CT: Yale University Press, 1985).

39 Mary Elizabeth Perry, *The handless maiden: Moriscos and the politics of religion in early modern Spain* (Princeton: Princeton University Press, 2005), pp. 5, 10; Fournel-Guérin, 'La femme morisque en Aragon', pp. 528, 533–4; Perry, 'Moriscas', pp. 274–5; Bruce Taylor, 'The enemy within and without: an anatomy of fear on the Spanish Mediterranean littoral', in William G. Naphy and Penny Roberts (eds), *Fear in early modern society* (Manchester: Manchester University Press, 1997), p. 89.

40 Perry, *The Handless Maiden*, p. 79; Perry, 'Behind the veil', pp. 40, 44.

41 Merry E. Wiesner, 'Women's response to the Reformation', in R. Po-chia Hsia (ed.), *The German people and the Reformation* (Ithaca, NY: Cornell University Press, 1988), pp. 148, 150–1; Alison Weber, *Teresa of Avila and the rhetoric of femininity* (Princeton: Princeton University Press, 1996), pp. 19–25.

42 Natalie Zemon Davis, 'Women on top: symbolic sexual inversion and political disorder in early modern Europe', in Barbara A. Babcock (ed.), *The reversible world: symbolic inversion in art and society* (Ithaca, NY: Cornell University Press, 1978), pp. 147–8; Laura A. Lewis, 'The "weakness" of women and the feminization of the Indian in colonial Mexico', *Colonial Latin America Review*, 5 (1996), 84; Merry E. Wiesner, *Gender, church and state in early modern Germany* (London: Longman, 1998), p. 85; Bennassar and Bennassar, *Les chrétiens d'Allah*, p. 235; Eric R. Dursteler, *Venetians in Constantinople: nation, identity, and coexistence in the early modern Mediterranean* (Baltimore: Johns Hopkins University Press, 2006), pp. 93–4; Eva C. Topping, 'Patriarchal prejudice and pride in Greek Christianity: some notes on origins', *Journal of Modern Greek Studies*, 1 (1983), 9–11.

43 Robert Mantran, *Istanbul au siècle de Soliman le Magnifique* (Paris: Hachette, 1994), p. 168; Bernard Lewis, *Islam and the West* (Oxford: Oxford University Press, 1993), pp. 49–50; Moktar Djebli, 'Takiyya', in H. A. R. Gibbs, et al. (eds), *Encyclopedia of Islam*, 2nd edn, 12 vols (Leiden: Brill, 1960–2004), 10.134–36; Madeline C. Zilfi, 'Muslim women in the early modern era', in Suraiya N. Faroqhi (ed.), *The Cambridge history of Turkey*, vol. 3: *the later Ottoman Empire, 1603–1839* (Cambridge: Cambridge University Press, 2006), p. 232.

44 Judith Lieu, 'The "attraction of women" in/to early Judaism and Christianity: gender and the politics of conversion', *Journal for the Study of the New Testament*, 72 (1998), 7; Rodney Stark, *The rise of Christianity* (New York: HarperCollins, 1996), p. 100. See also Ross S. Kraemer, 'The conversion of women to ascetic forms of Christianity', *Signs*, 6 (1980), 298–307.

45 Stark, *Rise of Christianity*, pp. 95–128. For a dissenting position, see Lieu, 'The "attraction of women"', p. 7.

46 John L. Esposito, *What everyone needs to know about Islam*, 2nd edn (Oxford: Oxford University Press, 2011), p. 105.

47 This view has been challenged as well; see Shannon McSheffrey, *Gender and heresy: women and men in Lollard communities, 1420–1530* (Philadelphia: University of Pennsylvania Press, 1995), pp. 138–9.

48 Peters, *Women in early modern Britain*, pp. 133–4; Dolan, *Whores of Babylon*, p. 27.

49 Nancy Roelker, 'The appeal of Calvinism to French noblewomen in the sixteenth century', *Journal of Interdisciplinary History*, 2 (1972), 402; Natalie Zemon Davis, *Society and culture in early modern France* (Stanford: Stanford University Press, 1975), p. 81; Susan C. Karant-Nunn, 'Continuity and change: some effects of the Reformation on the women of Zwickau', *Sixteenth Century Journal*, 12 (1982), 180.

50 Marc Baer, 'Islamic conversion narratives of women: social change and gendered religious hierarchy in early modern Ottoman Istanbul', *Gender & History*, 16 (2004), 426; Stephen Ortega, '"Pleading for help": gender relations and cross-cultural logic in the early modern Mediterranean', *Gender and History*, 20 (2008), 334–5.

51 Krstić, *Contested conversions to Islam*, pp. 162–3.

52 Bruce Masters, *Christians and Jews in the Ottoman Arab world* (Cambridge: Cambridge University Press, 2001), pp. 27, 34–5; Ronald C. Jennings, *Christians and Muslims in Ottoman Cyprus and the Mediterranean world, 1571–1640* (New York: New York University Press, 1993), pp. 139–41; Morris S. Goodblatt, *Jewish life in Turkey in the XVIth century: as reflected in the legal writings of Samuel De Medina* (New York: The Jewish Theological Seminary of America, 1952), p. 104; Paul Sant Cassia, 'Religion, politics and ethnicity in Cyprus during the Turkocratia (1571–1878)', *Archives Européennes de sociologie*, 27 (1986), 22–4; Eyal Ginio, 'Childhood, mental capacity and conversion to Islam in the Ottoman state', *Byzantine and Modern Greek Studies*, 25 (2001), 94–5.

53 Ortega, '"Pleading for help"', pp. 332–48; Eric R. Dursteler, 'Defending virtue and preserving reputation: gender and institutional honor on the early modern Dalmatian Frontier', *Journal of Early Modern History*, 15 (2011), 367–84.

54 Eric R. Dursteler, *Renegade women: gender, identity and boundaries in the early modern Mediterranean* (Baltimore: Johns Hopkins University Press, 2011), pp. 1–33.

55 Kim Siebenhüner, 'Conversion, mobility and the Roman inquisition in Italy around 1600', *Past and Present*, 200 (2008), 5–35.

56 Ella-Natalie Rothman, 'Between Venice and Istanbul: trans-imperial subjects and cultural mediation in the early modern Mediterranean' (Ph.D. dissertation, University of Michigan, 2006), pp. 133–4.

57 Bartolomé Bennassar, 'Conversions, esclavage et commerce des femmes dans les peninsules iberique, italienne ou balkanique aux XVIe et XVIIe siècles', *Dimensioni e problemi della ricerca storica*, 2 (1996), 106.

58 Cesarina Casanova, 'Il buon matrimonio di Anna Maria alias Cremesina, neofita lughese', in Claire E. Honess and Verina R. Jones (eds), *Donne delle minoranze. Le ebree e le protestanti d'Italia* (Turin: Claudiana, 1999), pp. 202–6.

59 Allegra, 'Conversioni dal ghetto di Torino', pp. 188–9; Dursteler, *Renegade women*, pp. 26–9; Siebenhüner, 'Conversion', p. 7.

60 Alice Kessler-Harris, 'What is gender history now?', in David Cannadine (ed.) *What is history now?* (New York: Palgrave Macmillan, 2004), pp. 101–2; Wiesner, *Gender, church and state*, p. 6.

61 Leslie P. Peirce, *The imperial harem: women and sovereignty in the Ottoman Empire* (Oxford: Oxford University Press, 1993), pp. 219–28; Judith E. Tucker, 'Rescued from obscurity: contributions and challenges in writing the history of gender in the Middle East and North Africa', in Teresa A. Meade and Merry E. Wiesner-Hanks (eds), *A companion to gender history* (Malden: Blackwell, 2004), p. 395.

62 Eric R. Dursteler, 'Fleeing "the vomit of infidelity": borders, conversion and muslim women's agency in the early modern Mediterranean', in Kent Shull and Christine Verhaaren (eds), *Living in the Ottoman realm: sultans, subjects, and elites* (Bloomington: Indiana University Press, 2016), pp. 182–93.

63 Chiara Povero, *Missioni in terra di frontiera: La Controriforma nelle Valli del Pinerolese. Secoli XVI–XVIII* (Rome: Istituto Storico dei Cappuccini, 2006), p. 371; Luciano Allegra, 'Modelli di conversione', *Quaderni storici*, 78 (1991), 903–4.

64 E. Natalie Rothman, *Brokering empire: trans-imperial subjects between Venice and Istanbul* (Ithaca, NY: Cornell University Press, 2011), p. 147. A study of Poland-Lithuania from 1754 to 1770 found a similar proportion of Jewish women converts to Christianity. See Magdalena Teter, 'Jewish conversions to Catholicism in the Polish-Lithuania commonwealth of the seventeenth and eighteenth centuries', *Jewish History*, 17 (2003), 262.

65 Minkov, *Conversion to Islam*, p. 170.

66 Bernard Heyberger, 'Frontières confessionnelles et conversions chez les

chrétiens orientaux (XVIIe–XVIIIe siècles)', in Mercedes García-Arenal (ed.), *Conversions islamiques: Identités religieuses en Islam méditerranéen* (Paris: Maisonneuve-Larose, 2001), p. 250 n. 36.

67 M'hamed Oualdi, 'D'Europe et d'Orient, les approches de l'esclavage des chrétiens en terres d'Islam', *Annales. Histoires et sciences sociales*, 63 (2008), 836–7. See Robert C. Davis, *Holy war and human bondage: tales of Christian-Muslim slavery in the early-modern Mediterranean* (Santa Barbara, CA: ABC-CLIO, 2009), pp. 37–66, 230–2; Salvatore Bono, *Un altro Mediterraneo: una storia comune fra scontri e integrazioni* (Rome: Salerno Editrice, 2008), p. 84. Cf. for a more modest estimation of the numbers of captives involved: Walter Kaiser (ed.), *Le commerce des captifs, les intermédiares dans l'échange et le rachat des prisonniers en Méditerranée xv–xviii siècles* (Rome: École française de Rome, 2008) and Gillian Weiss, *Captives and corsairs: France and slavery in the early modern Mediterranean* (Stanford: Stanford University Press, 2011). Cf. Jocelyne Dakhlia and Wolfgang Kaiser (eds), *Les Musulmans dans l'histoire de l'Europe*: vol. 2, *passages et contacts en Méditerranée* (Paris: Albin Michel, 2013).

68 Bennassar and Bennassar, *Les chrétiens d'Allah*, p. 291; Luis Alberto Anya Hernández, 'La invasión de 1618 en Lanzarote y sus repercusiones socio-económicas', in Francisco Morales Padrón (ed.), *VI coloquio de historia Canario-Americana*, vol. 3 (Las Palmas: Cabildo Insular de Gran Canaria, 1987), pp. 192–223.

69 Bennassar, 'Conversions, esclavage et commerce des Femmes', p. 102.

70 Joan W. Scott, 'Gender: a useful category of analysis', *American Historical Review*, 91 (1986), 1056; Sue Morgan, 'Rethinking religion in gender history: historiographical and methodological reflections', in Ursula King and Tina Beattie (eds), *Gender, religion and diversity: cross-cultural perspectives* (London: Continuum, 2005), p. 114.

71 Archivio di stato di Venezia, *Senato dispacci Costantinopoli*, b. 32, cc. 26^{r-v}, 12 September 1590; *Senato dispacci Costantinopoli*, b. 33, c. 360^r, 24 August 1591; *Senato deliberazioni Costantinopoli*, b. 10, copia 9 March 1604; *Senato deliberazioni Costantinopoli*, b. 8, 3 October 1591; *Senato dispacci Costantinopoli*, b. 32, cc. 235^v–236^r, 10 November 1590; 'Relation of Matteo Zane', in Eugenio Albèri (ed.), *Relazioni degli ambasciatori veneti al senato durante il secolo, decimosesto*, series 3, vol. 3 (Florence: Società editrice fiorentina, 1855), 9. p. 438; Maria Pia Pedani, 'Veneziani a Costantinopoli alla fine del XVI secolo', *Quaderni di studi arabi*, supplement to 5 (1997), 72–3.

72 Krstić, *Contested conversions*, p. 144.

73 Molly Greene, *A shared world: Christians and Muslims in the early modern Mediterranean* (Princeton: Princeton University Press, 2000), pp. 93–4.

74 Bennassar, 'Conversions, esclavage et commerce des femmes', p. 102.

75 Kessler-Harris, 'What is Gender History Now?', p. 102.

76 Anna Foa, 'Le donne nella storia degli ebrei in Italia', in Honess and Jones *Le donne delle minoranze*, p. 25.
77 Gillian Weiss, 'Commerce, conversion and French religious identity in the early modern Mediterranean', in Keith Cameron, Mark Greengrass, and Penny Roberts (eds), *The adventure of religious pluralism in early modern France* (Oxford: Peter Lang, 2000), p. 286.
78 Lewis R. Rambo, 'Theories of conversion: understanding and interpreting religious change', *Social Compass*, 46 (1999), 263.
79 Lieu, 'The "attraction of women"', pp. 7–8.
80 Jacqueline Eales, *Women in early modern England, 1500–1700* (London: UCL Press, 1998), p. 87.
81 Sîan Hawthorne, 'Religion and gender', in Peter B. Clarke (ed.), *The Oxford handbook of the sociology of religion* (Oxford: Oxford University Press, 2009), pp. 135, 142–4; Siebenhüner, 'Conversion', p. 9.

2

The quiet conversion of a 'Jewish' woman in eighteenth-century Spain

David Graizbord

> She responds that at present she holds and believes the articles of Our Holy Catholic Faith, which were made known to her by the Commissioner and in front of me, the notary, to whom she responded; and that the religion that she wishes to follow and profess in life and in death is the Catholic religion; and that she yearns for the same with intense and powerful desires to be baptized.[1]

The above quotation is a fragment of testimony recorded in Castile towards the end of the early modern period. Excerpts such as this are reminders that the centuries spanning that tumultuous era of nascent capitalism, religious wars, and the consolidation of absolutist states witnessed the creation in Europe of extensive institutional apparatuses designed to attract, convert, discipline, and thus 'save' souls. In the Iberian kingdoms, the tasks of religious correction, re-education, and absorption fell largely to the Holy Office. Spanish inquisitorial tribunals, which operated from the fifteenth century well into the nineteenth, have bequeathed to us an enormous trove of documents through which we may catch meaningful glimpses of the religious and social transformation of ordinary people. A question that engages this volume is how gender shaped these experiences. This chapter will approach that question microscopically through an examination of the inquisitorial case pertaining to the illiterate woman whose words are presented above. My response to the query will be tentative and requires ample qualification. The problematic nature of the inquisitorial documents upon which I have chosen to rely leave no other alternative. All the same, these sources allow us to isolate some of the subtle ways in which an early modern subject and her male interlocutors may have deployed normative ideas about femininity and masculinity in order to offer meaning to her identity and resolve her case. My discussion will focus specifically on ways in which an inquisitorial deponent and her interrogators manipulated gendered roles in order to construct a conversion narrative, one that may well have been at odds with non-normative aspects of the life that it was supposed to represent.

THE RELIGIOUS CONVERSION OF JEWS IN THE CONTEXT OF INQUISITORIAL ACTIVITIES

The would-be convert who interests us identified herself as a Jew. To contextualise her case, it is prudent to consider the historical relationship between the culture that generated the Spanish Holy Office on one hand, and on the other, Jews, both as actual human beings and as figments of Ibero-Christians' imagination. The conversion of Jews to Christianity in late medieval Spain and Portugal was often accompanied by much acrimony, and in many instances by violence. As historians know well, anti-Jewish agitation and riots engulfed these kingdoms in the late fourteenth and early fifteenth centuries. As many as two-thirds of the Castilian and Aragonese Jewish populations disappeared through forced baptism between 1391 and 1414. Largely owing to the propagandistic and popular qualities of the anti-Judaism that metastasised in the Iberian domains, changes in the cultural and social identity of Sephardic Jews were often dramatically public, and in that sense, 'loud'. We know this partly from Christian paintings and sermons that not only memorialised Jews' capitulation as a holy victory, but were also probably meant to stimulate the desire to convert them.

The 'loudest' converts were often those who accepted baptism of their own accord. Such people included the Dominican friars Pablo Christiani (b. thirteenth century) and Gerónimo de Santa Fe (1400–30), both of whom participated in religious disputations against their former coreligionists.[2] Less acrimonious conversions of Jews from the same and later periods have tended to escape scholarly attention because of their relatively quotidian and private nature, and I suspect, because the converts in such cases have often been women, whom no one expected to assume significant public roles as Christians, let alone to lead campaigns against Judaism. The conversion of Carlota Liot, a destitute widow and erstwhile merchant from the Holy Roman Empire who resided in Castile-La Mancha and who was probably baptised in 1790 or 1791, after voluntarily submitting to inquisitorial scrutiny, is one such inconspicuous or 'quiet' case.

By identifying as a person 'of Judaic nation' (fol. 16^r), Carlota Liot appealed to anti-Jewish motives and stereotypes that had been at the heart of inquisitorial endeavours in the Iberian domains since the Middle Ages. Specifically, she portrayed herself as a person with unique access to 'Jewish' criminality: from the outset, she declared that she knew of secret Jews in Andalusia, a claim she probably made because she knew that it would whet the Holy Office's appetite and help portray her as a helpful supplicant. Carlota's testimony also likened her to a category of suspects that had long interested the Holy Tribunals: allegedly crypto-Jewish women. Because of the roles they played in their households, these women became de facto custodians and principal transmitters of Iberian 'Jewish' culture, at least among New Christians of the first and second generations.[3] It is no surprise that inquisitorial edicts of faith and protocols for interrogating suspects depicted 'Judaism' in largely domestic terms, emphasising activities that women were expected to perform, such as cooking, cleaning, and educating young children in basic familial responsibilities.[4] In that sense, we may say that the Holy Office 'feminised' the figural Judaism that served as its original and most important target. As far as we can tell, *judeoconversos* (the Christianised descendants of Jews), as well as Jews who lived and travelled under assumed names in the Iberian peninsula, were physically indistinguishable from their 'Old Christian' counterparts. Material markers of confessional and ethnic identity pertained only to known foreigners. Among these subjects were but a handful of *Judíos de señal*: merchants to whom authorities granted special permission to trade temporarily in Spain on condition that the subjects wear a visible 'sign' of their Jewish status, for instance, a yellow cap or badge. There is no indication that Carlota Liot wore or otherwise displayed any such marker. One of the functions of the tribunals of the Spanish Holy Office, an institution that operated within a theoretically homogeneous Catholic society in which such markers were rare, was precisely to elaborate if not concoct material markers of cultural difference by 'finding' them in domestic and other private spaces – in suspects' kitchens, alcoves, hallways, and in parts of bodies that were usually covered (as in the case of circumcision).[5]

The sketchy 'Judaism' to which Carlota admitted was little more than the private, feminised, home-bound chimera just described. It conformed entirely to inquisitorial stereotypes and verbal formulae. In fact, she appears to have drawn her brief description of it directly from Christian folklore, inquisitorial edicts of faith, anti-Jewish sermons, and the like. For instance, she stated that the Jews 'worship a golden figure, like a calf', thereby repeating one of the oldest and most common polemical canards in the Christian anti-Jewish repertoire.[6] She also maintained that in her native country she and her family had observed the Jewish Sabbath from ten o'clock on Friday evenings, and that they did so with such rigour that they refrained from using even a single utensil (fol. 19ʳ). Both assertions betray a basic ignorance of Jewish religious practice, not to mention Jewish law.[7] It seems plausible that Carlota's testimony on this score was influenced by her interrogator or by another clerical or inquisitorial advisor. At any rate, her 'Judaism' is so predictable and caricatured that it is incredible to a modern eye.

The inquisitor who read transcripts of Carlota's words had his own doubts about it. Suffice it to note that the quality of her testimony concerning her 'Jewish' background leaves the strong impression that she was not and had never been a Jew. I would hazard that she merely knew that 'Jews' were the Inquisition's bogeymen, and, more importantly, that the Holy Office rewarded Jewish and other infidels who petitioned for conversion. Indeed, Carlota was probably counting on this, as had many other destitute or nearly destitute 'spontaneous declarants' over the course of the early modern centuries.

When Carlota Liot brought herself under the scrutiny of the Holy Tribunal of Toledo, that body had been in operation for over three hundred years. The perfect storm of late medieval anti-Judaic activity to which I refer above had long abated. Nevertheless, inquisitorial protocols had not changed significantly since the seventeenth century, when the tribunals were still busy prosecuting hundreds of alleged crypto-Jews, and fulminations against 'Judaism' issued like torrents from stages and pulpits during liturgical celebrations and other ceremonies. As significant for our purposes is the fact that the Iberian inquisitions had accumulated vast experience in evaluating and adjudicating travellers from foreign lands who claimed to be Jews and who declared their desire to become Catholics.[8]

On occasion, the aspiring converts were quasi-intellectuals whom the Holy Office could transform into 'learned' battering rams against the Jews. Such converts were highly atypical by the seventeenth century, however, and they could not match the exploits of late medieval arch-turncoats such as the religious disputants mentioned above. More common candidates for conversion in early modern Spain and Portugal included picaresque figures and other drifters who made of serial baptism a kind of personal strategy for material and social survival. An example of this type is Abraham Rubén. In 1624, Rubén admitted under interrogation that he had been baptised in Antwerp and in Madrid. His wife and travelling companion, María González, was a Portuguese Christian. She, too, confessed that she had been baptised twice: once as an infant and once after her first husband had left her and she had become Rubén's partner in subterfuge.[9]

This phenomenon of cultural commuting was a characteristic feature of the social margins of early modern Europe.[10] The extensive travels and chronic border-crossing of Ottoman Jews such as Abraham Rubén suggest that the same holds true for North Africa and the Levant, not to mention other distant imperial domains where the Ibero-Christian contest for pagan souls was still raging. Carlota Liot does not seem to have been a serial convert. Though she claimed to have travelled for much of her adult life, she does not appear to have been an adventurer of the most reckless sort. We may view Carlota, then, as a relatively unremarkable example of one-way cultural commuting within the European theatre of a much larger religious and political war for the allegiance and submission of individuals and communities.

INTRODUCTION TO THE SOURCE MATERIAL

In April and May of 1790, Carlota Liot appeared spontaneously before Silvestre Díaz Huerta, a parish priest and prior in the Castilian village of Consuegra, to declare that she wished to renounce her Jewish identity and embrace Christianity. This set in motion a largely standardised process of *'inquisición'*. A prosecutor of the Toledo tribunal quickly authorised Díaz Huerta to serve as his deputy, thereby enabling the prior to conduct Carlota's formal interrogation. Approximately eight months later, the process and attendant deliberations culminated when the prosecutor ordered that Carlota be examined by parish priests in Madridejos, Castile. They deemed her sincere, and so opened the way for her to be baptised. In this way, the Holy Office essentially authorised the delivery of an errant soul to 'the bosom of Our Holy Mother, the ... Catholic Church'.[11]

A main function of inquisitorial investigations was to generate meaningful narratives concerning the declarants' identities. Within the inquisitorial dossiers, notaries frequently recorded the life stories of suspects under the heading *discurso de su vida* – 'narrative of his/her life'. The particular *discurso* that interests us, along with some of Carlota's other testimony, tends, predictably, towards the formulaic and the obsequious. There are, however, important if subtle variations between her account and those of men in similar circumstances. So, too, the Holy Office reacted differently to her testimony than it did to similar testimonies offered by men. These differences point to gendered understandings of the self and its spiritual possibilities. Before dwelling on the differences, it is prudent to address the problematic nature of the sources that preserve the narratives in question.

Much of the information collected by the Iberian inquisitions against suspected religious criminals is of dubious reliability. Critics of naïve approaches to inquisitorial records point to the coercive nature of the inquisitorial process and setting. Sceptics also point to the hackneyed quality of many suspects' confessions, as well as to the fact that the Holy Office had a vested interest in producing incriminating evidence: simply put, the institution depended for its material viability on its capacity to confiscate the property of the people arrested at its behest. In light of these objections, it is understandable that an important minority of historians has approached the early modern Iberian inquisitions as factories for making religious criminals out of earnest (if ignorant) Christians, to loosely paraphrase the famous indictment of António Saraiva.[12]

Saraiva's categorical dismissal of the trustworthiness of inquisitorial dossiers overstates the case, however. Decades ago, Carlo Ginzburg, among others, showed that a systematic analysis of fragments of testimony that did *not* convey exactly what the inquisitors wished to hear may yield substantive material for the reconstruction of social and cultural history, including the history of gender.[13] A premise of this chapter is that a careful look at the inquisitors' responses to 'unscripted' testimony permits us a view of the normative models of Christian selfhood, with which these dutiful agents of religious discipline attempted to subjugate, and in so doing make 'sense' of unpredictable information in accordance with the orthodox standards of the Iberian churches.

It bears noting that in the late eighteenth century, the Spanish Holy Office was in decline. Spain was no longer the European hegemon and counter-reformist paragon. This meant that inquisitors were no longer an *avant-garde* in a worldwide crusade for Catholic discipline. The tectonic shifts of the Enlightenment and the French Revolution had begun to shake Spanish culture to its core, and would continue to do so during the Napoleonic wars.[14] All of this meant that, in 1790, when Carlota Liot entered the inquisitorial fray, the tribunals were driven by a need to produce documentation to justify their continued activity. Such material served to stake the Holy Office's claim to social relevance and political centrality at a time when its institutional weakness was deepening. In light of that need for documentation, we may conclude that from the inquisitors' point of view, Carlota's case had to be heard and resolved, however insignificant it may otherwise have been.

THE TALE(S) OF CARLOTA LIOT

Carlota Liot, aged twenty-nine, testified that she had been born to 'León' and 'Cecilia', people 'of [the] Judaic nation', in Hesse-Cassel, a province of the Holy Roman Empire. Carlota said she had been married to another 'León', known in Iberian lands as 'Antonio', who had recently died in a hospital in Málaga after a long career in petty commerce. Given the winding trajectory Carlota described in constructing the requisite account of her life, we may surmise that Antonio's mercantile pursuits had brought the couple to Andalusia:

> After the fairs [of Málaga] they [the declarant and her husband] went out to the towns of the county to sell [merchandise] without having a fixed domicile in any of them. She only stayed in the . . . city of Málaga for three years, at the time of the fairs. Though she left her [native] country eighteen years ago, more or less, six [of those] years she has been in Portugal, three in France, and the rest in Spain. She spent three of these [latter] years [in Málaga] as she has declared, and the six remaining [years] she was in Zaragoza, Pamplona, Valencia, and other cities, as well as in Barcelona, where a student for the price of half of a Piece of Eight prepared a certificate of marriage for her and Antonio. (fol. 25ᵛ)

Here Carlota was tacitly communicating something that women often conveyed to the tribunals of the Inquisition, namely that they were in no position to choose their places of residence, and that their husbands, fathers, and elder brothers were the ones who determined, through persuasion or coercion, where these women would live. For instance, María González, Abraham Rubén's wife, testified in 1625 that when her first husband, a field worker, had abandoned her and then (allegedly) died far away from their conjugal home in Santarem, Portugal, her new partner, Rubén, had persuaded her to travel with him to Madrid, whereupon she entrusted her young son to a neighbour and left the child behind. Rubén corroborated María's claim. He also confirmed her allegation that he had convinced her to pretend that she was Jewish and that she wished to become a Christian.[15]

Tales similar to that of María González are recorded in the dossiers of the few *conversas* (New Christian women) who had embraced Judaism in exile, returned from other lands to Iberia, and were investigated by the Toledo tribunal in the mid to late 1600s (in the eighteenth century such cases were rare). As I have noted elsewhere in my research, these women testified in almost identical language that their husbands had 'brought' them to Spain. The underlying message was uniform: as ordinary women of relatively modest means, they could scarcely travel on their own, for to do so was costly, dangerous, and unseemly.[16] More importantly, they did not possess the authority to decide where to travel and where to live. In other words, the women portrayed themselves as *innocent*, both in the sense of bearing no responsibility for their circumstances and for their religious lives, and in the sense of being 'decent' spouses, daughters, and sisters, that is, ingénues bonded to and living under the care of men. Neither age nor life stage was as relevant to religious penitence and conversion in these cases as was the condition of (gender-specific) dependency.

The life story that Carlota Liot built through her testimony is of someone who had been deprived of such guidance and attendant respectability, and was therefore adrift physically, economically, and spiritually. She described herself as virtually homeless and living hand-to-mouth on the margins of Andalusian society. She also implied that she had experienced little significant contact with more than a few people, especially after the death of her husband. The following excerpt is typical of what she told Prior Díaz Huerta during the inquisitorial proceedings:

> She does not know [on what] day Antonio died and was buried, because [she] had left the city of Málaga, in order to sell all kinds of [. . .] merchandise in the cities of Seville, Cordova, Ecija, and other towns, where she stayed for nine months. Upon her return to the city of Málaga she was notified that he had died ... about eight months earlier; and according to her calculation, [that is] about twenty-six months ago, more or less. He did not have a fixed home as his domicile in said city, as they lived in the streets where the fairs

that are frequent in that city were celebrated; such that when the [fairs] were [held] in the Calle de la Victoria, they took shelter and stayed by night in the house where a widow named Catalina has as her store, but that she does not recall her traits other than that she had her stalls and a large portal. For the lodging they paid five *reales* each night. When the fair took place in the ... Merchants' Street ... they spent the night at the Puerta de la Mar in a house that was a tavern. [The woman who hosted them there] was called María, a widow, to whom they paid four *reales* daily, but the house ... was leased. The declarant is not aware of the property's owner. When she went out to sell at the aforementioned time, Antonio was left in broken health in the Calle de la Victoria. She did not have any dealings or communication with people besides the two cited hostesses, Catalina or María, that was not through her sales, since after the fairs [the declarant and her husband] went out to the towns of the county to sell [merchandise] without having a fixed domicile in any of them [. . .] (fols 25^r–25^v)

[Later,] she became acquainted with and dealt with her countrywoman, Cristina, [who taught her the Law of Jesus Christ] in Vélez-Málaga. [Cristina] was the widow of an invalid whose name she does not know, and lived in a leased house located in the suburbs. She does not know the name of the street. Cristina lived from the work of her hands, threading and making buttons. Regarding [the] house, she cannot provide more details than that it stands apart, but that there are many little houses similar to it [that] stand alone. As for Cristina's personal traits, she can only say that she was a very old woman, of medium stature, with entirely white hair. She does not remember any more traits. (fols 25^v–26^r)

A few aspects of these tedious passages are noteworthy. The first is the high degree of independence and resourcefulness Carlota betrayed by outlining her life as an itinerant saleswoman and, indirectly, by doing so as an inquisitorial informant and candidate for baptism. Though it was probably not her intent, Carlota conveyed that she was perfectly capable of travelling by herself, and doing so constantly; of building relationships with women in various places; and of taking fateful decisions regarding her cultural orientation and spiritual status. An infantilised, upper-class housewife she was not. Her recourse to the Inquisition, and her probable fabrication of a Jewish background, may be viewed in this light as well. They suggest that she was desperate, to be sure, but that she was bold because of it. They may even hint at a capacity to connive. Holly Snyder speculates that Carlota's focus on a supposed religious mentor, the elderly 'Cristina', tells us that Carlota, in the manner of Martin Guerre, borrowed biographical details from the older woman (if, indeed, she existed), and perhaps some folkloric 'knowledge' regarding Jews as well.[17]

The second aspect I wish to underscore is related to the first. For all the autonomy she implicitly claimed, Carlota cast her life story in terms of her 'feminine' vulnerability. She was especially keen to convey that she suffered dire economic need and had been deprived of the respectable, sheltering authority and material sustenance of a man. As she put it virtually at the beginning of her first deposition, life had left her 'a poor *hostiatim* [Lat. 'victim'], because she has been robbed, and at present [she was] in a widow's state' (fol. 18ᵛ). Living 'off the grid' may well have made this narrative necessary. After all, Carlota asserted that she had no permanent home. She had no children, and no education. She was not even able to sign her own name. In other words, by her own admission she lacked the attributes of cultural power that would render her a stereotypical 'Jewish' or 'crypto-Jewish' woman, that is, someone capable of grave religious subversion, and hence of great interest to the Inquisition. What remained to Carlota was the option of an abject, 'womanly' surrender to a culturally 'male' institution – all inquisitors and, to my knowledge, all familiars were men. Rather than risk being branded as 'foolhardy, impudent, and arrogant', as so many women seers, *alumbradas*, and other religious dissidents had been, she offered her interrogators a tame, vulnerable, gendered soul on a silver platter.[18] What she could scarcely anticipate is that this strategy created a tension between her explicit normativity – her socially acceptable need for protection and spiritual guidance – and her implicit non-normativity – the fact that as a marginal traveller she did not conform to a traditionally respectable female role. I hazard that this ambiguity heightened the prosecutor's unease about her.

A third aspect to consider is the sheer vagueness of the information that Carlota provides in the above excerpt, as in much of her testimony. The prosecutor underscored this problem. He clearly suspected that Carlota was one of many shabby creatures who lied to the Holy Office about their origins, and approached baptism as a ticket to material and social comfort.[19] Noting several implausibilities and contradictions in Carlota's disclosures, the inquisitor cautioned Díaz Huerta not to fall for 'some fraud she may be trying to perpetrate' (fol. 27ʳ). The inquisitor's worry was probably that Carlota had already been baptised and was seeking a second (or third, or fourth) baptism. He further commanded the prior to interrogate her about the discrepancies in her story. Later still, the prosecutor complained that:

Her declarations still obscure the information that would be necessary to know whether she has been and is in reality a Jew, and whether she sincerely wishes to abjure that reprobate sect and receive the Holy Baptism. The fact that this woman is of vague quality, and does not cite a single person who can answer as to her civil status or moral character, and what is more, not even to her physical existence after so many years of traveling through so many towns and provinces of the realm, is a circumstance that recommends her very little with respect to the credibility of her statements. In certain terms it seems appropriate to the Prosecutor that for now a commission be given to ... examine the spontaneous declarant anew ... to ascertain whether in reality she has not received the Holy Baptism and has been of the Hebrew sect; and if her conversion is sincere; and she has been instructed in our holy Catholic dogmas; and it seems to them [that she] would persevere in Our Holy Catholic Apostolic Roman religion. (fols 36^r–36^v)

A 'WOMAN OF VAGUE QUALITY'

The prosecutor's scepticism had a firm basis. Already the officers whom he had sent to Málaga to try to find evidence that would corroborate Carlota's story had complained to him that the information she had provided was too scanty to make any determination as to its veracity. At the same time, I wonder whether it was Carlota's 'vague quality' *by itself* that put her credibility in doubt. To be more specific, I wonder whether the cultural models of femininity and masculinity through which the prosecutor regarded Carlota's narratives partly underlay his disbelief, or at least contributed to it. One way to address the question is to discuss instances – of which there were many – in which spontaneous supplicants for conversion who were men provided unspecific, even evasive information to the Holy Office, yet were not for that reason disbelieved. A case in point is that of Salomón Bergom, a 45-year-old carpenter and furniture-maker known in Spain as Carlos Bergamo.[20] One year after the closure of Carlota's dossier, the same inquisitorial tribunal that had had looked askance at her interrogated Salomón about his alleged Jewish past and activities in Spain. His responses were nearly as vague as Carlota's – even more so in some respects. The carpenter testified that he had fled his parents' home in Mantua at the age of nine, and joined the entourage of a nobleman whose last name he claimed not to know despite having served the knight for several years. Much like Carlota, Salomón said he had travelled extensively as his patron's dependant. After settling temporarily in various Austrian, Italian, and French cities and rural areas, Salomón had, in more recent years, become a journeyman carpenter in Galicia, Portugal, and finally, in Castile. He now found himself unemployed.[21]

There is virtually nothing in Salomón's 'recollections' to suggest that he had the slightest familiarity with Judaism. By and large his testimony did not even conform to more than two inquisitorial clichés regarding 'Jewish' practices. For instance, Salomón referred to only one of the quasi-ethnographic 'signs' by which the Holy Office purported to identify those who observed the 'Law of Moses': circumcision (see below).[22] He revealed no incriminating information about exotic cooking, eating, cleaning, and other rituals, though inquisitors routinely expected 'Jews' and 'Judaizers' to confess to such customs. Salomón's illicit 'faith', like that of thousands of inquisitorial deponents, bore little significant resemblance to the culture of early modern Jews – which, notably, they did not conceive as a 'religion', and did not call 'Judaism'.[23] At most, Salomón's 'Judaism' merely nodded in the direction of the sweeping presumption, articulated by the inquisitorial apologist Francisco Peña (among others) in 1587, that: 'It is an external sign of heresy when an action or word does not accord with the common practice of a Catholic people.'[24]

However, Salomón's discourse did hint at a patristic notion that Jews formed nothing more than a community of faith, one distinguished by its members' literal observance of the 'superseded' Law of Moses rather than the Law of Grace, and in that sense analogous to the Christian body of believers, for whom Christianity was a system of theological conviction and worship, not a shared, all-encompassing ethnic culture. Here is what little Salomón said about this fictive 'Judaism' and his supposed participation in it:

> He is not a baptized Christian because his parents reared him . . . in the Law of Moses, in which he has remained until now.
>
> He said that he believed in the Ten Commandments, as is taught in the Law of Moses, which is the one he had followed and held until the present day. [In his native country] the Christian religion is followed, except in the neighborhood of Elpuet[25] in the above-cited city of Mantua, in which that of Moses is followed, and they are circumcized according to it, as the declarant is as well.[26]

When his interrogator asked him why he now wished to embrace the Law of Grace, Salomón stated that it was because he had heard in some 'conversations of learned men' that although Christ could have redeemed the entire world with a single drop of His blood, He had opted to suffer exemplary travails for the benefit of all humankind. The carpenter added that he had also considered many times that 'the religion of Moses is abhorred everywhere'.[27] Consequently, Salomón said, he had come to the conclusion that the church's doctrines regarding Jesus' incarnation and salvific sacrifice, supported by the doctrine of divine omnipotence, were valid, while the error of the Jews was detestable, since Jews 'do not even [believe] the true Messiah has come, who is Jesus Christ, true God and man' (fol. 17^r). Elsewhere he reiterated that he had obtained 'light and instruction for knowing the truth' of Christianity only from 'a few private conversations, and sermons he has heard' (fols 17^v–18^r).

Salomón's inquisitorial case concluded quickly. At no time did his interrogator express any doubts about his veracity, despite the fact that, when prompted, the journeyman did not point an accusing finger at any 'secret Jews', and thus violated a centuries-old inquisitorial standard for establishing the moral reliability of those accused of 'Judaic error'. Furthermore, Salomón seemed to be oblivious to any specifically inquisitorial – as distinct from merely scholastic – conception of 'Jews' and 'Judaism'. How may we explain the leniency and gullibility of the Toledo tribunal in Salomón's case? I propose that the Holy Office deemed Salomón Bergom creditable because he possessed a number of attributes that afforded him certain advantages founded on normative gender roles to which the inquisitors subscribed.

For one thing, Salomón was literate. His inquisitorial dossier opens with a brief, neatly written, and suitably deferential letter in which he requests an audience with the Toledo tribunal and indicates that he is prepared to become a Christian.[28] The text offers a combination of Italian and Castilian orthography that probably lent credence to Salomón's claim that he was a native of Lombardy. To be sure, literacy was dangerous from an inquisitorial point of view, as it could expose individuals to heterodox ideas. Yet literacy could also confer respectability. This is demonstrated, for instance, by the favourable connotations that the masculine noun and adjective '*letrado*' (learned) bore in early modern Spain. By telling contrast, the feminine form, '*letrada*', was seldom if ever used, and carried no such associations.[29] Literacy and education in general were liabilities for the few learned women who figured as inquisitorial suspects, as these assets granted what churchmen often considered to be a socially inappropriate authority for people of the 'fragile sex'.[30] In the mid-seventeenth century, for example, an inquisitorial witness spoke of a New Christian '*doctora*' from Portugal who lived in France and taught other Iberian expatriates 'The Law of Moses'.[31] But the point of identifying her in this manner was to denounce the unharnessed, 'heretical' community to which she belonged. Consider also the inquisitorial condemnation that met educated women of high social status, such as the alleged *alumbrada* María de Cazalla (b. 1487), who may have quoted Erasmus, who wrote sophisticated letters to inquisitors in her own defence, and about whom one delator noted that she spoke 'with a great deal of wisdom for being a woman'.[32] Cazalla's case, like that of the more famous Teresa of Avila, underscores that the Inquisition persecuted women when they commanded a following based on their reputation as independent spiritual and intellectual leaders.[33]

Salomón Bergom also had in his favour the fact that he was a skilled artisan. He was someone who built things, rather than a person who merely trafficked in them; this in a society in which the term 'merchant' had been a euphemism for 'Jew'.[34] Unlike Carlota he was no itinerant seller, trapped in a geographic and social periphery for that reason. The fact that Salomón often travelled for a living and had no family did not seem to besmirch his character as far as the Holy Office was concerned. He was a journeyman carpenter, after all, and that was a traditionally acceptable, if humble, role for a male. Meanwhile, the very concept of a 'journeywoman' was entirely unknown. Carlota could scarcely hope to fit into such a category, as, in a sense, it did not exist. She was a woman out of her 'proper' place: she was a widow who had no permanent domicile and spent most of her days out of doors. This violated an early modern Ibero-Catholic ideal of women's enclosure that extended to homes, convents, and even brothels.[35]

Another of Salomón's advantages was his pious rhetoric. As we have seen, he said that he wished to become a Christian because he had been influenced by 'learned men', and declaimed his allegiance to Catholic dogma in formulaic language that is reminiscent of clerical sermons. Carlota, by contrast, alleged that she had been persuaded of and instructed in Christian doctrine by an old seamstress who lived in a rural shantytown. As a woman, and an indigent one at that, Cristina did not conform to normative images of religious erudition that the inquisitors presumed to embody, and to which they had given shape through the centuries in their role as cultural referees, prosecutors, and censors par excellence. To make matters worse, Carlota's alleged tutor was a foreigner, and someone whose existence the Holy Office was not even able to verify. Unlike Salomón Bergom, the young widow showed no particular enthusiasm in acknowledging the theological truth and praising the glory of Catholicism. Díaz Huerta did not challenge her to demonstrate her understanding of Christianity, despite her assertion that she knew 'some mysteries and prayers, such as the Credo, the Sacraments, the five Commandments of our Mother, the Church, the mystery of the Most Holy Trinity, how God is a remunerator, and the rest, in the native language [of Spain]' (fol. 19^v). It is as if the Priest assumed that his interlocutor was not worth the trouble of a thorough interrogation. Notice also that when Salomón was asked about his religious motivation he responded in lofty, if unspontaneous-sounding, terms. Carlota's response to the same question was comparatively trite and devoid of eagerness (though of course, we can only guess at the tone with which she delivered it):

> In the fifth [question] she was asked what cause, motive, or reason she has had and has for separating herself from the Judaic sect, and for wishing to follow and profess the Holy Catholic Faith of Our Mother the Roman Church. She responds: That being certain that if she dies a Jew it condemns her, and if she dies a Catholic she hopes to be saved and go to glory. (fol. 19^v)

From the foregoing it should be obvious that Carlota Liot's words painted her as a weak, demure, ignorant woman, yet one who was possibly deceptive and who lived an unconventional (though in reality quite common) life at the margins of Castilian society. So far, I have approached the emphasis she placed on her own helplessness, and the sketchiness of her information, as possible indications of bad faith. Yet we should consider the possibility that these qualities – especially the vagueness of which her prosecutor complained – may have been genuine.

Carlota's 'vague quality' at least allows us to question the authoritarian premise that guided her prosecutor, namely that she was either a calculating liar or an innocent. It is reasonable to surmise that by turning to her parish priest and to the Inquisition, Carlota was trying to escape a life of destitution and drift, but was not for that reason a complete cynic. The young woman's testimony engendered a tension between the gendered normativity to which she appealed as a supplicant, and the unconventional (if common) existence she led as a destitute or semi-destitute woman 'under the radar'. Yet this tension may have been beyond her powers to resolve. That task fell to the committee of clergymen who convened at the prosecutor's command to evaluate Carlota. Here is what they reported to him:

> Each and every one [of the Priests] interrogated and re-interrogated Carlota ... Each and every one of them found, and are of the common opinion that her desire to receive the Holy Baptism is true; so too that she has not received it to this day; yet, as to her knowledge of the Catholic doctrine, she is found to be very immature [...]
> When prompted, she has offered to remain in [the village of Madridejos] so that the Holy Sacrament is administered to her. (fol. 38^v)

Faced, then, with two normative interpretations of Carlota as a woman – Carlota as a religious criminal and deceiver interested only in her carnal survival, or as hapless ingénue – they chose the latter. Why they did so is anyone's guess. If Carlota's case had been heard one hundred years earlier, her fate might have been different. The religious temperature was much higher in the seventeenth century than it was in Carlota's day – too high, perhaps, to allow the committee the forgiving attitude on which they settled. What is clear is that in the eighteenth century, as in the seventeenth, being a pitiable soul, someone to whom the clergymen could safely condescend, was the price of admission to the bosom of the church and to the respectable society it purported to dominate. By setting this price, the men signalled their approval of a culturally sanctioned depiction of femininity as a condition of sinful fragility. Carlota was not fluent in the language of Ibero-Catholic power, with its obsessive concern with heretics and infidels, especially Jews; its role in warfare and empire-building; and its underlying appetite for control. However, she was consciously or unconsciously proficient in the cultural code that expressed clerical stereotypes of gender – just enough to make her case and win.

NOTES

1. Archivo Histórico Nacional, Inquisición de Toledo, legajo 159, expediente 11 1790–1791, fol. 19^r.
2. Documents pertaining to the disputations in which these converts participated, and a treatment of the broader phenomenon of medieval disputations against the Jews, are found in Hyam Maccoby (ed.), *Judaism on trial: Jewish-Christian disputations in the middle ages* (London: The Littman Library of Jewish Civilization, 1993).

3 On this phenomenon as it took shape in the fifteenth and sixteenth centuries, see for instance, Renée Levine Melammed, *Heretics or daughters of Israel? The crypto-Jewish women of Castile* (Oxford: Oxford University Press, 1999).
4 The scholarly literature on inquisitorial documents and procedures is vast. See for example Joaquín Pérez Villanueva, Bartolomé Escandell Bonet, and Angel Alcalá (eds), *Historia de la Inquisición en España y América*, 3 vols (Madrid: Biblioteca de Autores Cristianos, 1984–1993). On the Edicts of Faith, see Alicia Gojman Goldberg and Luis Manuel Martínez Escutia, 'La funcion del Edicto de Fe en el proceso inquisitorial'. http://biblio.juridicas.unam.mx/libros/2/700/19.pdf. Transcriptions of Edicts of Faith are found on various unscholarly websites. For example, an Edict from sixteenth-century Valencia is at http://www.gabrielbernat.es/espana/inquisicion/ie/proc/edictodefe/efevalencia/efevalencia.html.
5 On '*judíos de señal*', see Yosef Yerushalmi, 'Professing Jews in post-expulsion Spain and Portugal', in Saul Leiberman (ed.), *Salo Wittmayer Baron Jubilee Volume*, 3 vols (New York: Columbia University Press, 1974), II. 1023–1058. On modern anti-semitic discourse that fixates on supposed phenotypical features and associated psychological 'essences' and behaviours, see Sander Gilman, *The Jew's body* (London: Routledge, 1991).
6 See Pier Cesare Bori, *The golden calf and the origins of the anti-Jewish controversy*, trans. David Ward (Atlanta: Scholars Press, 1990).
7 Rabbinic law does not fix the beginning of the Sabbath to any particular hour, rather to the appearance of stars after sundown. Also, there is no categorical Halakhic prohibition against the use of utensils *per se* during the Sabbath; the prohibition applies to 'work', which legal authorities defined variously. The use of certain utensils was and is necessary for the celebration of the Sabbath according to rabbinic Halakhah.
8 On this subject, see for instance Bartolomé Benassar and Lucille Benassar, *Los cristianos de Alá*, trans. José Luis Gil Aristu (Madrid: Nerea, 1989; original edn. Paris, 1989); Michèle Janin-Thivos, 'Entre développement des affaires et convictions personnelles: la conversion des marchands étrangers devant l'Inquisition portugaise à l'époque moderne', in Albrecht Burkardt (ed.), *Commerce, voyage et expérience religieuse, XVIe–XVIIe siècles* (Rennes: Presses Universitaires de Rennes, 2007), pp. 275–86; Mercedes García-Arenal (ed.), *Entre el Islam y Occidente. Los judíos magrebíes en la Edad Moderna* (Madrid: Casa de Velázquez, 2003); Mercedes García-Arenal and Gerard Weigers, *A man of three worlds: Samuel Pallache, a Moroccan Jew in Catholic and Protestant Europe*, trans. Martin Beagles (Baltimore: Johns Hopkins University Press, 2003); and David Graizbord, 'A historical contextualization of Sephardi apostates and self-styled missionaries of the seventeenth century', *Jewish History*, 19 (2005), 287–313.

9 On Abraham Rubén and Maria González, see Richard L. Kagan and Abigail Dyer, *Inquisitorial inquiries: brief lives of secret Jews and other heretics* (Baltimore: Johns Hopkins University Press, 2004), pp. 88–118.
10 On cultural commuting by conversos and others, see the sources listed in n. 7, above. See also David Graizbord, *Souls in dispute: Converso identities in Iberia and the Jewish diaspora, 1580–1700* (Philadelphia: University of Pennsylvania Press, 2004); and Kim Siebenhüner, 'Conversion, mobility and the Roman Inquisition in Italy around 1600', *Past & Present*, 200 (2008), 5–35.
11 The quoted phrase was a Catholic formula, and commonplace. It appears numerous times in Carlota's dossier.
12 A heavily augmented restatement of Saraiva's thesis is António José Saraiva, The *Marrano factory: the Portuguese Inquisition and its New Christians 1536–1765*, trans. and augmented by H. P. Salomon and I. S. D. Sassoon (New York: Brill, 2001).
13 See Carlo Ginzburg, 'The inquisitor as anthropologist', in *Clues, myths, and historical method*, trans. John Tedeschi and Anne C. Tedeschi (Baltimore: Johns Hopkins University Press, 1986), pp. 141–8; and his classic study, *The night battles: witchcraft and agrarian cults in the sixteenth and seventeenth centuries*, trans. John Tedeschi and Anne C. Tedeschi (Baltimore: Johns Hopkins University Press, 1992).
14 On the decline and fall of the Holy Office, see for instance the historical survey in John Edwards, *The Spanish Inquisition* (Charleston: Tempus, 1999), pp. 109–34.
15 Kagan and Dyer, *Inquisitorial inquiries*, pp. 93–4, 101–5, 114–17.
16 Graizbord, *Souls in dispute*, p. 90.
17 Personal communication, 27 February 2012.
18 'Temeraria, atrevida, y arrogante', is what the Inquisition called mystically inclined *beata* it deemed undisciplined in 1576. Gillian T. W. Ahlgren, 'Francisca de los Apóstoles: a visionary voice for reform in sixteenth-century Toledo', in Mary E. Giles (ed.), *Women in the Inquisition: Spain and the New World* (Baltimore: Johns Hopkins University Press, 1999), p. 120.
19 Brian Pullan, *The Jews of Europe and the Inquisition of Venice, 1550–1670* (Oxford: Basil Blackwell, 1983), p. 244.
20 Bergom's case is preserved in Archivo Historico Nacional, Inquisición de Toledo, legajo 137, expediente 15 (1791–1792).
21 Ibid., fols. 15^v–16^r, 18^v–19^r.
22 The tribunal, for its part could have had Salomon examined by a physician, as was customary, to see whether he was circumcised. What is significant here is that it did not, as if his credibility were iron-clad.
23 Biblical Hebrew has no term that is neatly equivalent to 'religion'. To my knowledge, even writers and speakers of medieval and early modern forms

of Hebrew did not employ a biblical word denoting 'decree' (דת) to mean 'religion', as is the case with speakers of Modern Hebrew. The rabbinic word for 'faith' (אמונה) conveys 'allegiance', not 'theological belief' or 'confession', much less 'religion'. For its part, 'Judaism' may be viewed as the invention of nineteenth-century thinkers such as Moses Mendelssohn, whose aim was to reconfigure Jewish culture so that it would be comprehensible and politically acceptable to enlightened Protestants in existing and emerging central European nation-states. On this subject, see Laora Batnitzky, *How Judaism became a religion: an introduction to modern Jewish thought* (Princeton: Princeton University Press, 2011).

24 Francisco Peña (1587), quoted in Henry Kamen, 'Toleration and dissent in sixteenth-century Spain: the alternative tradition', *The Sixteenth Century Journal*, 19 (1988), 3–23.

25 This word is barely legible. It may convey 'El Puente' (the bridge), though I am not aware of any in the Ghetto of Mantua (est. 1610–1612). Given the city's location on a spur of land surrounded on three sides by a lagoon, however, this is not unlikely.

26 Archivo Histórico Nacional, Inquisición de Toledo, legajo 137, expediente 15 (1791–1792), fol. 16^v.

27 Ibid., fol. 17^r.

28 Here is Bergom's confession, from that letter: 'I declare that, being since birth [of], and reared in the Law of the Old Testament, for some years I have had the true desire to embrace the law of Jesus Christ, but experienced . . . some doubts that prevented me from following it. And now I have the[se doubts] convinced [*sic*.] and beg of you in surrender that you be so kind as to give an order of summons so that I am baptized and received in the bosom of the Holy Church, a grace which I hope to receive from Your Lordship's mercy.' (fol. 13^r).

29 Sebastián de Covarrubias's famous *Tesoro de la lengua Castellana o Española* (1611) defines 'letrado' (s.v., 'letra') in exclusively male terms, and does not include the theoretically possible term 'letrada' at all: 'Letrado, el que professa letras y han se alçado con este nobre los iuristas abogados' (http://fondosdigitales.us.es/fondos/libros/765/1083/tesoro-de-la-lengua-castellana-o-espanola/).

30 I borrow this formulation, which was commonplace in early modern Spain, from the inquisitorial defendant, the priest Jacinto Vásquez Araujo, Archivo Histórico Nacional, Inquisición de Toledo, legajo Archivo Histórico Nacional, Inquisición de Toledo, legajo 187, expediente 4 (1687–1688), fol. 228^v.

31 The case is mentioned in Carsten Lorenz Wilke, 'Un Judaïsme clandestin dans la France du XVIIe siècle: un rite au rythem de l'imprimerie', in Esther Benbassa (ed.), *Transmission et passages en monde juif* (Paris: Publisud, 1996), p. 308.

32 Father Gavriel Sánchez, in 'Document 12: excerpts from the trial of María de Cazalla, 1532–1534', in Lu Ann Homza (ed. and trans.), *The Spanish Inquisition, 1478–1614: an anthology of sources* (Indianapolis: Hackett Publishing, 2006), p. 114; more generally, see pp. 112–52.

33 On this phenomenon, see Gillian T. W. Ahlgren, *Teresa of Avila and the politics of sanctity* (Ithaca, NY: Cornell University Press, 1996).

34 On the stigma that attached to merchants in early modern Spain see, for example, Michell Cavillac, *Pícaros y mercaderes en el Guzman de Alfarache: reformismo burgués y mentalidad aristocrática en la España del siglo de oro*, trans. Juan M. Azpitarte (Granada: Universidad de Granada, 1994); and Edgar R. Samuel, 'The trade of the New Christians of Portugal in the seventeenth century', in R. D. Barnett and W. M. Schwab (eds), *The Sephardi heritage*, 2 vols (Grendon: Gibraltar Books, 1989), 2.100–14.

35 Mary Giles, 'Introduction' to Giles (ed), *Women in the Inquisition*, p. 10. On the ideal and its contested and uneven application, see for instance Mary Elizabeth Perry, *Gender and disorder in early modern Seville* (Princeton: Princeton University Press, 1990); María Dolores Pérez Baltasar, *Mujeres marginadas: las casas de recogidas en Madrid* (Madrid: Gráficas Lormo, 1984); and Alain Saint-Saëns and Magdalena Sánchez (eds), *Portraits of Spanish women in the Golden Age: images and realities* (Westport, CT: Greenwood Press, 1996).

3
'A father to the soul and a son to the body': gender and generation in Robert Southwell's *Epistle to his father*

Hannah Crawforth

Following his arrest in June 1592 the Jesuit priest and poet Robert Southwell (1561–95) was imprisoned in the Tower of London, where he underwent torture, including the recently adopted practice of hanging by the hands. Sir Robert Cecil, who attended his examinations, was later heard to say of this method that 'they had a new kind of torture, no less cruel than the rack, and such that no man could bear it'; nonetheless, 'he had seen Robert Southwell, being thus suspended, remain as dumb as a tree-stump; and it had not been possible to make him utter one word'.[1] Cecil's choice of metaphor is chillingly apt, for images of trees are central to Southwell's own writing, where they stand in for the idea of generation, in all its various senses. And it was of course Southwell's refusal to comply with the Protestant practices demanded of members of his generation that landed him in the Tower. Also of interest here is Cecil's curiously sexless phrase 'no man could bear it', which seems to place Southwell beyond gender boundaries, inviting the reader to consider whether his apparently superhuman feat of endurance transcends his physical, masculine, state.

Taking Cecil's remarks as its point of departure, this chapter is concerned with the relationship between the idea of generation and concepts of gender in Southwell's literary work. Both words ultimately derive from the same Latin root, *genus*, meaning 'stock', 'race', or 'kind', which gives rise to the verb *generare*, 'to create' or 'to beget'.[2] This constellation of terms is laid out in the earliest English dictionaries, which appeared shortly after Southwell's death during the first part of the seventeenth century. John Minsheu's etymological lexicon, *Ductor in linguas: the guide into tongues* (1617), traces 'Gender, as the masculine or feminine gender' to the Latin *genus*, from which 'Generation *or genealogie*' also derives, for example.³ In what follows I seek to understand the interplay of these related terms in Southwell's work as an underground Jesuit priest attempting to engender a process of conversion in his own family and the English population at large. In keeping with the aims of this collection as a whole, I contend that profoundly – indeed, productively – unstable notions of gender lie at the heart of early modern conversion narratives, an argument I here extend to embrace the etymologically related, and equally multivalent, concept of generation. Generation and gender are key terms through which Southwell encounters the world, defining the material and bodily experience that is central to his poetics and by which he seeks to effect conversion, a process I understand here as a mode of affiliation, in which identity is constructed through sensory practices, including speech.⁴

Southwell wrote a series of substantial prose works, printed by Henry Garnett's secret presses. These included the epistolary guide to enduring imprisonment and facing martyrdom, *An epistle of comfort, to the reverend priestes, & to the honorable, worshipful, & other of the laye sort, restrayned in durance for the Catholicke fayth* (Paris [London], 1578–79), a series of consolatory letters addressed to the recusant Earl of Arundel following a bereavement in 1591, printed posthumously as *The triumphs over death: or, a consolatorie epistle, for afflicted mindes, in the affects of dying friends, &c.* (London, 1595), and a spiritual guide written for the earl's wife, the Countess of Arundel, but directed towards pious Catholic noblewomen at large, *A shorte rule of good life, &c.* (London [Douai?], 1596–97). It is Southwell's poetry for which he is best known, and that has had most influence upon both his contemporaries and successors, however. Circulated in manuscript amongst the Catholic community during his lifetime, Southwell's lyrics attempted to reclaim the form, then inevitably identified with love poetry, as a vehicle for spiritual verse. They were published in the wake of his execution by the Protestant printer John Wolfe, who divested them of all references to overtly Catholic content (such as the Virgin Mary and the name of the author), and titled the collection *Saint Peters complaint, with other poemes* (London, 1595). The success of the volume is attested by the fact that seven further editions appeared over the following two decades.⁵ A need to redress imbalances of the kind introduced by Wolfe's interference has ensured that Southwell's Catholic faith has been the determining factor in many previous accounts of his poetics, with very few notable exceptions.[6] I proceed here from the presumption that scholarly attention to the question of Southwell's religion has eclipsed consideration of the other forces that drive him; his relationship to his family, particularly the older generations of Southwells, and a particular sense of gender identity, based upon an intensely physical understanding of bodily experience, are as much a part of his writing as his recusancy.

In 1595, after holding his silence for nearly three years, 'dumb as a tree-stump' even under torture, Southwell unexpectedly wrote to Cecil confirming his Catholicism and thus condemning himself to a long-awaited execution. His letter states that Southwell had returned to England from the relative safety of the Jesuit College in Rome in order to minister to his family, whose conformity to the reformed church he bitterly regretted, and whom he hoped to (re)convert, persuading them to return to the Catholic faith.[7] We might note here that in early modern England being 'born again' into true religion, whichever side of the doctrinal divide one stood upon, was known as the process of 'regeneration'.[8] The hope his family might be 'regenerated' in the specific sense I have just outlined also lies behind Southwell's shorter prose work *An epistle of a religious priest unto his father*, which was written upon his return from Rome in May 1586, and which Southwell signs 'Your most dutiful and loving son'.[9] Dutiful this letter may be, but loving it certainly is not. The text is extraordinary in its tone: belligerent, threatening, and seemingly lacking in any compassion for what Southwell sees to be his father's inevitable fate, should he fail to return to the Catholic faith. Moreover, there is none of the intergenerational deference, the respect for one's elders, that we might expect to find in such a document.[10]

Southwell's *Epistle* outlines a horrifying vision of his father's 'departing-bed', asking that he imagine himself 'burdened with the heavy load of your former trespasses, and gored with the sting and prick of a festered conscience', feeling 'the cramp of death wresting your heartstrings' (207). In lines that seem to pre-empt John Donne's more famous poem, 'The Apparition', Southwell laments, 'O how much would you give for one hour of repentence!' (207), evoking the Catholic concept of the deathbed revocation of sins.[11] The *Epistle* goes on to attack what Southwell sees as his father's decision to privilege worldly concerns over spiritual ones, by attempting to protect a vast fortune from recusancy fines. Using the terms of a business transaction he asks, 'Why then do you not at the least devote that small remnant and surplusage of these your latter days, procuring to make an atonement with God, and to free your conscience from such corruption as by your schism and fall hath crept into it?' (211). The schism alluded to here not only divides Southwell's father from what his son sees as the true church; it also divides him from his son.

The Southwell family's history was rife with conversions and reconversions, leading to multiple instances of intergenerational conflict of this sort. Whilst Robert Southwell, and quite probably his mother, would continue to adhere to Catholicism, his grandfather, Richard Southwell, had been responsible for the violent destruction of several monasteries in the area of Norfolk where Robert spent his childhood, including the ancient shrine of Our Lady of Walsingham, just a day's ride from the Southwell family home at Horsham St Faith.[12] The frequent recurrence of ruins among Southwell's poetic imagery attest to the rich associations these destructive acts held for him.[13] Southwell faced reminders of other damaging conflicts that characterised his family's recent history, too. His father, Richard Southwell, was the illegitimate son of another Richard Southwell, the product of an affair with a married woman who only later became his wife. This led to ongoing legal battles within the family, which would ultimately decimate the large Southwell fortune, and which made the poet poignantly conscious of the ongoing intergenerational battles that threatened to tear the branches of his family tree asunder.[14]

The image of familial interconnection conceived of as a tree is vividly rendered in the *Epistle*: 'O good Sir! shall so many of your branches enjoy the quickening sap and fry of God's Church, and daily shooting up higher towards Heaven, bring forth the flowers and fruits of salvation', Southwell asks his father, 'and you that are the root of us all lie barren and fruitless, still covered in earth and buried in flesh and blood?' (236-7). Southwell's metaphor might be construed as the archetypal image of generation, in its two most frequently used senses, suggesting both growth and – simultaneously – a group of offspring born to a parent. The term 'genealogy' is itself part of the nexus of words grouped around the Latin root *genus*, as the lexicographer Robert Cawdry makes clear in what is considered the first English dictionary: '*genealogie*, (greek) generation, or a describing of the stock or pedegree', he writes.[15] But Southwell here departs from the conventional life-giving associations of the figure of the family tree, adding a macabre twist: his father, 'root of us all', is 'buried in flesh and blood'. His misplaced faith, as Southwell sees it, has effectively buried him alive, just as he had been considered dead to his family upon his entry into the Catholic church. Generation has slipped into degeneration, and the tree is 'barren and fruitless'.

Southwell is not alone in subverting this traditional image of generation. It is an unfortunate consequence of Southwell's singular biography, and particularly the isolating effects of his recusancy, that his work is rarely read alongside that of other members of his generation.[16] Throughout this chapter I address the unexpected yet close relationship between Southwell and one of his peers, whose work was published in the same volume as some of his writings, and who shares some of his strikingly subversive imagery. Sir Walter Ralegh is the author of a peculiarly nasty and – for him – unconventional poem addressed 'To his son', which upsets the usual connotations of the image of the tree of life in ways familiar to readers of Southwell's *Epistle*. In what might be considered a drastically modified version of the advice letter, a genre of which we will encounter other examples below, Ralegh bitterly entreats his son to modify his behaviour or else face the consequences, which he unflinchingly articulates and of which he was all too aware (he wrote the verse from prison where he was awaiting trial for treason). The sonnet is tightly constructed – suffocatingly so, one might say – and hence needs to be quoted in full:

> Three thinges there bee that prosper vp apace
> And flourish, whilest they growe a sunder farr,
> But on a day, they meet all in one place,
> and when they meet, they one an other marr;
> And they bee theise, the wood, the wiide, the wagg.
> The wood is that, which makes the Gallow tree,
> The weed is that, which stringes the Hangmans bagg,
> The wagg my pritty knave betokeneth thee.
> Marke well deare boy whilest theise assemble not,
> Green springs the tree, hempe growes, the wagg is wilde,
> But when they meet, it makes the timber rott,
> It fretts the halter, and it choakes the childe.
> > Then bless thee, and beware, and lett vs praye,
> > wee part not with the at this meeting day.[17]

Critical readings of this poem have emphasised what has been perceived as its wittiness and tongue-in-cheek tone, interpretations that derive from the consoling final couplet which seems to lay the more disturbing implications of what has gone before to rest.[18] But the piece starts to look very different when one takes into account the fact that this final couplet exists in only one of the four extant manuscript copies of the poem, and that in the other versions the sonnet ends abruptly after the three quatrains and is left incomplete, interrupted by the gasping alliteration of 'it choakes the childe'.[19] In Ralegh's conceit the 'Three things' that grow together here – 'The wood', 'The weed' and 'The wagg' – are not generative but rather destructive, combining to prematurely end the life of his son. Rather than symbolising intergenerational relationships, the 'wood' here serves to make 'the Gallow tree'; like Southwell's image of his father as 'root of us all', this family tree is rotten through.[20]

How might we read Southwell's *Epistle to his father* in the light of this kind of iconographic subversion of the archetypal image of generation? It should first be noted that Southwell's concern in writing the letter is with the fate of his father's soul, rather than that of his body. As such, the regeneration of his spiritual life takes precedence over the merely physical relationship between father and son. Furthermore, Southwell understands the only truly meaningful familial relationship to be that between mankind and a divine Father. In a society where images of paternity proliferated, in offering an image of patriarchal power, as well as the Christian God, Southwell subjects biological fatherhood to this more metaphorical sense, an idea he also extends to maternity.[21] As Southwell makes clear in the *Epistle*, 'He cannot have God for his Father that refuseth to profess the Catholic Church for his Mother' (232). What Southwell terms 'carnal consanguinity' is coincidental (192); in yet another iteration of the tree imagery that recurs repeatedly in Southwell's work, flesh and blood are 'but bark and rind of a man' (193). Thus devotion to God supplants dedication to one's parents.

Such an idea seems difficult to reconcile to notions of piety, a word that was usually framed in compassionate terms during the early modern period, owing to its close relationship to the term 'pity'.[22] In a familial context 'piety' was often taken to explicitly imply a 'respect and devotion for parents', deriving from the Latin *pietas*, expressing dutifulness, and most commonly associated with respect and devotion to previous generations in classical literature. In post-classical Latin, however, the word *pietas* is extended to encompass a 'fervent attachment to the service of God and to the duties and practices of religion', and it is this latter sense that the *Epistle*'s concern for the spiritual life of Southwell's father thus seems to embody, at the expense of both blood ties and affect.

In seeking to contextualise this uncompromising stance further it is helpful to consider the particular restrictions under which early modern notions of tolerance functioned. Alexandra Walsham lays out what might seem to the modern reader the paradoxical status of this value in the English Renaissance. Whereas today tolerance is 'idealized as a virtue', at the time in which Southwell wrote it was more likely to be construed as a dangerous 'recipe for chaos and anarchy', she explains.[23] 'Together with other terms which implied a willingness to condone diversity and a conciliatory attitude towards doctrinal heterodoxy', toleration 'was a weapon in polemical controversy, a word used to wound, hurt, brand, stigmatise and slur'; some, she notes, 'even went so far as to boast of their intolerance'.[24] In sixteenth- and seventeenth-century thought tolerance was often held to be misguided, merited only where one wished to condone the spiritual practices of another, and wrongly applied at potentially great cost to the soul of the recipient. Such is Southwell's view of the dangers of sanctioning his father's conformity. One has to be cruel to be kind, his *Epistle* suggests, in its most basic terms, and the etymological relationship between 'kind', in the sense of generosity of spirit, and 'kind', in the sense of a familial or societal connection, is worth keeping in mind here.[25] The word 'kind' also owes its ultimate origins to the Latin *genus*, parent of 'generation' and 'gender' as we have already seen, and thus suggests both a fundamental underlying similarity (being of the same family, as in 'mankind') and a category of things (the means by which they are distinguished, as in a 'genre').[26]

Let us recall for a moment that a 'genre' is a 'kind' of text. The stylistic effects of Southwell's somewhat extreme rhetorical position become even more conspicuous if we consider the work alongside other, more conventional examples of the genre to which it belongs, and as which it would have been received: the letter of advice. This 'subdivision of the Conduct Book', as it has been described by Agnes Latham, was extremely popular in the late sixteenth, and particularly early seventeenth centuries, with notable examples produced by King James I, William Cecil (Lord Burghley), and Francis Osborne.[27] Such works usually contained guidelines on how to choose one's friends, one's wife, and one's wardrobe (in order of importance, we can only assume), and admonitions to avoid excessive eating, drinking, and talking. Most relevant here is that written by Ralegh, titled *Instructions to his sonne*, which was issued in the same volume as Southwell's *Epistle*, posthumously printed in 1632. The combination of these two works was a surprising one. Ralegh's work might be described as wholly conventional, in striking contrast to the poem 'To his son' which we have just read, whereas Southwell's *Epistle* makes several radical departures from the generic norm. The success of this co-publication is however evidenced by sales of the book, which went through five editions in four years, reaching an audience of potential converts far beyond its ostensibly domestic addressees.[28]

The most obvious way in which Southwell's *Epistle* subverts the generic expectations of the advice letter is through its reversal of the roles of advisor and advisee, a gesture that, while not unique amongst examples of the genre, is certainly unusual.[29] In just one instance of the way in which the English Reformation divided families and caused intergenerational conflict, the son here sees fit to lecture his father on his personal conduct. Southwell's second, and more interesting, departure from the conventions of the advice letter is to deliberately reverse the notion that wisdom is the fruit of experience, and thus, inevitably, the domain of one's elders. 'He may be a father to the soul that is a son to the body, and requite the belief of his temporal life by reviving his parent from a spiritual death', Southwell explains (195). 'Hoary senses are often couched under green locks', he says elsewhere, 'and some are riper in the spring than others in the Autumn of their age' (190–1). A model for this counter-intuitive logic is hinted at in Southwell's poetry, where we find an echo of this image in a description of 'Christes childhoode':

> In springing lockes laye couched hoary Witt
> In semblant younge a grace and aunciient port
> In lowly lookes high majestie did sitt
> In tender tungue sound sense of sagest sort.[30]

Christ's preternatural 'Witt', even at 'twelve yeres age', provides the ultimate example of natural wisdom for Southwell, who believes that an entire universe of understanding is collapsed into the short span of Christ's life. It is perfectly possible, he suggests, to be born with an inner spiritual intelligence that surpasses all other kinds of education, 'old in the cradle', to borrow a phrase from one of Southwell's better-known poems, 'Saint Peters complaynt'.[31] The pastoral role of the 'father' here supersedes any biological concept of paternity. Throughout Southwell's verse the intuitive knowledge of childhood is prized over the learned experience of age, and the passive acceptance of divine revelation over the active seeking out of learning. Childhood itself had an often paradoxical status in the period, serving as a metaphor for, or supplement to, gender categories.[32]

This figuration of the contradictory nature of divine wisdom seems to inform Southwell's poetry as a whole, in which he repeatedly employs the rhetorical device of the paradox in both structuring and elaborating his verse. Paradox, Southwell's writing reminds us, lies at the heart of Christianity; out of it grows true faith and through its distinctive form of logic the literary experience of this faith is generated. As he writes in 'A childe my Choyce': 'Though yonge yet wise though small yet stronge though man yet god he is'.[33] The configuration of man as God represents perhaps the most essential of these paradoxical truths for Southwell. 'Behould the father is his daughters sonne', begins 'The Nativity of Christ', an apparent impossibility that can only be resolved by the logic of faith.[34] The counterfactual instances of a daughter giving birth to her father, a mortal being delivering the immortal, and of Mary's immaculate conception ('Wife did she live, yet virgin did she die', begins 'Our ladyes spousals'), all reflect the ultimate conundrum lying at the heart of Southwell's Christian understanding: that of the Eucharist.[35] Paradox is thus key to any process of conversion (literally, a 'turning').[36] 'Of the Blessed Sacrament of the Aulter' uses language reminiscent of Southwell's poems on Mary's miraculous pregnancy to describe how 'The god of hoastes in slender hoste doth dwell'; the poem's animating force is generated by the obvious pun upon heavenly 'hoastes' of angels and the eucharistic 'hoste', in which two differing meanings coincide in a single term.[37] The Eucharist is for Southwell the supreme example of generation, operating according to the paradoxically generative logic of 'two-in-one', from which the Christian faith itself, not to mention the most hotly contested of debates between Catholics and Protestants, is begotten.

Southwell's subversion of the genre of the advice letter – by reversing the usual roles of advisor and advisee, father and son, and by conflating wisdom with youth, rather than age, in a manifestation of the greater paradoxes underpinning Christian experience itself – can be further understood by exploring connections between the *Epistle* and another subcategory of the conduct book, the mother's legacy. Authors of these extremely popular texts included Elizabeth Grymeston (*Miscellanea, meditations, memoratives*, [1604?]), Dorothy Leigh (*The mother's blessing*, [1616]), Elizabeth Josceline (*The mothers legacie to her unborn child*, [1622]), and Elizabeth Richardson (*The ladies legacy*, [1645]).

Considering Southwell's *Epistle* in the context of these volumes allows us to bring a third, etymologically related, key term into our discussions, addressing explicitly the role of gender in conjunction with the concepts of generation and ideas of genre that I have thus far considered.[38]

Let us begin by considering a particularly pertinent example here, that of an anonymous treatise in this tradition ostensibly written by a mother begging her recusant son, living and studying at the Catholic College at Douai, to recant his faith and return home. The martyrdom sought by the son is a mother's greatest fear. Published in 1627, *A mothers teares over hir sedvced sonne* follows Southwell's *Epistle* in its unflinching depiction of the inevitability of death, the ever-present implicit rhyme of womb and tomb.[39] A child 'may miscarry for want of thy care', its author reminds all mothers, but bleakly recognises 'so may it notwithstanding all thy care' (A4r). As she observes acutely:

> Thy child is a doubtfull commodity. There is a peradventure in all things good and evill under the Sunne, that may befall him, except one. It is borne, perhaps it may grow up, perhaps not, and so on, perhaps so, perhaps not. Thou canst not say, perhaps it may die, perhaps not: That is as certaine, as other things are uncertaine: if it doe grow up like the floure, it shall be cut downe like the grasse: no peradventure there . . .[40]

Like Southwell, the anonymous author of the tract derives her matter-of-fact tone from the metaphorics of business, comparing her child to a 'doubtfull commodity' just as the vocabulary of commerce permeates the *Epistle to his father*. There is something of the studied nonchalance of Ralegh's painfully witty sonnet here, too, as the apparently casual phrasing, 'perhaps it may grow up, perhaps not', belies a deeper anguish. Moreover, we see the traditional imagery of generation, so often figured in the growth of plants, savagely undercut in ways that reflects the governing trope of the *Epistle*, 'the floure' brutally 'cut downe like the grasse'. As the anonymous author goes on to say, a disobedient child is but 'a barren piece of mould' that 'brings forth nothing of it selfe but *briars* and *thornes*' (A4r). In a disturbing twist, metaphors of natural growth are turned to destructive effect at such moments; the imagery – like that of the *Epistle* – is all the more powerful because of its paradoxical qualities.

A mothers teares also contains an epistle from the son in which he defends his decision and denounces his mother's entreaties as an 'unreasonable, nay unnaturall' demand, in rhetoric that strikingly resembles that which Southwell directs towards his own father (B3ᵛ). This son's letter asks that his mother defer to the higher maternal authority proclaimed by adherents to the Catholic Church, that of the Virgin Mary: 'submit your selfe to her, who as a loving Mother would receive and embrace you', he urges, 'first be instructed by her, Deare Mother, and then shall you learne to governe and guide your owne Children in thinges that are good' (B4ʳ). As in the case of Southwell's *Epistle*, the traditional location of parental wisdom is transferred, here onto a very different mother figure, and, implicitly, onto the son who has chosen to supplant his own biological mother with that of his faith. In order to educate her children, he suggests, a mother must be educated herself in an act of childlike self-abjuration. The author of *A mothers teares* responds to such rhetoric by insisting to an unusual degree on the physicality of her experience of motherhood, the tears her son has brought her to and the aching of her 'bowels' (or to modern understanding, the womb), mirroring the prevalence of tears in Southwell's own affective vocabulary.[41] If the son's letter adopts the patriarchal condescension that characterises the popular posture of the father's advice letter to his child, the mother here puts her own gender at the forefront of her recasting of the genre in maternal form.

A mothers teares both borrows from and helps to solidify the emerging conventions of its own genre.[42] Its author refers to many of the popular examples of the form listed above in a preface in which she self-consciously takes on her precursors' mantle, situating her work firmly within this ongoing literary history, much as the publication of Southwell's *Epistle* alongside Ralegh's work positioned the text within the genre of advice letters written by fathers to sons. As Marsha Urban has recently observed, seventeenth-century mother's advice books are typically pious in content and deferential in tone, with their authors making much show of their inadequacy as writers and the unsuitability of their scribblings for publication, a display deliberately calculated, it seems, to offset any readerly sense of the impropriety of female authors.[43] *A mothers teares* is a pious document in this tradition, displaying all the signs of (false) modesty associated with such works, including the trope of reluctance to publish: 'I could not, whether for want of witt, or too much propensitie to talke (both if thou wilt, it is no great impeachment to a woman) coutch my answer within the scantling of a letter', its author explains, 'whence it hapned, that a friend desiring a Copy, tooke a readier way for 500, then he could with his pen transcribe one, and so printed it beyond the seas' (A2ᵛ). Responsibility for the decision to publish is thus put onto the shoulders of the 'friend', in a gesture wholly characteristic of writing by both women and men in the early modern period.

At the same time, as I have suggested, its author departs from such conventions in provocative ways, including for example the interpolated voice of her son, both in the form of his own epistle and a series of interjections in her text, which takes the atypical form of a dialogue. In the introduction to an important collection of essays considering the relationship between genre and gender in early modern England, Michelle Dowd and Julia Eckerle somewhat contentiously argue that 'the experimentation with form was a fundamental characteristic of women's life writing', inferring a self-conscious literariness in such works.[44] Citing Nigel Smith's case for directly relating the 'generic inventiveness and eclecticism' that characterises seventeenth-century women authors to the way in which autobiographical forms such as the advice book construct identity and function as 'a means through literary structure of exploring potentials and acknowledging limitations in relation to the world', Dowd and Eckerle more persuasively suggest that 'the categories of genre, gender, and identity were thus mutually constitutive in early modern England'.[45]

We see precisely this dynamic at work in Elizabeth Grymeston's *Miscellanea*, a gathering of diverse textual fragments that expands the genre of the advice book to include poems, 'A madrigall' and proverbs, as well as the '*Prayers. Meditations. Memoratiues*' mentioned in the subtitle to the work. Addressing herself to Bernye Grymeston, '*My dearest sonne*', the author's preface draws an explicit and physical connection between the experience of motherly love and the form this love takes upon the page: the advice book. In a series of connected subclauses that render each of her points the inevitable logical outcome of its predecessor, Grymeston writes that

> there is no thing so strong as the force of loue; there is no loue so forcible as the loue of an affectionate mother to her naturall childe: there is no mother can either more affectionately shew her nature, or more naturally manifest her affection, than in aduising her children out of her owne experience, to eschew euill, and encline them to do that which is good.[46]

Gender blends seamlessly into the etymologically related question of genre here; writing guidance for a child 'out of her owne experience' is presented as the natural culmination of motherhood itself.

Like the author of *A mothers teares*, and in a way highly reminiscent of Southwell's *Epistle*, Grymeston places physical experience at the heart of the entreaties she makes to her son. An allusion to her own bodily suffering, a 'languishing consumption' as she calls it in the preface to the *Miscellanea*, resonates throughout the text in its repeated evocations of the torments of Christ on the cross, suggesting an understanding of identity as constituted through bodily, material, and sensory practices in a manner I have here also attributed to Southwell (to whom Grymeston was related through the poet's grandfather).[47] In an extraordinary and intricately interconnected series of metaphors Grymeston figures the resurrection (and the processes of martyrdom that imitate this pattern of extreme physical pain as a path to spiritual rebirth) as a

> Silkworme [who] first eateth hir selfe out of a very little seed, and groweth to be a small worme: afterward when by feeding a certain time vpon fresh and greene leaues it is waxed of greater sise, eateth it selfe againe out of the other coate, and worketh it selfe into a case of silke; which when it hath once finished, in the end casting the seed for many yoong to breed of, and leauing the silke for mans ornament, dieth all white and winged, in shape of a flying thing...[48]

The culmination of the silkworm's existence is at once creative and destructive, engendering future generations while dying out itself; its final act is also an aesthetic one, as it takes on a new and wondrous form even at the moment of extinction. Grymeston goes on to compare this process to that of becoming a martyr, drawing parallels to the way that 'when the persecution is greatest, they finally as need requireth, shed their blood, as seed for new offspring to arise of', an act of creative destruction just like that of the silkworm, with the similarly productive effect 'that though the ripe fruit of the Church bee gathered, yet their blood engendreth new supply, and it increaseth the more, when the disincrease therof is violently procured' (E2ʳ). Grymeston emphasises the physicality of martyrdom, its violence, and bloodshed in a way designed to provoke not only contemplation but also spiritual action. As such she addresses dual audiences, recalling Southwell's own *Epistle*; her son serves as a stand-in for a wider community of possible converts to whom the text implicitly speaks.

As such, her writing shares with Southwell's poetics an emphasis upon physical experience, which both authors utilise in the hope of galvanising their dual readerships to act in the service of their faith.

Southwell's verse is written with the aim not only of generating a consolatory body of work, and thus building an alternative church of the imagination, but also of inspiring its readers to action. The physical suffering of Christ is emphasised at every turn, in a mode that recollects that of medieval lover-knight lyrics. 'Christs bloody sweate' belongs firmly to this tradition, beginning with a stunning example of *versus rapportatus*, the first four lines forming a 'magic square' that can be read horizontally or vertically, and even across some of the diagonals:

Fatt soyle,	full springe,	sweete olive,	grape of blisse
That yeldes,	that streames,	that powres,	that dost distil
Untild,	undrawne,	unstampde,	untouchd of presse,
Deare fruit,	cleare brooks,	fayre oyle,	sweete wine at will

Thus Christ unforc'd preventes in shedding bloode
The whippes the thornes the nailes the speare and roode.[49]

The magic square is not simply a dazzling display of virtuosity designed to inspire awe in Southwell's readers, and to feed their religious devotion, although this is indeed part of its effect. It is also a poetic form that requires an active reader, one who will traverse and reverse its lines, dismantling and rebuilding the poem for themselves. Recusancy in late-Elizabethan England necessitated precisely the doublings and redoublings embodied in Southwell's verse here, poetry made flesh. In requiring his readers to treat his poem in this way, Southwell creates in miniature a mimetic representation of the active form of piety he demands of them. The word 'convert' is used more often as a verb than a noun in the early modern period; Southwell's understanding of true faith is fundamentally physical, a process of doing rather than a state of being; he hopes to effect conversion by provoking his reader to act.

Southwell's poetry is richly invested with etymological puns and verbal play upon semantic histories that seek to engender this particularly active response in his reader. One of his favourite such devices is the manipulation of the differing senses of 'kind' that I have explored in this chapter. In the longer version of 'Saint Peters Complaynt', for instance, he describes sorrow as 'Sinnes eldest child: / Best, when unkind in killing who it bred'.[50] Sorrow is 'unkind' in yet another sense of the word: 'uncharitable'. But sorrow is also 'unkind' in that in 'killing who it bred', sin, it commits an unnatural act, patricide, transgressing the familial relation and thus behaving as if from a different 'kind' or family. Elsewhere in Southwell's verse we encounter productive etymological play upon Saint Peter's 'stony name' ('Peter' derives from the Greek *petros*, meaning 'rock') and a nod to the popular account of the origins of the name 'God' in 'goodness', in 'I dye without desert': 'god murdred in the good', Southwell writes.[51]

On other occasions we find simpler play upon shared linguistic origins. Southwell reminds his readers of the distance between God's creatures and his act of divine creation, miraculously bridged, in 'Looke home', observing that 'The mind a creature is, yet can create'.[52] In 'Lew'd love is losse', it is the aural similitude between two words falsely hinting at a shared etymological root that produces Southwell's line, 'A locke it proves that first was but a looke'.[53] And, a strikingly Spenserian piece of verse, 'In all things mutable, but mutabilities', from 'Fortunes falsehood', enacts the processes of semantic generation by which words give rise to other words, the same in 'kind' yet not the same, their grammatical offspring.[54] At moments like these, Southwell's poetry is generative, in the fullest sense of this word. His language generates yet more language; his poetry grows out of the etymological and semantic possibilities of the individual word, seeking to bring about a change in religious affiliation by changing his readers' relationship to their own linguistic universe.

The aim of what I have termed Southwell's generative poetics is then singular and transparent. Writing was Southwell's chosen means of ministering to the subterranean Catholic community, for his generation a 'congregation denied a church', which he saw as 'souls denied access to emotional engagement with their God'; Anne Sweeney makes clear that his poetry 'was written to redress that loss'.[55] It is difficult to ascertain the extent to which Southwell succeeded in constructing his virtual church. The wide circulation and influence of his poetry and prose amongst both Catholic and Protestant audiences, of his own and subsequent generations, suggest some measure of success, although not always of a kind Southwell himself would have desired or envisaged. His effectiveness in converting genre and gender conventions into a poetics that privileges bodily experience is more readily apparent. Likewise, we have no record of Richard Southwell's response to the *Epistle* from his son. But, in 1600, five years after Robert Southwell's death, Henry Garnett wrote to Acquaviva, Superior General of the Jesuits, to tell him: 'Mr Southwell, Robert's father, has just died a Catholic.'[56]

NOTES

1 Cecil's remarks are reported by Father Henry Garnett, in a posthumous account of Southwell's torture and execution written in Italian and addressed to Acquaviva. Dated 7 March 1595, the document is held in the Jesuit archives at Farm Street and quoted in Pierre Janelle, *Robert Southwell the writer: a study in religious inspiration* (London: Sheed & Ward, 1935), 66–7. Cecil's apparent admiration for Southwell's extraordinary silence under torture is recorded in Henry More's *Historia missionis Anglicanae Societas Jesu* (1660), 193, translated by Francis Edwards as *The Elizabethan Jesuits* (London: Phillimore, 1981), 243. Edwards considers Cecil's comments apocryphal.
2 *OED*, 'generation, n', and 'gender, n'.
3 John Minsheu, *Ductor in linguas: the guide into tongues* (London, 1617), pp. 213, 214.
4 In arguing that bodily experience is inseparable from the spiritual in Southwell's writing my argument moves in the opposite direction to that of Gary Kuchar, who posits that the fashioning of the 'ideal recusant subject' in *Mary Magdalen's funeral teares* (London, 1591) involves a 'transition from an inwardly divided, melancholic attachment to Christ's literal body to [a] recognition of a spiritual, and consequently more complete, relation with the resurrected Christ'. See Kuchar, 'Gender and Recusant melancholia in Robert Southwell's *Mary Magdalene's funeral tears*', in Ronald Corthell et al. (eds), *Catholic culture in early modern England* (Notre Dame, IN: University of Notre Dame Press, 2007), p. 136.
5 See Pollard, Alfred W., *A short-title catalogue of books printed in England, Scotland, and Ireland, and of English Books printed abroad, 1475–1640*, 2nd edn, revised and enlarged by Katharine F. Panzer, 3 vols (London: Bibliographical Society, 1976–91), 22956–22962.
6 The late Anne Sweeney's work has been instrumental in redefining Southwell studies, urging critics to move beyond heavily biographical readings of Southwell's poetry through the lens of his martyrdom, and to consider political, social, and other factors. See her *Robert Southwell: snow in Arcadia: redrawing the English lyric landscape, 1586–95* (Manchester: Manchester University Press, 2006). The previously prevailing martyrological approach is typified by Scott Pilarz's *Robert Southwell and the mission of literature, 1561–1595: writing reconciliation* (Aldershot: Ashgate, 2004); and Christopher Devlin's *The life of Robert Southwell, poet and martyr* (London: Longmans, Green & Co., 1956).
7 Southwell had left England for the Catholic colleges of Douai and, subsequently, Rome in June 1576, remaining there for a decade, during which time he petitioned for, and was later granted, admission to the Jesuit order (his initial application was refused). So long was his absence that, on his

return, Southwell had to relearn his mother tongue in order to minister to the English recusant community, according to Sweeney, *Robert Southwell*, 99–100. See also Nancy Pollard Brown, 'Southwell, Robert (1561–1595)', *Oxford Dictionary of National Biography* (Oxford: Oxford University Press, 2004), hereafter abbreviated to *ODNB*.

8 See the entries for '*regenerate*, borne againe', and '*regeneration*, a new birth', in Robert Cawdry, *A table alphabeticall, conteyning and teaching the true writing, and understanding of hard usuall English wordes* (London, 1604), H2^r.

9 The *Epistle* was first printed by Garnett's second secret press, appended to *A short rule of good life. Newly set forth according to the authours direction before his death* (London, 1597) [STC2 22968.5, ESTC (*English Short Title Catalogue*) S95268]. Because this volume is exceedingly rare, and because we still lack a modern scholarly edition of this work (J. W. Trotman's 1914 Catholic Library text is extremely problematic), my citations here are taken from a more readily accessible subsequent edition, printed at St Omer by John Heigham in 1622 [STC2 22970, ESTC 106293], 240. Subsequent page numbers appear in the text.

10 'The maintenance of three basic hierarchies was deemed essential to an ordered household – and, by implication, an ordered society: ideally, husbands should govern wives; masters and mistresses their servants; and parents their children', writes Alexandra Shephard, *Meanings of manhood in early modern England* (Oxford: Oxford University Press, 2003), p. 3. Southwell's lack of subservience might thus be interpreted as a political gesture as much as a familial one.

11 Whilst Louis Martz, in a seminal study of meditative verse, has explored Southwell's influence upon a subsequent generation of devotional poets, most notably George Herbert, his role as a possible source for 'The Apparition' has been thus far overlooked. See the chapter on 'Southwell and Herbert' in Louis L. Martz, *The poetry of meditation: a study in English religious literature of the seventeenth century* (New Haven, CT: Yale University Press, 1954).

12 See Pollard Brown, 'Southwell, Robert (1561–1595)', and Stanford Lehmberg, 'Southwell, Richard (1502/3–1654)', *ODNB*.

13 'The prodigall chylds soule wracke' describes the eventual salvation of one who has been an exile from faith, for example, 'Till mercy raysed me from my fall, / And grace my ruines did repaire'. I quote Southwell's poetry here and throughout this chapter from *Robert Southwell: collected poems*, ed. Anne Sweeney and Peter Davidson (Manchester: Fyfield Books for Carcanet Press, 2007), p. 38. This edition is the first to offer an adequate representation of his verse as it initially circulated in manuscript, before it was sanitised for the 1595 publication.

14 The sixteenth-century saw a rising interest in genealogy, the tracing of one's family tree; see Graham Parry, *Trophies of time: English antiquarians of the seventeenth century* (Oxford: Oxford University Press, 1995); and Angus Vine, *In defiance of time: antiquarian writing in early modern England* (Oxford: Oxford University Press, 2010).

15 Cawdry, *Table alphabeticall*, C3^r.

16 Alison Shell has attempted to correct this oversight in *Catholicism, controversy and the English literary imagination* (Cambridge: Cambridge University Press, 1999), ch. 2.

17 *The poems of Sir Walter Ralegh*, ed. Agnes C. Latham (London: Routledge & Kegan Paul, 1929), p. 102.

18 Latham's commentary on this poem sets the tone, declaring that it was 'written in a light hearted moment', *Poems of Sir Walter Ralegh*, p. 186.

19 See again Latham's commentary, which notes that '*MS Malone omits ll. 13, 14 and has instead* God blesse the Child', *Poems of Sir Walter Ralegh*, p. 186.

20 In Southwell's poetry one is likewise never far from a reminder of the darker side of the human covenant with God, and its ability to destabilise relationships between successive generations. Imagining Mary's torments in 'The virgin mary to Christ on the Crosse', Southwell adopts her voice:

> Thou messenger that didst impart,
> His first discent into my womb,
> Come helpe me now to cleave my heart,
> That there I may my sonne intombe.

Like Ralegh's very different poem 'To His Son', the deadening rhyme of 'womb' with 'tomb' here serves as a harsh reminder that children sometimes die before their parents. See Southwell, *Collected poems*, p. 61.

21 On the political applications of the metaphor of fatherhood, see Su Fang Ng, *Literature and the politics of family in seventeenth-century England* (Cambridge: Cambridge University Press, 2007).

22 It was not until the seventeenth-century that the separation of the two words was completed. See 'piety, *n*' and 'pity, *n*', *OED*.

23 Alexandra Walsham, *Charitable hatred: tolerance and intolerance in England, 1500–1700* (Manchester: Manchester University Press, 2006), p. 1.

24 Walsham, *Charitable hatred*, p. 5.

25 Southwell deploys a similar rhetoric in his letter to Cecil confessing his Catholicism and asking for the martyrdom he would soon receive: 'in extreme courses it hath ever been counted a kind of pity to kill quickly and an argument of some mercy to be but a while unmerciful', he writes. See *Two letters and short rules of good life*, ed. Nancy Pollard Brown (Charlottesville, VA: University Press of Virginia for the Folger Shakespeare Library, 1973), p. 77.

26 The etymological equivalence of the two words is masked by the effects of what is known by linguists as Grimm's law, according to which 'g' sounds become 'k' over time. See John Algeo and Thomas Pyles, *The origins and development of the English language*, 6th edn (Boston: Wadsworth, Cengage Learning, 2005), pp. 71–3.

27 Agnes Latham, 'Sir Walter Ralegh's *Instructions to his son*', in Herbert Davis and Helen Gardner (eds), *Elizabethan and Jacobean studies (presented to Frank Percy Wilson in honour of his seventieth birthday)* (Oxford: Oxford University Press, 1959), p. 199. The examples mentioned above are: James I, *[Basilikon Doron] or his majesties instructions to his dearest sonne, Henry the prince* (Edinburgh, 1603) (the work had been anonymously issued four years previously); William Cecil, *Certaine precepts, or directions, for the well ordering of a mans life: left by a father of eminent note and place in this kingdome* (London, 1615); Francis Osborne, *Advice to a son; or, directions for your better conduct* (Oxford, 1655).

28 See STC2 20641.5–20646.

29 A fascinating, Protestant, analogue is James Wadsworth the younger's account of his father's recusancy, *The English Spanish pilgrime* (London, 1629). As Helen Smith also notes in her chapter in this volume, Wadsworth denounces his father's Catholicism, celebrating his own return to 'his true mothers bosome, the Church of England', on the title page. Wadsworth only published his 'advice' after his father's death, however. See A. J. Loomie, 'Wadsworth, James [*pseud*. Diego de Vadesfoote] (b.1604)', *ODNB*.

30 Southwell, *Collected poems*, p. 10.

31 *Ibid.*, pp. 63–85.

32 See Naomi J. Miller and Naomi Yavneh, 'Early modern children as subjects: gender matters', in Miller and Yavneh (eds), *Gender and early modern constructions of childhood* (Farnham: Ashgate, 2011), p. 1. See also the chapter by Abigail Shinn in this volume.

33 Southwell, *Collected poems*, p. 12.

34 *Ibid.*, p. 6.

35 *Ibid.*, p. 4. Paradox is also central to martyrdom; the notion of dying in order to embrace an eternal life is an idea that is ever-present in Southwell's work as one can only assume it must have been in his life. Even the process of becoming a martyr was infused with paradox, with the outcome of a trial often resting on a prisoner's answer to what was known as 'The Bloody Question', in which they were asked to choose whether they would side with the Pope over the Queen if his forces invaded England. Neither answer was acceptable, an inescapable dilemma sure to result in charges of treason.

36 The relationship between conversion and paradox merits further exploration: Richard Lanham succinctly summarises the rhetorical figure as: 'A seemingly self-contradictory statement, which is yet shown to be (sometimes

in a surprising way) true.' Lanham, *A handlist of rhetorical terms*, 2nd edn (Berkeley & Los Angeles: University of California Press, 1991), p. 107. Conversion – to the view of Jesuit missionaries like Southwell – is a process of revealing the truth that has underlain a contradictory exterior all along.

37 Southwell, *Collected poems*, p. 23.
38 The term 'gender' had its grammatical significance before it was used to denote the distinction between male and female, see 'gender, *n*', *OED*.
39 *A mothers teares over hir seduced sonne* (London, 1627). Subsequent page numbers appear in the text. Compare Augustine's account of his mother's attempts to convert him to Christianity in Book 3 of *The confessions*, trans. Henry Chadwick (Oxford: Oxford University Press, 2008).
40 *A mothers teares*, sig. A4^r.
41 See, for instance, 'A vale of tears', in Southwell, *Collected poems*, pp. 36–8, and his prose-poem, *Marie Magdalens funeral teares*. The latter's influence beyond Catholic circles is attested by Thomas Nashe's imitation of it in *Christs teares over Jerusalem* (London, 1593), noted – and mocked – by Gabriel Harvey. See Pilarz, *Robert Southwell*, p. xx.
42 On the genre see Jennifer Heller, *The mother's legacy in early modern England* (Aldershot: Ashgate, 2011); Edith Snook, *Women, reading, and the cultural politics of early modern England* (Aldershot: Ashgate, 2005); and Marsha Urban, *Seventeenth-century mother's advice books* (New York & Basingstoke: Palgrave Macmillan, 2006).
43 Urban, *Mother's advice books*, p. 5.
44 Michelle Dowd and Julia Eckerle, *Genre and women's life writing in early modern England* (Aldershot: Ashgate, 2007), p. 4.
45 *Ibid*. See also Nigel Smith, *Literature and revolution in England 1640–1660* (New Haven, CT: Yale University Press, 1994), p. 5.
46 Grymeston, *Miscellanea*, A2^r.
47 On Grymeston's familial and literary connections to Southwell, see Ruth Hughey and Philip Hereford, 'Elizabeth Grymeston and her *Miscellanea*', *The Library*, Fourth Series, 15.1 (June 1934), 78–9.
48 Grymeston, *Miscellanea*, E1^v–E2^r.
49 Southwell, *Collected poems*, p. 17.
50 *Ibid*., pp. 64–85.
51 *Ibid*., p. 42. Hence Christ's famous declaration, 'I will build my Church upon this rock' (Matt 16:18).
52 *Ibid*., p. 49.
53 *Ibid*., p. 54.
54 *Ibid*., p. 56.
55 Anne Sweeney, 'Introduction' to Southwell, *Collected poems*, xiii.
56 Quoted in Devlin's *Life of Robert Southwell*, p. 203.

4
Gender and reproduction in the *Spirituall experiences*

Abigail Shinn

This chapter explores how female authority is connected to the reproduction of religious experience in the collection of Protestant conversion narratives *The Spirituall experiences of sundry beleevers*.¹ This was the first anthology of conversion narratives to appear in print when it was published in 1653. The model was soon copied and in the same year the minister John Rogers produced a similar collection, titled *Ohel or Bethshemesh*, which was aimed at the gathered churches in Ireland. Bruce Hindmarsh cites the *Spirituall experiences*, alongside other collections of conversion stories published in 1653, as evidence for the increased popularity of the genre, and notes that texts such as these were designed to provide evidence for an individual's admission to a church community.²

The popularity of the Protestant conversion narrative in this period is allied to a growing eschatological impatience on the part of members of the gathered churches (independent congregations of both separatist and non-separatist believers).³ These were radical Protestants who had survived the Civil War and witnessed the increasing religious confidence of their peers during the 'Barebones' parliament (1653), known as the 'Parliament of Saints'. The conversion narrative provided these believers with a means of inscribing and disseminating their religious experiences in order to highlight their elect status and to gather more souls before the coming apocalypse. This eschatological impetus was also reflected in the writings of female prophets, including Sarah Wight and the fifth monarchist Anna Trapnell, whose experiences and prophecies were disseminated in print.⁴ Importantly, this community of radical believers

81

was shaped by its reading and writing practices, most obviously when engaging with scripture, but also when composing and reading texts which outlined the parameters and effects of conversion. As Andrew Cambers argues, 'reading was a crucial strand of puritan self-identity' which 'bound the godly together'.[5] The conversion narrative consequently operates as one of the literary forms which had the potential to turn individual readers into a congregation of believers. It is to this textual culture that the *Experiences* belong.

A small-format (12mo) but lengthy volume, the *Spirituall experiences* is divided into three parts. The first two contain sixty-one stories of experience delivered by individuals who are identified only by their initials.[6] The third addresses the 'Practice of the Gathered Churches', including a letter-template indicating the procedure for expelling a member of the church, complete with blank spaces to be filled in with the names of the minister and the expelled member.[7] The full title of the collection indicates that the various narratives of experience may originally have formed testimonies delivered orally at the moment of an individual's entrance to a church congregation: *The spirituall experiences of sundry beleevers held forth by them at severall solemn meetings and conferences to that end*. The only named individual in the whole text (apart from a series of men whose efficacious preaching is noted by the converts), is the Welsh Independent minister Vavasor Powell, whose name appears on the title page and at the end of a commendatory preface. Kathleen Lynch identifies Powell, a vociferous critic of Cromwell's Protectorate, as 'one of the most forceful and active of the millenarians in Wales'.[8]

Powell's preface to the anthology incorporates a definition of religious experience, identified as 'the inward sense and feeling, of what is outwardly read and heard' (A1^v). This establishes that the *Experiences* is concerned with the interior effects of the Word (via both reading and hearing) upon the (feeling) soul of the believer. Using a similitude which underlines this sensate understanding of experience, Powell argues that 'like salt to fresh meat it [experience] seasons brain-knowledge' (A2^r–A2^v). This image of experience as heightening taste, which is further emphasised by the repeated description of the text's 'sauory worth' (title page), positions the anthology as a source of spiritual nourishment. Powell goes on to state that '*Experience* is a Copy written by the Spirit of God upon the hearts of beleevers' (A3^r). 'Copy' is related to transcription and imitation as well as copiousness, and Powell thereby simultaneously associates experience with the inscription of God's grace upon the soul of the convert and with an endlessly replicable process of conversion.[9] This is a system of experiential copying that perhaps has its echo in the action of the printing press which produced the *Experiences*, an action which was frequently described using gendered terminology.[10] As we will see, Powell's understanding of experience as nourishing and perpetuating is indelibly connected to the reproductive power of the female body.

Powell is unlikely to be the minister to the congregation or the editor of the *Spirituall experiences*; he instead acts as a reviewer or licenser of the work. Nigel Smith has persuasively argued that the narratives were collected by Henry Walker, the editor of parliamentary newsbooks who also had a chequered career as a preacher.[11] Walker may be the preacher 'Master *Walker*' (B10ᵛ) who is mentioned by a number of converts in their narratives, but nowhere does his name appear as the editor. The text is in fact startlingly reticent in relation to named authority.[12] No principal author or editor is identified and the experiences contained within are identified only through the initials of the convert. Where it is possible to determine gender, however, women outnumber men, testifying to the important role played by women in the gathered churches. Rogers' *Ohel or Bethshemesh*, for example, not only includes many narratives composed by women (although, unlike in the *Experiences*, most of the converts are named), but also incorporates a treatise on the value of women preachers.[13] These texts, as Keith Thomas argues, mirror the emphasis placed upon the 'spiritual equality of the two sexes' by Protestant sects during this period.[14]

In this chapter I argue that the employment of authorial anonymity, coupled with the preponderance of female gender signifiers, foregrounds female experience in such a way as to frame the *Experiences* as a reproductive object. This bias is achieved, in part, because a number of narratives which are identified as being by men in the contents pages do not incorporate masculine pronouns or mention familial relationships which identify their gender in the narrative itself. Where men can be identified in the *Experiences* it is often because of their occupation and behaviour rather than their position within families or households. For example, one convert, T. R., identifies himself as a sailor, another as a 'Souldier' (Q6ᵛ). A further man, T. G., initially leaves his gender uncertain, but mentions 'unlawfull gameing' (O11ʳ), smoking 'Tobacco' (O11ᵛ), and the evils of 'drinke' (O12ʳ) before finally noting that he has a wife. In contrast, female converts are not only identified in the contents pages, but frequently refer to themselves as daughters and mothers, and mention husbands. The narratives composed by women are also often more elaborate and richer in biographical detail, so there is greater scope for gender to be identified by the reader. The result is a text which encourages a gendered hermeneutics: the reader goes looking for the gender of the convert and more often than not finds a woman.

In order to explore the reproductive effects of this gendered bias I will look firstly at how the use of authorial anonymity confers a feminised moral authority upon the text. I will then move on to examine the importance of fertility as a spiritual trope for radical Protestants, before considering in detail how the *Experiences* utilises the symbolic associations of motherhood in a number of narratives composed by women. I will argue that the compositional techniques employed by converts, as well as by the unnamed editor, promote a feminised ventriloquism designed to draw the reader into a fertile, and ever-expanding, textual congregation. I conclude with a detailed examination of the longest, and one of the richest, narratives from the *Experiences*, the story of a woman identified as M. K.

Marcy North has argued that anonymity not only conceals identity but also highlights the 'moral character' of the hidden author.[15] This effect was reinforced by the legacy of scriptural anonymity which was often used as a precedent by both Protestant and Catholic writers after the Reformation. Anonymity therefore not only provided protection for religious radicals but also brought them into a congregation of believers which included the anonymous scribes of biblical texts. The *Experiences*' employment of anonymity can be framed in the same way, as a gesture towards the ultimate authority which is God. This is complicated, however, by the emphasis the text places upon female voices, as anonymity is creatively figured as a form of female moral authority rather than male. Female anonymity might also be linked to the modesty topos frequently utilised by women writers as a means of demonstrating self-deprecation and feminine virtue, particularly as silence was often equated with godliness in women.[16] For example, Phyllis Mack argues that female prophets were 'paradoxically described as dumb' as they were mute on everything apart from God.[17] Female anonymity, if equated with a gendered silence, thereby confers upon women spiritual modesty and moral authority as a conduit for God's grace.

The women in the *Experiences*, however, are far from silent. Their gendered voices, lacking the specificity of a proper name, potentially act as a mouthpiece for the divine, rather than articulating individual concerns, but nonetheless remain the voices of women. This ensures that their stories can be moved away from the personal and specific in favour of a universal understanding of religious experience and conversion allied to female symbolism. The eliding of individuality achieved by anonymity always remains gendered; while personal names disappear from the text, female voices dominate the anthology's stories of experience and conversion. This is mirrored by the fact that, unlike many female prophets, the women in the *Experiences* always use the first person ('I', 'me', 'my') rather than explicitly adopting the voice of God or using the third person to render themselves the 'object' rather than the 'subject' of their discourse.[18] The combining of anonymity with female voices in the text also has the effect of potentially allowing those narratives without any gender signifiers to become female. The reader becomes so accustomed to reading the stories of women that they can transfer a sense of femaleness to narratives which are in fact empty of explicit gender references.

This reading of anonymity as promoting female moral authority can be linked to a particular aspect of Puritan textuality which emphasised the gendered instrumentality of religious writing. As Sylvia Brown has argued in relation to John Bunyan, for radical Protestants texts were 'reproductive agents', 'they were autonomous, they acted on human subjects rather than being produced by them and they were fertile'.[19] Protestant writers and readers understood the action of both reading and writing via feminine systems of reproduction to such an extent that religious writing, whether by men or women, was always feminised. This was particularly the case for books such as the *Experiences*, which were designed to bear witness to the process of spiritual change, but also to convert others. The converting power of the conversion narrative was frequently attested to by both converts and their witnesses; the puritan Rose Thurgood directs her conversion narrative, *A Lecture of Repentance* (1637), to a female readership and emphatically states that her story is designed to be followed by others: 'And thus loving mothers & sisters I have sett you a patterne, how you may gett the love of God'.[20] Devised in such a way as to produce a particular effect upon the reader, conversion narratives are arguably the ultimate reproductive text.

The urge to generate further conversion via the reading process is illustrated by the *Experiences*' third section, titled the 'Practice of the

Gathered Churches', which aims to instruct the reader as to the models and structures of congregation-building for Protestant sects. This section emphasises that the text is designed to act as a pattern or guidebook for those wishing to create their own congregation of experienced believers. This is further emphasised by the fact that most of the stories of experience follow a similar pattern: vacillation between despair and 'comfort'; an intense moment of spiritual awareness (comfort outweighs despair); a recitation of 'promises' taken from scripture; and a numerical list of proofs of the individual's conversion in the form of 'testimonies', 'particulars', or 'evidences'.[21] The scriptural 'promises' which are incorporated into the narrative are frequently repeated across different stories. For example, the quotation from Matthew 2:28, 'come unto mee all yee that labour and are heavy laden and I will give you rest' is used on twenty-four different occasions.[22] This patterning of religious experience along loosely prescribed parameters ensures that the process of conversion is endlessly replicated in such a way as to incorporate the reader themselves into the conversion process: all they need do is mimic the progress from despair to comfort via scriptural 'promises' in order to reach the 'evidence' of their conversion. The result of this patterning and repetition is the awareness that the text is designed to perpetuate more experiences, more converts, more congregations, more texts – it is intended to reproduce.

The reproductive nature of the *Experiences* can also be tied to its material and textual organisation. While small in size, perhaps to ensure its portability, it is a copious text whose narrative patterns are replicated over and over again. We can therefore connect its composition to the motions and effects of dilated discourse (related to *dilatio* or swelling speech) and the actions of *partitio* (a logical division into partitions via rhetorical walls). *Partitio* is a way of controlling the expanding text by dividing it into different parts or 'members'; Patricia Parker has brilliantly connected this process to the qualities of the female body as a symbol of *copia*, dilation, and fertility.[23] The *Experiences*' privileging of female voices, coupled with its use of partitions in the form of both printed divisions and the containment produced by the replication of narrative patterns (the reader knows that one narrative is about to end and another begin when the convert enumerates the proofs of their conversion), thereby connects the text to modes of dilation and partition associated with the female body.

This fertile instrumentality is directly tied to the *Experiences'* emphasis upon female religious experiences as a source of spiritual nourishment. These include stories of women whose husbands and children are killed or injured in the Civil War, women who are pregnant, elaborate dream narratives experienced by women, and the description of women's relationships with their husbands. Often these female experiences are accompanied by a resonant biblical symbolism which allies them with female scriptural types such as the Virgin Mary, the woman at Canaan, and Mary Magdalene. The most dominant female symbol, however, is that of the pregnant and maternal woman: the most potent image of spiritual reproduction available to the convert.[24]

One of the women whose experiences operate in this way is M. W. She was living in Ireland but then travelled to Liverpool where she lost a child and her husband in one of the battles of the Civil War. Despairing and traumatised, after the battle she shelters in a barn with her remaining children, one of whom has been badly wounded, and takes comfort from a 'piece of the Bible' (B6^v) she has found, self-consciously echoing the tableau of the nativity as well as elements of the pietà: 'I ... did rejoyce with my wounded Childe, and a little daughter, in a Barn where we were put, having gotten a peece of an old Bible; and then and since I have found much setlednesse in my faith from severall Promises of the Lord, revealed in his holy Word' (B6^v–B7^r). Having lost her husband and one of her children, it is a fragment of scripture which gives her comfort. Crucially, the setting in which she reads the 'Word' also allows her to inhabit the position of the Virgin Mary, both at the moment of Christ's birth and at his death (although her child is wounded rather than dead). The framing of her experiences around her role not just as a mother, but as an inheritor of Mary's maternal qualities and virtues, is what allows her to 'rejoyce'.

There are also stories which recount how women who are suicidal are prevented from killing themselves because of the intercession of their children, an instance of a child acting as a conduit for God in much the same way as Christ, the son of both God and a human woman, enacted the divine on earth. The power of fertility is frequently referenced in the Bible. From the despair felt by Rachel when she cannot conceive and her joy when God finally gives her a son, to Moses' invocation to the Israelites in Deuteronomy 7:13 that the lord 'will love thee, and bless thee, and multiply thee: he will also bless the fruit of thy womb, and the fruit of thy land', fertility is equated with God's grace and blessing.[25] The intercession of children in these narratives therefore maps directly onto the understanding of the fruitful womb as an act of (literally) saving grace.

The *Experiences*' contents pages place particular emphasis upon the role played by children in saving the lives and souls of women. This stresses the importance of maternal feeling and pregnancy for religious transformation by distilling a convert's conversion down to a single sentence in which the role of children dominate. For example, the conversion of L. P. is described as being prompted 'By thoughts touching a childe in her wombe, when Satan tempted her to destroy her selfe' (A5ᵛ); the conversion of D. M. is inspired 'By a young infant, when she went to a Pond to drown her self' (A4ʳ); and the reference to C. M. reads 'By trouble about some miscarriages towards her children' (A5ᵛ), thereby highlighting the role played by her maternal feeling in her conversion, but also raising the spectre of a stillbirth which is analogous with sin. The contents pages consequently highlight for the reader the power of motherhood as a catalyst for conversion.

As is outlined in the contents, D. M. determines not to commit suicide by drowning herself in a pond near Leeds because of the young child she has with her:

> By the providence of God, having a great love to a young infant I had then, I tooke that childe in my armes; and when I came to the place, I looked upon the childe, and considered with my selfe, what, shall I destroy my selfe and my poor childe? . . . me thought at last, I heard the Lord saying to my soule, as he did to *Paul, Trust in me, my grace is sufficient for thee*. And then I found some comfort . . . and so I went away back with much joy, beleeving that I should have the favour of God. (C6ᵛ–C7ʳ)

Mimicking the pose of mother and infant found in iconographic depictions of Mary and Jesus, D. M. carries her child to the edge of the pond but is unable to enter the water if it means killing the child along with herself. She then hears God speaking the lines he directed to Paul (the archetypal male convert), '*Trust in me, my grace is sufficient for thee*'. The movement from a powerful maternal image to the words uttered by God to Paul, transposes two scriptural precedents onto D. M.'s conversion. While one is female and the other male, they point to the inherently replicable and generative nature of conversion within the gathered churches, phenomena which find their root in the fertile symbolism of D. M.'s own body.

Another woman, L. P., is only prevented from doing herself harm because she is pregnant:

> Had I not been with child, and affected with natural inclination to the Babe in my womb, I had been in danger ... to have destroyed my self ... thus considering the innocency of the childe, which the Lord put into my minde, it (through Gods mercy) became a meanes to stay my hand from laying violence upon my selfe. (L7^v– L8^r)

L. P. is recounting an incident which occurred 'some twenty years since' (L7^r) indicating that by the time of writing, she is likely to have been beyond her childbearing years. The fruit of her womb at this moment in her story provides the transition point between despair and comfort which will set the pattern for the rest of her life as a member of the gathered churches. Her generative body saves both her life and her soul.

In both these cases from the *Experiences* the woman's role as a mother overrides her feelings of despair, but the resulting imagery also recalls the relationship between the Virgin Mary and Christ, as well as numerous images of fertility found in scripture. Motherhood, however, could also be the source of a convert's despair. A. A. recounts how her husband was wounded, perhaps in fighting during the Civil War, something she 'tooke as a great trial, not having above a month to goe with childe' (D10^v). Heavily pregnant, her husband's injury leaves her vulnerable. She then loses her two sons to smallpox, leaving her with only a daughter who she had not previously valued:

> All my children were sicke together of the small pox ... one of my children dyed suddenly, when I thought hee had been neare well ... suddenly the Lord stroke the elder of my two children then living, which was a Boy, my other, which is a Girle, I did not so much value, but now I doe, and know Gods mercy in sparing her, but my childe that then dyed, was the chiefe comfort that my heart was fixed upon in this world. (D10^v–D11^v)

The death of her children leaves A. A. so traumatised that she believes that their deaths are her fault. Reading the loss of her sons as an indictment by God she remained 'between hope and despair' (D12^r) until she found 'comfort' by considering how '*Pauls* life was subject to temptations' (D12^v). Like D. M., A. A. moves from despair to hope via a gendered trajectory which takes her from motherhood to the archetype of masculine conversion, St Paul.

While this movement again reinforces how scriptural types aid in the patterning of conversion, providing a template which the potential convert is able to follow, there may be a further layer of gendered meaning attached to these two women's use of Paul. Paul was the man previously known as Saul who persecuted Christians only to convert on the road to Damascus and become the greatest of the Apostles, men who were charged by Christ with spreading the Gospel. Paul was therefore a convert, but also a teacher who brought about the conversions of others. One of the often repeated 'evidences' of conversion espoused by converts in the *Experiences* is the desire to proselytise to others. W. F., an individual whose gender is not marked in his/her narrative, desires 'that my life may be a patterne of holinesse unto others' (O10^r), while D. M., the woman saved from drowning herself in a pond by her child, hopes 'it is possible to convert sinners' (C10^r). These converts read their desire to bring others into their congregation as proof of their elect status, their movement from convert to converter aligning them with the dynamic found in the life of Paul. This is also a shift which can be read via the symbol of female reproduction. Upon being spiritually remade the convert hopes to become a procreative site, a fertile source for further conversions. Paul, while male, may in fact be a useful symbol for the generative power of the convert analogous to that of the Virgin Mary.

So potent is the image of mother and child for those who are in the spiritual wilderness that two dream narratives contained in the *Experiences* also incorporate the intercessions of children. The stories of E. R. and T. M. do not identify the gender of the convert in the narrative itself, although E. R. is identified as a woman in the contents pages (A7^v) and uses a number of scriptural women as exempla: 'it pleased the Lord to bring many promises into my minde, and that example also of *Mary Magdalen*, and also of the Woman of *Canaan* beleeving; that as Jesus Christ had been gracious to them, so he would also to me' (R4^r). E. R. dreams of 'a little childe in white' (R2^v) identified as Christ by her companions, who 'told me That it was Jesus Christ that had appeared in the shape of a Childe' (R3^r). T. M. dreams of a child who rescues him or her from a red dragon:

> There appeared a great red Dragon; before it came at me, there appeared a little Childe, and it was put into my armes . . . I asked it what was its name; it said *Emanuel*; I asked it who was its father; it said *I am*; I asked, who was its Mother; it said *Eternity*; I asked from whence he came, he said, *from my Father out of* heaven. (R5^v–R6^v)

The child who appears in these dreams identifies himself as Christ (*Emanuel*) and is read as such by authorities other than the dreamer. In both cases, the lack of any clear indication of the convert's gender (E. R.'s identification as a woman in the contents pages notwithstanding) nonetheless frames the dreaming believer as maternal. This is particularly clear when T. M. has the child 'put into' his or her 'armes', mirroring the stance of the Virgin Mother as she holds the infant Christ. The maternal image is so powerful for converts that it not only overlays the quotidian with scriptural iconography, but follows them into the dream realm as a protective force.

This foregrounding of the spiritual bond represented by parental relationships is also echoed at the end of the *Experiences* in 'A Confession of faith' (U8r), a numerical list of beliefs which appears to have been designed as a verbal, and communal, speech act attesting to a congregation's faith. Beginning with the assertion that 'WEE believe, That the Scriptures contained in the Old and New Testament are the Word of God, written by the Prophets' (U8r), the 'Confession' goes on to outline a belief in original sin which frames the members of the congregation as children: 'We beleeve, That through the guilt and corruption of *Adams* sin, he and all his posterity, are by nature the children of wrath' (U8v–U9r). Emphasis is also placed upon Christ's mortal lineage through his mother Mary: 'We beleeve, That God the Son tooke upon him the nature of man, but without sinne, was conceived by the holy ghost, borne of a virgine' (U9r). In this way both believer and saviour are figured as children, although one is sinful, the other 'without sinne'. While this potentially highlights the inevitable subordination of the child to the heavenly father, the text's emphasis upon the child as the product of the female body in the narratives which have preceded the 'Confession', ties the congregation which speaks these lines in one voice to the procreative capacity of the feminine: the convert is a child, saved by a child, and both are the product of women.

The image of the female convert inhabiting the position of the divine mother Mary is also to be found in a conversion narrative which encapsulates the child's ability to educate their parent. In a reversal of the traditional familial hierarchy the convert I. B. finds that she is called to account by her young son. Following the stricture of Psalm 8:2, 'Out of the mouth of babes and sucklings hast thou ordained strength', the six-year-old boy provides the catalyst for her conversion when he refuses to play with other children who swear. The child,

Robert, is one of the few individuals who is not a preacher to be named in the text:

> About seventeen years since, a Childe of mine about six yeares of age, when I have bid him goe forth to play, he hath come in againe very solitary because other Children would swear . . . I would ask him, *Robert*, what ayleth you, why doe you not goe to play? . . . they could not be (said he) Gods children. I would say, Why not Childe? then he would say, No Mother, though I am but a little way in my Booke, yet I have learnt, that God will not pardon such sinnes, as swearing . . . And many times I had such conference with that Childe . . . I was much afflicted in soule, considering that my Childe, so young, should give me such instructions; which hath proved a blessing to me, to bring me home to him. (D2^r– D3^r)

Like the children who we have seen preventing women from committing suicide and appearing as Christ in people's dreams, Robert acts as a conduit for God's grace. He reminds his mother that swearing is a sin and that his 'Booke' tells him so, thus acting as an interpreter of scripture for his parent. Robert's repetition of the word 'Mother' in this excerpt reinforces the nature of their bond, but also emphasises that she has given birth to the very agent who will secure her salvation and 'bring her home' to another child: Christ.

Is the symbolic power of female generation only harnessed in the stories of women in the *Experiences*? A number of the male narratives in the collection highlight specifically male behaviours, including gambling and smoking, and the narrative of T. R. describes in elaborate detail a number of sea voyages in which he is saved from kidnap, shipwreck, and starvation due to the intercession of God, indicating that he is a sailor by trade. These stories don't always include specific gender signifiers, as is the case of H. N. who takes part in 'gameing on the Lords day' (Q5^r), but it is probably safe to assume that it is unlikely that a female convert would be employed as a sailor or confess to spending her time drinking, smoking, and gambling. Out of the sixty-one narratives in the *Experiences*, however, only four describe specifically masculine pursuits or occupations, the stories of T. R., H. N., T. G., and the 'souldier' S. P.

Several narratives employ male signifiers in the form of relationships. N. B., for example, dates his conversion away from the 'Church of *Rome*' to his 'wives perswasions' (N1^v), but it is often the case that male narratives defer any identification of gender. The story of H. W. fails to note his gender until towards the end of the narrative when he states 'That though I was a sinful man, yet it was my comfort that the Lord was my God' (F6^v), and another convert, W. F., says that 'God in all his dispensations to mee is my father, and I stand as a son in his presence' (O9^v), but this is the only hint that the writer is a man. It is therefore often the case that male narratives are far from explicit and instead force the reader to examine the text with a forensic eye in order to ascertain gender. This may mean that given the dominance of obviously female narratives in the collection, the reader is likely to mistake a male narrative for a female one before the text tells them otherwise.

Narratives identified as male also occasionally adopt female signifiers. This is the case in the story of W. W., identified in the contents pages as being a man, but devoid of gender signifiers in the body of the text. W. W. describes how the 'great tempter of mankind' (P4^v), Satan, lay siege to his soul and specifically genders his soul female: 'He then immediately, like a sharpe accuser, steps in upon my poor drooping soule, laying in her sight the wrath of God in his justice for sin' (P5^r). The battle which W. W. outlines, between a masculine Satan and a feminine soul, underlines his soul's weakness at this point in his conversion experience, but also indicates that spiritual identity can be gendered female even if the convert is male.

Despite the potential for gender to appear unstable in these male narratives it is not the case that any of them use the language of maternity in the same way as the female narratives. There is one potential exception to this reading, however. There are a number of narratives which fail to identify gender in the body of the text, but which nonetheless describe the convert as a parent. These include the story of A. L. who opens his or her narrative by describing their 'griefe' at the death of a daughter who they believe 'made away her selfe' (C10^r); C. M. who describes being 'seduced touching my children, that hath brought some trouble upon them, by my parting with them' (M1^r); and A. H., who talks of a new found love of God which supersedes any love they feel for their child: 'I find my heart really to desire to love God above all, and am jealous over my selfe, least my child, or any worldly thing should withdraw my love from my God' (N9^v). C. M. and A. H. are both identified as women in the contents pages, but remain ungendered in the body of their narratives, while A. L.'s gender is not identified. As the raising of children was traditionally the purview of women, however, the early modern reader would almost certainly have attributed all these stories to women.

The effect of these phenomena upon the collection as a whole (the relative scarcity of male narratives which describe explicitly male behaviours; male narratives which frequently defer the identification of gender; the use of a feminised spiritual language by male converts; and the identification of converts as parents even if their gender is not explicit) is both to downplay masculine identity and also to detach female qualities from biological gender.

The importance of female and maternal symbolism for converts is closely allied to the generative qualities of the female body and the understanding of conversion as a re-birth. As Mack points out, the capacity to give birth ensures that it is the female body which best encapsulates the process of religious change and conversion: 'The paradigm for the experience of spiritual striving and ultimate union with God was the relationship between the mother and her infant child. The labor of childbirth was the archetypal metaphor for the agony of spiritual transformation.'[26] The female (unnamed) subject is consequently shown to embody the process of reproductive religious transformation which has to be achieved by all converts, including men, a process (a labour) which the *Experiences* seeks to both contain and perpetuate.

All of the narratives of experience, despite the converts being unnamed, are littered with pronouns, to the extent that the repetition of 'I' and 'me' encourages the reader to inhabit the position of the penitent believer as they suffer their labour of faith. This is illustrated by the following quotation taken from the story of the woman E. C.:

> *I* am so little affected to the world, that *I* account it nothing; *I* can willingly leave all for God, and *I* hope suffer any thing for God, if he should please to call *me* to it, so farre as *I* can judge of *my* owne heart, but herein trusting in the power of Christ. [emphasis mine] (C4ʳ)

The rhythm of the sentence, imposed by the use of punctuation, places stress upon the pronouns 'I', 'me', and 'my', before ending upon the unstressed 'Christ'. This appears to subsume a sense of the personal into Christ while also conferring an oral quality onto E. C.'s evidence of her conversion: we can almost hear her speak. Alongside the proliferation of repetitive pronouns, the use of female gender-signifiers frequently promotes a self-consciously female ventriloquism on the part of the reader. We can see this in the earlier quotation from I. B. where she recreates the question and answer dialogue which occurred between herself and her son Robert ('I would ask him', 'then he would say').

This effect is further encouraged by the text's incorporation of prayers and moments of speech in italics, allowing not only for a form of commonplacing but also for the reader to 'speak with' or even 'for' the female and male converts. The individual narratives consequently have a verbally cumulative quality achieved through the amassing of scriptural precedents and personal proofs. This sense of a spiritual aggregate is not only emphasised via the repetition of the personal pronouns 'I' and 'me' (particularly in the numerical proofs/evidences), but is also complicated by the incorporation in the third and final section of the *Experiences* of 'scripts' which appear to be intended to be read aloud, in concert, by members of a newly gathered church. For example, 'A Confession *of* Faith', as previously noted, begins with the words 'WEE believe' (U8r). This not only makes the reader ventriloquise the experiences of the convert, but organises the disparate narratives in the collection around a community of voices: the text becomes a congregation. The dominance of female voices without named authority has the effect of gendering this textual congregation female. This woman-centred textual space, however, is designed to utilise the generative power of the female body without necessarily conferring authority upon particular individual women.

This feminised act of communal ventriloquism can be connected to Peter Stallybrass's argument that the personal name is the 'name of deprivation'; the act of naming strips the individual of their social function. Stallybrass is here talking about mimesis, doubling, and costume on the Renaissance stage, but I think it is possible to connect the deprivation of naming to the *Spiritual Experiences*' focus upon gender at the expense of named identity.[27] In stripping its congregation of their proper names the *Experiences* allow the reader to inhabit the text via gender rather than individual personas. If the personal name of the convert had been incorporated into the text then the image of the convert as a fertile soul whose experiences can be endlessly replicated would have been marginalised in favour of a more masculine, and less fruitful, image of the conversion process. This is also the phenomenon which allows for the textual congregation to be joined by the reader as they are not circumscribed by the individual personal name, but rather embraced by a universal femininity.

The most elaborate of all of the narratives of experience, by either a man or a woman, is the story of the woman M. K. Appearing at the end of the first section of the *Experiences*, her story serves as an example for the reproductive qualities of female experience in the text as a whole.[28] She begins with a theatrical metaphor which imbues her story with drama, self-consciousness, and also irony: 'When I take a view of my life upon the stage of this world, I may very well compare it to a comicall Tragedy, or a tragical Comedy, or a labyrinth from one sin to another' (H8ᵛ). The 'daughter of very godly and honest parents' (H9ʳ) she was singled out from her eleven siblings by her mother: 'she told me it was because she saw something ... more tractablenesse and diligence to please her than in the rest' (H9ʳ). M. K. was instructed in matters of religion by her mother who allotted her a 'portion of Scripture every day' and 'likewise a part of *Erasmus Rotterdamus* upon the foure Evangelists' (H9ʳ) as a part of her spiritual education. M. K. appears to have read these texts alongside her mother, rather than privately, as she notes that 'we took great delight' (H9ᵛ) in reading. She then ruminates upon the example set by the Marian martyrs and asks herself '*What wouldest thou doe, if thou should be tempted to deny Christ, and be called to suffer for his sake, as some of thy kindred were in Queene Maries time? Wouldest thou not deny thy master?*' (H9ᵛ). She determines that '*I would not*; and if the Lord would be pleased to try me, he would see how valiantly I would fight under his banner' (H10ʳ).

When M. K. was twelve, her mother died and she found herself her 'fathers house-keeper, so as it were a mother to ten children' (H10ʳ). Due to her new status she believed herself to have 'advanced ... amongst the chiefest of the Parish, who were my mothers companions, I representing her person when I was amongst them' (H10ᵛ). This caused her to act with pride. Both her religious education and her sin therefore originate from the maternal line. When her father also died, M. K. tells us she fell into despair believing she had sinned by omission. Her friends, wearied by her 'excessive sorrow' (H11ᵛ) sent her to London as the 'word of God was more plentifully preached there' (H11ᵛ). Upon arrival she fell into a friendship with the wife of 'Doctour *Page*' (H11ᵛ), a minister at Deptford whose eldest son she later married. Her husband, falling into bad company, slipped into idleness and drinking and M. K. found herself compelled to murder the friend who she blamed for his changed condition: 'the devill set his foot into my heart, and perswaded me that by the committing of one sinne, I should prevent many, and so stirred me up to murther him, to which suggestion I cowardly yeelded' (H12ᵛ). She only ceased in her murderous intent when, in the midst of a dream in which she was with the man in a chamber surrounded by weapons, she went to attack him and was stopped by the voice of God saying 'Vengeance is mine' (I1ʳ).[29]

M. K. later found comfort in the ministry of 'Mr Dod' (I5ᵛ) in Westminster and attended sermons 'constantly' (I5ᵛ) until she was encouraged to petition God. This petition is reproduced in italics and takes the form of M. K. directly beseeching the Lord to enact her conversion: '*Heale me O Lord, and I shall be healed; turne me, and I shall be turned; convert me, and I shall bee converted*' (I8ᵛ). Vocalising her desire for spiritual renewal in this manner appears to increase M. K.'s resolve, 'when the Lord had opened my mouth to speake unto him, I gathered a great deal of strength' (I9ʳ), and meditating upon Christ on the cross and John 17 she finally finds a sense of faith, ending her narrative with a list of nine proofs of her position as a member of the elect.

M. K.'s narrative of experience, with its seemingly endless oscillation between hope and despair, the incorporation of a divine dream, and a moment of evil intent and divine providence, follows many of the typical patterns of Protestant conversion texts as well as echoing the format utilised by many of the converts in the *Experiences*. Importantly, however, her movement towards God is structured by her position as a daughter, a housekeeper filling the shoes of her dead mother, a female friend, and a wife anxious about her husband's soul. Her familial and domestic relationships shape her experiences and sins to the extent that her repeated use of the pronoun 'I', particularly in the nine proofs which can potentially operate as statements of faith for the reader, is explicitly gendered female (although it is worth noting that she does not mention having any children).

The length of M. K.'s story, and its inclusion of a high level of biographical detail, ensures that the reader is given multiple opportunities to identify her gender. Her eloquence and ability as a storyteller – evidenced by her confident use of rhetorical tropes and the creation of an atmosphere of suspense, particularly at the moment when she recounts wishing to murder her husband's friend – makes this narrative a compelling read which borrows from some of the conventions of popular gallows confessions, even if she is prevented, through divine inspiration, from actually committing a crime. The combination of the quotidian and the extraordinary in her story also allows the reader to imagine that their own lives and spiritual struggles can be patterned in a similar way. The unapologetic identification of M. K. as a woman, and the space which she is afforded in the text, indicates that this textual congregation happily incorporates female experience. The focus which is placed upon M. K.'s inheritance of the traditional female roles of daughter and wife, however, makes her story inherently replicable, particularly for the female reader. M. K.'s conversion thus serves as a model for the importance of the female voice superseding individual named authority in such a way as to foreground the imitative and fertile nature of both her individual story and the text as a whole.

The use of authorial anonymity, the dominance of female gender signifiers, and the recollection of uniquely female experiences, particularly those associated with motherhood, all combine to shape the *Experiences* into a reproductive text. The eloquence and complexity of some of the female narratives in the anthology also signal that female voices, in as much as they operate as a feminised conduit for God's grace, are to be valued and assimilated. While this bias potentially reflects the important role played by women in the radical sects which emerged during the Civil War and Protectorate, it is ultimately the generative and dilatory symbolism of the female body which informs the text's construction. Crucially, the fertile instrumentality that this promotes is designed to function as a proselytising and converting force which will expand the congregation of the gathered churches by subsuming the 'sober and spirituall Reader' (title page) into the text.

NOTES

I would like to thank Helen Smith, Simon Ditchfield, and Kathleen Lynch for their comments and encouragement.

1 Kathleen Lynch, *Protestant autobiography in the seventeenth-century anglophone world* (Oxford: Oxford University Press, 2012), p. 130.
2 D. Bruce Hindmarsh, *The evangelical conversion narrative: spiritual autobiography in early modern England* (Oxford: Oxford University Press, 2005), pp. 45–6.
3 *Ibid.*, p. 43.
4 Sylvia Brown discusses how the roles of women in radical sects were often linked to a millenarian timetable, 'Introduction', to Brown (ed.), *Women, gender and radical religion in early modern Europe* (Leiden: Brill, 2007), pp. 6–8.
5 Andrew Cambers, *Godly reading: print, manuscript and Puritanism in England, 1580–1720* (Cambridge: Cambridge University Press, 2011), p. 7.
6 On the hermeneutic flexibility of initials see Marcy North, *The anonymous Renaissance: cultures of discretion in Tudor-Stuart England* (Chicago: Chicago University Press, 2003), pp. 67–75.

7 *The spirituall experiences of sundry beleevers* (London, 1653), U1^r. According to the title page, this is the 'second impression' of the *Experiences*, the first has since been lost. There were no further editions published after 1653.
8 Lynch, *Protestant autobiography*, p. 131.
9 *OED*, 'Copy, *v*.1', def. 1.a.; 'Copy, *n*. and *adj*.', def. 1.c.
10 On the role played by gendered language in legitimising publication see Wendy Wall, *The imprint of gender: authorship and publication in the Renaissance* (Ithaca, NY: Cornell University Press, 1993), p. 6. See also Douglas Brooks (ed.), *Printing and parenting in early modern England* (Farnham: Ashgate, 2003).
11 Nigel Smith, *Perfection proclaimed: language and literature in English radical religion 1640–1660* (Oxford: Clarendon Press, 1989), p. 43. On Walker's career as a preacher, and his expulsion from a number of congregations, see Lynch, *Protestant autobiography*, pp. 138–40.
12 Lynch argues that this ambiguity reflects the 'unsettled state of the gathered churches', *Protestant autobiography*, p. 131.
13 In the body of the text we can identify seven men and ten women, six of whom are also identified as mothers. Forty-four narratives contain no gender signifiers. When looking at the contents pages we can identify a further twelve men and a further seventeen women, one of whom is identified as a mother. This takes the total count of men to nineteen, the total count of women to twenty-seven, and the total count of mothers to seven. It may also be significant that in the body of the first narrative, composed by T. A., the convert employs the figure of the Christian everyman, 'I think a man cannot repent before he have faith: A man must first taste of the love of Christ' (B1^v), but does not use any gender signifiers, although in the contents T. A. is identified as a man. The following twelve narratives identify the convert as either a woman (seven women, five of whom are mothers), and there are no gender signifiers (five) until the narrative of the man H. W. at F4^r. This means that the beginning of the collection is overwhelmingly dominated by female voices.
14 Keith Thomas, 'Women and the Civil War sects' *Past & Present*, 13 (1958), 44. As Thomas points out, this equality was confined to the spiritual realm, p. 53. See also, Smith, *Perfection proclaimed*, pp. 12–13. For a detailed examination of how 'ideals of masculinity' were fractured during the Civil War see Diane Purkiss, *Literature, gender, and politics during the English Civil War* (Cambridge: Cambridge University Press, 2005).
15 North, *The anonymous Renaissance*, p. 4. Conversion narratives composed by women were frequently published posthumously; Elaine Hobby, *Virtue of necessity: English women's writing 1649–88* (London: Virago Press, 1988), p. 66. The story of Anna Trapnell's conversion contained in *A legacy for saints* (London, 1654) includes a prefatory justification for publication

endorsed by John Proud and Caleb Ingold (Elder and Deacon respectively of Trapnell's church of Great All Hallows, London), in which it is asserted that the publication of Trapnell's experiences was prompted by her imprisonment in Bridewell and 'otherwise had waited the death of the Testatrix, as she fully purposed' (A2^v). Men, often the convert's husband, also edited, and thereby controlled, female narratives, a practice which Hilary Hinds reads as an act of 'silencing', *God's Englishwomen: seventeenth-century radical sectarian writing and feminist criticism* (Manchester: Manchester University Press, 1996), p. 58. One example of this phenomenon is the conversion narrative belonging to the Baptist convert Jane Turner, published in the same year as the *Experiences*. This incorporates a lengthy dedicatory epistle composed by Turner's husband John, *Choice experiences of the kind dealings of God before, in, and after conversion* (London, 1653). Similarly, the story of the conversion of Sarah Wight was published and edited by Henry Jessey, *The exceeding riches of grace advanced* (London, 1647). On Jessey's editorial practices see Smith, *Perfection proclaimed*, pp. 45–9.

16 Hinds, *God's Englishwomen*, p. 57. On the prevalence and power of the modesty topos for women writers see Patricia Pender, *Early modern women's writing and the rhetoric of modesty* (Basingstoke: Palgrave Macmillan, 2012).

17 Phyllis Mack, *Visionary women: ecstatic prophecy in seventeenth-century England* (Berkeley and Los Angeles: University of California Press, 1992), p. 32. The weaker status of women was also thought to make them more susceptible to ecstatic prophecy, a justification utilised by the fifth monarchist Anna Trapnell; Nicholas McDowell, *The English radical imagination: culture, religion, and revolution, 1630–1660* (Oxford: Clarendon Press, 2003), pp. 16–17.

18 Diane Purkiss, 'Producing the voice, consuming the body: women prophets of the seventeenth century', in Isobel Grundy and Susan Wiseman (eds), *Women, writing, history 1640–1740* (London: B. T. Batsford, 1992), p. 142.

19 Sylvia Brown, 'The reproductive word: gender and textuality in the writings of John Bunyan', *Bunyan Studies*, 11 (2003/2004), 23. Similarly, Purkiss reads maternal metaphors as having an 'underlying linkage between female reproduction and the production of the Word', 'Producing the voice', p. 153.

20 Rose Thurgood, 'A Lecture of Repentance', in Naomi Baker (ed.), *Scripture women: Rose Thurgood, 'A lecture of repentance' & Cicely Johnson, 'Fanatical reveries* (Nottingham: Trent Editions, 2005), p. 16.

21 The importance of despair for the reception of grace in Protestant theology is highlighted by John Stachniewski when he argues that 'a sense of God's anger ... was the flashpoint for conversion': *The persecutory imagination: English puritanism and the literature of religious despair* (Oxford: Clarendon Press, 1991), p. 18.

22 Instances of this quotation appearing as a scriptural 'promise' include sigs. M11^v, N2^v, N11^r, P1^v, P12^v, Q4^v, S7^r, S9^v, and S11^v. Similarly, the following quotation from Isaiah 1:18 appears on a number of different occasions, '*though your sinnes be as scarlet, they shall be as white as snow*', including sigs. P8^v and P11^r. On the repetitive features of the *Experiences*, including the recurring use of particular scriptural quotations see Owen C. Watkins, *The Puritan experience* (London: Routledge & Kegan Paul, 1972), p. 41.

23 Patricia Parker, *Literary fat ladies: rhetoric, gender, property* (London: Methuen, 1987), pp. 13–14.

24 For an illuminating exploration of the importance of this trope for the seventeenth-century visionary Jane Lead see Julie Hirst, '"Mother of love": spiritual maternity in the works of Jane Lead (1624–1704)', *Women, gender and radical religion*, pp. 161–87. Explorations of attitudes to maternity in the period can be found in Patricia Crawford, 'The construction and experience of maternity in seventeenth-century England', in Valerie Fildes (ed.), *Women as mothers in pre-industrial England* (London: Routledge, 1990), pp. 3–38, and Sara Mendelson and Patricia Crawford, *Women in early modern England 1550–1720* (Oxford: Clarendon Press, 1998), pp. 148–64.

25 *The Bible: authorized King James Version with Apocrypha*, ed. Robert Carroll and Stephen Prickett (Oxford: Oxford University Press, 1997), p. 226. All further King James Version quotations are from this edition.

26 Mack, *Visionary women*, p. 39.

27 Peter Stallybrass, 'Naming, renaming and unnaming in the Shakespearean quartos and folio', in Andrew Murphy (ed.), *The Renaissance text: theory, editing, textuality* (Manchester: Manchester University Press, 2000), p. 108.

28 Watkins argues that M. K.'s story is an example of the 'Puritan spiritual autobiography as popular literature', *The Puritan experience*, p. 43.

29 On M. K.'s divine dream see Alec Ryrie, 'Sleep, waking and dreaming in Protestant piety', in Jessica Martin and Ryrie (eds), *Private and domestic devotion in early modern Britain* (Farnham: Ashgate, 2012), p. 90.

Part II: Material conversions

5

'The needle may convert more than the pen': women and the work of conversion in early modern England

Claire Canavan and Helen Smith

In 1622, Henry Gunter narrated the conversion of his wife, Marie, an orphan 'nousled and misled ... in Popery' by an aged guardian until the age of fourteen, when, her Catholic protector having died, she was taken into the house of a relative, Lettice Dudley, Countess of Leicester.[1] Gunter endeavoured to persist in her Catholic faith, determined to cross the seas and become a nun as soon as the occasion presented itself.[2] 'But she could not', Henry records, 'so closely carry her secret deuotions and intentions, but that by the carefull eye of her Honourable Lady, they were soone discouered'.[3] The implacable Dudley 'tooke from [Gunter] all her Popish books, Beades and Images, and all such trumpery', a term that ties together material presence, low value, the trappings of religious ceremony, and practices of deceit or imposture.[4] Dudley enforced attendance at household prayers; appointed Gunter as the reader of the additional prayers 'her honour daily vsed to haue in her priuate chamber with her women'; and scrutinised her correspondence and social connections, as well as testing Gunter on the sermons she heard, 'the rather because it was constantly obserued by all the women in that honorable Family, to come together after the last Sermon, and make repetition of both' sermons they attended each Sunday.[5]

Thanks to this panoptical religious regime, Gunter experienced 'a staggering in her old way' (G7ᵛ) and was finally 'wonne to beleue the Truth, and renounce her former superstition and ignorance', a moment which is marked in the text with a printed marginal note celebrating 'Her new birth' (G8ʳ). Deriving from the Latin *convertĕre*, meaning variously 'to turn about, turn in character or nature, transform, or translate', the

English term 'conversion' is similarly capacious, embracing a 'turning in position, direction, destination'.[6] Gunter's 'staggering', then, can be read as the necessary stumbling that allows for a change of direction; in the terms of the queer phenomenology proposed by Sara Ahmed, 'in order to become orientated ... we must first experience disorientation'.[7] Gunter's conversion or reorientation, however, was neither final nor complete; she endured 'five or six' years of spiritual turmoil before devising a rigorous regime of bible-reading and prayer that established temptation not as a continual 'molestation' but as a kind of devotional salt: 'a sweet seasoning of her whole life' (H3r).

Having changed church as a teenager, Marie Gunter was – at least according to her husband's account – forever a convert, constantly alert to the perils of religious doubt, but also to the possibility of replicating and extending the conversion experience. As Henry put it: 'as it is the property of a true Conuert, being conuerted her selfe shee endeauoured the conuersion of others' (G8v–G9r). His *Short relation* of Marie's life participates in this conversionary dynamic: a designedly exemplary narrative, it declares on its title page that it is 'to be looked vpon, both *by Protestants* and *Papists*', confirming the faith of the former through readerly participation in a dramatic tale of error, redemption, and spiritual trial, and extending Marie Gunter's – and before her, Lettice Dudley's – pastoral work by effecting further confessional shifts within the Catholic community.

Scholars have long recognised the importance of religion to early modern women's identity and self-expression. Nonetheless, women's literary explorations of religious commitment have frequently been taken as evidence of their passive obedience to patriarchal mandates and, as Erica Longfellow notes, assumed to belong to 'a less transgressive and therefore less interesting aesthetic' than other genres.[8] Historians, too, whilst recognising women's roles in maintaining and articulating the religious identity of the household, have paid little attention to the wider social and cultural force of women's devotional practice. Arguing for the need to study 'female religious beliefs', Patricia Crawford suggests that this topic has been neglected precisely because 'it seems as if the godly woman was the successfully socialised woman', of little interest to historians seeking evidence of women's subversion of the patriarchal order. Nonetheless, Crawford posits, 'if we examine the lives of godly pious women then we can see how belief could become an individual matter which women could transform into something of their own'.[9] Even this, however, accepts the premise that women's religious culture was an individual and internalised domain. As the example of Marie Gunter suggests, religion, whilst deeply felt, was far from being simply 'an individual matter'; it was, both within the extended household of Lettice Dudley and within the wider community in which Gunter laboured to reproduce her own conversion, an essentially social phenomenon, and one in which women's agency and influence extended far beyond the self.

Women's religion was understood as both affective – a site for the revelation and expression of religious feeling – and effective – able to prompt change in others. Scholars have been rightly suspicious of idealising posthumous accounts such as that of Henry Gunter, which expressed and attempted to reproduce 'powerful and formative cultural discourses'.[10] Nonetheless, we want to suggest that the popularity of such accounts – attested most notably in Philip Stubbes' report of the godly life and death of his wife, Katherine, which went through thirty-four editions between 1591 and 1693 – is evidence not simply of patriarchal *mores*, but of the cultural visibility and force of women's devotional routines and actions. In her outline of a queer phenomenology, Ahmed argues that the experience of 'turning' – of recognition or misrecognition, but also of taking on new orientations – is central to identity formation. This chapter takes on Ahmed's description of gender as 'a bodily orientation, a way in which bodies get directed by their actions over time' in both figurative and literal terms, considering how women's actions as converts and converters intersected with ideologies of gender and shaped the religious experience of those around them, before going on to analyse how material expressions of women's devotion served to direct and orientate the bodily and spiritual responses of observers.[11]

Our particular example is that of women's needlework: a practice which has, as much if not more than religion, been read as symptomatic of women's internalisation of patriarchal prescriptions, and their corresponding exclusion from the realms of self-expression or influence.[12] Given the prevalence of biblical themes in women's needlework of the late sixteenth and seventeenth centuries, scriptural stitching might seem to offer a compelling example of women's lack of agency. Yet drawing on a series of texts which attest to the public and conversionary effects of women's decorative craft, we argue that women's devotional needlework possessed a significant charge as a pervasive and effective technology for the conversion or confirmation of others. Women's religious practices should be understood neither as straightforwardly private, nor as taking place within a controlled and strictly feminine domain, but as evolving within and shaping a range of gendered relationships and encounters. Elaborated and performed within domestic and social contexts, women's religious experience formed part of a web of sexed encounters that influenced the aspirations, behaviour, and identity of both men and women.

'SHEE ENDEAUOURED THE CONUERSION OF OTHERS': WOMEN AND RELIGIOUS CHANGE

As Frances Dolan notes, among early modern Protestant commentators, it was assumed 'that women were more likely than men . . . to convert to [Catholicism]'.[13] Dedicating his 1609 *A letter to Mr. T. H. late minister; now fugitiue* (an attack upon the recent Catholic convert, Theophilus Higgons) 'To All Romish Collapsed Ladies, of Great Britanie', Sir Edward Hoby asked his readers to consider that '*were [the Jesuits'] grounds of such soundnes, as they beare you in hand, they would not so busily swarme about your sexe, which, by reason of your lesse abilitie of iudgement, is soonest inueigled with their wiles*'.[14] Appealing to women's discernment about their sexes' lack of discrimination, Hoby essays the difficult task of remonstrating with a group of readers stereotyped as lacking reason and being all too ready to succumb to flattering persuasion.

It was not only Catholicism that was understood to possess a particular fascination for women. In 1646, the Protestant controversialist John Bastwick, railing against the Independents, noted women's propensity to follow one another's example, complaining: 'If these grolls seduce but any giddy-headed Gentlewoman that is rich or but any inferior Lady, and make them but turne Independents, what a noise there is by & by through the Kingdom of it, and how staggering other poor unstable women begin to be.'[15] In Bastwick's account, women are easy converts, but also exemplary converters, whose fashionable religious practice is liable to exert a profound influence on observers of courtly life. The replicability of women's conversion was reproduced and reinforced in print; 1608, for example, saw the English publication of *The conuersion of a most noble lady of Fraunce . . . A most Christian epistle, written by her, to the ladyes of Fraunce, to resolue them in the cause of her conuersion from popery . . . and aduising them to imitate her religious example*. The anonymous translator addressed his translation (or 'conversion') of the Duchess of Tremoille's letter, 'To those mis-led Ladies and Gentelwomen of *England*, whome seducing Seminaries and Popish Priests haue too much preuailed withall, to the great danger of their soules.'¹⁶

Whilst women were seen as perilously liable to convert, they were also seen as able to effect confessional change in others. As Hoby puts it, in a distinctively gendered image, if Jesuit priests could '*once win the night-crow, to sing their dittie, then make they no doubt, but that the whole house will soone dance after their pipe*'.¹⁷ In particular, women were seen as capable of converting their husbands, as well as members of their extended family and community. From 1625, intense suspicion surrounded the marital and political influence of Henrietta Maria, Charles I's openly Catholic queen consort; an anonymous pamphlet, *The great eclipse of the sun, or Charles his waine* (1644) insisted that Henrietta Maria had successfully persuaded Charles 'that Darknesse was Light, and that it was better to be a Papist, then a Protestant'.¹⁸ In more positive terms, in 1622, William Gouge insisted 'it is the maine drift of *S. Peters* exhortation to beleeuing wiues, about their conuersation, to draw on their vnbeleeuing husbands to the true faith'. Gouge's suggestion that wives can 'draw' their husbands to religion resonates with Ahmed's questions: 'What does it mean for sexuality to be lived as orientated? What difference does it make "what" or "who" we are orientated toward in the very direction of our desire?'¹⁹ Women's 'conversation' within the context of a heterosexual union can, in Gouge's account, become a means to re-orientate the desires of the husband, both towards his marital partner and towards God. Celebrating the conjugal as well as spiritual benefits of such influence, Gouge reflects: 'If it please the Lord to giue such a blessing to the endeuour of an husband or wife, as to be a meanes of the conuersion of their bedfellow, then will the partie conuerted both intirely loue the other, and also heartily blesse God . . . that euer they were so neerely linked together.'²⁰

One Catholic woman, herself a convert, delighted in the ability of her sex to work upon men's souls; in a document newly recovered by Arnold Hunt, a 'Catholique Lady', whom Hunt tentatively identifies as Lady Mary Lovell, a 'cradle Catholic' and prominent figure among English Catholic exiles in the Low Countries, responded to Hoby's accusation that Jesuit priests preferred to work upon women by declaring that priests 'are more glad to confer with a wise and learned man . . .

than with an ignorant woman'. Her letter goes on, however, to celebrate the honest 'politie' of priests who 'make use of woemen of qualitie, witt, and worth, to further the conversion of their husbands and friends'. Referring to women's influence in the patronage of church livings, and thus highlighting the power of some elite women within the local religious community, Lovell argues that Catholic priests do no more, in seeking the support of women, 'than any minister of yours wold be glad to use to procure him selfe a benefice if he supposed the help of any lady or chambermayde of your profession might further his suite therein'.[21]

Their role as domestic educators meant that women had a particular influence on the religious choices and constancy of their children.[22] In a funeral sermon for his wife, Alice (d. 1647), Sir John Bramston recalled that 'she was a virtuous and religious women, a most careful and indulgent mother to her children, instructed them in the church catechism, teaching them the Lord's Prayer, the Ten Commandments, and the Creed'.[23] Crawford notes that nearly a quarter of the young men who entered the English College at Rome testified that their mothers had influenced their conversion and vocation, sometimes in opposition to their Protestant fathers.[24] The relationship between maternal care and religious faith was writ large in the commonplace metaphor that imagined the church as the true mother of her subjects; James Wadsworth, a convert first to Catholicism and then to Protestantism, was described on the title page of his *The English Spanish pilgrime* (1629) as being 'newly conuerted into his true mothers bosome, the *Church of England*'. This gendering of the church allowed for the exploration of male religiosity in affective terms, with converts, depending on the affiliation of the commentator, troped either as cruel sons acting against a suffering mother or as prodigals returning to a welcoming maternal embrace.

In larger households, a concern for the devotional economy, exemplified in Lettice Dudley's strictly enforced religious routines, extended beyond the immediate family to wards, as we have seen in the case of Marie Gunter, and also to servants and the extended community. Mary Rich, Countess of Warwick, paid particular attention to the souls of her servants. She allegedly reshaped her household as a pathway to Christian practice, 'scattering good Books in all the common Rooms and places of attendance, that those that waited might not lose their time, but well employ it, and have a bait laid of some practical, useful Book, and fitted to their capacity, which might catch and take them'.[25] The language of bait and snare establishes Rich as a fisher for souls within a rich biblical and iconographic tradition.[26] In a smaller establishment, the nonconformist minister, Richard Baxter, recalled of his wife Margaret (née Charlton), that 'she had an earnest desire of the conversion and salvation of her servants, and was greatly troubled that so many of them (though tolerable in their work) went away ignorant, or strange to true godliness, as they came: And such as were truly converted with us she loved as children', though Baxter does not record whether Margaret's efforts to save the souls of her servants were connected to the household's high turnover of domestic staff.[27]

Within a Catholic context, Margaret Mostyn, later Margaret of Jesus and Prioress of the English Carmelite Convent at Lierre, was said to have 'much delighted in reading ye saincts liues, and other pious bookes, often spending whole howers in reading to ye saruants, by wch she conuerted too soules yt ware protistance [Protestants]; in fine she gaue light and instruction both to ould and young in ye house'.[28] Margaret's youth – she was around eight years old, according to this account – speaks to the converting power of childish innocence, explored by Abigail Shinn in the previous chapter. In a manuscript life of Dorothy Lawson, a Catholic matriarch living near Newcastle, William Palmes describes her success in converting her husband's brothers and sisters, as well as her new household servants, so that her husband reportedly 'between jest and earnest, tould her, his family was become Papists ere he perceived it'.[29] Claiming that Lawson converted 'above a hundred' members of the local community to Catholicism, Palmes reminisced that 'when any was to be reconcil'd there-about, shee played the catechist, so as I had no other share in the work but to take their confessions'.[30] So committed was she to her evangelical duties, that even a fall from her horse whilst 'riding to an ancient servant falne from his faith' could not prevent Lawson from reaching the old man's deathbed in time to convert 'the miserable apostate'.[31]

A little further south, in Yorkshire, Lady Margaret Hoby also combined personal piety with a commitment to conversion. Hoby's diary makes it clear that the management of devotional activity was a central aspect of her household and estate duties: private and household prayer, sermon attendance, religious reading, and godly conversation with her chaplain, friends, servants, and neighbours, form dominant motifs in her record of her daily actions. In 1599, Hoby recorded that she had 'Instructed Tomson wiffe in some principles of relegion', and that, with her chaplain, Mr Rhodes, she had 'som speech with the poore and Ignorant of the som [sic] princeples of religion' in her kitchen.³² In January 1601, Hoby recorded the imbrications of her godly, medical, and social duties within an explicitly cross-confessional context:

> After priuat praier I did eate, then dressed my patients, reed of the bible, and then saluted some strangers : after, praied and then dined : after, I kept Companie tell they departed and, after, reed and talked with a yonge papest maide: and when I had giuen order for things in the house, I went to priuat examenation and praier and, after that, to supper...³³

Hoby's husband, Sir Thomas Posthumous Hoby, was a strict Puritan who frequently clashed with the local recusant community; Margaret's record of reading and talking with a local Catholic woman must be read as a conversion attempt or process, and testifies to her sense that it was her role to cure the souls as well as the bodies of her charges. Hoby seems to have been keen to collect evidence to support her conversionary acts, recording in her diary that on 10 April 1600 she not only 'hard Mr Smith defend the truth against the papest' at York Minster, but that, after returning home, she 'went to the church wher I hard Mr Stuard handle this question betwene the papests and vs – whether we were Iustefied by faith or workes'.³⁴ She also heard her chaplain, Mr Rhodes, 'read of the principles of poperie out of one of their owne bookes', 'read of a popeshe booke', and 'Read of a booke against some newe spronge vp herisies'.³⁵

Women's proselytising acts were licensed by biblical and church history: Bastwick, for example, argued that 'all Christians and all the Servants of the Lord in all ages studied to teach their friends and families *the knowledge and fear of the Lord*', and directed his readers' attention to the 'woman of *Samaria* how quickly she brought her neighbours and fellow citizens unto Christ after shee was converted'.³⁶ In similar terms, sources as diverse as *The Roman martyrology* and Protestant commentaries recorded on the one side that Saint Gudelia 'conuerted very many to the faith of Christ',³⁷ and, on the other, that it was 'reported of *Cicilia*, in the history of the Church, a poore Virgin, that by her gracious behauiour in her martyrdome, she was the means of converting four hundred to Christ'.³⁸ The converting activities of St Augustine's mother, Monica, were also frequently invoked as incentives to good living. Women's religious activity, then, was not confined to personal devotion or to the assertion – or denial – of particular forms of selfhood, but encompassed the extended household and local community. In their roles as domestic educators, householders, and charitable neighbours, women worked to instil and confirm the faith of their children, husbands, neighbours, and servants: acts that in themselves might spark the re-orientations of conversion, whether understood as the kindling or intensification of religious feeling or as a change in confessional affiliation and devotional practices.

'SANCTIFY MY CUSHIONETS': NEEDLEWORK, DEVOTION, AND CONVERSION

Biblical stories predominate in seventeenth-century English embroideries, making up 43 per cent of the examples surveyed in Ruth Geuter's catalogue of English embroidered needlework.[39] In contrast with earlier scholarship, which saw women's needlework as a practical exercise in self-regulation, more recent criticism argues that women's use of pertinent examples, and interpretations of popular themes, 'can ... sometimes reveal the subjective patterns of female piety'.[40] Susan Frye, for example, suggests that a 'woman's embroidery of biblical Women Worthies allowed her to express connections with female exemplars known for their personal virtue and beauty, as well as for adventures marked by eroticism and violence, all within the socially sanctioned activity of sewing'.[41] Yet Frye's insistence that sewing was 'socially sanctioned' registers a tension between the search for traces of women's self-expression and a sense that needlework – like religion – was an essentially constrained and constraining arena, with seventeenth-century embroideries constituting, at best, 'a vehicle for sporadic self-expression', as women re-worked biblical exemplars and applied them to their own socio-political and personal circumstances.[42]

Like acts of prayer, religious reading, and local conversions, women's sewing was far from being an inherently 'private' activity. In his *Anatomy of melancholy*, Robert Burton explained, 'insteed of laborious studies, [women] have curious Needle-workes, Cut-workes, spinning, bone-lace, and many pretty devises of their owne making, to adorne their houses, Cushions, Carpets, Chaires, Stooles'. Whilst Burton's comment appears dismissive, explicitly contrasting women's needle-work with the laborious studies of male melancholics, he recognises the intricacy of this 'curious' work, and goes on to establish such activity as shared and social, observing, in faintly weary tones, that these are skills which women 'shew to strangers'.[43] The complex and highly ambitious needlework 'stories' produced by women constituted alternative sites of knowledge production, and even proselytising activity. As Morrall puts it, women's needlework 'formed part of the habitus of the pious household in which embroidery and religious devotion were integral and related parts of a daily routine'.[44] Stitchcraft was highly visible, shaping the experiences of those who viewed, touched, and admired it, and possessing an orientating function which positioned men and women in relation not only to domestic and devotional space, but to the social order and to the divine.

The funeral monument of Dame Dorothy Selby of Ightham Mote in Kent highlights the visibility of women's embroidery, calling her

> a Dorcas,
> Whose curious needle wound the abused stage
> Of this leud world into the golden age,
> Whose pen of steel and silken inck enroll'd
> The acts of Jonah in records of gold.
> Whose arte disclosed that plot, which had it taken,
> Rome had tryumph'd, and Britain's walls had shaken.[45]

Situating Selby's work as part of the religio-political labour of repairing and maintaining the 'walls' of Protestant Britain, the tomb establishes an explicitly confessional context for Selby's work. The monument records the sumptuous appearance of Selby's embroidery of Jonah, as well as her needlework account of the gunpowder plot, shown in Figure 5.1. Selby's vivid embroidery copies and elaborates a popular print, *The double deliverance*, after Samuel Ward, which responded to the proposed Spanish Match of 1621 by reminding viewers of England's victory over the Spanish Armada, as well as the more recent revelation of the Gunpowder Plot. Selby was not the only needleworker to be inspired by this print; a second canvas-work version by an anonymous needleworker is held at the Lady Lever Art Gallery.[46] Done predominantly in shades of yellow and blue, and elaborated with popular stitched motifs, including animals and a mermaid, the embroidery is vibrant in comparison with its monochrome source, presenting the viewer with a dynamic and affective image.

The trend for biblical needlework was satirised in Jasper Mayne's 1639 comedy *The city match*. Sharing with the deceased Selby a name which recalls the biblical maker of tunics and clothing for widows, Dorcas is a zealously Puritan servant. Her mistress, Aurelia, locates Dorcas's energies as explicitly evangelical, complaining:

Figure 5.1 Dorothy Selby, 'The defeat of the Armada and the Gunpowder Plot', needlework picture.

> Yesterday I went
> To see a Lady that has a Parrot, my woman
> While I was in discourse converted the fowle.
> And now it can speak nought but Knoxes workes,
> So theres a parrot lost.[47]

Although Dorcas's devotion is ultimately revealed to be a subterfuge, it is manifest in every aspect of her household labours. In the kitchen, 'she will make / The Acts and Monuments in sweet-meats; Quinces / Arraigned and burnt at a stake; all my banquets / Are persequutions . . . and we eat Martyrs'. Dorcas's religiosity extends to stitchcraft: Aurelia details the variety of domestic and sumptuary locations that might feature devotional needlework:

> She works religious petticoats; for flowers
> She'll make church-histories. Her needle doth
> So sanctify my cushionets; besides,

> My smock-sleeves have such holy embroideries,
> And are so learned, that I fear, in time,
> All my apparel will be quoted by
> Some pure instructor. (E1ʳ)

Promising alternative employment, Banesworth offers Dorcas the position of 'usher' to 'Your schoole-mistresse, that can expound, and teaches / To knit in Chaldee, and work Hebrew samplers', a joke that emphasises the increasing seventeenth-century scholarly interest in biblical languages as well as the overlap between learning textile skills and attaining basic alphabetic literacy.[48]

The 1601 inventories of Elizabeth Shrewsbury's (Bess of Hardwick) Derbyshire properties give some sense of the variety and extent of godly scenes that might feature in the varied fabrics of an elite Protestant household. In her Withdrawing Chamber in Hardwick New Hall, hangings featuring personified virtues and portraits of royalty and nobility rubbed shoulders with 'fowre peeces of Arras of the storie of Abraham [and the angels], everie peece twelve foote deepe' and a table carpet 'of nedleworke of the storie of David and Saule', whilst the Long Gallery contained 'Thirtene peeces of deep Tapestrie hanginges of the story of Gedion [Gideon] everie peece being nyntene foote deep', and long cushions showing 'the storie of the sacryfice of Isack' and 'the Judgment of Salomon betwene the too women for the Childe'.[49] 'Toby's chamber' and 'Jacob's chamber' both took their names from the suites of biblical tapestries with which they were lined. The lower chapel featured 'a Crucefixe of imbrodered worke'. Four painted cloths, which are not included in the inventory, but whose borders feature Bess's initials and heraldic attributes, show the conversion of St Paul, and his own proselytising work in the Middle East, before Agrippa, and in Malta, a further reminder of the self-replicating and proliferating dynamic of conversion. The richness of these visual materials contributes to recent scholarship which has sought to unpick the apparent divide between Catholic iconophilia and Protestant austerity, pointing out the extent to which Protestant devotion might encompass or rely upon visual as well as textual cues.[50]

Though many of the tapestries, hangings, and painted cloths that cloaked the home were professional, not amateur, and, in large part, the work of men, women's stitched work can be understood to have formed part of the domestic environment, exhibited for 'strangers', and a familiar presence for family members and servants. 'A poeticall view of Ashridge in the Com. Bucks' composed by Marie Burghope in 1699, celebrated the superiority of textiles over texts, remarking 'The Hangings Keep those Storys fresh in view, / That scarce the Pen or Presse cou'd ever doe', and admiring the 'Sumptious Rooms of State. / Their Hangings wrought with Skillfull Ladys Hands', in terms which explicitly situate textile work as female.[51]

The intricacy and elaborate scope of needlework made it a commonplace means to conceive of the divine order.[52] In 1658, Anthony Burgess noted that scriptural sources frequently compare 'the *workmanship of our body, to the curious needle work of some skilfull woman*'.[53] Several women elaborated these material metaphors in their writing. Lady Anne Southwell (1574–1636), compiler of an important manuscript miscellany, recorded God's hexameral creation in textile terms:

> In six days god made this admired balle,
> this verdantcoutch, with lyllyes over spread:
> ingrayld it with a liquid christall walle
> and hungg a double valence over head.[54]

In a manuscript composed between 1672/3 and 1684, Protestant gentry woman Dorothy Calthorpe inscribed 'A discription of the Garden of Edden' which features sumptuous descriptions of a 'green plush hill imbroidered with roses Lilles and flowerdeluces' and comments that 'the very grass was perfect green velvett'.[55]

Given this potent and commonplace association of divine and domestic craft, it is perhaps unsurprising that needlework was understood to work upon the viewer. As Ahmed puts it, objects serve as orientation devices: 'to be orientated is . . . to be turned toward certain objects, those that help us to find our way'.[56] The loose papers of a former occupant of Ashridge, Elizabeth Cavendish Egerton, collected into a manuscript volume by her husband, John Bridgewater, contain four additional 'pieces' written by John. 'A contemplation, vpon the sight of a cushion' neatly illustrates how household objects might direct observers towards metaphysical speculation:

> I cannot see so slight a thing, but I presently think of ye ease w:^{ch} God hath graciously been pleased to allow, to those he hath set in high place w:^{ch} they ought to improve to his glory, y^t God hauing allowed them ease for their bodyes, their hearts & soules may be y^e more earnest & industrious to set forth his praise.[57]

Figure 5.2   WA 1947.191.316 Anonymous British, book cover with biblical scenes, mid-seventeenth-century, Ashmolean Museum, University of Oxford.

Bridgewater does not record whether the cushion in question featured a biblical narrative, though many embroidered cushion covers did so; crucially, his meditation highlights the extent to which the decorative arts of the household might direct viewers' and users' attention to their own spiritual state.

Some needleworkers represented scenes of religious transformation. One unusual embroidered book cover shows the conversion of Paul brought into a dynamic relationship with the stories of Abraham and Isaac and of a triumphant Samson, exemplary of the trials of the true Christian (Figure 5.2).[58] Whilst Geuter, Frye, and Morrall all emphasise the presence of female figures in embroidered designs, with Morrall suggesting that the examples of biblical heroines were 'literally inured into [girls'] being through the act of making', these male figures, caught in scenes of debasement and debilitation, in the case of Paul, and in the act of violently severing social and familial ties, in the cases of Abraham and Isaac Lot, prompt us to consider the forms of masculinity which were scripted and licensed by biblical needlework, as well as women's investment in the forms and stories of the biblical patriarchs.[59]

Even scenes which did not directly articulate narratives of conversion could prompt spiritual transformation. On 9 July 1636, the University of Oxford received a piece of embroidery from a 'heroina'.[60] The work was celebrated in a manuscript of poems addressed 'To the Right vertuous the Ladie Elizabeth Powlet upon her Present to the Vniversitie of Oxon being the Birth, Death, Resurrection and Ascension of our Saviour wrought by her selfe in Needle-worke'.[61] In the poem which opens the volume, William Cartwright of Christ Church College praised Powlet as a 'Shee=Evangelist['s]', commenting that her vivid embroidery had rendered

> Faces so Quick and Liuelie, that wee may
> Feare, if wee turne our backs, they'll steale away.
> Postures of Greife so true, that wee may sweare
> Your Artfull fingers haue wrought Passion there. (1ʳ)

Cartwright's poem was joined by six others, attributed to Samuel Evans, Thomas Gawen, Edward Marrow, Edward Dalby, John Beesley, and Rod. [Ralph] Brideoake, all of New College, indicating that the needlework formed the subject of a lively coterie verse exchange. The poems are also reproduced in several manuscript miscellanies and printed verse collections.[62] Combined with the poets' references to people 'flock[ing] to Oxford' (9ᵛ) to view the work, this suggests that Powlet's handiwork attracted considerable contemporary interest, within and beyond Oxford. The social presence of biblical embroidery adds an additional charge to Calabresi's observation that 'For the early modern auditor or reader of English in particular, *sowing* – planting in one's own or another's mind, disseminating, distributing abroad – and *sewing* – needlework . . . – were not only homophonic and orthographically identical but also conceptually similar'.[63] 'Shown to strangers', women's biblical needlework, with its floral frames and motifs, 'sowed' in two senses the seeds of divine inspiration.

Like Cartwright, Dalby also considered Powlet's work as gospel, declaring:

> Your Worke's all miracle, and you
> Our fifth Evangelist, whose skillfull Clue
> Hath made a Rode to Bethlem; (7ʳ)

The reference to Powlet's 'clue', or ball of thread, renders her embroidery labyrinthine, and the track of her needle directive. It literalises Ahmed's observation that:

> Following a line is not disinterested: to follow a line takes time, energy, and resources, which means that the "line" one takes does not stay apart from the very line of one's life, as the very shape of how one moves through time and space. We then come to "have a line," which might mean a specific "take" on the world, a set of views and viewing points, as well as a route through the contours of the world, which gives our world its own contours.[64]

In turning the lines of Powlet's thread into lines of poetry, the Oxford wits do not simply celebrate her devotional needlework, but follow and reproduce it as a means of orientation. The transformation of Powlet's embroidery silk into a track along the labyrinthine road to salvation directs the attentive viewer, guided by these poetic fictions, into the embroidery, orienting him or her towards the act of religious meditation and conversion.

For Ahmed, objects both extend the body and 'seem to measure the competence of bodies and their capacity to "find their way"'.[65] The poems celebrate the fabric's realism in ways which blur the line between object and feeling, both presenting and encouraging the bodily effects of emotional and devotional engagement. Imagining another woman's attempt to copy Powlet's intricate work, Gawen insists 'You being th'Evangelist, Her Prophetesse', and suggests 'For, who obserues the Arte, will moue a strife/ Whether the Threds be more of Silke or Life' (3^v). Dalby too stages the act of viewing as one of conversation and commentary: 'His side seemes yet to bleede & leaus a stayne. . ./See howe hee faints, ye Crimson silke turnes Pale,/ Changing its Graine' (7^{r-v}). In this reading, the embroidery takes on the emotional and embodied characteristics of the tortured Christ, and the skilful needle does not simply represent but enacts the scene. Punning on the varied meanings of 'prick', Gawen insists that the sewn thorns that 'Crowne the Crucifixe' allow the image to pierce the viewer: 'I thought o' your Needle, but you Thread more pricks' (3^v).

This vivacity also provoked fears that the work was capable of turning viewers in the wrong direction. For John Beesley, 'This is a Worke so accurately trimme . . ./ That the precisest tempted is to spy/ And Seeke a guilt of sweet Idolatrie', a comment which acquires an added resonance in the context of his fellow-poet Gawen's subsequent conversion to Catholicism (8^{r-v}). Beesley's concerns appear amplified by Powlet's crucificial subject which prompts him to conjecture:

> Could Rome shew such a Crucifix, she might
> Purchase each minute a newe proselyte

Could the proud Pontifye but once commande
Such a liue sacrifice, wee all should stand
His pliant Convertites; (8ᵛ–9ʳ)

These uneasy speculations hint at the effects of Catholic needlework and point obscurely to the work of recusant women who wrought vestments used in household worship. As Sophie Holroyd highlights, finely embroidered vestments constituted important 'devotional structure[s]' which were appreciated for their 'power to move and impress', with Jesuit John Gerard proclaiming that even the Protestant 'heretics' who raided the Vaux household 'were amazed' at the Mass vestments they found.[66] At once postulating and dismissing the possibility that Powlet's work might stir Catholic impulses, Beesley both acknowledges and seeks to re-orientate the potential of recusant embroidery to transport its viewers. Ultimately, Powlet's compelling embroidery is claimed as a victory for the reformed faith. As Brideoake concludes 'The Jesuits only hope is by some tricke/ To make this Protestant turne Catholicke'.[67]

Laudian supporter Cartwright rejoices in the ability of Powlet's embroidery to stir the conscience of the viewer, announcing that: 'The Needle may convert more then the Pen;/ When Faith may come by Seeing, & each Leafe/ Rightly pervs'd proue Gospell to the Deafe' (1ᵛ). Invoking the rich iconic and biblical significance of stitched flowers, and the tradition of embroidered pictures of the tree of life, the term 'Leafe' also conflates the leaves of Powlet's needlework trees and the pages of the gospel, as Cartwright declares 'That the Whole seemes not so much wrought, as Writt' (1ᵛ). This continuity between text and textile is reinforced by Cartwright's description, in the printed version of his poem, of the lively movement of Powlet's silks in terms that conflate the lines of fabric with scriptural verses, and with the span of time as well as the direction of the track or trail: 'Here runs this tract, thither we see that tends / But cannot say, Here this, or there that ends.'[68] Though written within a context of patronage and flattery, and thus designedly hyperbolic, these poems celebrate the vivid effects of Powlet's embroidery not just as a visual surface but as a made object capable of prompting and directing intense feeling, imitation, and – ultimately – conversion.

Women's activities as converts and converters were distinctly gendered in early modern England, with women at once troped as vulnerable to the dis- and mis-orientations of religious change and celebrated as influential models, whose examples and actions were liable to spark and confirm further conversions. The gendered structures of the household established women as central to children's religious education and as the moral and devotional compass for their husbands, at the same time that the celebration of women's devotional ability, and the understanding of women's cure as extending to the wider household and estate, emphasised women's potential influence across a far wider community. Even as male writers sought to establish women's devotion as safely contained within the bounds of patriarchal strictures, men's own impulses to replication and reproduction established women's religion as public and influential. This dynamic is redoubled in accounts of women's needlework, presented at once as a socially sanctioned and specifically feminine activity and as a distinctly visible resource able to prick the conscience, and prompt the conversion, of male viewers and users. In the turns and re-orientations of conversion, religious and gendered identity coincided; both were reproduced and at the same time re-made through the disorientations and directions of religious change.

NOTES

We wish to thank participants in the Gender and Conversion workshop at the University of York in July 2012, and the 'Texts and Textiles' conference in Cambridge in September 2012 for their comments and feedback.

1 Thomas Taylor, *The pilgrims profession.* . . . *To which (by his consent) also is added, a short relation of the life and death of the said gentle-woman* (London: I. Dawson for Io: Bartlet, 1622), G3^v.
2 For details of English Catholic children conveyed from northern ports to the post-Reformation convents and monasteries of France and the Spanish Netherlands, see Leona Rostenberg, *The minority press and the English crown: a study in repression, 1558–1625* (Nieuwkoop: B. De Graaf, 1971).
3 Taylor, *Pilgrims profession*, G5^{r-v}.
4 *OED*, 'trumpery', n., defs 1, 2a–d, 3.
5 Taylor, *Pilgrims profession*, G6^r, G7^{r-v}.
6 *OED*, 'conversion', n., def. 1.
7 Sara Ahmed, *Queer phenomenology: orientations, objects, others* (Durham, NC: Duke University Press, 2006), p. 5.
8 Erica Longfellow, *Women and religious writing in early modern England* (Cambridge: Cambridge University Press, 2004), pp. 10–11.
9 Patricia Crawford, *Women and religion in England, 1500–1720* (London and New York: Routledge, 1993), p. 4.

10 Mary Ellen Lamb, 'Inventing the early modern woman reader through the world of goods: Lyly's gentlewoman reader and Katherine Stubbes', in Heidi Brayman Hackel and Catherine Kelly (eds), *Reading women: literacy, authorship, and culture in the Atlantic world, 1500–1800* (Philadelphia: University of Pennsylvania Press, 2008), pp. 15–35.
11 Ahmed, *Queer phenomenology*, p. 15.
12 For an influential example, see Rozsika Parker, *The subversive stitch: embroidery and the making of the feminine* (London and New York: Routledge, 1989).
13 Frances Dolan, *Whores of Babylon: Catholicism, gender, and seventeenth-century print culture* (Ithaca, NY: Cornell University Press, 1999), p. 27.
14 Edward Hoby, *A letter to Mr. T. H.* (London: F[elix] K[ingston] for Edward Blount and William Barret, 1609), A2^v.
15 John Bastwick, *The utter routing of the whole army of all the Independents . . . by John Bastvvick, captain in the Presbyterian army* (London: John Macock for Michael Spark, 1646), Ddd2^v.
16 Charlotte Brabantina, Duchess of Tremoille, *The conuersion of a most noble lady of Fraunce*, anon trans (London: Thomas Purfoot for Nathaniel Butter, 1608), A2^v.
17 Hoby, *A letter*, A3^r.
18 See Michelle White, *Henrietta Maria and the English Civil Wars* (Aldershot: Ashgate, 2006); *The great eclipse of the sun, or Charles his waine over-clouded* ([London]: G.B., 1644), A1^v.
19 Ahmed, *Queer phenomenology*, p. 1.
20 William Gouge, *Of domesticall dvties eight treatises* (London: John Haviland for William Bladen, 1622), Q8^{r-v}. Gouge goes on to clarify: 'This dutie of winning one another, is to be applied to such as are maried not only to plaine infidels, but also to Papists or other like Idolaters, to Atheists, or any other profane persons, to heretiques, separatists, schismatiques, or any that beleeue not aright'
21 Lambeth Palace Library, MS 446, f. 414.
22 Margaret Spufford notes that most of the seventeenth-century autobiographers whose accounts she has studied 'learnt to read with a variety of people, mostly women, before starting writing with the "formal" part of their education at seven, if they got that far' ('First steps in literacy: the reading and writing experiences of the humblest seventeenth-century spiritual autobiographers', *Social History*, 4 (1979), 407–35; at 410). See also Kenneth Charlton, *Women, religion and education in early modern England* (London: Routledge, 1999), pp. 188–241 and Femke Molekamp, *Women and the Bible in early modern England: religious reading and writing* (Oxford: Oxford University Press, 2013), pp. 89–101.
23 *The autobiography of Sir John Bramston*, ed. Lord Braybrooke (London: Camden Society, 1845), 111; quoted in Charlton, *Women*, p. 295.

24 Crawford, *Women and religion*, pp. 60–1.
25 Anthony Walker, *Eureka, Eureka. . . . At the funeral of that most excellent lady . . . Mary, Countess Dowager of Warwick* (London: for Nathanael Ranew, 1678), F3^r; cited in Andrew Cambers, *Godly reading: print, manuscript and puritanism in England, 1580–1720* (Cambridge: Cambridge University Press, 2011), p. 88.
26 Walker, *Eureka, Eureka*, F3^v–F4^r.
27 Richard Baxter, *A breviate of the life of Margaret, the daughter of Francis Charlton . . . and wife of Richard Baxter* (London: for B. Simmons, 1683), L3^v.
28 Darlington Carmelite Convent, County Durham (Lierre archive), L13.7, cited in Nicky Hallett, *Lives of spirit: English Carmelite self-writing of the early modern period* (Aldershot: Ashgate, 2007), p. 181.
29 William Palmes, *The life of Mrs Dorothy Lawson, of St. Antony's near Newcastle-on-Tyne*, ed. and with an introduction by G. Bouchier Richardson (London: Charles Dolman, 1855), pp. 16; 19–20.
30 *Ibid.*, pp. 21, 45.
31 *Ibid.*, p. 46.
32 Margaret Hoby, *The private life of an Elizabethan lady: the diary of Lady Margaret Hoby, 1599–1605*, ed. Joanna Moody (Stroud: Sutton Publishing, 1998), pp. 3, 9.
33 *Ibid.*, pp. 63–4.
34 *Ibid.*, p. 73.
35 *Ibid.*, pp. 83, 54.
36 Bastwick, *The utter routing of the whole army*, Ddd2^r.
37 *The Roman martyologe, according to the reformed calendar*, trans G.K. ([Saint-Omer]: Imprinted *with Lecence*, 1627), X1^v.
38 Jeremiah Burroughs, *An exposition of the prophesie of Hosea* (London: for R. Dalwman, 1652), Aaaa2^v.
39 Ruth Geuter, 'Embroidered biblical narratives and their social context', in Andrew Morrall and Melinda Watt (eds), *English embroidery from the Metropolitan Museum of Art, 1580–1700: 'twixt art and nature* (New Haven, CT: Yale University Press, 2008; published for The Bard Center for Studies in the Decorative Arts, Design, and Culture, New York), pp. 57–77; at 57.
40 Andrew Morrall, 'Regaining Eden: representations of nature in seventeenth-century English embroidery', in Morrall and Watt (eds), *English embroidery*, p. 85.
41 Susan Frye, *Pens and needles: women's textualities in early modern England* (Philadelphia: University of Pennsylvania Press, 2010), p. 118.
42 Andrew Morrall and Melinda Watt (eds), 'Introduction', to Morrall and Watt (eds), *English embroidery*, p. xii.
43 Robert Burton, *The anatomy of melancholy*, ed. Nicolas K. Kiessling, Thomas C. Faulkner, and Rhonda L. Blair, vol. II (Oxford: Clarendon Press, 1990), p. 95.

44 Andrew Morrall, 'Representations of Adam and Eve in late sixteenth and seventeenth-century English embroidery', in Celeste Brusati, Karl A. E. Enenkel, and Walter S. Melion (eds), *The authority of the word: reflecting on image and text in northern Europe, 1400–1700* (Leiden: Brill, 2012), pp. 313–53; at 314.

45 This verse appears on Selby's funeral monument on the East wall of St Peter's Church, Ightham, Kent.

46 LL5295 (WHL4144), 'The defeat of the Armada and the Gunpowder Plot', after 1621. The work is described in Xanthe Brook, *The Lady Lever art gallery: catalogue of embroideries* (Stroud: Alan Sutton, 1992), 18–21; a small image is displayed at http://www.liverpoolmuseums.org.uk/picture-of-month/displaypicture.aspx?id=328. Selby's embroidery is pictured and briefly described in Katharine A. Esdaile, 'Gunpowder plot in needlework: Dame Dorothy Selby, "Whose arte disclos'd that plot"', *Country Life* (18 June 1943), 1094–6.

47 Jasper Mayne, *The citye match A comoedye* (Oxford: Leonard Lichfield, 1639), E1^{r-v}.

48 On the connection between learning to sew and learning to read, see Bianca F.-C. Calabresi, '"you sow, Ile read": letters and literacies in early modern samplers', in Hackel and Kelly (eds), *Reading women*, pp. 79–104.

49 Santina M. Levey, *Of household stuff: the 1601 inventories of Bess of Hardwick* (London: The National Trust, 2001), pp. 47–9.

50 See especially Tara Hamling, *Decorating the Godly household: religious art in post-Reformation Britain* (New Haven, CT: Yale University Press, 2011); Matthew Milner, *The senses and the English Reformation* (Farnham: Ashgate, 2011).

51 Betty S. Travitsky, *Subordination and authorship in early modern England: the case of Elizabeth Cavendish Egerton and her "Loose Papers"* (Tempe, AZ: Arizona Center for Medieval and Renaissance Studies, 1999), pp. 254–5.

52 On needlework as an intra-biblical and especially psalmic trope, see Michelle Osherow, 'Mary Sidney's embroidered psalms', *Renaissance Studies*, 29 (2015), 650–70; esp. 650–5.

53 Anthony Burgess, *A treatise of original sin* (London: [Abraham Miller for Thomas Underhill], 1658), Zz1^r.

54 *The Southwell-Sibthorpe commonplace book: Folger MS V.b.198*, ed. Jean Klene (Tempe, Ariz: Medieval & Renaissance Texts and Studies, 1997), 60.

55 Dorothy Calthorpe, *Writings*, Osborn MS b421 v.1, 8^v, 9^v–10^r. For further discussion of this manuscript, see Michelle M. Dowd and Julie A. Eckerle, 'The devotional writings of Dorothy Calthorpe', *ANQ: A Quarterly Journal of Short Articles, Notes and Reviews*, 24 (2011), 89–98.

56 Ahmed, *Queer phenomenology*, p. 1.

57 Travitsky, *Subordination and authorship*, p. 207.

58 Mary M Brooks, *English embroideries of the sixteenth and seventeenth centuries in the collection of the Ashmolean Museum* (Oxford and London: Ashmolean Museum, in association with Jonathan Horne Publications, London, 2004), p. 56. The conversion of St Paul also features alongside the stoning of St Stephen in an early-seventeenth-century needlework valence panel, made in England or France, Christie's London, *The country home: early furniture and works of art*, 1 December 2015, Lot 9.

59 Morrall, 'Representations of Adam and Eve', p. 314. Geuter suggests that the stories women chose to embroider 'were characterized predominantly by their focus on women, children, and relationships between husbands and wives' ('Embroidered biblical narratives', p. 59).

60 Reg. Conv. R. 24 fol. 129^b, cited in William Dunn Macray, *Annals of the Bodleian Library, Oxford; with a notice of the earlier library of the University*, 2nd edn (Oxford: Oxford University Press, 1890), p. 65.

61 MS Bodl. 22, 1^r.

62 For example, Cartwright's poem is copied in Bodleian MS Eng. poet. e. 4, p. 34; Bodleian MS Rawl. poet. 153, 25^v–26^r; Bodleian MS Rawl. poet. 84, fol. 90$^{v\text{-}r}$; and, in abbreviated form from the 1656 printed version, in Bodleian MS Eng. poet. e. 4; William Cartwright, *Comedies, tragi-comedies, with other poems* (London: Printed for [T.R. &] Humphrey Moseley, N4^r–N4^v. Cartwright's poem is attributed to John Cleveland in *J. Cleaveland revived ... with some other exquisite remains of the most eminent wits ... that were his contemporaries* (London: for Nathaniel Brook, 1659), E7^v–E8^v. The poems of Cartwright, Dalby and Gawen are collected in Abraham Wright (compiler), *Parnassus biceps. Or severall choice pieces of poetry* (London: for George Eversden, 1656), L1^v–L5^r.

63 Calabresi, 'You sow, Ile read', p. 80.

64 Ahmed, *Queer phenomenology*, p. 17.

65 *Ibid.*, p. 110.

66 Sophie Holroyd, '"Rich embrodered churchstuffe": the vestments of Helena Wintour', in Ronald Corthell, et al. (eds), *Catholic culture in early modern England* (Notre Dame, IN: Univeristy of Notre Dame Press, 2007), pp. 73–116, esp. 75-7. For this and further examples of recusant women embroidering, see John Gerard, *The autobiography of a hunted priest*, trans. Philip Caraman (Chicago: Thomas More Press, 1988), pp. 40, 75–6, 256.

67 MS Bodl. 22, 12^r.

68 Wright (compiler), *Parnassus biceps*, L1^v; *OED* 'Tract', n. 2; n. 3, I.1; II.4, 5; IV.8, 9, 10. The connection between 'track' and 'tract' is manifested in MS Bodl. 22, which renders the lines: 'Here runnes This Track wee see, thither That tends,/ But cann't say here This rose, or there that ends (1^r).'

6

Uneven conversions: how did laywomen become nuns in the early modern world?

Elizabeth A. Lehfeldt

∾

'The maiden that shall be made nun.'[1] This medieval description of a novice on the brink of her profession ceremony is simple and yet profound. It highlights the point at which a young woman, after her novitiate, announced her intentions to become a full member of the convent community. At the same time it obscures or at least elides the dramatic transformation that underlay her decision to become a nun. Because taking the veil and becoming a nun was such a customary feature of the religious landscape of early modern Europe, it is easy to pass over its significance. Though not a conversion in the sense of adopting a new faith, the moment at which a (typically) young woman entered a monastic community signalled a profound conversion of her lifestyle as she rejected the earthly realm and took up her responsibilities as a bride of Christ. At the same time, life within the monastic community blurred the very distinctions that she pledged to uphold, marking her conversion as uneven or incomplete.

This chapter examines three parts of a nun's experience – her profession, her habit, and enclosure – to explore the character of a nun's 'conversion' to the religious life. Because these three topics touch upon ceremony, material culture, and discipline, respectively, they allow us to probe various facets of female monastic experience. In each instance, this chapter seeks to balance the nun's experience of these things against the expectations of male ecclesiastics. A nun's habit, for example, was an item that shaped her daily lived experience – it constrained her body in various ways while at the same time representing her membership of a community of shared values and traditions. For male ecclesiastics the habit signified various features of the female monastic life such as obedience and virginity. These two interpretations of the habit, as we will see, were not always consistent with one another.

We begin with the formal ceremony by which a young woman moved from being a novice to a nun. While we might regard the text and actions associated with a nun's profession as formulaic, we need to appreciate that for the novice in question this would be the first – and presumably only – time that she would say these words and perform these actions. So, for her, they undoubtedly resonated more deeply. In addition, a survey of these acts reveals that ceremonies of profession varied – by geography, religious order, and time period. It is impossible to do justice to this diversity in a single chapter, but a sampling will suffice to highlight the variety.

We have a remarkably complete account of the script for such a ceremony from a fifteenth-century guide for English Benedictine nuns.[2] The event took place at the altar of the convent church with the other nuns looking on from their stalls in the choir. The novice read her profession in the presence of a priest, made the sign of a cross in the book of profession, approached the altar with her novice mistress, kissed the altar, bowed, and sang several lines, echoed by the choir. She prostrated herself, and the priest and nuns alternated singing various lines. The priest said four collects over her. She then stood and her veil was consecrated. Surrounded by several nuns, the veil was put on her. Finally, she recited the words of profession to the prioress. She prostrated herself again while the priest sang and said three more collects. When the ceremony was over, the prioress led her to the choir stall where she stood. She was then supposed to receive the Eucharist.

This text probably has some features that may be particular to England or to Benedictine nuns or even to the fifteenth century, but overall it highlights a few salient features that transcended these and other distinctions: the ceremony was performed in the convent precinct and in the presence of a male ecclesiastic and members of the convent community. A few other details that may be unique to this document stand out: the physical posturing of the young woman, the importance of recited words, and the use of space. The novice was required to prostrate herself – an extreme act of humility and obedience – twice. Language – both spoken and sung – was central to the act. Not unlike the legal requirements that made a secular marriage valid, the novice was supposed to utter her intentions aloud. In addition to her prostration before the altar, other uses of space also marked the transition.³ The conclusion of the ceremony, for example, installed the novice in the choir, among her new sisters, marking her full membership in the community.

Evidence from other parts of Europe and the Atlantic world suggest that there were significant variations on the script outlined above. As Kate Lowe has noted, there could be at least four steps to the process of becoming a nun: entrance into a convent, putting on the habit (vestition), profession itself, and consecration and veiling. The case from late medieval England above clearly conflates some of these steps, and Lowe, too, finds that the process was often simplified to just vestition and profession, with veiling taking place during the act of profession.⁴ Overall, the additional embellishments to the ceremony centred on the presence of laypeople and visual pageantry. Though the text from fifteenth-century England limits the participants to the novice, choir nuns, and the priest, other evidence makes this seem somewhat unusual, if not idealised. Across Europe and the colonial Americas, the families of the women professing attended the ceremony. The nun chronicler of Le Murate in Florence described lavish profession ceremonies, attended by so many family members that the event was held in one of the convent's larger rooms.⁵ These same families often gifted the convent with fabrics – that might be turned into ecclesiastical vestments – and other precious items. In colonial Mexico, a young woman's family expected to be able to attend her profession ceremony and to turn it into an expensive affair that showcased the family's wealth and prestige.⁶ Similar displays of family pride and wealth occurred in France in the seventeenth century.⁷

Perhaps because laypeople were often in attendance, additional evidence reveals that there was often a high degree of visual pageantry. In late medieval German convents, for example, nuns often added a coronation ceremony to the act of profession.⁸ In this case, the crown was 'a white linen circlet with overlapping bands forming a cross worn over her veil'.⁹ Even though ecclesiastical law specified that this ritual was not supposed to take place until after profession and that the nun was supposed to be at least twenty-five before she was 'crowned', visitors' reports reveal that this was routinely ignored. Defiance of these prohibitions reveals the importance that nuns and their convents attached to this act and these crowns. In imitation of bridal wreaths, these crowns signified the nuns' mystical marriage and her privileged status within the community. Significantly, it was an honour that set her apart from lay sisters and novices. Nuns in colonial Mexico also received crowns as part of their profession ceremony. By the eighteenth century, these ceremonies and the attendant items became ever more elaborate. The novices wore high headdresses of wax flowers and carried wax flowers, a candle, a crucifix, or a figure of the Christ child. 'A nun in this regalia was as richly dressed as the most exalted bride in an eloquent display of pomp.'[10]

Lavish ceremonies that included a nun's natal family, headdresses, and visual commemorations all point to the significant overlap between secular weddings and convent professions. The similarities also illustrate, of course, the ecclesiastical expectations for a young woman's profession. She was literally becoming a bride of Christ. The veil that was bestowed in some profession ceremonies signified submission and modesty.[11] A fifteenth-century set of guidelines for a profession instructs the officiating priest to reference the New Testament story of the wise virgins who were prepared for the bridegroom's coming.[12] An early-sixteenth-century manuscript, detailing the profession ceremony at St. Mary's, Winchester features various nuptial parallels, including blessing the rings that the nuns receive.[13] A late-seventeenth-century sermon preached at the profession of a nun at Santa Clara in Mexico emphasised these features verbally. Addressing the nun, the priest said: 'Your husband is Christ and you are the Bride . . . the house of your wedding is this convent of Santa Clara; your bridal bed is the sacrament that makes God and the soul one.'[14] As we have already seen, this similarity between a secular wedding and a nun's profession was not lost on their families who invested these events with comparable levels of pomp and ostentation.

It seems, in fact, that profession ceremonies became more elaborate over the course of the early modern period. Asunción Lavrín has observed, for example, that the nun portraits of colonial Mexico that families commissioned became increasingly ornate by the eighteenth century. In the seventeenth century, nuns were represented in their religious habits, holding items that signified virtues, such as a lily for purity. But by the eighteenth century 'the fashion was to wear a high headdress in the shape of crown of wax flowers' and to hold various items.[15] The nuns of the Concepcionist order also had breastplates or *escudos* depicting various religious scenes made to commemorate their profession, which became additional adornments in their portraits. The reasons for this change, however, varied. Sharon Strocchia has tied the rise in these lavish displays and the attendance of more and more laypeople to the rising stakes of Florence's dowry market. As secular dowries rose, so, too, did convent dowries and this, in turn, led to an increasing preoccupation with demonstrating a family's wealth and social status – whether a daughter was being wed to Christ or to an earthly husband.[16]

Chronology shaped the profession ceremony in other ways. Post-Tridentine professions, for example, demonstrated a marked concern with the language of intention, as convents, bishops, and others showed their compliance with the Council of Trent's decrees. The Council had insisted that women making a profession be at least sixteen and that no one should force a woman to profess. Further, the chronicler of Le Murate in Florence noted in her account that Trent required more austere ceremonies and that these clashed with the long-standing tradition of families staging more elaborate observances.[17] In the convents of Valladolid, Spain, in the early seventeenth century, references to Trent were scattered throughout the profession ceremonies. At Santa María de las Huelgas, the text stated that in accordance with the Council of Trent it was necessary to ascertain whether or not a woman's profession was voluntary. The young woman was to respond that she was making her decision of her 'free will'.[18] At the Cistercian convent of Nuestra Señora de Belén, María Duque de Estrada affirmed that she was making her profession in compliance with 'the holy Tridentine council'.[19]

The act of professing and entering a convent came with other attendant acts that marked the transition. Some of these were legal. In Spain, which practised a system of partible inheritance, a nun received what amounted to an advance on her inheritance when she professed. This sum became her dowry and it was transferred from her natal family to the communal property of the convent. It was not unusual for families to also provide other items, typically clothing and bedding, and in Spain this was actually referred to as a trousseau (*ajuar*). Whether due to constrained convent finances or the desire of families to showcase their wealth, families also made various other gifts to convents when their daughters professed. Some even paid 'tips' (literally *propinas*) that were meant to cover the expenses of the profession ceremony.[20] Practices such as these were echoed in the convents of Spanish colonies.[21] This transfer of property also required another legal act: that the nun make a will or *renuncia*. This document was supposed to signify her receipt of her dowry and her renunciation of any claims to future inheritances. As Francisca Manríquez noted in her *renuncia* in 1577, she would 'have no need of temporal things'.[22] And even in regions that lacked a system of partible inheritance, such as England and Italy, a nun was still required to pay an entrance fee and bring various items of clothing and bedding.[23]

Other rites of passage underscored the conversion that a young woman experienced at her profession. Nuns often took new names when they entered a convent. Doing so was meant to represent the ways in which they severed their ties to the world and 'detached a nun from her previous secular self'.[24] As Sharon Strocchia has observed, the naming practices in Florentine convents of the period highlighted spiritual exemplars from early Christianity (which displaced medieval saints), celebrated the cult of the angels, and commemorated deceased nuns by passing their names on to new members of the community.

Nuns themselves experienced the profession ceremony in profound ways. The experience could be deeply moving. According to a nun professing in the eighteenth century at a Capuchin convent in Mexico: 'Immersed in my interior, I entered humbly in the choir and I felt as if the sun penetrated me; my understanding cleared, my will was inflamed.'[25] In addition to the ways that nuns' families celebrated these events, convents, too, endowed the ceremony with significance. In English and Italian convents this could include music composed for the occasion.[26] In Spanish convents it might include poems composed for the occasion. The famous Spanish writer, Sor Marcela de San Félix, composed various dramatic monologues to celebrate the occasion of novices making their professions. In one of them she rehearses the familiar trope of the novice as Christ's bride:

> Christ will take full possession of her.
> How tenderly He gazes upon her,
> how galantly [sic] He woos her
> and lavishes her with riches.[27]

After teasing the convent community about the extravagance and feasting associated with professions (in turn suggesting that these could be, in part, lighthearted affairs), she concludes with advice to the young novice:

> She must remember
> that she will become more virtuous
> through repentance and reform;
> ...
> May she neither neglect nor offend
> holy meekness,

who is sister to humility
and close kin to peace. If she heeds this advice, no doubt
she will be so accomplished and perfected
that God will be praised
and glorified in her.[28]

What unites all of this evidence is the effort to mark the significance of the transition that took place when a young woman professed. Whether these markers were language, physical postures (e.g. prostration), items of clothing (e.g. crowns), commemorative traces (e.g. portraits), legal transactions (e.g. wills), or the presence of witnesses (ecclesiastic or lay), this was a striking event meant to transform a young woman as she renounced the world and her family and entered a new community. Overall, then, the profession of a young woman into a monastic community was a highly gendered affair. In image and word and action she was consistently reminded of her status as a bride of Christ. Her family engaged in rituals (elaborate ceremonies) and transfers of property (dowry, trousseau) that underscored the similarities with secular weddings. Adhering to these acts, and this transition, were the attendant ideologies of female submission, obedience, and passivity.

As we saw in the profession ceremony, items of clothing or adornment were significant markers of the transition or conversion taking place. Clothing remained important even after a woman professed. In some profession ceremonies the nun donned her new habit. Habits – though meant to conform to monastic standards of simplicity and austerity – nonetheless had considerable variety and were an important source of identity for nuns. To begin with, different religious orders distinguished themselves by their habits. Benedictines wore black mantles, for example, whereas the garb of Franciscan sisters tended to be a grey-brown colour. The habit, whatever its colour, typically regulated the body and the senses, often in unanticipated ways. As an Italian nun playwright noted, 'the harmony of verse can little be heard by the ear that is bound by a thick wimple'.[29] Such remarks should serve as necessary reminders of the sensory and bodily limitations of nuns living their lives attired in this way.[30]

Male ecclesiastics clearly believed that the habit played a critical role in defining a nun's vocation. Sarah Salih has suggested that the act of veiling a nun during her profession marked 'her body as one devoted to the enactment of virginity'.[31] Priests did not miss the metaphorical potential of the habit. An English sermon of the fifteenth century preached for the nuns at Carrow for the feast of the Virgin Mary's Assumption highlights the various features of the habit: the smock, for example, represented contrition and confession and the girdle represented the restraint of the individual will in order to serve God's.[32]

For nuns, the habit was a more malleable canvas. Visitation records provide telling cases of how habits could be sources of contention. To begin with, nuns often rebelled against the required dress code and embellished their habits. In the 1490s at the convent of San Daniel de Gerona, for example, the male visitor warned the nuns that they were not supposed to mix colours in their habits or adorn them. The habit was supposed to be completely black (it was a Benedictine convent), and he was concerned because 'the diversity [of colours] was very irregular'.[33] At the convent of Le Vergini in Venice the nuns were reprimanded for wearing silk and other expensive fabrics.[34] At the convent of Wix in England a visit from the bishop in 1509 exposed irregular dressing habits and he forbade the nuns to wear 'silver or gilt hairpins and kirtles of fustian or worsted'.[35] The intentions behind these variations in dress are unclear: were they simple acts of rebellion, manifested in wardrobe; particular statements of identity as expressed through items of clothing; or some combination thereof? Did nuns dress with this kind of ornamentation and flair because they were bringing secular fashion inside the cloister? Male visitors to the convents cited all of these possible explanations and railed against such visible signs of disobedience.

There were, however, other acts of sartorial disobedience that are less attributable to rebellion or an incomplete break with the secular world. Instead nuns often used their habits to make powerful statements about female monastic identity. The case of Santa Clara of Barcelona highlights this dramatically. Although Franciscan, the convent had a history of wearing the Benedictine habit. The community traced its origins to the rule drafted for Saint Clare by Cardinal Hugolino in 1219. Because there was a ban on new religious orders at the time, the cardinal had placed the women under the Benedictine Rule. Years later, visitors to Santa Clara noted this discrepancy, and ordered that the nuns wear Franciscan garb.[36] The nuns resisted and ultimately transferred the convent to the Benedictine Order, a decision upheld by the papacy in the face of the Franciscan Provincial's objections. At Le Vergini, when the convent came under the control of the observant branch of the order in the early sixteenth century, there was a clash of habits. The original members of the community wore white, but the newcomers wore grey. An agreement was reached to wear white, but when the lay sisters adopted this colour for their habits, conflict erupted. The solemnly professed nuns wanted to be certain that the colour of their habits signified their distinction from the lay sisters.[37] Thus, as these battles demonstrate, habits could represent the history and traditions of a community and were an important source of communal identity.

Just as a habit confined and defined a nun's body, so, too, did the discipline of enclosure. As a monastic ideal, male ecclesiastics believed that enclosure provided protection – both from the threats of the outside world and from the nuns' own proclivities as weak women to stray and be tempted. Thus, monastic claustration was a highly gendered ideal that sharply differentiated the female monastic experience from the male one. It enshrined and safeguarded a nun's most precious virtue: her chastity. The stakes were high. Any violation of her chastity was 'a direct offense against her Spouse, the King of Heaven'.[38] There was no comparable peril if a monk violated his vows. Thus, although there are scattered examples of monasteries that sought to practice strict claustration, it was overwhelmingly an ideal imposed upon nuns. As Roberta Gilchrist has noted 'space was used to construct and reinforce a gendering of women's bodies which emphasised chastity and purity'.[39] Enclosure was the spatial dimension of the same ideals the profession ceremony and habit sought to have the nun embody. She became the obedient bride of Christ, clothed in a modest habit and cloistered within the convent.

For nuns from elite families, this policy of confinement was perhaps not radically different from the life they had experienced outside the convent. We know that young women were directed to conduct themselves modestly, remain within the confines of the home whenever possible, and to move about in public with chaperones and tremendous care. Juan Luis Vives' famous 1524 manual directing the behaviour of Christian women captures these sentiments in dire terms: 'She will appear in public on occasion, but as rarely as possible, for many reasons. First, because every time she issues forth in public she undergoes what we might almost call a fatal judgment of her beauty, modesty, prudence, propriety, and integrity, since there is nothing more fragile or more vulnerable than the reputation and good name of women.'[40] Though prescriptive texts such as these undoubtedly faltered in the face of lived experience, they still embodied an ideal similar to that of monastic enclosure. Claustration would not have been a dramatic departure from the way some young women had conducted their lives before entrance into the convent.

Some recent research for the later Middle Ages has also begun to plumb the comparison between secular domestic interiors and architecture and the space of the convent.[41] It would be intriguing to know the extent to which the protected and enclosed space of the convent echoed the experiences young women had in their natal homes. We do know, certainly, that some wealthier nuns had nearly private 'apartments' within their convents. These could include plush furnishings, rich textiles, and other adornments that undoubtedly mimicked the homes they had left behind. Yet however familiar the enclosed life of the convent might have been for a newly professed nun, we should also be attentive to the ways in which the language of enclosure and its enforcement created a particular culture for the women living by its strictures. Enclosure assumed not only that the world outside the cloister was a dangerous place, but also that the women within, because they were women, would be unable to withstand its temptations. In the opinion of one seventeenth-century moralist, even nuns required this protection; they were weak since they could not divorce themselves from their nature as women.[42] Thus, though some have suggested, and some nuns even cited, the opportunities that enclosure fostered, it still meant accepting an ideology that devalued their worth as women and was suspicious of their ability to protect their own chastity.

Given the high and gendered stakes that male ecclesiastics attached to it, enclosure required vigilant enforcement. This was achieved in various ways. Curiously, foundational texts such as the Benedictine Rule did not specify the bounds of enclosure, stating only that: 'The monastery should be planned, if possible, with all the necessities – water, mill, garden, shops – within the walls. Thus the monks will not need to wander about outside, for this is not good for their souls.'[43] Some religious rules added it as an expectation for nuns, but not monks.[44] More often, it was articulated in other sets of instructions such as an order or convent's constitutions. Benedictine constitutions printed in Spain in 1612 provided rigorous instructions: the fence surrounding the convent was supposed to be at least four bricks high without any small doors or openings. Any windows that looked outside had to have iron grillwork so dense that an arm could not fit through and latticework so fine that a 'nun looking through them cannot be recognized by anyone outside'.[45] Overall, these constitutions communicated an exacting architectural precision. Seemingly, nothing was left to chance and no aperture in the building could escape the attention of its authors. In this, the constitutions betrayed an obsession with protecting female chastity. And the Benedictines were not alone in this preoccupation. Franciscan constitutions from the same period specified that the convent door could not have any windows or shutters. The *torno* (revolving window through which the convent conducted business) had to be made of strong materials and constructed along dimensions that would not allow 'any person to enter or leave through it'.[46] The stakes for the built environment were high since they protected the virtue of the nuns.

Visitation records also shed light on the enforcement of enclosure in convents. These are littered with injunctions and specifications regarding the creation and maintenance of claustration. A series of visits to convents in the region of Catalonia in the late fifteenth century cited various infractions and their perceived remedies. Concerned about the ability of the nuns at Santa Clara of Barcelona to see a nearby monastic foundation, San Daniel, the visitors ordered changes to the windows. At the convent of Pedralbes they instructed the nuns not to use the door of the convent, but to conduct all of their business through the *torno*. At San Daniel de Gerona it was necessary to require the construction of a *torno*. At Valldonzella the nuns were asked to put a grille on the window in the kitchen.[47]

What is perhaps more revealing is less that the visitors policed the built environment so carefully, but rather that they often mitigated the meaning of enclosure. In the words of Sarah Salih their instructions worked to 'authorize potential variations' in the dictates of religious rules and other prescriptive texts.[48] Visitation records from England illustrate this well. When Bishop Richard Fox visited the convent of Romsey he issued a set of injunctions requiring the nuns to better secure the various doors of the convent. He also instructed them to close a particular kitchen window because the nuns were conversing with outsiders beyond the proper time – thereby suggesting that there was a time when such behaviour was acceptable.[49] At the convent of Wix, in 1509, the nuns were cautioned that they could not go on pilgrimages or otherwise leave the convent without the diocesan's permission.[50] The implicit message, then, was that such excursions could take place, provided they had proper approval.

These, then, were the expectations, but what was enclosure like as a part of daily life within the cloister? Nuns, as women who had taken vows of obedience, understood that they were expected to restrict their contact with the world. And so, they lived accordingly – walking the sheltered corridors of the convent, sitting behind curtains or grilles in the visiting parlour, participating in the Mass from the protected confines of their separate choir in the convent church, and conducting their business at the convent's revolving window (*torno, ruota*). And yet, the available evidence also suggests that when necessary, nuns routinely left the convent and interacted with the secular world in order to conduct their affairs. As we saw with variations in nuns' habits, the temptation is to read this as evidence of transgression and rebellion, but the circumstances of these violations of enclosure are often more complex than such a reading would allow.

If we begin, for example, to compile a list of activities that would take nuns outside the cloister it looks like this: seeking alms, seeking patrons and having art works evaluated in the local marketplace, visiting seigneurial jurisdictions, managing estates, performing agricultural tasks, providing spiritual guidance to other women, attending the funerals of patrons, and visiting sister convents. In short, the officers of late medieval and sixteenth century convents left the cloister to fulfil a variety of responsibilities.[51] As we accumulate more and more examples of breaches of claustration, it appears that the business of female monasticism often required nuns to step beyond the cloister wall in ways that were legitimate and certainly not transgressive. Thus, the discipline of enclosure provides a convenient starting point from which to interrogate the extent of a laywoman's 'conversion' into a nun. Although it was meant to mark a transformation of her life and a movement from the secular world to a distinctly ecclesiastical environment, traces of her former life remained. Certainly, enclosure was incomplete. We would do well to adopt Sharon Strocchia's concept of 'open reclusion':[52] an attitude or posture whereby enclosure was mostly observed but put aside when the business and relationships of the convent demanded otherwise.

Ironically, the legal traces of the profession ceremony were the grounds upon which nuns maintained ties with the secular world. Nuns often battled with their natal families over dowry payments and other transactions emanating from their entrance into the convent. In 1602 the convent of Santa María de las Huelgas in Valladolid initiated a lawsuit for two of its nuns, Rafaela and Juana de Heraso y Herrera, claiming that they had been deprived of the full sum of their dowries.[53]

At a daughter's profession families also often agreed to provide a yearly maintenance allowance (*alimentos* in Spain). These, too, could become contentious sums. In 1662 the convent of Santa Catalina, on behalf of Bernarda de Mercado, entered into a lawsuit with her father's estate, claiming that sufficient payment on her *alimentos* had not been made.[54] Thus, the very acts meant to sever a nun's ties from the secular world kept her intricately bound to it as she and her convent defended her ongoing financial interests.

In more routine fashion, nuns had regular contact with outsiders. Male personnel – priests and doctors – entered the cloister to provide necessary services. Passive enclosure was also 'violated' when visitors came to the convent. Families, in fact, expected this kind of access to nuns. It became another instance in which the rules were mitigated. Rather than forbid these conversations, they were regulated and monitored. Most convents, for example, had a visiting parlour that provided an approved space for such interactions. Constitutions and other guidelines specified that the nuns should be separated from their visitors by partitions of cloth or grillework or wood, or all three. Older members of the community were typically appointed as 'listeners' (in Spain, literally 'escuchaderas' or 'escuchas') and were supposed to eavesdrop on the conversations to make sure they remained edifying. Again, the very obligations that nuns were supposed to leave behind upon their profession – in this case, family ties – intruded upon the space of the convent. The transformation of becoming a nun often seemed incomplete.

While we might expect that the Council of Trent's enclosure decree would put an end to such mitigations, this was not necessarily the case. In 1596 the convent of Santa Isabel in Valladolid was enmeshed in a debate about the definition of enclosure. The issue was the entrance of outsiders into the cloister and what was acceptable. In the end, the ecclesiastical visitor distinguished between two types of clausura, *perpetua* (perpetual) and *decente* (modest), 'having two modes of enclosure, one strict where they do not leave nor do men or women enter ... and the other more moderate where they do not leave nor do men enter, but women do'.[55] Ultimately, he reasoned that the nuns had previously followed the moderate standard and that this was adequate and they should not have to alter their tradition.

Modifications such as this one at Santa Isabel in the late sixteenth century, some thirty years after the decrees of the Council of Trent had been made the law of the land in Spain, speak to the complicated process by which young women with religious vocations separated themselves from the world and family and prepared to live in a monastic community. And the evidence from Italy suggests that there, too, enclosure was implemented slowly and irregularly, if at all.[56]

A nun professing at the priory of Little Marlow in 1528 spoke the following words:

> And for this intent and purpose I here renounce for ever and utterly forsake the world, and property of temporal substance and goods of the same and all other worldly delights and pleasures, taking upon me wilful poverty; vowing also and promising ever to live in pure chastity during my life: to change my secular life into regular conversation and religious manners.[57]

No doubt she intended these words to be true. And this very profession ceremony, the habit she would don, and the monastic discipline she would observe worked to ensure the verity of her claims. And yet, as we have seen, enclosure was malleable, dowries needed protecting, and families continued visiting. The conversion that she perhaps sought and that male ecclesiastics anxiously regulated through liturgical rituals, clothing, and spatial discipline, would always be uneven.

NOTES

1 Quoted in Sarah Salih, *Versions of virginity in late medieval England* (Woodbridge: Boydell & Brewer, 2001), p. 130. I have modernised the spelling.
2 Nancy Bradley Warren, 'The ritual for the ordination of nuns' in Miri Rubin, ed. *Medieval Christianity in practice* (Princeton: Princeton University Press, 2009), pp. 318–23.
3 Asunción Lavrín notes that Bridgettine nuns in colonial Mexico had to lie face down during part of their profession ceremony. See Lavrín *Brides of Christ: conventual life in Colonial Mexico* (Stanford: Stanford University Press, 2008), p. 76.
4 K. J. P. Lowe, *Nuns' chronicles and convent culture in Renaissance and Counter-Reformation Italy* (Cambridge: Cambridge University Press, 2004), p. 228. See also her 'Secular brides and convent brides: wedding ceremonies in Italy during the Renaissance and Counter-Reformation', in Trevor Dean and Lowe (eds), *Marriage in Italy, 1300–1650* (Cambridge: Cambridge University Press, 1998), pp. 41–65.
5 Cited in Lowe, *Chronicles*, p. 233. See the recent edition of this chronicle: Sister Giustina Niccolini, *The chronicle of Le Murate*, ed. and trans Saundra Weddle (Toronto: Centre for Reformation & Renaissance studies, 2011).

6 Lavrín, *Brides of Christ*, p. 77.
7 Elizabeth Rapley, *A social history of the cloister* (Montreal: McGill-Queen's University Press, 2001), p. 181.
8 Julie Hotchin, 'The nun's crown', *Early modern women: an interdisciplinary journal*, vol. 4 (2009), 187-94.
9 Hotchin, 'The nun's crown', 187.
10 Lavrín, *Brides of Christ*, p. 77.
11 Salih, *Versions of virginity*, p. 127.
12 Nancy Bradley Warren, *Spiritual economies: female monasticism in later medieval England* (Philadelphia: University of Pennsylvania Press, 2001), p. 4.
13 *Ibid.*, p. 26.
14 Quoted in Lavrín, *Brides of Christ*, p. 78.
15 *Ibid.*, p. 77.
16 Sharon Strocchia, *Nuns and nunneries in Renaissance Florence* (Baltimore: Johns Hopkins University Press, 2009), pp. 1-38.
17 Niccolini, *Chronicle of Le Murate*, pp. 213-18.
18 Archivo Histórico Nacional (hereafter AHN), Clero, leg. 7910, 'espontanea voluntad'.
19 AHN, Clero, leg. 7761, 'el santo concilio de Trento'.
20 Elizabeth A. Lehfeldt, *Religious women in Golden Age Spain* (Aldershot: Ashgate, 2005), p. 76.
21 Lavrín, *Brides of Christ*, pp. 24-5, 72-4.
22 Lehfeldt, *Religious women*, pp. 85-7.
23 Marilyn Oliva, *The convent and the community in late medieval England* (Woodbridge: Boydell & Brewer, 1998), pp. 48-9.
24 Sharon Strocchia, 'Naming a nun: spiritual exemplars and corporate identity in Florentine convents, 1450-1530', in William J. Connell (ed.), *Society and individual in Renaissance Florence* (Berkeley: University of California Press, 2002), p. 216.
25 Quoted in Lavrín, *Brides of Christ*, p. 76.
26 Anne Bagnall Yardley, *Performing piety: musical culture in medieval English nunneries* (New York: Palgrave Macmillan, 2006) and Lowe, 'Marriage', p. 53.
27 Amy Katz Kaminsky (ed.), *Water lilies / Flores de agua, an anthology of Spanish women writers from the fifteenth through the nineteenth century* (Minneapolis: University of Minnesota Press, 1996), p. 360.
28 *Ibid.*, pp. 365-6.
29 Cited in Elissa Weaver, *Convent theater in early modern Italy* (Cambridge: Cambridge University Press, 2002), p. 180.
30 See also Nicky Hallett, *The senses in religious communities, 1600-1800: early modern 'convents of pleasure'* (Farnham: Ashgate, 2013).

31 Salih, *Versions of virginity*, p. 127.
32 Oliva, *Convent and community*, p. 63.
33 *Acta visitationis*, Real Biblioteca del Monasterio de San Lorenzo de El Escorial, Madrid Ms. V. II. 14, 224 $^{r-v}$.
34 Lowe, *Chronicles*, p. 213.
35 'Houses of Benedictine nuns: Priory of Wix', in William Page and J. Horace Round (eds), *A History of the County of Essex: Volume 2* (London: Victoria County History, 1907), pp. 123–5. http://www.british-history.ac.uk/vch/essex/vol2/pp123–125 (accessed 4 June 2016).
36 One modern scholar has trivialised this distinction, suggesting that the nuns preferred the more elegant Benedictine habit to the drab, grey Franciscan one. Cited in Lehfeldt, *Religious women*, p. 153. Laura Hodges' *Chaucer and clothing* (Woodbridge: Boydell and Brewer, 2005), and especially her chapter on the Prioress' garb, provides a useful critique of scholarly assumptions about female monastic attire.
37 Lowe, *Chronicles*, pp. 209–10.
38 Quoted in Warren, *Spiritual economies*, p. 7.
39 Roberta Gilchrist, *Gender and material culture: the archaeology of religious women* (London: Routledge, 1993), p. 57.
40 Juan Luis Vives, *The education of a Christian woman: a sixteenth century manual*, ed. and trans. Charles Fantazzi (Chicago: Chicago University Press, 2000), p. 125.
41 Marilyn Oliva, 'Nuns at home: the domesticity of sacred space', in Maryanne Kowaleski and P. J. P. Goldberg (eds), *Medieval domesticity: home, housing and household in medieval England* (Cambridge: Cambridge University Press, 2009), pp. 145–61.
42 Antonio de Andrade, *Libro de la guia de la virtud, y de la imitación de Nuestra Señora: segunda parte* (Madrid, 1644), pp. 610–11.
43 Anthony C. Meisel and M. L. deMastro (eds), *The Rule of Saint Benedict* (New York: Image, 1975), p. 102.
44 'The Rewle of sustris menouresses enclosid', in R. W. Chambers and W. W. Seton (eds), *A fifteenth century courtesy book and two fifteenth-century Franciscan Rules* (London: K. Paul, Trench, Trübner & Co, 1914), pp. 81–119.
45 *Constituciones de la congregacion de San Benito de la Observancia, que tuuo principio en el Real Monasterio de San Benito de Valladolid* (Madrid, 1612).
46 *Constituciones generales para todas las monjas, y religiosas sujetas a la obediencia de la orden de N.P.S. Francisco* (Madrid, 1642), p. 27.
47 All of these appear in the *Acta visitationis*.
48 Salih, *Versions of virginity*, p. 113.
49 Hampshire Record Office, Register of Bishop Richard Fox, vol. 2, f. 42^v–43^v.
50 'Houses of Benedictine nuns: Priory of Wix', pp. 123–5.

51 Oliva, *Convent and community*, pp. 35–6; 86.
52 Strocchia, *Nuns and nunneries*, p. 79. The issue of monastic business beyond the cloister, however, does raise the question of lay sisters. These were women who did not take solemn vows, but who adopted partial monastic vocation. They were often given the tasks that more strictly enclosed nuns could not perform. The subject of lay sisters is quite understudied and requires more attention.
53 AHN, Clero, leg. 7810.
54 AHN, Clero, leg. 7847.
55 AHN, Clero, leg. 7907, 'abiendo dos modos de clausura una estrecha donde no salen ni entran honbres ni mugeres . . . y la otra mas moderada donde no se salen ni entran honbres sino mujeres'.
56 P. Reneé Baernstein, *A convent tale* (New York: Routledge, 2002) and Craig Monson, *Disembodied voices: music and culture in an early modern Italian convent* (Berkeley: University of California Press, 1995).
57 'Houses of Benedictine nuns: The priory of Little Marlow', *A History of the County of Buckingham: Volume 1* ed. William Page (London, 1905), pp. 357–60. British History Online http://www.british-history.ac.uk/vch/bucks/vol1/pp357-360 (accessed 4 June 2016) My thanks to Elizabeth Makowski for this citation.

7
Domus humilis: the conversion of Venetian convent architecture and identity

Saundra Weddle

Despite their institutional significance, Venice's early modern convents were among the city's more ordinary religious structures. Like monumental religious buildings, convent complexes relied upon architectural features such as enclosing walls to make their function apparent, producing associations with and for their inhabitants and imparting meaning to local sites. But whereas monumental buildings obviously adhered to a coherent and legible typology – a consistent formal model that corresponded to particular functions and expressed a fixed identity – Venetian convents articulated and combined their common features in idiosyncratic ways that bore witness to processes of conversion experienced by the women who founded and inhabited them.

Taken as a whole, the convent complex served as both the result and the evidence of dynamic development processes that saw the conversion of buildings and identities over time, so that change was the most dominant distinguishing characteristic of Venetian convents. While providing an orienting architectural and spatial syntax, convent architecture connected convent communities to the place they occupied and established a discursive public relationship with local contexts of various sorts; almost paradoxically, these communities made enclosure, anonymity, and modesty imperative.[1] As products and producers of their urban contexts, convent complexes responded to and expressed particular connections and conditions. Vernacular materials and marginal site conditions (usually at the city's edges) made manifest convents' humble and, often, informal origins (Figure 7.1). An assemblage of disorderly

Figure 7.1 Map of Venetian convents showing parish boundaries.

building volumes whose specific functions remained unidentifiable to the outside viewer reflected the ways in which convents responded to changing needs using an accretive approach to site development. Eventually, unifying enclosing walls conveyed the achievement of a formalised institutional identity, giving an impression of communal order that did not always exist in reality.

The improvised and evolutionary nature of Venetian convents' architectural and spatial features follows in part from topographic and urban conditions. Unstable subsoil and dependence on water-based transportation presented a variety of logistical challenges to the construction process, and the city's relatively dense development effectively frustrated the execution of idealised architectural plans. Relying upon already-extant building fabric was simply more practical than building *ex novo*. But the challenge of building on the lagoon's mudflats and integrating into the city's urban fabric hounded every Venetian architectural project. Why, then, were convent complexes more likely than other institutional sites to involve the appropriation and modification of existing buildings, a conversion of architecture that corresponded to a conversion of identity? This chapter will demonstrate that the architecture of most

Venetian convents resulted to some extent from patterns of patronage and processes of development that demanded flexibility in response to changing identities and circumstances. Increasing convent populations and the changing expectations of nuns, their families, their patrons, and their superiors followed from complex religious, social, political, and economic contexts, causing convent architecture to be transformed on a relatively regular basis.[2]

The degree to which convent architecture exhibited the disorderly characteristics of change over time depended to some degree on its foundation date. Richard Goy draws a distinction between 'great and ancient foundations like [the Benedictine convent of] San Zaccaria, traditionally patronized by powerful members of the nobility and by the doge himself' and 'minor institutions in a distant corner of the city, with few wealthy benefactors'.[3] The origins of differences in patronage patterns and convent status can be traced to Venice's early development, when powerful families assumed responsibility for establishing parishes. A parish's boundaries generally followed the edges of the island it occupied; most islands had their share of modest and palatial houses, workshops, and businesses, along with the parish church and its campo.[4] Patricians were frequently responsible for the foundation of the church in the neighbourhood around their compound, a benefaction that gained them the privilege of *iuspatronatus*, which allowed them to influence parish administration.[5] Landowners in a given parish also played the role of *vicinus*, and were required by civic statutes to fund public works in the parish, paying a share proportionate to their property ownership.[6] Like parish churches, Venice's oldest convents enjoyed consistent and generous patronage from neighbouring prominent patrons, many of whom sought a reputable home for their unmarried kinswomen.

Most Venetian convents fall into Goy's category of 'minor institutions'.[7] Eventually, patricians extended their patronage of religious institutions beyond their home parish, a practice that was not limited to convents.[8] Dennis Romano has shown, for example, that Venetians often lived and worked in different neighbourhoods, and it was not uncommon for them to choose to be buried outside their parish. While on one hand this shift expanded the population of potential convent patrons, on the other, it meant that local patronage could not be relied upon to the extent it once was.

So-called 'minor institutions' evolved differently than their more established and distinguished predecessors. The ad hoc nature of

Venetian convent complexes resulted as much – if not more – from the circumstances of their foundation and subsequent development than from their physical urban context. Although their enclosing walls were intended to suggest otherwise, convents were not isolated objects; they shaped and were shaped by dynamic communities with complex relationships both inside and outside the enclosure.

Beginning around the fourteenth century, convent histories commonly include a charismatic and pious woman – sometimes identified as a widow, sometimes referred to only as *fondatrice* – who, together with like-minded companions, established a hermitage, hostel, or hospice.[9] Not all foundresses were widows, but many were, and this might be explained in part by the fact that convents often evolved from hospices for poor women, especially widows.[10] Occupying the threshold between secular and religious, these foundresses oversaw the conversion of their community – and the buildings that housed them – into a convent sanctioned by church and civic authorities. Of course, they did not operate in isolation, but rather on behalf of and in collaboration with their community.[11] While it might be overreaching to call their approach to convent foundation a strategy, the examples that follow show that these women used their liminal status and the flexibility that accompanied it to their advantage, achieving their devotional goals, often despite the initial absence of patrician support.

It should come as no surprise that widows were inspired to found a convent; they were likely to identify with nuns' lives. Although early modern conduct guides functioned as prescriptions more than mirrors of reality, they described the ideal widow as one who engaged in spiritual and bodily disciplines: praying, fasting, confessing, regularly attending religious services, giving alms, and reading the scriptures, all while denying herself worldly pleasures, activities around which the nun's life also centred.[12] Widows' empathy for women religious is not only evidenced in their interest in founding convents, but also in their testaments, which often included a donation to a convent – or multiple convents.

The motivations behind widows' patronage patterns likely extended to their interest in philanthropy. Widows' status liberated them from the obligation to seek, secure, and cultivate a husband's approval of their patronage.[13] Citing institutions such as the Casa delle Zitelle (for girls in danger of becoming prostitutes), the Casa delle Convertite (for reformed prostitutes), and the Casa del Soccorso (for prostitutes and adulterous wives), Monica Chojnacka has extended Brian Pullan's thesis that the sixteenth century in particular saw a general increase in philanthropic support of the poor, noting that wealthy women, especially widows, focused their patronage on the plight of impoverished and dishonoured women.[14] Chojnacka proposes that the focus on prostitution resulted not only from counter-reformation zeal, but also from civic concerns that recent political and economic problems were divine punishment for the city's slack morality; Chojnacka claims that laymen and laywomen sought to reverse this trend by caring for 'these women and other unfortunate groups'.[15] Some, such as Girolamo Priuli, equated convents with brothels and blamed nuns' lax observance for Venice's reversal of fortune.[16] It is possible, then, that the establishment of more rigorous convents was also understood as a way to counteract the effects of immorality. As earlier reform efforts and the condemnations of early modern preachers show, these concerns were not new to the sixteenth century.

Understanding the relationships between the economics and status of widowhood and convent foundation helps to explain why many convents evolved from informal communities into established institutions, with their architecture developing through a process of accretion that chronicled their conversion. A widow who did not re-marry and was childless, or whose children were adults, controlled her own dowry, providing her more financial freedom than most other women.[17] While not all widow-foundresses came from the patrician class, the average value of the patrician dowry provides some indication of the sums widow-foundresses might have been working with. The average amount of the patrician dowry was about 650 ducats during the trecento, but it grew substantially in the centuries that followed: in 1420 the Venetian Senate capped dowries at 1000 ducats; in 1535 the limit was set at 4000 ducats, and in 1551 at 5000 ducats.[18] The setting of limits and the steadily increasing sums (fuelled to some extent by inflation) suggest that actual patrician dowries were generally higher.[19] Even a portion of such funds could make a substantial contribution toward convent foundation, but additional assistance would inevitably have been required. The legitimising effect of conversion to a recognised convent would have raised the profile of the community, the institution, and the complex, and would have both required and attracted outside patronage.

The data on convent building costs in surviving account books are inconsistent, but it is worthwhile to establish some context about relative expenses. To assess the relative value of a dowry and the cost of convent construction, the example of the Corte Nova almshouses is especially informative, not only because it provides a sort of economic datum for construction costs for a modest complex intended to house a small community, but also because some convents were adapted from buildings that originally functioned as almshouses. The Corte Nova almshouses were constructed in the 1440s in an undeveloped area of Cannaregio with the aim of accommodating twenty residences.[20] The site had to be constructed, so the development perched upon an estimated 15,000 piles – stakes driven into the subsoil and then covered with stone slabs that formed the foundation. Like much convent construction, the almshouses were built of brick, a lightweight material that was less expensive and easier to transport and lay than stone, which was reserved for window frames, doorways, and brackets that supported the roof eaves. Wood was used for stairs and interior partitions. The complex was modular, comprised of repetitive units for the almshouse's residents. The project's total cost was 3600 ducats, including approximately 600 ducats spent on the foundations.[21] This may serve as a low reference point for fifteenth-century costs to build from scratch a structure of size and material similar to a small-scale convent.

Of course, compared with almshouses, convent communities had more complicated needs related to their devotional lives and the practical requirements of enclosure; even without accounting for the church and campanile, the cost of building a convent complex was, naturally, higher than that for almshouses. The Clarissan convent of Santa Maria dei Miracoli can serve as a gauge of the upper limits of fifteenth-century convent construction costs since it was built *ex novo*. It was founded in the 1480s as an afterthought, when funds remained in the building fund of the opulent neighbouring church of the same dedication. The Miracoli convent's façade on the Calle dei Miracoli bears a striking resemblance to the façade of the Corte Nova almshouses, but the complex itself was larger, with networks of spaces on multiple floors organised around a courtyard, and a walled garden space in the rear, bordered by porticos on three sides (Figure 7.2). The first order of business was to acquire the site, originally occupied by houses and a dyeworks, bought from the Barozzi family for the exceptional sum of 2800 ducats and razed before construction commenced.[22] The fifteenth-century chronicle of the Amadi family, the original owners of the miracle-working painting

Figure 7.2 Façade of the convent of Santa Maria dei Miracoli, Venice.

for which the church of Santa Maria dei Miracoli was constructed, states that the convent itself cost 8000 ducats.[23]

The total cost of constructing new building fabric would have been considerable even if it was added on to an existing building, and individual widow-patrons were therefore unlikely to possess adequate resources to operate as the sole patron of a new convent project.[24] It would have been necessary to supplement their support in a variety of ways. Convents produced more than prayers as nuns engaged in various commercial activities and gained additional income and resources from their real-estate holdings, but they also depended on their patronage networks to support their everyday income and their building projects.[25] The combination of considerable and varied economic demands and somewhat unpredictable income meant that convent construction usually happened in a piecemeal fashion.

As formidable as the financial challenges could be, however, they were not the only factors that contributed to convent architecture's extemporaneous qualities. The scarcity of buildable land gave exceptional significance to construction projects in Venice and had implications not only for a building's inhabitants, but also for their neighbours, with whom convents competed for space. Although some convents mitigated this situation to some degree by building at the city's edges, no complex evolved without constructing at least part of its site with pilings, or by acquiring neighbouring properties that were either demolished for the purpose of building on a cleared site or incorporated into the enclosure. Acquiring permission to build and executing the construction also involved considerable time. These factors meant that the process of conversion from informal community of laywomen to recognised convent, and from modest structures to unified complexes clearly expressed and contributed to public understanding of changes in a convent community's identity.

This complex of interests may have informed the foundation and development of the convent of San Sepolcro, whose roots can be traced to Elena Celsi, the widow of Marco Vioni. Celsi's testament of 2 January 1410 stipulated that one-half of a large house located on the Riva degli Schiavoni, where the Grand Canal meets the lagoon, should be used as a residence for 'good and honest widows', while the other half should be used as a hostel for female pilgrims.[26] After the arrival of Beatrice Venier and Polissena Premarin at the residence following the fall of Nigroponte to the Turks in 1471, the place's identity began to shift: in 1499 the women received approval from Pope Alexander VI to become a community of Third Order Franciscans.[27] With first-hand knowledge of the uncertainties unmarried women faced, Celsi, Venier, and Premarin provided a socially acceptable and institutionally stable option to women in this liminal state.

The accretive nature of San Sepolcro's development was natural given the unpredictability of the community's income and changing identity. With Celsi's house as a starting point, a small chapel was added and, during the first quarter of the sixteenth century, neighbouring properties were attached to the original core. Among these were some small houses, contiguous to the main property, which the institution initially used for rental income, as well as houses and shops purchased from the Molin family.[28] As the community's population expanded so did the complex. San Sepolcro purchased one *casa da statio* – a large family compound – from Luca di Andrea Molin in 1514, and another, 'with courtyards and gardens', from Marco di Luca and Andrea di Henrico Molin in 1523.[29] This enlargement of the site was not well received by everyone in the neighbourhood. Priests from the parish of San Giovanni in Bragora protested against San Sepolcro's expansion, which claimed

Figure 7.3 Detail of bird's eye view of Venice from the south, woodcut by Jacopo de'Barbari, *c.*1500. A: Santa Marta; B: Sant'Andrea della Zirada; C: Santa Chiara; D: Santa Croce; E: Corpus Domini; F: Santa Lucia.

a significant portion of built and buildable land, thereby threatening local resources the parish relied upon.[30] In this hostile and competitive context, which was not unique to San Sepolcro, development proceeded in fits and starts.

Changes in urban development and shifts in institutional identities also fuelled conflicts between communities of women, as the examples of Sant'Andrea della Zirada and Santa Lucia show (Figure 7.3). When Sant'Andrea was founded in 1329, four noblewomen – identified as *matrone* or matrons – sought and received approval from the parish of Santa Croce to erect a hospital for poor women, widows, and *cittadine* (women from the citizen class), along with an oratory dedicated to Saint Andrew.[31] The neighbouring Clarissan convent of Santa Chiara protested, claiming that their Rule restricted new monastic foundations in such close proximity to existing houses. Although Santa Chiara succeeded in delaying the construction for three years, the matter was finally settled in Sant'Andrea's favour.[32] In 1346, the Maggior Consiglio agreed to allow the women to construct a convent, with the Doge being awarded the privilege of *iuspatronatus*. Not coincidentally, this approval came the same year that the two surviving foundresses received approval to accept the Augustinian order.

Sites such as Sant'Andrea, at the city's edges, were typical, demonstrating how and why convent architecture was regularly in flux. Such locations had obvious advantages because they were not as densely developed as the city centre, and offered the opportunity for expansion. As was often the case, building Sant'Andrea's complex was not simply a matter of occupying an existing site, but of constructing the site itself. The phrase used here is *atterrare parte della laguna*, or 'to make into land', a process of making the mudflats suitable for building, making a kind of platform by driving wooden pylons into the mud and bedrock. Thus, in April 1330, permission was granted to construct an area 15 *passi* long and 4 *passi* wide; such permission was also granted in 1337 (30 *passi* beyond the initial concession), 1383 (an unspecified area), 1411 (to build a garden), and 1420 (to build a sepulchre).[33] The complex continued to grow as neighbouring buildings were acquired.[34] Significant reconstruction of the church occurred in the fifteenth century, with the Senate dedicating 1000 ducats to the project; the new church was consecrated in 1502.[35] This slow expansion of the site contributed to the improvised appearance of convent complexes.

The foundation of Santa Lucia also provoked conflict with a neighbouring convent related to changes in status and site limitations (Figure 7.3). Originally known as La Nuntiata, the convent traces its origins to some point in the early fifteenth century when a group of women established residence in a house in the parish of Santa Lucia, near an existing church dedicated to the Annunciation.[36] The women lived as Augustinian tertiaries and initially took the church's dedication as their own. According to the community's chronicle, the site was very constricted; only a narrow *calle* separated the tertiaries from the Dominican convent of Corpus Domini, a condition that ultimately provoked discord between the neighbours.[37] Eventually, it became necessary to expand the tertiaries' living space, so they purchased some adjacent houses and made a cloister, occupying the site in 1459. In 1461, Patriarch Andrea

Bondumier, himself an Augustinian, introduced three nuns from the convent of San Daniele to educate the tertiaries in the monastic discipline, preparing them to join the Augustinian order.[38] Following this transition, the community's reputation and number grew, and the community attempted subsequent building campaigns with particular interest in erecting a church, since they still had none of their own. Corpus Domini claimed that the planned construction conflicted with the Dominican Rule, which they said stipulated that two convents must be no less than 90 *canni* (roughly 300 metres) apart, citing the noise of the bells and other distractions as obstacles to their devotional life.[39] Despite this protest, the patriarch ruled that the difficult paludal building conditions that characterised the Venetian lagoon necessitated an exception to this regulation.[40] The Dominican nuns then attempted an appeal to Pope Pius II, but the Venetian Senate ordered its ambassador in Rome to uphold the patriarch's decision, and the Pontiff agreed, allowing the nuns of La Nuntiata to expand their site.[41] Even if Corpus Domini's objections centred on spatial considerations, there can be no doubt that they extended to concerns about competition for patronage with another convent: as long as the women of La Nuntiata lived nearby as tertiaries, Corpus Domini took no notice of them or their house; only after their identity changed and the community gained status by becoming a fully fledged convent was animosity expressed.

Fierce competition for financial support also likely informed the next phase of the dispute between these convents. Although given approval to build their church, the Augustinians made little progress on the project because they lacked sufficient funds. In 1476, they found a solution, however, in the nearby church of Santa Lucia, where the popular relics of the homonymous virgin martyr attracted the attention and alms of a great number of pilgrims. Aware that in 1466 Pope Eugenius IV had granted Corpus Domini possession of the parish church of Santa Lucia, including its relics, the nuns of La Nuntiata successfully appealed to Pope Sixtus IV to transfer the saint's body to their convent in order to raise funds. Another maelstrom ensued: Corpus Domini sent letters of protest to civic and religious authorities, and, under cover of night, stole the relics, hiding them in their cloister. Outraged, the Council of Ten ordered the doors of Corpus Domini to be walled up until the nuns relinquished the saint's body. Within two days the matter was resolved, with Corpus Domini receiving 50 ducats in recognition of the financial hardship it would bear as a result of losing the relics. To formalise their legitimate possession of the relics, La Nunziata changed its name to Santa Lucia. Construction at the site continued into the seventeenth century, with a family chapel and a new high altar commissioned by Leonardo Mocenigo from Andrea Palladio.[42] The ambitious project stalled when the patron died in 1575, but ultimately led to the convent church's reconstruction, including its re-orientation, with the entry facing the Grand Canal, providing the convent with a kind of public exposure usually reserved for patrician palaces.

A house that combined many of the characteristics evidenced at San Sepolcro, Sant'Andrea, and Santa Lucia, was Santa Marta, where a woman of disputed status founded an institution for others in need; although the complex occupied a site at the city's far western limit, the project provoked controversy with neighbouring religious institutions (see Figure 7.3). The foundress was Giacomina Scorpioni, a resident of the parish of San Nicolò dei Mendicoli. She received permission in 1315 to found a hospital for the people of her neighbourhood, relying on financial support from Marco Sanudo and Filippo Salamon. The project, which also included a church, moved so slowly that excommunication was threatened if construction was not finished in good time.[43] As the job neared completion, Scorpioni changed her mind and proposed the foundation of a convent instead of a hospital, launching a controversy not only with the patrons, but also with parish priests from San Nicolò, who argued that a convent was not part of the original agreement. They even attacked Scorpioni personally, saying that she had no right to be there because she was already a *conversa* (servant nun) at the convent of San Mauro di Burano.[44] Their arguments were overruled and the convent of Santa Marta was established. On 20 October 1317, the Augustinians, led by Scorpioni, *patrona, funditrix et hedificatrix,* were liberated from the parish church's jurisdiction, but more than a century later the old conflicts over neighbourhood territory resurfaced.[45] With its church in disrepair and a need for more space, the nuns sought to expand their complex by building on public land. A process not unlike that described at Sant'Andrea followed, with the convent granted permission to 'make land' in 1432, 1446, and 1451 'to build the monastery'.[46] The priests' attempts to stop the project proved unsuccessful, and the new, single nave church was consecrated in 1480.[47]

The bas-reliefs that decorated the doors to the convent church and the convent itself (now transposed to the other churches, one of which is shown in Figure 7.4), may have functioned in the way *capitelli* did,

Figure 7.4 Bas-relief originally at the convent of Santa Marta, now at the church of Angelo San Raffaele, Venice.

with the intention of inspiring decorous behaviour on the city's rough and remote edges, but this image of the Virgin Mary sheltering kneeling nuns also recalls the Misericordia's iconography, suggesting that the reliefs also served as talismans, protecting the convent against its hostile neighbours.

The practice of adapting existing secular buildings to monastic uses was common in early modern Italy, but the conversion of a monastic complex previously used either by men or by nuns of another order occurred just as often. Monastic complexes were seized and re-assigned when a community did not respond to reform efforts and its persistent breaches of decorum became publicly known. In the offending community's place, Church authorities installed a proven, devout group with the hope that it would attract like-minded individuals and grow to become a stable and respected institution. In such cases, there is no known evidence to suggest that significant architectural changes accompanied the introduction of a new community. The new institution's identity was conveyed more by the invisible than the visible: a convent whose nuns were not seen and were heard only from the privacy of their choir or their side of the parlour grate adhered to the ideal. The architecture of their complex served as both the instrument and the symbol of nuns' piety.

San Daniele, located in the Castello neighbourhood near the Arsenale, offers an example of a change of identity without a corresponding architectural change.[48] The church of San Daniele was founded by the Bragadin family at an unknown date thought to correspond with the city's foundation. In 1138, a Cistercian monk was given permission to build a monastery next to the church, but by the late fourteenth century the monks' religious fervour had waned. They were removed and, in the early fifteenth century, the complex was given over to a devout woman named Chiara Ognibene, who attracted other religious women who joined her in a life of reclusive devotion. In 1437, Pope Eugenius IV placed them under the Augustinian Rule with no known significant modifications to the complex or its church. The change in the institution's identity became evident when a small group of nuns from San Daniele was sent to educate the burgeoning convent of Santa Lucia, discussed above.

The Franciscan convent of Santa Croce also experienced this sort of conversion (see Figure 7.3).[49] The convent traced its origins to a parish church that gave its name to one of Venice's six administrative districts. In 1109, the Badoer family, founders of the original church, led a group of patrons in the construction of a monastery for Cluniac monks on the site. Over time, the monks' observance grew more lax, and, in 1342, they were evicted from the complex, which then functioned for several decades as a Priorate. By 1460, a group of tertiaries established residence in a nearby house, where, in 1470, church authorities eventually sent professed nuns from the convents of San Bernardino in Padua and Santa Chiara in Murano to educate the women in the Franciscan *vita regolare*. Before long the entire monastic complex of Santa Croce was ceded to the nuns. Archival records, which are fragmentary, offer no indication of significant building on the site until the late sixteenth century, when the church was rebuilt. Santa Croce's shift in identity can also be confirmed by Church authorities' decision to send a number of the convent's pious nuns to reform the neighbouring convent of Santa Chiara.

The Franciscan convent of Santa Chiara on the island of Murano is an unusual case because, unlike other institutions whose inhabitants changed from male to female and from one order to another, it was its name that changed. The circumstances of the original monastery's foundation are not clear. Known as San Nicolò della Torre (a reference to the church's campanile), it seems first to have been inhabited by Augustinian friars and then, from the fourteenth century, by Benedictine nuns. After a scandal whose specifics have not been recorded, Pope Eugenius IV ordered, in 1439, not only that the nuns leave the site, but that the Protonotary Apostolic, Fantino Dandalo, and the Bishop of Macerata and Recanati, Tommaso Tommasini, personally escort the nuns from the convent and situate them in other institutions. These events coincided with an effort on the part of a Venetian Senator, Stefano Trevisano, to relocate his widowed sister from a Clarissan convent in Treviso; she and some of her sisters were transferred to the Murano convent, changing the institution's name to reflect their adherence to Saint Clare's rule and the name of their home institution. Before long, these women became known for their religious devotion and members of the community were sent to found other Franciscan convents in Venice, including Santa Croce and Santa Maria dei Miracoli, or to reform a house where religious fervour had waned, as at Santa Maria Maggiore.[50] In this case, then, changing the institution's name communicated to the public the initiation of a conversion process; the nuns' enactment of and reputation for piety effectively secured this change of identity for the site.

Unlike the conversions of convent architecture and identity that followed from foundation practices, reform efforts attempted to impose conversion from outside the enclosure. Whether they focused on individual houses or took the form of decrees addressed to all the city's nuns, attempts to transform decadent communities into pious ones were nearly constant in early modern Venice. Until the start of the sixteenth century, most attempts to impose discipline on Venetian convents issued from the Pope. Beginning with the fall of Constantinople in 1453, however, the Venetian state began to experience a crisis of confidence caused by military and economic challenges that intensified and eventually climaxed in 1509 with its defeat at the hands of the League of Cambrai at Agnadello, resulting in the dramatic reduction of Venetian territory on the *terra firma*. The unpredictability of commerce at the same time further threatened the lagoon city. Beginning in 1502, both the city and the church had attempted to impose discipline on convents, but a dramatic change in approach can be traced to 1519, when Patriarch Antonio Contarini gained support from Doge Leonardo Loredan and Pope Leo X for a plan to reform eight convents.[51] Convents previously overseen by no authority other than the pope were now forced to answer directly to the patriarch, and the way of life followed by many Venetian nuns was set to disappear, with no personal possessions and the enforcement of enclosure regulations.

At the heart of the controversy were the practices of Conventual nuns whose relaxed practices caused great scandal in comparison with the behaviour of Observant nuns, whose practices were strict and severe. Essentially, the reform called for the sequestration of Conventual nuns within their convents – a kind of house arrest, while Observant nuns from other houses were introduced and given the right to manage the community's affairs. All new abbesses and new members were to be Observant, leaving the Conventual faction to wither as the nuns aged and died.

The case of Santa Maria delle Vergini, one of Venice's oldest convents, exemplifies how this particular effort relied upon architecture inside the convent enclosure, not to convert individual Conventual nuns but, in essence, to re-found and convert the entire community's identity. Since its foundation, the Vergini had enjoyed a special connection to the Doge, confirmed at each new abbess's election with the Doge's presentation of rings to the convent's new leader. The convent enjoyed exceptional freedom and privileges. When confronted with the reform's requirements, the nuns claimed that they were exempt from observing monastic rules because they professed no vows; their principal obligation, which they claimed to have fulfilled, was the recitation of divine offices.[52] Diarist Marin Sanudo reports that some of the canonesses' kinsmen attempted to plead their case at the Collegio, but they were sent away.[53] Within a few weeks, the patriarch, his vicar, and a group of builders forcibly entered the convent complex to construct walls that would divide the Conventuals from the Observants, but some days later the nuns destroyed them. From their hasty construction and demolition, we might conclude that they were composed of timber studs and timber or dried reed lath, covered by plaster, a common technique in vernacular Venetian architecture, but they also could have

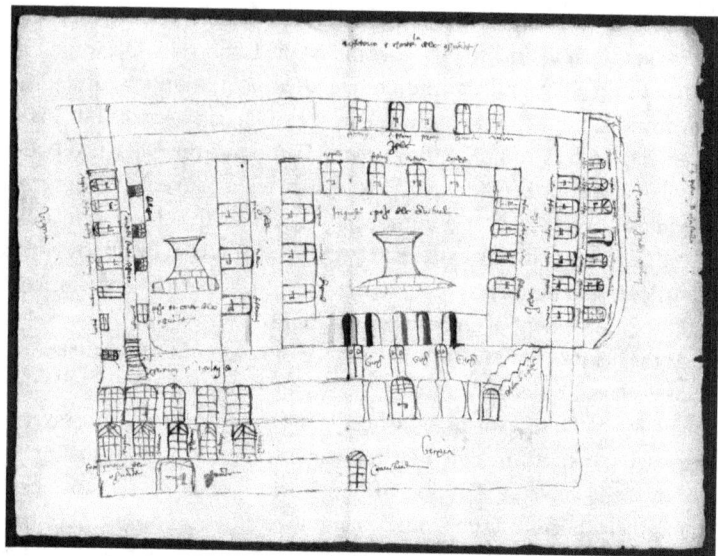

Figure 7.5 Sketched plan of the convent of Santa Maria delle Vergini, Venice, after 1519.

been masonry walls. Weeks of wrangling followed, but on 4 July, five Observant nuns and two servant nuns from the Augustinian convent of Santa Giustina were introduced. The divisions were reconstructed. A surviving sketch depicts how the two constituencies were accommodated in separate zones of the complex, with cells arrayed around each of the convent's courtyards (Figure 7.5). It is difficult to imagine how these convents functioned once the walls were in place, since mundane spaces such as kitchens and laundry rooms, and more significant spaces such as the nuns' choir would not have been duplicated within the complexes, but would have had to be shared. Conflict and protest continued until the last Conventual nun died in 1537.[54] Whether the conversion of the Vergini to an Observant convent was truly achieved is difficult to assess, but it seems that the nuns wished to make a public architectural statement of a change of identity because, after 1537, they launched a major renovation of the most public part of their complex, the church, under the direction of *proto* Gugliemo Grigi.[55]

It should come as no surprise that even after the Contarini reform nuns continued to resist and even disregard reform efforts, and ecclesiastical authorities continued to try to use architecture not only to secure the enclosure as a way of forcing nuns to change their behaviour, but also to communicate to the public that convent practices in general had been modified. In 1521, the city formed a committee to resolve problems of behaviour and financial mismanagement that came to light during Contarini's reform campaign, and, in 1528, the magistracy was made a permanent institution. These attempts to govern Venetian convents were bolstered by the Council of Trent's decrees, issued in 1564, giving civic efforts the authority of religious law, but enforcement was still a concern. In 1569, the Council of Ten ordered the *Provveditori sopra i Monasteri* and the patriarch to inspect the city's convents and ensure that the architecture was not facilitating lax observance.[56]

In 1591 and 1592, respectively, Patriarch of Venice Lorenzo Priuli and Bishop of Torcello Antonio Grimani issued constitutions designed to codify and unify convent practices.[57] The two texts have much in common with regard to matters of behaviour and administration, and Grimani's in particular explains how convent architecture could serve as a durable barrier between the enclosure and the world outside. Grimani wrote that his text was the product of convent visits he already made in compliance with the Council of Trent, when he saw for himself what needed to be changed.[58] Once the Constitutions were published, there was no excuse for inconsistent observance, and Grimani reserved 'the right to give greater and more severe penalties' to those who violated his rules.[59]

Both Priuli and Grimani ordered that windows and doors that could provide views into or out of the convent be walled up, unless the light in the room was insufficient, in which case the existing windows should be covered with grills.[60] Convents were to have no more than three doors – one giving on to land; one, which should be opened only very rarely, giving on to water; and another for the *cavana*, or dock. The three doors had to be locked at all times, with only the abbess or prioress in possession of the keys. The doors were to be fitted with grills covered with a black cloth so that no one could see in, but the porter could communicate with and identify those who approached. Any additional doors had to be walled up.[61] With openings in the convent walls closed or strictly monitored, convent architecture was again used to convey to the public a definitive conversion of monastic practices; it identified the site and the community that lived within the complex with an ideal of observance and discipline.

Architectural historians commonly distinguish between 'space' and 'place', the former being almost neutral, defined by a formal void fixed by its surroundings, the latter being understood as a location whose built features are identified with particular individuals or events. A building need not be monumental to function as a place. During the period when the communities themselves transformed from informal groups of pious women to sanctioned convents governed by vows and rules, the architecture responded to identity shifts by slowly acquiring typical convent features, communicating publicly the place's function. As examples of re-assigned and reformed convents show, however, once the institution was more established, the architectural changes were more specific, sometimes hidden within the enclosure, sometimes defining the enclosure itself. Although the enclosure wall came to embody the stability and constancy associated with the convent as an ideal institution, in fact, Venetian convent architecture changed regularly in response to more specific, localised conditions that were often in flux, responding to both internal and external pressures. Despite the ordinariness of their architecture, Venetian convents consistently exhibited attributes that identified them with the women who occupied them, making convents places with clear, localised associations, which included processes of change over time.

NOTES

1 I wish to express my sincere gratitude to Helen Smith and Simon Ditchfield for their patient and careful comments on this chapter. On architecture's capacity to express and 'organise' identity through form, space, and the body, see Helen Hills (ed.), *Architecture and the politics of gender in early modern Europe* (Aldershot: Ashgate, 2003), pp. 3–22.
2 For general studies of Venetian convents, see Jutta Sperling, *Convents and the body politic in late Renaissance Venice* (Chicago: University of Chicago Press, 1999); and Mary Laven, *The virgins of Venice: broken vows and cloistered lives in the Renaissance convent* (New York: Viking, 2002).
3 Richard John Goy, *Building Renaissance Venice: patrons, architects and builders, c. 1430–1500* (New Haven, CT: Yale University Press, 2006), p. 60.
4 For some discussion of this pattern, albeit for a patriarchal seat rather than a parish church, see Areli Marina, 'From the myth to the margins: the patriarch's piazza at San Pietro di Castello in Venice', *Renaissance Quarterly*, 64 (2011), 353–429.

5 Dennis Romano, *Patricians and popolani: the social foundations of the Venetian Renaissance state* (Baltimore: Johns Hopkins University Press, 1987), pp. 15 and 162, n. 10.
6 Elizabeth Crouzet-Pavan, 'An ecological understanding of the myth of Venice', in John Jeffries Martin and Dennis Romano (eds), *Venice reconsidered: the history and civilization of an Italian city-state* (Baltimore: Johns Hopkins University Press, 2002), p. 62, n. 33.
7 Most of Venice's earliest convents were established by patrician families, who donated land and funded construction; these institutions were viewed, at least in part, as sanctuaries for their unmarried daughters.
8 Romano, *Patricians and popolani*, pp. 79–81, 114–18.
9 Flaminio Corner, *Notizie storiche delle chiese e monasteri di Venezia, e di Torcello* (Padua, 1758) commonly uses the term *fondatrice* to refer to a convent foundress, and occasionally, while providing biographical detail about these women, explains that they were widows. For more on this subject, see Allison Mary Levy (ed.), *Widowhood and visual culture in early modern Europe* (Aldershot: Ashgate, 2003). For Renaissance Milan, see P. Renée Baernstein, 'In widow's habit: women between convent and family in sixteenth-century Milan', *Sixteenth Century Journal*, 25 (1994), 787–807. See also Mary Martin McLaughlin, 'Creating and recreating communities of women: the case of Corpus Domini, Ferrara, 1406–1452', *Signs*, 14 (1989), 293–321; and Carolyn Valone, 'Roman matrons as patrons: various views of the cloister wall', in Craig Monson (ed.), *The crannied wall: women, religion and the arts in early modern Europe* (Ann Arbor: University of Michigan Press, 1992), pp. 49–72.
10 Examples of convents that began as hospices or houses sited near an existing oratory include San Sepolcro, San Giovanni in Laterano, Santa Lucia, San Girolamo, Gesù e Maria, Ognissanti, Santi Cosma e Damiano, and Zitelle.
11 Helen Hills, 'Introduction', to Hills (ed.), *Architecture and the politics of gender*, p. 10.
12 Catherine E. King, *Renaissance women patrons: wives and widows in Italy c. 1300–1550* (Manchester: Manchester University Press, 1998), pp. 29–39.
13 *Ibid.*, 3–5.
14 Monica Chojnacka, 'Women, charity and community in early modern Venice: the Casa delle Zitelle', *Renaissance Quarterly*, 51 (1998), 68–91; Chonjacka cites Brian Pullan, 'La nuova filantropia nella Venezia cinquecentesca', in Bernard Aikema and Dulcia Meijers (eds), *Nel regno dei poveri: arte e storia dei grandi ospedali veneziani in età moderna 1474–1797* (Venice: Arsenale, 1989), pp. 17–34. See also Katherine A. McIver, *Women, art, and architecture in northern Italy, 1520–1580: negotiating power* (Aldershot: Ashgate, 2006), pp. 194–202.
15 Chojnacka, 'Women, charity and community', p. 72.

16 *I diarii di Girolamo Priuli*, ed. Roberto Cessi, *Rerum italicarum scriptores*, 24:12–14 (Bologna, 1938–41), p. 115. Nuns' debauchery was common knowledge. See, for example, Marin Sanudo, *Venice, città excelentissima: selections from the Renaissance diaries of Marin Sanudo*, ed. Patricia Labalme and Laura Sanguineti White, trans. Linda L. Carroll (Baltimore: Johns Hopkins Press, 2008), p. 381. For a more subtle analysis, see K. J. P. Lowe, *Nuns' chronicles and convent culture in Renaissance and Counter-Reformation Italy* (Cambridge: Cambridge University Press, 2004), pp. 193–213.

17 As Stanley Chojnacki explains, most widows with children postponed the recovery of their dowries, living in their husband's home and relying on their husband's estate to support the family, claiming their dowry only after their children had grown, but no more than thirty-one years and one day following their husband's death. 'Getting back the dowry', in *Women and men in Renaissance Venice: twelve essays on patrician society* (Baltimore: Johns Hopkins University Press, 2000), pp. 95–114.

18 Comparison with the prices of common provisions sets dowry sums in context. In 1582, a *staio* of wheat (approximately 83 litres) cost 1 ducat, a *mastello* of wine (approximately 75 litres) cost 0.4 ducats, and a *libbra* of pork (approximately 0.47 kilograms) cost 0.375 ducats. Sperling, *Convents and the body politic*, p. 242. According to Norbert Huse: 'To be well-off in the sixteenth century was to have an income of 1,000 ducats and more; to be rich was to enjoy more than 10,000 ducats in income.' *The art of Renaissance Venice: architecture, sculpture, and painting, 1460–1590* (Chicago: University of Chicago Press, 1993), p. 66.

19 Stanley Chojnacki, 'Dowries and kinsmen in early Renaissance Venice', *Journal of Interdisciplinary History*, 5 (1975), 571. Julia DeLancey's forthcoming work on the status of Venice's colour sellers will demonstrate that dowries could soar to double the limits established by the Venetian Senate. On challenges to the Venetian economy in the sixteenth century, see Brian Pullan, 'Wage earners and the Venetian economy, 1550–1630', in Pullan (ed.), *Crisis and change in the Venetian economy in the sixteenth and seventeenth centuries* (London and New York: Routledge, 2013), pp. 146–74.

20 Goy, *Building Renaissance Venice*, pp. 48–50.

21 Approximately 600 ducats were spent on the foundations for the Corte Nova project, leaving 3000 ducats for construction of the almshouses themselves. Goy, *Building Renaissance Venice*, p. 50.

22 The price of the site was excessive due to animosity between the Barozzi property holders and the convent procurators, resulting from a dispute over ownership of the miracle-working Madonna that prompted the construction of the church and the convent.

23 This did not include the cost of building the church, which in most convent complexes would have been a significant expense. Biblioteca del Museo

Correr, Gradenigo-Dolfin 56, *Memorie lasciate da Francesco Amadi della sua familia*, f. 15. Originally intended for no more than twenty-five women, the convent eventually housed as many as forty-four. The limit on the number of inhabitants to twenty-five came from the papal bull authorising the convent's foundation. Archivio Storico del Patriarcato di Venezia, Liber diversorum E, f. 88. Pastoral visitation records show that forty-four nuns lived there in 1594. Sperling, *Convents and the body politic*, p. 245. A chronicle published in 1664 states that the number of nuns – twelve – had multiplied five times since the convent's foundation, and that the cost of building the convent was 15,000 ducats, including the 2,800 ducats for the property. D. S. R., *Cronichetta dell'origine, principio e fondatione del Monastero, Chiesa, e Madonna detta de' Miracoli di Venetia* (Venezia: Baba, 1664), p. 25. The anonymous author claims to have consulted a variety of old writings, including a 200-year-old manuscript describing the foundation of the church, which may have been the Amadi chronicle.

24 Resourceful foundresses might have taken a more economical approach to initiating a community by renting a residence for as little as five ducats per year. Monica Chojnacka estimates the average rent for an apartment in a working class neighbourhood was about eight ducats a year. By comparison, a 'prosperous wool merchant rented comfortable lodgings in a nicer part of town for 76 ducats a year'. *Working women of early modern Venice* (Baltimore: Johns Hopkins University Press, 2001), pp. 6 and 146. Indeed, it seems that Venetians favoured renting over owning their residences. Patricia Fortini Brown, 'Behind the walls: the material culture of Venetian elites', in John Jeffries Martin and Dennis Romano (eds), *Venice reconsidered: the history and civilization of an Italian city-state, 1297–1797* (Baltimore: Johns Hopkins University Press, 2002), p. 304.

25 No focused study of Venetian convent economies exists, but for Florence, see Sharon Strocchia, *Nuns and nunneries in Renaissance Florence* (Baltimore: Johns Hopkins University Press, 2009), especially pp. 72–151.

26 The year of the testament is listed as 1409, but because the Venetian calendar year began on 1 March, the year in the modern style is 1410. Celsi also ordered that the institution, known as the Pilgrims' Hospital of Ca' Vioni, be administered by six gentlemen and six gentlewomen. This inclusion of women in a supervisory group is unusual, but Celsi's request may not have been honoured because the convent archive includes only the names of male commissioners. Archivio di Stato di Venezia (henceforth ASV), San Sepolcro, b. 1, f. 3^{r-v}. See also, Corner, *Notizie storiche*, pp. 116–25, and Giuseppe Tassini, 'Iscrizioni dell'ex chiesa e monastero del S. Sepolcro in Venezia', *Archivio Veneto*, 17, 18 (1879), 274.

27 Documents assert that the women asked to be affiliated with the Third Order, rather than having it assigned to them. Third Order nuns professed simple

vows rather than the solemn vows of chastity, poverty, and obedience, and they were not obliged to observe enclosure regulations until Pope Pius V issued his constitution, *Circa pastoralis* in 1566. However, Pope Alexander VI (r. 1492–1503) had already stipulated that the nuns at San Sepolcro would remain enclosed and would be supervised by the Observant Friars Minor at San Francesco della Vigna. Given these restrictions, it is not clear how these nuns' lives differed from those of Second Order nuns. On the church and convent, see Matteo Ceriana, 'La chiesa e il monastero del Santo Sepolcro di Venezia ai tempi di Chiara Bugni', in Reinhold C. Mueller and Gabriella Zarri (eds), *La vita e i sermoni di Chiara Bugni Clarissa Veneziana (1471–1514) Temi e testi* 89 (Rome: Edizioni di Storia e Letteratura, 2011), pp. 31–61.

28   ASV, San Sepolcro, b. 1, f. 3^v and 5^r.
29   *Ibid.*, 5^{r-v}. The first property was purchased for 1040 ducats; the transaction was recorded by notary Mattio Tura. The second was purchased for 2000 ducats. No notary is noted.
30   *Ibid.* and Corner, *Notizie storiche*, p. 119.
31   Gaetano Moroni, *Dizionario di erudizione storcico-ecclesiastica da S. Pietro sino ai Nostri Tempi* (Venice: Tipografia Emilia, 1854), p. 178. The entry on Sant'Andrea della Zirada confirms that the women intended to support the hospital with their own funds.
32   Emmanuele Antonio Cicogna, *Delle inscrizioni Veneziane raccolte ed illustrate da Emmanuele Antonio Cicogna*, v. 6 (Venice: Tipografia Andreola, 1853), pp. 5–155.
33   *Ibid.*, p. 12.
34   *Ibid.*; in June 1338 a house was donated, and, in 1347, another was acquired.
35   *Ibid.*, p. 7.
36   Corner, *Notizie storiche*, p. 252 states only that this group of tertiaries was formed before 1459.
37   ASV, Santa Lucia, b. 3, f. 17v. I would like to thank Daniel Bornstein for bringing this source to my attention. See also Maria Pia Pedani, 'Monasteri agostiniane a Venezia', *Archivio Veneto*, V:125 (1985), 35–78.
38   ASV, Santa Lucia, b. 3, f. 18^v–19^r.
39   ASV, Santa Lucia, b. 3, f. 20^r. A variety of rules provided guidelines for the siting of mendicant houses. Pope Alexander IV (r. 1254–61) offered to some Franciscan houses a distance of 300 *canni*, and Clement IV (r. 1265–68) extended the rule to all Mendicant foundations. In 1268, he reduced the distance to 140 *canni*. Gabriel Le Bras, *Histoire de l'eglise depuis les origines jusqu'a nos jours* (Paris: Bloud & Gray, 1964), p. 507.
40   Corner, *Notizie storiche*, 253.
41   Because both convents were destroyed to make way for the Venice train station, and site plans lack detail, it is difficult to assess the degree to which La Nuntiata actually encroached on Corpus Domini.

42 Tracy E. Cooper, *Palladio's Venice: architecture and society in a Renaissance republic* (New Haven, CT: Yale University Press, 2005), pp. 163–173.
43 Cicogna, *Inscrizioni Veneziane*, V:101 says that a family known as Centraniga or Barbolana had built a church dedicated to Santa Marta in 1018, but this could not be verified. Filippo Salamon was the son of Giovanni Salamon of the parish of Santa Maria Formosa, and Marco Sanudo was from the parish of San Severo, thus neither lived in this neighbourhood.
44 This assertion is supported by the convent archive, which describes Scorpioni as an '*onesta matron*', who left San Mauro di Burano to live in Venice as a tertiary. ASV, Santa Marta, b. 7, f. 239. Scorpioni is described as a noblewoman in Paola Malpezzi Price, *Moderata fonte: women and life in sixteenth-century Venice* (Cranbury, NJ: Associated University Presses, 2003), p. 150, n. 1. If this were the case, it would be highly unlikely that she would have been a *conversa*, but I have found no other sources to describe her status.
45 ASV, Santa Marta, b. 2, document labelled LRI records the convent's liberation from the parish of San Nicolò and this reference to Scorpioni as patron, founder, and builder.
46 ASV, Santa Marta, b. 2, pages labelled LKI, LSSI, and LKKI.
47 On 15 September 1451, Maestro Piero dall'Oglio was hired to build the peak of the convent's church to match that of Santa Maria della Carità. Presumably this refers to a scalloped pattern of brickwork. ASV, Santa Marta, b. 7, fasc. 100. See also Cicogna, *Inscrizioni Veneziane*, V:102. Cicogna cites a confirmation of the convent's exemptions issued by Antonio Saracco, archdeacon of Castello and patriarchal Vicar General, dating from 1467. Saracco consecrated the church. By the time the convent was suppressed, the church had seven altars, and included sepulchres for the Patarol, Gioliti, and Duodo families. Cicogna, *Delle Inscrizioni Veneziane*, V:102–3.
48 Corner, *Notizie storiche*, pp. 100–6.
49 *Ibid.*, pp. 380–3.
50 The Trevisan convent of Santa Chiara was previously known as La Cella, a Franciscan convent that had been reformed by nuns from a Franciscan convent in Mantua.
51 Biblioteca del Museo Correr (henceforth BMC), Cicogna 2570 is filled with examples of papal briefs, patriarchal pronouncements, and findings from archiepiscopal visitations. Observant nuns were introduced to Santa Maria delle Vergini, Santi Biagio e Cataldo, Santa Marta, Santa Chiara, La Celestia, San Secondo, San Zaccaria, and Sant'Anna. Nuns from Ognissanti were sent to Santi Biagio e Cataldo; from San Giuseppe to Santa Marta; from San Sepolcro, Santa Croce, and Santa Maria dei Miracoli to Santa Chiara; from San Daniele to La Celestia; from Santi Cosma e Damiano to San Secondo; from San Servolo to San Zaccaria; and from San Giovanni Laterano to

Sant'Anna. A similar effort was made at San Giovanni di Torcello, which took in Observant nuns from from Santa Caterina di Mazorbo. Corner mentions that San Lorenzo was also divided between Conventuals and Observants, but this seems to have predated Contarini's reform. *Notizie storiche,* p. 136.

52 BMC, Correr 317, *Cronica del monastero delle Vergini di Venetia,* f. 58^r.
53 Sanudo, *Venice, cità excelentissima,* pp. 386–93. The Collegio was an executive body that included the Doge and twenty-two councillors.
54 *Ibid.*
55 ASV, Santa Maria delle Vergini, b. 43.
56 ASV, Provveditori sopra i monasteri, b. 1, f. 29^v.
57 Lorenzo Priuli, *Ordini et avvertimenti che si devono osservare ne' monasteri di monache di Venetia* (Venice: s.n., 1591). Priuli's Constitutions are transcribed in BMC, Cicogna 2570, f. 172–206. Antonio Grimani, *Costitutioni dell'illustrissimo et reverendissimo Monsignor Antonio Grimani Vescovo di Torcello* (Venice: Giovanni Battista Meietti, 1592).
58 Grimani, *Constitutioni,* proemio.
59 Grimani, *Constitutioni,* p. 4.
60 *Ibid.,* p. 57.
61 *Ibid.,* p. 58.

8

Converting the soundscape of women's rituals, 1470–1560: purification, candles, and the *Inviolata* as music for churching

Jane D. Hatter

∽

There was only one ceremony or blessing in the late medieval Catholic rite that was reserved for laywomen – the ritual purification or churching of a woman after childbirth. This ceremony functioned primarily as an articulation of the transition of the woman from the authority of a female midwife to a male priest and also as a marker of the end of the new mother's period of seclusion and celibacy as she returned to public life and the reproductive cycle.[1] Although there was significant regional variation, the basic churching ritual was experienced not only by almost every properly married Christian woman during the fifteenth and sixteenth centuries but also by unmarried mothers, who often went to great lengths to secure the rite for themselves despite their exclusion by ecclesiastical authorities.[2] Early modern women's churching ceremonies were closely associated with Candlemas, or the Feast of the Virgin Mary's Purification, and the two shared many elements: in particular, processions with candles and, as discussed in this chapter, music. For members of the urban middle class of the early sixteenth century, both Catholic and early Lutheran, music was an expected enhancement for important life events and appropriate at all three stages of churching rites – simple music for processions; chant, hymns, and polyphony for the ritual itself; and instrumental and vocal music for entertainment during and after a festive meal. Although churching provides a rare opportunity to connect music to a central aspect of early modern women's lives, there has as yet been no study of the soundscape of churching ceremonies nor any exploration of how this soundscape was converted for early Protestant practice.[3]

The stakes around churching were high since the death of women in childbirth was extremely common during the fifteenth and sixteenth centuries and the bodies of women who had not been churched were not usually allowed burial in sacred ground.[4] The high mortality of childbearing women is reflected in one of Luther's statements that is very discordant to modern ears:

> Women are created for no other purpose than to serve men and be their helpers. If women grow weary or even die while bearing children, that doesn't harm anything. Let them bear children to death; they are created for that.[5]

Merry Wiesner has shown that Luther's views contributed significantly to a restriction of women's freedom to be active participants in intellectual and social life outside the home, essentially limiting women to their roles as wives, mothers, and dependants of men.[6] Luther's remark is nonetheless revealing of the mortal peril faced by childbearing women in the early sixteenth century. For early moderns, as the moment of the emergence of a new life approached, death was equally present. A pregnant woman relied on the strength and resourcefulness of the community of women around her to guide her, for both her baby's health and her own survival. Failure meant the loss not only of lives, but also of salvation. Not only were women's unchurched bodies barred from sacred ground, but it was only during childbirth that a woman, the midwife, was given the authority to provide the sacrament of baptism if the infant was unlikely to survive long enough to be baptised by a priest.[7]

Depending on the circumstances, churching rites could be simultaneously expressive of multiple meanings – from a celebration of the woman's accomplishment and survival to the return of the woman to her husband's bed and the renewal of her cycle of fertility. This ceremony could also be a sorrowful public acknowledgement of the loss of an infant, symbolised by the woman carrying an unlit rather than a lit candle during her churching procession.[8] Women's rituals often slip through the cracks of history, leaving little trace in the written record even though they are fundamental to the structure of a society.[9] For this reason, this kind of research project must bring together evidence from a wide variety of sources – including polyphonic and chant manuscripts, illuminations and altar paintings, ritual books and calendars, and even travellers' accounts – weaving together information on three interrelated topics. The first of these is Purification, which was of two different types: the Feast of the Purification of the Virgin Mary, or Candlemas, celebrated on 2 February, and the purification or churching of a woman three to six weeks after childbirth. The second is a category of objects – blessed candles. Candles blessed at the church door during the celebration of Candlemas were believed to have protective qualities. An illumination from a portable Benedictine psalter from Ghent, made about 1320, depicts women and men holding candles that are being aspersed with holy water during Candlemas.[10] These candles were taken home to be burnt to avert damage from storms and at other dangerous times, such as during and following the birth of a child.[11] Candles were also carried during processions, including churching, although it is unclear if these candles necessarily needed to be blessed. Finally, the plainchant sequence *Inviolata, integra et casta es Maria* was sung for the blessing of candles during Candlemas and was extremely popular as the musical and textual basis for polyphonic compositions; around fifty different pieces with at least one hundred occurrences are extant in manuscript and print sources from between 1470 and 1580.[12]

As a simple prayer that was regularly carried beyond the boundaries of the church in Marian processions, the *Inviolata* was part of the shared memorial archive of music known by both clerical and lay people. It is a prime candidate for use as a musical embellishment of churching rituals because of its association with blessed candles, childbirth, and purification rituals. The fact that it existed in so many different musical settings, including some popular printed collections, implies that it was sung more frequently than just during the liturgically prescribed moments around Candlemas, an idea that I will explore more fully below. Pieces using the *Inviolata* regularly crossed confessional boundaries, and were converted for use in Protestant sources, where they occur with revised texts. Despite the vulnerability of the traditional ceremony to charges of superstition, churching itself was retained in or reintegrated into early Protestant practices, including Lutheran, Calvinist, and Anabaptist ceremonies.[13] Like the *Inviolata* chant and related musical settings, these ceremonies were adapted, with controversial elements, such as blessed candles, expunged or reinterpreted. How can blessed candles illuminate the gradual conversion of the churching rite and the process of negotiation? And what can study of the persistence, use, alteration, and reuse of settings of the *Inviolata* contribute to our understanding of the struggle of women for continuity in ritual and musical expressions of female reproductive power?

FEAST OF THE PURIFICATION OF THE VIRGIN OR CANDLEMAS

To begin to understand early modern churching we must look at the Feast of the Purification of the Virgin celebrated on 2 February, or forty days after Christ's birth. This feast is derived from the second chapter of the Gospel of Luke, which conflates two events, stating that 'after the days of her [Mary's] purification, according to the law of Moses, were accomplished, they carried him [Jesus] to Jerusalem, to present him to the Lord'.[14] For this reason there is some ambiguity about what was actually happening at this biblical moment, resulting in two names for images associated with it – the Purification of Mary or the Presentation of Christ. In late medieval Catholicism, however, this moment was celebrated as one of the five main Marian festivals of the church year and it was also universally retained in early Protestant calendars because of the centrality of Christ to the event.[15] Catholic celebrations included processions of men and women through the streets carrying candles, hence the common English name for this feast is Candlemas. Psalter calendars from the thirteenth and fourteenth centuries, like the one from Ghent mentioned above, sometimes include illuminations depicting Candlemas processions, and laywomen are regularly the most prominent or sole participants, confirming the strong connection between Mary's purification and laywomen.[16] In his *Golden legend*, a thirteenth-century collection of saints' lives that was widely diffused in the later middle ages and early modern period, Jacobus de Voragine described Candlemas processions and justified some of the secular aspects of the celebration. He wrote 'As related to the day's procession: candles are blessed and exorcised, then lighted and given into the hands of the faithful, and the people go into the church singing hymns'.[17] Voragine emphasised candles, shown in the illuminations, but also the singing of hymns by lay people, confirming the importance of participatory music-making to these processions.

Candles and music are also both present in a mid-fifteenth-century altar painting by Johann Koerbecke – the candles are carried by a group of diminutive men and the singing is performed by a choir of angels surrounding God the Father who is looking down from heaven on the holy family.[18] This painting is an ideal demonstration of the multivalence of a late medieval understanding of this moment in the story of salvation as presented in Luke's gospel, and also the interconnectedness of the narratives of the lives of Christ and his mother in the early modern imagination. Koerbecke's image blends elements of four distinct events. First, Christ's Presentation and meeting with Simeon and the Prophetess Anna in the temple, the central image of the painting. Second, Mary's Purification, clearly identified with the offering of two turtledoves shown in Mary's hands as she approaches the altar. The birds are included in Luke's account and also aligned with ancient Mosaic law.[19] Next, the early modern practice of processing with candles on Candlemas is indicated by a procession of diminutive men, probably donors, depicted in the foreground. And, finally, this image also illustrates aspects of the churching rituals of early modern women, made evident by the three women standing behind the Virgin Mary, signifying her churching procession.[20] These women were probably intended to represent some configuration of those who, according to apocryphal and popular literature, attended to Mary during childbirth and confinement, perhaps including some combination of her midwives, the more memorable being Salome, her mother Anne, and her two sisters, the other Marys.[21]

There is much evidence to suggest a strong connection between Candlemas and early modern women's rituals surrounding childbirth. According to Voragine, the purpose of Candlemas was 'to recall the procession that occurred on this day, when Mary and Joseph and Symeon and Anna formed a solemn procession and presented the child Jesus in the Temple. On the feast day we too make a procession, carrying in our hands a lighted candle which signifies Jesus, and bearing it into the churches'.[22] According to Voragine, Candlemas was understood as a contemporary re-enactment of the Gospel of Luke, including both Mary's Purification rite and the Presentation of Christ, but also mixing late medieval practices with the biblical account.

Voragine provided two stories of contemporary miracles associated with Candlemas; both involve women, and perhaps 'women's issues'. The first recounted how a pious woman, having given away all of her possessions to the poor, found herself unable to attend Mass on 2 February, having literally nothing to wear. She was blessed with a vision of a procession of virgins, headed by a queen who may represent the Virgin Mary. During her dream she was given a candle and the opportunity to participate in the ritual but she refused to present her candle to the priest like the other women. She therefore wound up in a physical struggle with a messenger sent by the virgin queen to retrieve the candle until it broke into two pieces. She awoke abruptly holding the broken candle from her vision, which she saved as a relic, later finding that it had healing powers.[23] The second miracle story tells how a pregnant woman who had been plagued by dementia was restored to her senses by spending the entire day of the Feast of Mary's Purification in a church listening to the cycle of the office and Mass for the feast. The delusion she was suffering from involved her perception that her breasts were unable to retain the 'faith of Christ' which she believed she had literally clasped between them.[24] These accounts suggest that women were understood to have a particularly strong and embodied connection to the Virgin through the celebrations surrounding her ritual purification, an event that would have been common to the experience of all properly married childbearing women in fifteenth-century Europe.

CHURCHING OF WOMEN

Churching straddled the secular and ecclesiastical divide, essentially articulating the return of new mothers from the temporary authority of a female community headed by a midwife to the jurisdiction of male priests and the public life and work of the family. Susan Karant-Nunn and Paula Rieder have shown that although there was significant variation according to regional custom and liturgical use, churching ceremonies in both Catholic and Protestant areas were usually divided into three distinct parts: a procession of well-dressed women to the church; a ritual purification or blessing and offering in the church; and finally a communal meal in the home of the new family.[25]

To give a sense of an ideal, and perhaps exaggerated, expression of churching, I turn to an account of the churching of an English Queen, Elizabeth Woodville, as recounted in the published travel diary of a German visitor to London in 1465, Gabriel Tetzel. This narrative demonstrates the centrality of music to these rituals. First we hear about an elaborate procession, including at least three distinct musical ensembles, which I have italicised in the text.

> The Queen left her child-bed that morning and went to church in stately order: accompanied by many priests bearing relics and by many *scholars singing and carrying lights*. There followed a great company of ladies and maidens from the country and from London, who had been summoned. Then came a great company of *trumpeters, pipers, and players of stringed instruments*. The *king's choir followed, forty-two of them, who sang excellently*. Then came twenty-four heralds and pursuivants, followed by sixty counts

and knights. At last came the Queen escorted by two dukes. Above her was a canopy. Behind her were her mother and maidens and ladies to the number of sixty.[26]

After this Tetzel briefly mentions the ceremony, including the 'singing of an Office' followed by a procession back to the palace.[27] It seems likely that, as an outsider, the writer was not invited to attend the actual ceremony, which may have been a more private event reserved for the Queen, her sixty female attendants, and probably only a portion of the two hundred people mentioned as participating in the procession. Even if this description is exaggerated, it still indicates that music was central to both the procession and the service.

From Tetzel's account it seems that a queen might expect her churching to be its own separate service, a distinct event dedicated to her relatively private ceremony. For ordinary women, however, this ceremony and blessing was usually integrated into the weekly Mass on Sunday, publicly marking a woman's return to the normal activities of the family as well as preceding her sanctioned return to her husband's bed.[28] For her book on medieval purification in northern France, Rieder has surveyed a large number of *rituales* and practical manuals for secular clergy. Rieder shows that there were two main events for the woman:[29]

(1) *Ad introducendam mulierem in ecclesiam*
  (Introducing the woman into the church)
  – the woman was greeted at the North door by the priest
  – she was blessed, aspersed, and ritually led into the sanctuary by the priest
  – she was seated in a special section, usually close to the altar, for the Mass
(2) *De purificatione*
  (On the purification)
  – at the end of Mass she was called to the altar and blessed
  – the opening of the Gospel of John was read over the woman
  – the woman received the first piece the pain bénit (blessed bread), which was then distributed to everyone – the bread seems often to have been baked by the woman

The first, *Ad introducendam mulierem in ecclesiam*, involved the woman being greeted and aspersed with holy water at the church door before Mass. Rieder points out that this was often the North door, a special door associated with practices intended to thwart evil and sometimes referred to as the Devil's door. There is evidence for various local traditions about how the woman should be led into the church by the priest, often involving a special crossing of left (*sinistra*) and right (*dextra*) hands, believed to force unwanted spirits to flee; in some areas the woman was required to grasp the priest's stole rather than his hands.

During the celebration of Mass women being churched were often seated in a special pew. At the end of the service these women received a final blessing, *De purificatione*, during which they were again aspersed and the beginning of the Gospel of John was read over them. Finally, a woman being churched would receive the first piece of the *pain bénit*, a kind of blessed bread, which was then also distributed to the community, but not full communion. Rieder also notes that some manuals include a separate rite for women who were too ill to leave home, indicating again the importance of being churched to ensure salvation after death. Modern scholarship on purification has struggled with the complexity of meanings in these rituals.[30] While it contains aspects that affirm female roles and experiences and also showcase a woman or group of laywomen, the rite ultimately reinforces a patriarchal social order and focuses on an implicit belief in the impurity of childbearing women and their need to be cleansed before resuming their active role in the home and in public life.

To return for a moment to Elizabeth Woodville's churching, after the service, in the afternoon, there was an elaborate meal where the segregated groups finally mixed: 'Then all who had joined the procession remained to eat. They sat down, women and men, ecclesiastical and lay . . . and filled four great rooms . . . After the banquet they commenced to dance . . . After the dance the king's choristers entered and were ordered to sing.'[31] Although this account describes the practices of the royal court as recounted by a foreign traveller, it is nonetheless indicative of the centrality of music to an idealised celebration. The well-known illumination of the Virgin Mary's Purification from the sumptuous book of hours prepared for the Duke of Berry between 1411 and 1416 offers a sense of what an elite woman's churching procession might have looked like as it approached the local church, including the display of finery, the segregation of the participants into groups of women, men, and clergy, and the candle held prominently by the central female figure.[32] Contemporary accounts and spiritual writers, including Martin Luther, often attempted to censure the ostentatious displays of women of all social classes during churching. In his 'Sermon on Soberness and Moderation' from 1539 Luther said: "'Sober" means that we should not overload the body, and it applies to excess in outward gestures, clothing, ornament, or whatever kind of pomp it may be, such as we have at baptisms and the churching of women.'[33] It is likely that for aspiring women of the middle class, the excessive display of fine clothes would be complemented by equally fine music.

ILLUMINATING THE SOUNDSCAPE OF CHURCHING RITUALS: THE MARIAN SEQUENCE *INVIOLATA, INTEGRA ET CASTA*

Despite the fact that music resounded through the sacred space of the church, and also in the streets and homes of lay people, during their churching celebrations, modern scholarship remains silent about the soundscape of these rituals.[34] I argue that while noble women might hire 'scholars' to sing while carrying candles, groups of laywomen could themselves sing repetitive processional chants and spiritual songs or simple polyphony like *laude*. While there is a body of plainchant associated with regular church services, it seems likely that for an important life event, couples of means would provide funds for the performance of special polyphony, consisting of motets and Mass settings. And, finally, appropriately themed vocal and instrumental music was certainly performed at the communal meal. While much of this might have been secular and perhaps even bawdy in nature, there is no reason that some of it might not have been related to the liturgical events of the day.[35] Like the sweet smoke of the blessed candles burning in birthing chambers and winding through the streets, I believe that the chants associated with the feast of Mary's Purification were used to extend the sacred space of the church into the homes and lives of early modern laywomen during these moments of great danger and great joy.

As noted above, the piece of plainchant that constitutes the strongest connection with churching is the sequence *Inviolata, integra et casta es Maria*, shown in Figure 8.1. The melody of the *Inviolata* sequence developed in the eleventh century and was set to the current text in the twelfth.[36] The most stable version is extant in at least forty late medieval sources, including manuscripts and prints used by both monastic and secular clergy.[37] This piece is a prosa or sequence, a chant genre most often associated with the Alleluia, but also used in other places within and outside of the liturgy.[38] It seems to have been derived from the end

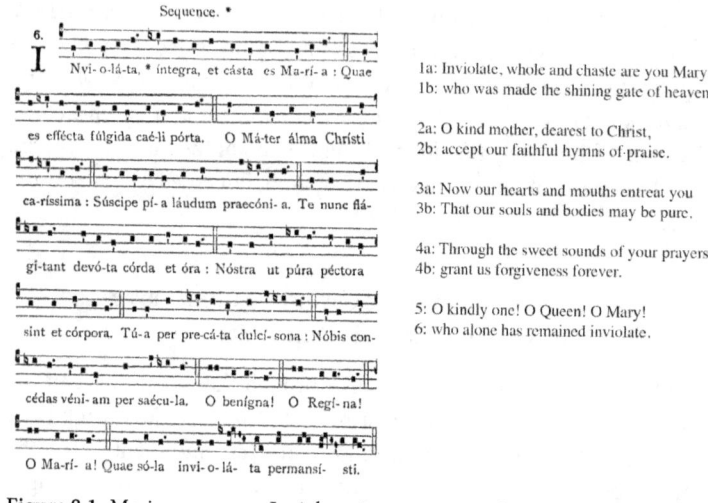

Figure 8.1 Marian sequence *Inviolata, integra et casta* from the *Liber usualis* (1961), 1861–62.

of the responsory chant *Gaude Maria*.[39] In its oldest extant musical source, a twelfth-century monastic antiphoner from Saint-Maur-des-Fossés, it can be seen scribbled into the space above an older set of words used for the same tune, following the *Gaude Maria*.[40] In most of the sources it is assigned to the Feast of Mary's Purification, but in a few it was also associated with other Marian festivals. While most sequences were removed from use after the Counter Reformation, this chant is retained in a special section of votive Marian music in the modern *Liber usualis*, indicating its popularity and cultural significance. But most importantly for our purposes, it was employed for the blessing of candles by c.1500.[41]

As a sequence, the *Inviolata* has a musical and textual form called double versicle, which means that each pair of lines uses a distinct poetic structure. Each line of the pair is set to the same musical phrase, resulting in direct musical repetition. This pattern is broken after the fourth pair of lines, which is followed by a trio of invocations of the Virgin Mary (line 5), emphasised by 'O'. This trio of laudatory titles introduces the final line, which features a textual and musical quotation from the *Gaude Maria* responsory – 'inviolata permansisti'. The emphasis both on Mary's role as a mother and on the desire of devotees for purity in soul and body would have made this chant an ideal musical embellishment for churching events.

As a simple *prosa* that was regularly carried beyond the boundaries of the church in Marian processions, the *Inviolata* would have been part of the shared memorial archive of music known by both clerical and lay people. Although Voragine does not cite the names of any specific pieces, this is a 'hymn' appropriate to be sung during Candlemas processions. The repetitive melody and narrow vocal range indicate that it could easily have been memorised and sung by people without any formal musical training. As such it would have been ideal music for groups of laywomen enacting their own purification, in emulation of the Virgin Mary. As in the performance of this same chant recorded by the amateur Spanish ensemble *Polifónica Turolense*, sixteenth-century women might have alternated singing lines as solos.[42] The fact that at least one printed setting of the *Inviolata* features only every other phrase of the chant in simple polyphony around the basic tune, indicates that there might also have been a tradition of *alternatim* performance, common for well-known hymns and sequences, where singers alternated phrases of plainchant with improvised polyphony based on the pre-existent melody.

I have found fifty different polyphonic settings of the *Inviolata* from the late fifteenth and early sixteenth centuries, making it among the most popular tunes for polyphonic setting in the Renaissance. The one hundred sources for these pieces are distributed over a hundred-year period from the 1470s to the 1580s, with a clear peak around 1540, as shown in Figure 8.2.

The large number of pieces based on this tune indicates that the *Inviolata* was appropriate for use more often than just at Candlemas, a single feast of the church calendar. In addition, I have discovered that at least twelve of the sources (eight manuscripts and four prints) include two different settings, and the Leiden manuscript has three (see Table 8.1).

It is striking that so many sources, including the widely distributed motet anthologies of Petrucci and Rhau, found it felicitous to include multiple settings of the same chant. In Rhau's anthology two simple anonymous settings are separated by only one piece, which is also based on a Marian plainchant for the closely related feast of the Nativity of Christ.

The generic division of this repertoire would make it appropriate for both the sacred and secular aspects of churching celebrations. These

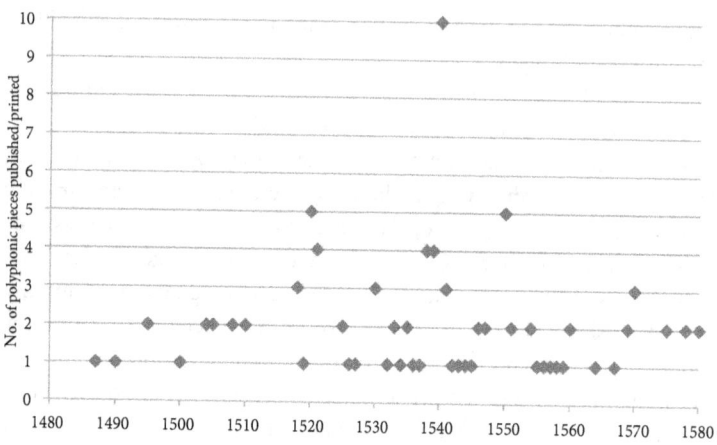

Figure 8.2 Distribution of one hundred sources of polyphonic pieces based on the *Inviolata* chant.

settings range from large-scale polyphonic masses and grand motets for up to twelve voices, like the one that is transmitted in three German sources from c.1540, to simple chant elaborations like the anonymous setting in Petrucci's *Motetti libro 4*. As Figure 8.3 shows, the vast majority of these settings are motets, a genre that was appropriate for use in a variety of sacred and secular contexts and the most common genre for musical commemoration of important events, including many occasional motets written for individuals.

The many simple anonymous, *cantus firmus*-based motets would make excellent adornments sung by a choir of clerics or school boys as special music for an ordinary Sunday service that also included a churching ceremony. There are more challenging settings for more advanced ensembles with a variety of lengths, like Josquin's beautiful motet for five voices, which states the entire melody in canon between the tenor and alto, but reduces the time interval of imitation in each section.[43] A polyphonic Mass, like the one Palestrina published in 1567, could constitute a more appropriate choice in the case where a prominent citizen capable of making a more substantial donation was being churched. In both cases, the highly recognisable melody, which many lay people sang in processions on Candlemas, would have resonated with the new mother, her husband, and the community gathering around to see her dressed in her finery, having survived childbirth and contributed to her

Date	Location and source ID or title and printer.	No.	Type
c.1525	Copenhagen. Det Kongelige Bibliotek. MS Ny Kongelige Samling 1848, 2	2	MS
1537–44	Berlin. MS XX. HA StUB Königsberg Nr. 7	2	MS
c.1540	Bologna. Civico Museo Bibliografico Musicale. MS Q27	2	MS
c.1540	Casale Monferrato. Archivo e Biblioteca Capitolare, Duomo. MS D(F)	2	MS
c.1540–60	Leiden. Gemeentearchief. Archieven van de Kerken. MS 1442	3	MS
1569–78	Regensburg. Bischöfliche Zentralbibliothek. MS A.R. 786–837	2	MS
c.1570–75	Treviso. Biblioteca Capitolare del Duomo. MS 29	2	MS
c.1583	Munich. Mayerische Staatsbibliothek Musiksammlung, Musica MS 1536	2	MS
1505	Venice. Petrucci's *Motetti libro 4*	2	P
1547	Valladolid. Valderrábano's *Libro de musica de vihuela intitulado Silva*	2	P
1538	Wittenberg. Rhau's *Symphoniae iucundae atque adeo breves quatuor vocum*	2	P
1578	Madrid. Cabezón's *Obras de musica para tecla arpa y vihuela*	2	P

Table 8.1 Sources with more than one *Inviolata* setting.

family's hopes for status and longevity. Rieder has shown that during the late medieval period there was a significant push from the clergy to limit churching to properly married women, as part of a general movement by the clergy to regulate marriage and reproduction.[44] Both of these ceremonies involved substantial fees, an issue that became even more explicit in Protestant discourse, where fee structures had to be redefined and justified.

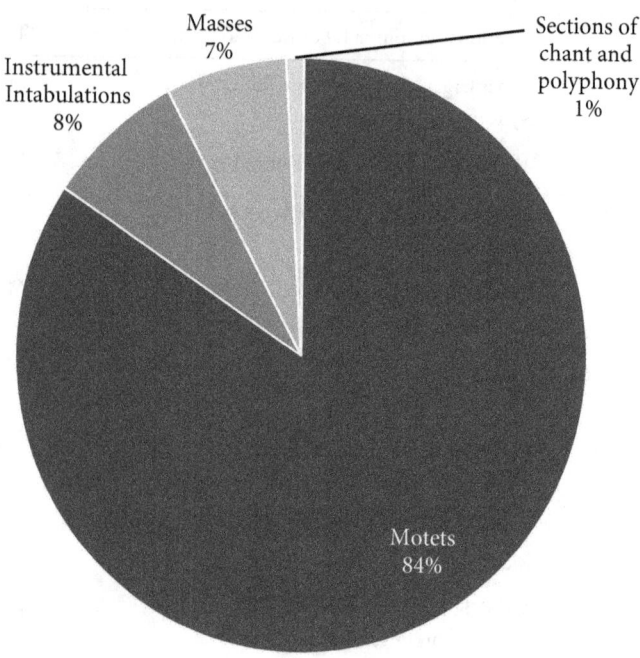

Figure 8.3 Generic division of *Inviolata* settings.

We do not have to look far to find music for the final element of a churching celebration – the communal meal, also known as the gossips' feast.[45] Josquin's motet is included in the motet anthology, *Novum et insigne opus musicum,* printed by the firm Berg & Neuber in Nuremberg in 1558. As the prefaces to the motet anthologies of Berg & Neuber clearly state, Josquin's motet, like the rest of the motets in the anthology, would have been appropriate for performance by ambitious amateurs singing around the table after a festive meal.[46] A woman's churching would make an excellent excuse for bringing friends together to take on this stimulating piece. It is clear that instrumental music was appropriate for feasting and we have multiple intabulations of the *Inviolata* by musicians such as Cabezón and Valderrábano.[47] Hans Gerle even arranged and printed an intabulation of Josquin's famous motet for lute in Nuremberg in 1533. At the beginning of Gerle's arrangement the chant tune is clearly audible, as are, a little later, the long descending lines that are distinctive features of Josquin's motet.[48] Of the sources that include two different *Inviolata* settings, two are printed volumes of intabulations, suggestive of a range of practices for arranging settings of this tune for a variety of instruments and perhaps of improvisation as well.

EVOKING FEMALE EXPERIENCE AND FEMALE VOICES IN POLYPHONY

It is often difficult to connect women to polyphony because the best-documented venues for performance of polyphony were within churches and monasteries, where most of the singers, in both Catholic and Protestant areas, were men and boys. Recent research has expanded our understanding of the musical world of female monastics, but I propose that the *Inviolata* enhances our understanding of how a specific musical repertoire was integral to the experience of laywomen in their social role as wives and mothers, and also as sisters and friends.[49] Some of these pieces are among the most famous and widely distributed compositions of the era, such as Josquin's five-voice motet, transmitted in over thirty different sources, while others are without composer ascription and survive in a single source.[50] It is of course clear that there are inter- and intra-musical or structural reasons that the *Inviolata* chant appealed to composers. This broad range of compositional activity, however, is indicative of a significant need for a large number of different musical settings of this particular chant with a spectrum of lengths and difficulties. Churching, which probably happened on an almost weekly basis in parish churches, is a good candidate for such an event, especially when these rituals are understood as closely related to the chant's liturgical source, Candlemas, or the ritual commemoration of Mary's Purification.

Although polyphonic music in the church was performed by men and choirboys, I propose that the *Inviolata* settings provide a rare opportunity to study affective representations of female experience and femininity that would have been accessible to women. The link with women is audible in some of these settings. The anonymous setting from Petrucci's *Motetti C* features the *Inviolata* as a *cantus firmus* primarily in the soprano, a fairly rare feature in motets of this time. If you compare the soprano voice part from the original print with the melodic outline of the sequence in Figure 8.4, you can see that the composer set the sequence tune in longer and more regular note values than the other voices. The tune is made audible in this way in the soprano in fully half of the twelve sections of this motet.

MATERIAL CONVERSIONS

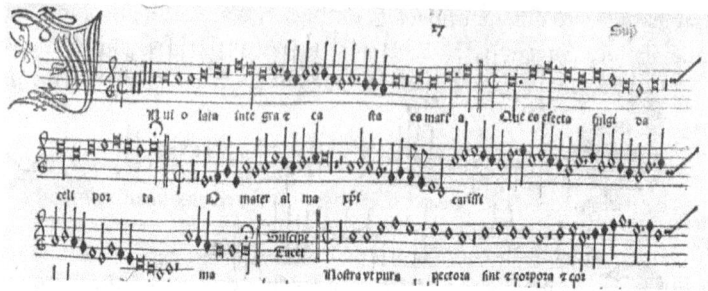

Figure 8.4 *Inviolata* in the soprano part from an anonymous setting in Petrucci's *Motetti C* (Venice, 1504).

While the high register of this *cantus firmus* could be evidence of a generic link to *alternatim* hymn paraphrase and simple polyphony, the tessitura might also represent the sound of women singing. Although women were not part of the church choirs, their voices were appropriate for processions like those on Candlemas and also those for their own churching. Thus, even when sung by young boys during a Mass, the associations of this chant with processions would evoke the sound of women's voices. I have found two other settings that place the *Inviolata* chant in the top voice, an anonymous piece for twelve voices and a setting by Ghiselin, shown in Table 8.2.[51]

Like the setting from *Motetti C* in Figure 8.5, the anonymous motet for twelve voices regularly places the *Inviolata* melody in the highest voice in even note values of longer durations than the other voice parts, making it both suggestive of a female voice and easily audible.[52] In addition to placing the *cantus firmus* at the top of the texture, in his setting Ghiselin supports it with three lines in ranges most comfortable for female voices, an extremely rare voicing for motets during this period. Regardless of whether this setting was performed by choirboys, was transposed down for performance by a male ensemble, or was actually performed by women, setting the *Inviolata* in high clefs signifies the sound of female voices and experiences through the chant's association with purification, churching rituals, and childbirth.

PROTESTANT RE-WORKINGS AND THE RE-EMERGENCE OF CHURCHING

One of the particularly surprising features of this repertoire is that, despite the social and religious turmoil of the early Reformation, and

Composer	Sources	Remarks
Anon.	*Motetti C* (Venice: Petrucci, 1504)	–12 sections –features the tune in the soprano in 6 sections
Ghiselin	*Motetti libro 4* (Venice: Petrucci, 1505)	–features the tune in the soprano throughout –three lower voices are also in high register
Anon.	CopKB 1872, copied at Lyon *c*. 1525 KasL 38, copied in Kassel *c*. 1535 *Tschudi Liederbuch*, copied in Switzerland *c*. 1540	–for 12 voices –regularly features the tune in the soprano

Table 8.2 Settings of the *Inviolata* featuring the tune in a high register.

Figure 8.5 Josquin's *Inviolata a 5*, Tenor from Berg & Neuber, *Novum et insigne opus musicum* (1558–59).

anxieties in Protestant areas about the excessive Marian devotions of late medieval Catholicism, print and manuscript sources for *Inviolata* settings exist in both Catholic and Protestant areas, regularly crossing the confessional divide. Some of these feature altered texts, which demonstrate a common Protestant re-interpretation of Mary as a more docile, subdued figure, often referred to as the *Hausmutter*.[53] If we look at the music for the opening of Josquin's famous motet in the tenor partbook of Berg & Neuber's print, shown in Figure 8.5, we notice a textual alteration from the original chant in the second staff, where an appeal to 'Christ the Son of God' is substituted for a plea to his mother, 'O kind mother, dearest to Christ'. Comparing the Protestant version of the text with the original prayer reveals a marked reduction of Mary's role in redemption.

PROTESTANT TEXT FROM BERG & NEUBER (1558–59)	ORIGINAL CHANT TEXT
1a: *Inviolate, whole and chaste are you Mary:*	
1b: *you who have become Christ's beautiful mother.*	1b: who was made the shining gate of heaven.
2a: *O Christ, son of God and a virgin,*	2a: O kind mother, dearest to Christ,
2b: *accept our faithful hymns of praise.*	
3a: *We ask of you with devout hearts and mouths*	3a: Now our hearts and mouths entreat you
3b: *that our souls and bodies may be pure.*	
4a: *Despite our sins against you,*	4a: Through the sweet sounds of your prayers
4b: *grant us forgiveness forever.*	
5: *O Christ the King, O redeemer, O victim,*	5: O kindly one! O Queen! O Mary!
6: *who has paid for all the sins of the world.*	6: who alone has remained inviolate.

This new text originated in the second volume of a motet anthology series issued by another Nuremberg printing firm in 1539.[54] Lines 2a, 4a, 5, and 6 are all Marian prayer requests redirected towards Christ, while line 1b seems intended to emphasise Mary's role as an earthly mother.[55] The powerful prayers and praises of the final lines, 'O benigna, O regina, O Maria!' have become 'O rex Christe, O redemptor, O victima!' If one is familiar with the original version of this powerful motet, one can imagine the sonic and emotional impact of altering the ardent requests of this final homophonic section, especially for someone who was familiar with the original chant and its associations.[56] It is notable that one of the manuscript sources that was copied from the same exemplar, the anthology printed by Grapheus, restored the original text of the sequence, indicating the endurance of the *Inviolata* as a musical-textual unit.[57]

Overall, while the alterations in Berg & Neuber's print redirect the appeals of this text to Christ, the result is actually an accentuation of

Mary's maternal role. The new text does not obscure the emphasis on purification at all, perhaps making it even more appropriate for early modern churching rituals.[58] Although early reformers initially suppressed churching, it was quickly restored in most areas in response to complaints that women were dying because they were being made to return to work too soon after childbirth.[59] Andreas Hohndorff's calendar expresses a typical mid-century Lutheran view of churching. He states that: 'Although in the New Testament the Law of Moses concerning the purification of the post-parturient woman is repealed . . . still natural decency, the need of the woman lying in to return to bodily strength and health and the warm love of the married couple . . . requires that the husband spare his wife with hard work for six weeks, and looks after her more with drink and food.'[60]

Women's churching rituals suggest multiple registers of conversion over the course of the late fifteenth through the early seventeenth centuries – the ritual transformation of a woman from a girl to a mother (at least at a first churching) and from unclean to blessed, the change from a state of darkness to light through blessed candles, and the alteration of chant-based compositions from Catholic to Protestant use involving a conversion from a female to a male deity (Mary to Christ). Examination of the fifty settings of the *Inviolata* sequence and their cultural contexts provides vital information about the soundscape of women's devotions and rituals and also reveals ways in which the fundamental issues of gender and faith were expressed by early modern women and men and regulated by church authorities. While a greater consideration of the ritual use of candles illuminates the shadowy and neglected lives of early modern laywomen, so, too, their association with the *Inviolata* chant and its polyphonic settings reinvigorates the early modern soundscape with the voices of laywomen.

Although women's voices are generally overlooked as part of early modern church services they were clearly present and at times intrusive. Karant-Nunn cites an early-seventeenth-century visitation record from Nassau-Saarbrücken that specifically enquires whether women were regularly arriving late for their churching in the middle of the sermon, disrupting the male preacher with their physical entrance into the church, and, it is implied, also with their chatting.[61] Like the high vocal register evoked in the *Inviolata* motets in Table 8.2, these female voices interrupted the male-dominated soundscape of public rituals and religious life. Assessed through the lenses of churching and blessed candles, these compositions, texts, and musical sources reveal evidence for the ways laywomen negotiated the rapidly changing cultural and societal expectations of early modernity and the centrality of music to their identity as a community of wives, midwives, and mothers, and also of sisters, companions, and friends.

NOTES

1 In some literature, including the poem by Robert Herrick quoted in footnote 35 below, it is viewed as another wedding night.
2 Paula Rieder, *On the purification of women: churching in northern France, 1100–1500* (New York: Palgrave Macmillan, 2006), pp. 41–2.
3 The only discussion of music and churching is Sue Niebrzydowski's brief article on the chanted soundscape of the churching ceremony, but she deals primarily with the texts and does not engage with the chant tones, melodies, or polyphony. '*Asperges me, Domine, hyssopo*: male voices, female interpretation and the medieval English purification of women after childbirth ceremony', *Early Music*, 39 (2011), 327–33. For recent studies of soundscapes see Alexander Fisher, *Music, piety and propaganda: the soundscape of Counter-Reformation Bavaria* (Oxford: Oxford University Press, 2014); and Giovanni Zanovello, '"In the Church and in the Chapel": music and devotional spaces in the Florentine church of Santissima Annunziata', *Journal of the American Musicological Society*, 67 (2014), 379–428.
4 See Jacques Gélis, *History of childbirth: fertility, pregnancy, and birth in early modern Europe*, trans. Rosemary Morris (Cambridge: Polity Press, 1991); Jacqueline Musacchio, *The art and ritual of childbirth in Renaissance Italy* (New Haven, CT: Yale University Press, 1999).
5 Martin Luther, *D. Martin Luthers sämtliche Werke*, ed. E. L. Enders, 26 vols, 2nd edn (Erlangen and Frankfurt: Heyder and Zimmer, 1862–85), XX.84.
6 Merry E. Wiesner, 'Luther and women: the death of two Marys', in J. Obelkevich and Lyndal Roper (eds), *Disciplines of faith: studies in religion, politics and patriarchy* (London: Routledge & Kegan Paul, 1987), pp. 295–308.
7 There are accounts of women's bodies being churched after death to allow them burial within the churchyard. On midwives administering emergency baptism see Kathryn Taglia, 'Delivering a Christian identity: midwives in northern French synodal legislation, c. 1200–1500', in Peter Biller and Joseph Ziegler (eds), *Religion and medicine in the Middle Ages* (York: York Medieval Press, 2001), pp. 77–90.
8 Adolph Franz, *Die kirchlichen Benediktionen im Mittelalter*, 2 vols. (Freiburg im Breisgau: Herder, 1909), II.214.

9 See Joan Wallach Scott, *Gender and the Politics of History* (New York: Columbia University Press, 1999), esp. Introduction.
10 Bodleian Library MS. Douce 5, fol. 1ᵛ.
11 Eamon Duffy, *The stripping of the altars: traditional religion in England. c. 1400–c. 1580*, 2nd edn (New Haven, CT: Yale University Press, 2005), pp. 16–17; and Robert Scribner, 'The impact of the Reformation on daily life', in Lyndal Roper (ed.), *Religion and culture in Germany (1400–1800)* (Leiden: Brill, 2001), p. 292.
12 For an example of a polyphonic motet based on the tune, listen to the anonymous setting on *Eternal music of the Sistine Chapel*, performed by De Labyrintho, dir. by Walter Testolin, 2008 (Berlin Classics: B0012RW6EI). This motet is for twelve voices and features the *Inviolata* tune as a *cantus firmus*, meaning as a melody in one of the voices in regular note values. The tune is especially audible at the very beginning in the highest sounding voice.
13 Scribner, 'The impact of the Reformation', 291.
14 Luke 2:22, *Douay-Rheims and Latin Vulgate Online*, 2001–2013, web, http://www.drbo.org.
15 Bridget Heal, *The cult of the Virgin Mary in early modern Germany: Protestant and Catholic piety, 1500–1648* (Cambridge: Cambridge University Press, 2007), pp. 84–6.
16 Other examples I have found in the collection of the Bodleian Library include a Franciscan Missal (MS. Douce 313), fol. 257ᵛ; and two Flemish psalter calendars (MS. Douce 49), fol. 4ᵛ; and (MS. Auct. D. 4. 2), fol. 4.
17 Jacobus de Voragine, *The golden legend: readings on the saints*, vol. 1, trans. William Granger Ryan (Princeton: Princeton University Press, 1993), pp. 147–8.
18 This painting is in a private collection but a high-quality version, usually titled 'Presentation at the Temple', is viewable online through the Frick Collection (http://images.frick.org/). It can be found within the Image Archive in the collection of Library Negatives as record W1244. A colour version is also available on WikiGallery.
19 Dorothy C. Shorr, 'The iconographical development of the presentation in the Temple', *The Art Bulletin*, 28 (1946), 17.
20 Rieder gives some excellent statistics showing the connection between churching and purification images. *On the purification of women*, pp. 124–7.
21 Salome lost her hand when she doubted and checked the status of Mary's postpartum virginity. For the story of Salome, see Edgar Hennecke, *New Testament Apocrypha*, ed. Wilhelm Schneemelcher, trans. R McL. Wilson, 2 vols (Philadelphia: Westminster Press, 1963) I.383–85; or Voragine's version, *Golden legend*, trans. Ryan, vol. 1 (1993), p. 38.
22 Voragine, *Golden Legend*, I (1993), p. 149.

23 *Ibid.*, pp. 150-1.
24 *Ibid.*, p. 151.
25 Susan Karant-Nunn, *The reformation of ritual: an interpretation of early modern Germany* (London: Routledge, 1997); Rieder, *On the purification of women*.
26 Gabriel Tetzel, *The travels of Leo of Rozmital through Germany, Flanders, England, France, Spain, Portugal, and Italy, 1465-1467*, ed. and trans Malcolm Letts (Cambridge: Cambridge University Press, 1957), pp. 45-6.
27 *Ibid.*, p. 46.
28 Rieder, *On the purification of women*, pp. 81-103.
29 *Ibid.*, pp. 85-94.
30 Karant-Nunn provides an excellent summary of the various approaches in her chapter on churching in *The reformation of ritual*. Also notable is Adrian Wilson's chapter on the English ceremony, 'The ceremony of childbirth and its interpretation', in Valerie Fildes and Dorothy McLaren (eds), *Women as mothers in pre-industrial society* (London: Routledge, 1990), pp. 68-107.
31 Tetzel, *Travels*, p. 48.
32 This illumination decorates the office of Nones in the Hours of the Virgin, on fol. 54^v. This image is reproduced in many sources including online in Artstor (http://www.artstor.org/). The figure carrying the candle is not Mary, but perhaps her midwife, Salome.
33 This sermon was printed in Augsburg in 1542. *Luther's Works* (1955-), LI: 296.
34 The exception is Sue Niebrzydowski, see footnote 3 above.
35 Bawdiness is certainly suggested in the poem by Robert Herrick, 'Julia's churching, or purification' which after describing the churching ceremony, includes the lines 'All rites well ended, with faire Auspice come . . . home; / Where ceremonious Hymen shall for thee / Provide a second Epithalamie. / She who keeps chastely to her husband side . . . / Brings him not one, but many a Maiden-head.' In *The complete poetry of Robert Herrick*, ed. J. Max Patrick (New York: New York University Press, 1963), p. 377.
36 Clemens Blume, '*Inviolata*, der älteste Marien-tropus im brevier. Geschichte des textes und der melodie', *Die Kirchen musik*, 9 (1908), 41-8; and Peter Wagner, *Einführung in die gregorianische melodien: ein handbuch der choralwissenshaft*, 2 vols (Fribourg: Universitätsbuchhandlung, 1895), I.293.
37 Blume, '*Inviolata*', p. 64. The *Cantus* database has entries for twenty-five sources: http://cantus.uwaterloo.ca/. See also Marie Louise Göllner, '*Praeter rerum seriem*: its history and sources', in Wolfgang Osthoff, Frank Heidlberger, and Reinhard Wiesend (eds), *Von Isaac bis Bach—studien zur älteren deutschen musikgeschichte: festschrift Martin Just zum 60. Geburtstag* (Kassel: Bärenreiter, 1991), pp. 41-51.

38 For more information on sequences see Richard L. Crocker, *The early medieval sequence* (Berkeley: University of California Press, 1977); and David Hiley, *Western plainchant: a handbook* (Oxford: Clarendon Press, 1993).
39 Blume, 'Inviolata', p. 64.
40 http://gallica.bnf.fr/ark:/12148/btv1b6000531z/f117.image.
41 *Liber usualis*, ed. by the Benedictines of Solesmes (Tournai: Desclee Company, 1961), 1861–62. This was specified in a printed Missal from Troyes. See Göllner, 'Praeter rerum seriem', p. 50, n. 10.
42 This track is available for purchase or preview at: http://www.amazon.com/Inviolata/dp/B00R9WFD9K. It comes from the album *Musica gregoriana*, perf. Polifónica Turolense (Classic Records Gold, 2014).
43 For an excellent recording, listen to Josquin des Prez, 'Inviolata a 5', tracks 25–7 on *Josquin: Missa de beata Virgine et motets à la Vierge*, performed by A Sei Voci (Astrée 8560, 1995).
44 Rieder, *On the purification of women*, pp. 39–59.
45 For more on the 'gossips' feast' in English practice see David Cressy, 'Purification, thanksgiving and the churching of women in post-Reformation England', *Past & Present*, 141 (1993), 106–46.
46 Facsimile available as vols. 27–9 of *Renaissance music in facsimile*, ed. Howard Mayer Brown, et al., 50 vols (New York: Garland Publishing, 1986–88). Extant copies show that these anthologies were owned by Latin schools and citizens alike, indicating that they were used both in church and at home.
47 Valderrábano's *Libro de musica de vihuela intitulado Silva* (Valladolid, 1547); and Cabezón's *Obras de musica para tecla arpa y vihuela* (Madrid, 1570).
48 For Ron Andrico's excellent performance of Gerle's intabulation of Josquin's *Inviolata* a 5, listen to *Harmonia caelestis: 16th-century motets for voice and lute*, Duo Mignarda (2010).
49 On the musical lives of female monastics, see Anne Bagnall Yardley, *Performing piety: musical cultures in medieval English nunneries* (New York: Palgrave Macmillan, 2006); and Craig Monson, *Disembodied voices: music and culture in an early modern Italian convent* (Berkeley: University of California Press, 1995).
50 Stephen Rice discusses the connections between four later compositions which based their settings of the *Inviolata* on the remarkable *cantus firmus* of Josquin's famous five-voice motet. 'Resonances of Josquin in later *Inviolata* settings', in Katelijne Schiltz and Bonnie J. Blackburn (eds), *Canons and canonic techniques, 14th–16th centuries: theory, practice, and reception history* (Leuven: Peeters, 2007), pp. 197–220.
51 I have not yet been able to study the music for all of the settings, since many are not transcribed or reproduced in modern facsimiles, so it is possible that there are more that use this technique.

52 See footnote 12.
53 Beth Kreitzer, *Reforming Mary: changing images of the Virgin Mary in Lutheran sermons of the sixteenth century* (Oxford: Oxford University Press, 2004); and Donna Spivey Ellington, 'Impassioned mother or passive icon: the Virgin's role in late medieval and early modern Passion sermons', *Renaissance Quarterly*, 48 (1995), 227–61.
54 *Secundus tomus novi operis musici, sex, quinque et quatuor vocum...* (Nuremberg, 1538). The repertoire and format of the anthologies of Berg & Neuber are heavily dependent on those of Grapheus.
55 Line 3a seems to be an improvement on the grammar of the original, rather than a change in meaning.
56 To hear this listen to the transition between track 26 and 27 on the recording by A Sei Voci in footnote 43 above.
57 The source is a single *altus* book from a set of partbooks, Munich, Bibliothek der Ludwig-Maximilians-Universität, Mss. 8° 326, available at http://epub.ub.uni-muenchen.de/12048/1/Cim._44b-1.pdf. The *Inviolata* is on fol. 5'–6. For the stemmatic filiation of the sources see William Elders' commentary to vol. 24 of the *New Josquin Edition*, ed. Elders (Utrecht: Koninklijke vereniging voor nederlandse muziekgeschiedenis, 2007), p. 62.
58 The fact that Lutheran pastors often had to assert the official view that women are not unclean after childbirth may indicate that this belief was not widely held by the populace.
59 Quoted by Scribner as being in 1528, 'The impact of the Reformation', pp. 290–1.
60 Andreas Hohndorff, *Calendarium sanctorum & historiarum* (1587), p. 74.
61 See Karant-Nunn, *Reformation of Ritual*, p. 229, n. 47.

Part III: Travel, race, and conversion

9

Narrating women's Catholic conversions in seventeenth-century Vietnam

Keith P. Luria

In 1634, a recently deceased Christian woman appeared on a mountaintop in a globe of fire. Her neighbour, also a Christian woman, quickly reported the apparition to the Jesuit missionary Alexandre de Rhodes. The witness told the missionary that the deceased had complained bitterly about her family not doing enough to help her in her misery. The Jesuit said masses for her, and once he had done so, she made no further appearances.[1] The vision occurred in Vietnam, but readers of de Rhodes's account in Europe would have quickly understood its significance.[2] They knew the dead could appear to the living to plead for assistance in gaining release from purgatory. The apparition and the success of the masses the Jesuit said would have confirmed their belief in the doctrine of purgatory, which was under Protestant attack. But if those European readers were imbued with the spirituality of the Catholic Reformation, then their response might have been cautious and ambivalent. The vision was of a woman who appeared to another woman. The Catholic Reformation church did not reject apparitions of women or women visionaries. However, proper ecclesiastical control had to be exercised, since the church increasingly found supernatural events involving women suspicious. What is more, both the woman who appeared in the vision and the one who saw her were Vietnamese converts to Catholicism. Could European readers willingly accept that they were true Catholics, firm in their new faith, and clear in their understanding of proper doctrine? Or was the vision evidence that such converts were still attached to their traditional, and for Europeans, 'false' religion?

Such uncertainties could arise not because the mission accounts singled out women converts; they celebrated male neophytes just as much. Rather, it is the specific roles that some Vietnamese Christian women played in the reports, namely as miracle workers, which would have provoked suspicion. Many of the women converts the accounts describe, though from an exotic land, would have looked perfectly recognisable and acceptable to European Catholic readers. They were important leaders and protectors of Catholic evangelising efforts, pious wives or celibates zealously guarding their chastity. Each exemplified a different aspect of the Catholic Reformation's views of proper female piety.

The Catholic Reformation church acclaimed pious women who fulfilled specific roles in its devotional life. Chief among them were women who followed a celibate life, and the church worked to enforce their strict enclosure in religious houses.[3] But it also depended on others who promoted the Catholic cause outside convent walls. It valued more than ever before the pious lives of women (and men) within marriage. And it relied on women of elite families to advocate new forms of devotion, patronise and finance new religious orders or communities, and serve as spiritual examples to men as well as other women.[4] When Europeans read mission accounts of heroic Vietnamese mandarin women who protected the missionaries, or wives who, along with their husbands, undertook charitable works and risked persecution, they could recognise them as pious figures, fully in accord with church attitudes about women. Despite the cultural differences that separated them from the Vietnamese, they could feel a bond with them, and perhaps overcome whatever doubts they might have about whether people so different from themselves could ever be true Catholics. And when Vietnamese women risked the anger of their families and powerful men to resist marriage and remain chaste, Europeans could see their piety as truly heroic.

But recognition and acceptance became more complicated when the mission accounts turned to other types of holy women, miracle workers and visionaries, especially those who had been possessed by demons. Europeans were well acquainted with holy women – mystic nuns, lay beatas, ecstatic visionaries – 'living saints', whom the faithful perceived as having a special relationship with divine power that allowed them to petition God for miracles.[5] The church did not reject them; indeed, they were religious figures of great importance. But the church was always suspicious of them, in part because their individual relationship with the divine threatened to bypass the clergy's supervision and control, but also because of the fear that the power these women had came not from God but from the devil. And the clergy believed women to be even more vulnerable to demonic influence than men. Each case required an assessment, with increasingly elaborate procedures, to ascertain if the woman was truly holy or under the devil's influence. When overseas missionaries made such determinations, the issue was even more complicated. They saw their work as primarily a battle against the devil. The people who followed 'false religions' were subjected to the devil. The clergies of these religions, for example, Vietnamese Buddhist monks, served as the devil's instruments in maintaining people in subjection, but women were particularly susceptible to the devil's control.

Moreover, when women played important roles in local religious life, as was the case in Vietnam, they were even more suspect of being in thrall to the devil. The evangelisers' battles with demons for these women were fierce, but victory was especially rewarding. Or at least it was if the missionaries could convince their readers that when such women were baptised, their conversions were sincere and their new Catholic faith was profound. And to do that, the miraculous had to defeat the demonic. If a convert worked a healing deemed miraculous, then the depth of her Christianisation was clear. If she had a truly divine vision, then God's favour was evident for all to see.[6] Mission accounts had to show these results. However, could they do so convincingly? After all, the apparition of the deceased woman in the globe of fire could demonstrate the truth of purgatory, but it could also remind her living relatives of the veneration the Vietnamese traditionally owed their ancestors. The missionaries' task was to convince their readers that their converts' extraordinary experiences revealed Catholic truth, not demonic deceptions.

THE VIETNAM MISSION

Vietnam in the seventeenth century was, in principle, a kingdom united under the rule of emperors of the Lê dynasty, but it was actually divided into two polities: the north, known to Europeans as Tonkin, under the control of the Trinh clan, and the south, known as Cochinchina, ruled by the Nguyen.[7] The two kingdoms were often at war during the seventeenth century. Jesuits undertook the first sustained Catholic mission in Vietnam, arriving in Cochinchina in 1615. They started in Tonkin in 1626.[8] Because missionary orders in Asia operated under the Portuguese *padroado* system, their reception in Tonkin and Cochinchina often depended on the state of relations between the Portuguese and local rulers, who wanted military alliances with the Europeans. In the seventeenth century, periods when Christian evangelisation was tolerated alternated with periods of fierce persecution, during which the missionaries were arrested, went into hiding, or were expelled. Their followers risked imprisonment, torture, mutilation, and death.

Still, for the Jesuit missionaries Vietnam was an unquestionable success story, which they described in their letters to Rome and in a rich collection of publications about the mission. In Europe, the 'annual letters' far-flung Jesuit missionaries sent home were edited and issued in letterbooks.[9] In addition, missionaries composed other works, usually titled 'Relations' or 'Histories', which recounted their overseas endeavours, sometimes combined with descriptions of the exotic countries in which they worked. It is these sources I have relied on here. To judge from the number of letterbooks, relations, and histories published and their widespread distribution, the European audience for the accounts of overseas missions was large.

That audience included, first, their fellow Jesuits. Part of the purpose of missionary reports of all sorts was to glorify the society's accomplishments and inspire other Jesuits to take up the missionary calling. Beyond members of their own order and other Catholic clerics, the missionary texts attracted devout lay readers. The stories missionaries told reaffirmed the readers' faith by offering them compelling exemplary tales of the piety and courage of evangelisers and foreign converts, and they helped build a sense of identification between devout Europeans and overseas Christians. However, the most extensive of the accounts offered much more than edifying examples of faith, and they probably found other – and not necessarily Catholic – readers. 'Relations' and 'Histories' also contained travelogues and adventure stories. They related information helpful to other travellers, merchants for instance, on routes, local conditions and products, peoples, governments, customs, and flora and fauna.

Thus the accounts were capable of gaining a large readership. Cristoforo Borri's *Relatione della nuova missione delli PP. della Compagnia de Giesu al Regno della Cocincina* was published in 1631, and within two years it appeared in French, Latin, Dutch, German, and English translations. The existence of Dutch and English translations suggests that the book was not confined to a Catholic readership.[10] Giovanni Filippo Marini's *Historia et relatione del Tunchino e del Giappone*, published in 1665, went through seven editions in the next two decades.[11] And Antonio-Francisco Cardim's account was translated from Italian to French.[12] The most celebrated of the Jesuit missionaries in Vietnam, Alexandre de Rhodes, was also its most prolific, producing a 'Relation', a 'History', and travel accounts, along with a Vietnamese–Latin–Portuguese dictionary (he is well known for his romanisation of the Vietnamese alphabet) and a Vietnamese–Latin catechism.[13]

Given the absence of Vietnamese sources independent from the missionaries' accounts, it is difficult to know what Vietnamese converts thought about the new religion. However, we do know what the missionaries reported about Vietnamese enthusiasm for it. De Rhodes recorded in his *Histoire du Royaume de Tunquin* that he baptised over 5600 people in Tonkin between 1627 and 1630.[14] His colleague Cardim was more specific, listing 9797 baptisms in 1634, 9874 in 1635, 8176 in 1636, 7121 in 1637, 9707 in 1638, and so on.[15] Other Jesuit accounts offered more extraordinary totals. Joseph Tissanier stated that, at the time of his arrival in 1654, Christians in the northern kingdom of Tonkin numbered 300,000, no doubt a very inflated figure.[16] Cochinchina was tougher going since Christianity faced heavier persecution there. But de Rhodes claimed some 50,000 Cochinchinese had received baptism by the time of his departure in 1645.[17] Even if we discount these numbers for exaggeration, it is likely that the Jesuits baptised many in Vietnam in the first half of the seventeenth century. We cannot ascertain how many of the converts were women and how many were men. The mission accounts offer total numbers and illustrative examples of converts of both sexes.

Missionaries described Vietnamese converts as the image of ideal Christians. Like his brethren, Metello Saccano commented that when he heard confessions he found the converts so innocent that there was little or nothing for which to give them absolution.[18] In describing the port city of Faifo, where there was a community of both Vietnamese and Japanese expatriate Christians, Christoforo Borri remarked, 'that the church ... might compare with many in Europe; such was [the faithful's] piety, zeal, frequenting of sacraments, and other godly works'.[19] For Joseph Tissanier, the Tonkin church was simply 'a paradise'.[20]

Hence, for the Jesuit missionaries the Vietnam mission was a miracle, and their accounts depict their passage through the Vietnamese kingdoms as bathed in a miraculous aura. Not only did they win many converts, but wondrous healings, visions, and exorcisms accompanied their work. The periodic persecutions confirmed converts and missionaries in the faith and produced martyrs the church could celebrate.[21] In accounts of missions within Europe and from elsewhere around the world, it was common enough for missionaries to appear as miracle workers. They were charismatic; they attracted crowds; their oratory prompted conversions; they healed the sick; and they exorcised demons. While the Vietnam accounts present the missionaries as preaching to large crowds and winning converts, when it came to working miraculous healings and confronting demons, the miracle workers were just as often the people the missionaries converted.

Chief among them were the male catechists Jesuits trained to teach, baptise converts, and direct worship when, as was often the case, the missionaries were unavailable or banished. The catechists were also miracle workers. Armed with holy water, crosses, and images of the Virgin, they spread into the provinces, curing the sick. But women converts, especially those from elite families, also provided leadership. They offered examples of fortitude, sacrifice, and chastity. And they were in contact with divine power through receiving or working miracles. It is precisely in the reports of these miracles that tensions become apparent between the missionaries' presentation of Vietnamese Catholicism and the religion promoted by the Catholic Reformation church.

MANDARIN WOMEN

Missionary texts recount the conversions of Vietnamese women belonging to every social level, from those in humble fishing villages on the Tonkinese coast to those at the royal courts. But new Christian women from the mandarin elite stand out in the accounts and receive individual mention, which most of the poorer women do not. Missionary texts extolled their conversions and their pious good works. The missionaries saw such women as comparable to widely publicised noblewomen converts in Europe.[22] In Vietnam they were important for protecting the nascent Christian community, for exercising influence over politically important men, and for helping to win over others, including, sometimes, their husbands. Saccano reported that the courage and piety of imprisoned Christians in Cochinchina so impressed a disgraced mandarin official, who was also in prison, that he converted along with his wife. What particularly moved the wife, the missionary added, was having heard daily prayers said in the missionaries' home. She asked that catechists be sent to instruct her. They did this so well that she announced publicly that Christianity was the true religion 'because it taught not only what was necessary for each particular [individual] but also for the public necessities and the prosperity of the king and his state, notwithstanding that he was persecuting the Church'.[23] Rulers in both Tonkin and Cochinchina feared that the missionaries might be the agents of the rival state or Portugal. If the convert did make such a declaration, or if the missionary writer put the words in her mouth, it could have been an offer of reassurance that the missionaries posed no threat. But Saccano attributed the words to the devout wife not her disgraced husband.

Mandarin husbands most often resisted conversion. For example, de Rhodes reported that the wife of one provincial governor in Tonkin, baptised as Anne, convinced a number of others to convert but not her husband. Another provincial governor also refused baptism, even though he was well disposed to the missionary, protected him when he was ordered into exile, and allowed his wife and daughter to convert.[24] Cardim recounted similar cases from Cochinchina of governors who would not convert, but were willing to see their wives and daughters baptised.[25] Presumably, it was difficult for officials, even if they were well disposed to the evangelisers' message, to put their careers at risk by turning against the rulers' commitment to Confucianism. But the missionaries offered a different reason for mandarins' reluctance to convert. The texts presented them as being too attached to their concubines. Jesuits in Asia were often willing to accommodate local customs that they could define as non-religious, but polygyny they would not accept. They pressed potential converts with multiple wives to retain one and send the others away. Mandarin officials often were unwilling to do so; they could not overcome their 'attachments of the flesh'.[26]

The missionaries hailed the Christian wives of powerful families as models of devotion and sacrifice; they 'ceded nothing to men in their piety'.[27] De Rhodes reported that the spouse of a Cochinchinese governor 'compare[d] in her fervor and devotion to any of the most pious of European women'.[28] Saccano related that the wife of another governor in Cochinchina came secretly to worship with the missionaries at night, always departing before daybreak so that persecutors would not notice her. Like many of the elite women converts, she became a model of good works. She supported twelve catechists (the number is no doubt significant), bought them a house to live in, and built a chapel, in which the Mass could be celebrated.[29] She also hid missionaries while they clandestinely administered sacraments to Christians and won more conversions.[30] Such women suffered for their faith, as did, for example, the Cochinchinese 'noble matron' Paule, who was arrested and endured torture with constancy. So, too, did her adopted daughters, Luce and Ruffine, who refused to renounce Christianity, despite being tortured.[31]

Perhaps the most notable of the women protectors of the church was Minh Duc Vuong Thai Phi, baptised as Marie-Madeleine, the great aunt of the Cochinchinese ruler, who appeared frequently in the Jesuit accounts. Although she had been very devoted 'to idols', once she heard Francisco de Pina preach, she renounced her errors and asked to be baptised. Other converts followed her example, including two granddaughters, young princesses of the Cochinchinese court.[32] She constructed a hospital for Christians, prevented the destruction of local churches, and supported the catechists in their work. She also hid de Rhodes during persecutions. The chapel she maintained in her palace provided Christians with a place to worship, even when they were being harassed.[33] Cardim recorded, or put in her mouth, a speech made to fellow Christians during a persecution:

> Do you not realize, my brothers, that brave soldiers should boldly put their lives at risk for their lord and king, being assured that the king will reward them? So too should we put our lives at risk for the just purposes of our God, to defend his holy law ... Without doubt he will repay us, not with some temporal and perishable reward but with the glory that never ends. Do you not see how our masters, the Fathers of the Company [the Jesuits] remain firm and constant in maintaining the holy law of our God. We should imitate them without ever weakening.[34]

Thus Marie-Madeleine was an important guardian of the church as well as a model of steadfastness to other Vietnamese and to Europeans reading the missionary accounts.

The Christian wives of mandarins who did not convert, such as Marie-Madeleine, appeared in the texts as independent women capable of resisting political pressures and of acting decisively in public life. De Rhodes referred to these Christian women as 'courageous amazons', the same designation used in Europe to celebrate female defenders of the church against heresy.³⁵ These women were of high rank and considerable political influence. De Rhodes' description of Marie-Madeleine pointed out that her great-nephew, the Cochinchinese ruler, was accustomed to consulting her on political issues. Conversion does not appear to have disrupted their public lives during periods when the missionaries were tolerated. But during periods of persecution even their high rank and political influence did not protect them. During the 1644 crackdown in Cochinchina, the king ordered Marie-Madeleine's chapel destroyed.³⁶

Soon after his arrival in Tonkin in 1627, de Rhodes met a sister of the king, who was mourning the recent death of her husband. She inquired of the missionary if he could in some way help her deceased spouse. De Rhodes replied that there was nothing he could do; he was in Tonkin to proclaim the Gospel to the living not to dead infidels, and she should think of her own salvation. Apparently she refused, but some of the court women present were so impressed by his blunt honesty that they converted, as did the royal sister's very ill mother-in-law, who was renamed Anne.³⁷ Another royal sister, baptised as Catherine, was useful to the church in various ways. She stood up to her brother's pressure to renounce Christianity. She instructed other court women in doctrine. And she made holy objects, such as silk Agnus Dei, which the missionaries distributed to converts around the country. Her daughter, also named Catherine, put her education in Chinese poetry to use in composing a historical catechism in verse.³⁸

In certain cases, women converts provided examples that went beyond heroic piety to saintliness. Colombe, a Tonkinese Christian, built an oratory in her home, gave money to the poor, and supported catechists. She was buried with a cross, and forty days after her death her body was found to be intact, a sure sign of holiness. Another convert in Tonkin, Lina, decorated churches, supported catechists, and, on her deathbed, received an 'illumination' from an image of the Virgin. In both cases, the signs of saintliness were clear to European readers accustomed to descriptions of divine favour bestowed on holy women.³⁹

CELIBATE WOMEN

While most women converts appeared in the missionary texts as pious wives or widows, some followed the alternative model of Catholic womanhood by taking vows of celibacy. Their chastity demonstrated to readers the purity of the Vietnamese church.[40] Men also took such vows, most notably the catechists, but others too. De Rhodes reported that, in the Tonkinese province of Nghéan, where missionaries had some of their greatest successes, young people of both sexes 'conserv[ed] themselves outside of marriage'.[41] But the accounts gave few details about these men. With the exception of the catechists, the exemplary stories are of women who refused marriage and suffered as a result.

As they are presented in the accounts, celibate women provoked violent reactions, presumably because they resisted family marriage plans and the social alliances they could bring.[42] Married women, even if they were Christians, did not pose the same problem, which was one reason why mandarin officials might not object when their wives were baptised. The pious women who converted with their husbands also did not upset traditional marriage patterns or expectations, though it is possible that Christianity encouraged a more companionate marriage than had traditionally been the case.[43]

Female converts, who took vows of virginity or resisted the marriages their families expected them to make, stood by their vows courageously. The adopted daughter of the Christian wife of a Cochinchinese governor had such love for 'Our Lord' that she resolved never to marry, which, as Saccano pointed out, was 'a rare thing in this country especially for a girl of such high extraction, who was sought after by the most advantageous parties in the kingdom'.[44] Conversion also offered a way to avoid a concubine's life. For example, a Tonkinese mandarin sought to make a concubine of a woman named Darie. She refused and the Christians of her locality hid her. They suffered the consequences as the spurned man took out his anger on them. They were forced to flee to the capital with Darie, where a Christian mandarin woman protected them. Another woman, Pie, was raised by a gentleman to be his concubine. Conversion saved her from this fate; as de Rhodes put it, she 'conceived a love for the purity of her body against her parent's and the gentleman's wishes'. He beat her as a result, and she too fled to another Christian woman who protected her.[45]

De Rhodes also recounted the story of three young women – Vitte, Monique, and Nypmh – who, to protect their chastity, resisted soldiers who wanted to rape them. Taken before the king, they openly declared themselves to be Christians. As punishment they were buried in the ground up to their necks, until Christians rescued them. Apparently their plight only encouraged others; de Rhodes reported that six more young women soon joined them. They were a 'small choir of virgins, like angels'.[46] As Tara Alberts has pointed out, it is striking that the women themselves, rather than the priests, appear to have taken the initiative in establishing groups of celibates like this one. She speculates that their actions may have reflected local traditions of 'autonomous female religious organization'.[47] Indeed, it is possible, though difficult to determine from mission accounts, that chaste women and men understood celibacy according to local traditions and not strictly in Catholic terms.

But later in the century, evangelists from the French organisation, the Missions Étrangères de Paris (who took over leadership of the Vietnam mission in the 1660s) channeled the desire for celibacy into a more recognisable Catholic institution. François Deydier, who worked in Tonkin, reported that in his travels he came across young girls 'living in chastity while awaiting the opening of a community that would allow them to live with the many others in the kingdom with the same desire'. Widows and 'virtuous girls' were living 'in common with a fidelity and edification that cede[d] nothing to women religious [*religieuses*] in Europe'. Some had practised chastity for fifteen to twenty years.[48] At the end of his visit to the country in 1669, the Missions Étrangères bishop, Pierre Lambert de la Motte, drew up a set of regulations for these women, which stressed their life of penance and their responsibilities for instructing young girls, taking care of women who were ill, baptising moribund infants, and rescuing dissolute women from bad lives. The rules became the basis for the formal community of the Amantes de la Croix that Lambert started in 1670.

WOMEN AND DEMONS

Pious wives, courageous amazons, angelic virgins, all these women practised their new faith in ways familiar to European Catholics and encouraged by the Catholic Reformation church. They advertised the success of the Vietnam mission, but none of them presented it at its most miraculous. The missionaries' truly dramatic successes came in curing and converting women possessed by demons. Since Catholic missionaries understood their task as a worldwide campaign against Satan and his false religions, their foremost task was to combat demonism. Anyone who obstructed them was the devil's ally, and none did so more spectacularly than women suffering from possession. The missionaries were well acquainted with the usefulness of demonic possession in polemical battles against rival religions. During the late sixteenth and early seventeenth centuries, Catholic clerics in France turned possession cases against Protestantism. When exorcists succeeded in expelling Satan's minions from the bodies of possessed women, the departing demons frequently identified Huguenots as their allies. Some of these cases were widely publicised, such as that of Nicole Obry in 1565, Marthe Brossier in 1599, and the Ursuline nuns of Loudun in the 1630s, though the early Jesuit missionaries in Vietnam would not have known of this last one before their departure from Europe.[49]

In many of the overseas places missionaries worked, they confronted ecstatic cults, which they understood in Catholic terms as instances of demonic possession.[50] Although the phenomenon was not the same in each place, women were often at the centre of the struggle between missionaries and demons. As Haruko Nawata Ward has shown, Jesuits in Japan were quick to characterise the Shinto-Buddhist nuns, prophetesses, and priestesses they encountered as witches, and they had a long-running conflict with them. The battle was often fought over cases of demonic possession that the missionaries accused the witches of provoking; new Christians seemed especially susceptible. Jesuit exorcists and local women healers competed over the bodies of these suffering converts: 'Jesuits depicted the body of the possessed as a battleground between the God of the Kirishitans and the devil of Shinto-Buddhism.' Men were afflicted as well as women, but for the missionaries women were the instruments by which demons most easily worked their will. The Jesuits deployed the rituals and sacred objects that successfully fought demons – exorcism, baptism, holy water, relics, and crosses. In Vietnam, too, they proved to be powerful weapons.[51]

In 1644 in the Cochinchinese city of Halam, a mother who had mistreated her virtuous Christian son was herself tormented horribly by demons until she accepted baptism. Once the Holy Spirit was 'lodged within [her]', she never again felt under demonic attack.[52] Also in Cochinchina, a venerable Christian by the name of Paul preached, instructed new converts, and delivered the possessed of their demons. God had given him such 'absolute empire' over demons that none could resist him. De Rhodes saw Paul deliver one poor tormented woman of evil spirits. She had been running through the forest and engaging in a 'thousand extravagances'. Paul had the ability to calm possessed women and prepare them for baptism, which restored them to health. Baptism was frequently the cure for possession. The missionary told of a Cochinchinese 'enchanter and master of superstitions', which is to say a Taoist ritual specialist, who had heard of the marvels the missionaries had performed and took it upon himself to study Christian ideas. He started reading a catechism, but Satan immediately afflicted him with eye problems and tormented his body. The prayers of local Christians helped drive out the demon, but they did not cure the eye illness. And the expelled demon quickly possessed the body of the enchanter's wife. They both suffered until he had a dream in which a 'venerable matron' told him that only baptism would cure them. As, indeed, it did.[53]

The Jesuits exorcised demons from the possessed, as de Rhodes did for two women in the Cochinchinese province of Ranran. The first one demonstrated her possession by speaking in languages she could not have known and by doing things she could never have done without the added strength of the demon within her. The Jesuit remarked that his first exorcism drove the demon out; it was a relatively easy case. The other was more difficult because the woman was a 'pythoness'.[54]

De Rhodes took the term pythoness from ancient Greek oracles to describe the women involved in spirit possession rituals, which played a large part in customary Vietnamese religion. Women spirit mediums were particularly important in the cult of the Princess Liễu Hanh, which was part of the Cult of the Mothers (otherwise known as the Three Palaces or Four Palaces Cult). It started in the sixteenth century and was spreading at the time the Jesuits arrived.[55] Male spirit mediums were also common, especially in the General Tran cult, but the missionaries did not say much about them. Female mediums delivered prophetic messages about how to obtain peace and happiness or avoid sickness and misfortunes, but the Jesuits, particularly de Rhodes, portrayed them as involved in funerals and ancestor devotion. As he described it, after a burial, members of the deceased's family would visit a medium, who, after reciting magical invocations, would summon a demon under the name of the deceased to come and console the family. The demon would enter the medium's body and agitate it with furious movements. Her face would become red and inflamed, or pale, or frighteningly black. The demon speaking through her and counterfeiting the voice of the deceased would call relatives by name and speak to them on some private matter known only to them. In tears, the family would prostrate themselves to revere the spirit of the deceased and then would pose questions to which the demon would give obscure oracular responses. De Rhodes insisted that the mediums were either frauds, which is why the demon always recommended a good food offering to the pythoness, or they were suffering from demonic possession.[56] But, of course, the missionaries read the Vietnamese practices in terms of their understanding of possession in Europe, the controversies possession cases provoked there, and the Catholic theological understanding of possession, which, as Moshe Sluhovsky has shown, was changing at the time Catholic missionaries were spreading around the globe.[57]

Like other traditional ritual specialists, pythonesses posed serious competition to the missionaries. But their tormented demon-possessed bodies also presented a dramatic stage setting for missionaries' victories over the devil. In the case referred to above from Ranran province, the demon had tormented the pythoness night and day for seven years. De Rhodes' attempts over several days to exorcise the demon failed; it was too strong and too habituated to the pythoness's body. Finally the priest convinced the woman that only baptism would work. The moment the missionary poured the water over her head, her frightening face calmed and she gained such repose that everyone present proclaimed it a miracle.[58]

De Rhodes worried that these former pythonesses, who had served the devil, would be especially susceptible to the devil taking revenge on them once they had converted. That is what appeared to happen to a Tonkinese baptised as Monica. She had been a pythoness; evil spirits had often possessed her and driven her into 'maniacal furors'. After her baptism, the missionary warned her that the devil would try to take her back. He advised her never to leave her house, from which demons had been expelled, without first making the sign of the cross and carrying with her some holy water. One day she forgot, and sure enough, as soon as she was outside the devil entered her body and threw her into strange contortions. Her eyes were on fire and she screamed threats. Her pious Christian husband got her back inside and sent for the Jesuit. De Rhodes exorcised the demon, who finally departed when Monica agreed to make her confession.[59]

Yet former pythonesses turned Christians were not only a battleground in the combats between missionaries and demons. Once they had converted, their previous association with demons now gave these women power over them. For example, a Cochinchinese convert, Therese, another former pythoness, had a gift for expelling demons. She had served them, but once converted she became their greatest foe. When she approached people suffering from possession, they would throw themselves on the ground, and her prayers would chase the demons out.[60]

It should be added that not all the victims of possession were women; some were men, as in the case of the 'enchanter' mentioned above. Nonetheless, it is notable but not surprising that almost all the cases of possession in the missionary reports concerned women. The accounts give the impression that, for the Vietnamese, women were the most likely to have contact with spirits, good or evil, and were likely also to suffer what Europeans characterised as possession. Similarly women did not monopolise the power of expelling demons. Obviously the missionaries could, and so too could certain devout men, especially the catechists. But the missionary and his readers were predisposed to see women more than men as associated with the demonic world. They shared a presupposition about women as mentally and physically weak and thus more prone than men to 'diabolic attacks and temptations, as well as to deceptions and simulations'.[61] As Sluhovsky reminds us, under European assumptions, the spirits to which women were susceptible could be either demonic or angelic. Thus, 'the idiom of possession ... created spiritual possibilities for women at the same time that it suspected them'. But 'the paradox of women's susceptibility to both diabolic and divine spirits ... increased anxieties concerning possessions'.[62]

Thus one reason why spirit possession loomed so large in the missionaries' stories of conversion is because of its customary role in Vietnamese culture. But another is that European Catholics had their own highly developed demonological tradition. Catholic missionaries and their readers at home understood demons and spirits, their bodily effects, the theological explanations for such phenomena, and the means the church offered for controlling them. Therefore, a missionary writer like de Rhodes could use the cases of spirit possession to convince readers that the conversions he won were true. Describing the changed interior dispositions of the converts' souls after they adopted the true faith was insufficient, even if the mission reports stressed the outward manifestations of such changes in pious behaviour and good works. True conversion had to be seen as manifested physically in bodies, and cases of possession and successful exorcisms provided the most dramatic examples, even if they more often involved female rather than male bodies.[63] However, it was precisely because they featured women's bodies that these examples of conversion could prove problematic to European readers.

The entire issue of spirits, whether in possessions or in visionary experiences, underwent a reassessment in Europe from the late Middle Ages to the Catholic Reformation. The church's redefinition of belief and practice concerning spirits was part of a battle carried out on two fronts, one against Protestantism and the other against growing scepticism.[64] As Sluhovsky explains, the development of the science of spirit discernment, which would enable clerics to figure out if the spirits possessing women were demons, led to the increasing possibility that women's mystical experiences would be reinterpreted as demonic rather than divine. In Vietnam, the spirits possessing pythonesses or other women were, according to the missionaries, always demonic, but the women who expelled demons from the possessed became miracle workers. European clerics developing the science of spirit discernment would not have felt comfortable with the idea of women expelling evil spirits. That was the male clergy's job.

Women miracle workers were increasingly suspect within a church concerned with gender boundaries as much as with the boundaries between the clergy and the laity, the sacred and profane, or true and false religion. Catholic reformers championed devout nuns enclosed within their convents, or wives living piously and obediently with their husbands, or, slowly, women organised into supervised groups dedicated to charitable work. It was the women whose ecstatic experiences put them into direct contact with supernatural power who came increasingly under suspicion. Sometimes, after close examination, clerics accepted the divine nature of these women's experiences; they might even become saints. Often they were rejected and their experiences deemed demonic. European readers could recognise such women as holy figures once the demons possessing them were driven out. The abbess of the Loudun Ursulines, Jeanne des Anges, worked miraculous healings after the end of the possessions in her convent.[65] But the church could not easily accept the notion of such women combating demons and expelling them from possessed bodies.

In attributing that capability to women, the Jesuits in Vietnam risked bending the gender boundaries the Catholic Reformation was trying to impose. In other words, to incorporate Vietnamese Catholics into the universal body of the church, missionaries told stories of victories over demons in battles fought out in women's bodies and of women whose experiences with demonic power made them miracle workers. But, in so doing, the Vietnam missionary campaign entangled itself in an issue which was controversial and undergoing changes at home that would impose a stricter gender distinction between the acceptable and the unacceptable in contact with the spirit world.

The true and the false in religion were also at stake in the case with which I started, the vision of a woman in a globe of fire complaining that her relatives had done little to succor her in her suffering. Was this a lesson about the obligation of the living to work for the release of souls from purgatory? Or was it a message from the spirit of a deceased relative, which required proper rituals and offerings to be placated? Perhaps it was both. The missionaries in Vietnam sought to inculcate pure Catholic belief and practice. But they had to work with what Vietnamese culture gave them – the need to pacify spirits to heal illness or avoid misfortune and the importance of women mediums who could communicate with spirits. To convince their readers that they had successfully transformed these beliefs and rituals into acceptable Catholic doctrine and practice, the missionaries constructed exemplary narratives of Vietnamese women's conversions and pious activities. But doing so was fraught with problems not only because of the importance of women's customary religious functions in Vietnam but also because women's religious roles in Europe were changing. The stories of Vietnamese women converts reveal the ambiguities of religious change in their own country, but these stories were also caught up in the transformation of religious life underway on the other side of the world.

NOTES

1 Alexandre de Rhodes, *Les voyages et missions du P. Alexandre de Rhodes de la compagnie de Jésus en la Chine et autres Royaumes de l'Orient, Nouvelle édition par un père de la même compagnie* (Paris: Julien, Lanier et Cie, 1854), p. 259.
2 Early modern Europeans used the Chinese term *Annam*, 'pacified south', to refer to the country.
3 For efforts towards, and the limits upon, enclosure, see Chapter 6 in this volume.
4 The literature on this issue is large, but, for a brief overview, see Merry E. Wiesner-Hanks, *Women and gender in early modern Europe*, 3rd edn (Cambridge: Cambridge University Press, 2008), pp. 207–32. On elite women, see Barbara B. Diefendorf, *From penitence to charity: pious women and the Catholic Reformation in Europe* (Oxford: Oxford University Press, 2004).

5 Gabriella Zarri, 'Living saints: a typology of female sanctity in the early sixteenth century', in Daniel Bornstein and Roberto Rusconi (eds), *Women and religion in medieval and renaissance Italy*, trans. Margery J. Schneider (Chicago: University of Chicago Press, 1996), pp. 219–303.

6 Leslie Tuttle, 'French Jesuits and Indian dreams in seventeenth-century New France', in Ann Marie Plane and Leslie Tuttle (eds), *Dreams, dreamers and visions: the early modern Atlantic world* (Philadelphia: University of Pennsylvania Press, 2013), pp. 180–2.

7 Peter C. Phan, *Missions and catechists: Alexandre de Rhodes and inculturation in seventeenth-century Vietnam* (Maryknoll, NY: Orbis Books, 2005), pp. 6–8; Alain Forest, *Les missionnaires français au Tonkin et Siam, XVIIe–XVII siècles: analyse comparée d'un relatif succès et d'un total échec*, 3 vols (Paris: Éditions l'Harmattan, 1998); and Tara Alberts, *Conflict and conversion: Catholicism in Southeast Asia* (Oxford: Oxford University Press, 2013).

8 Phan, *Mission and catechists*, pp. 10–13.

9 John Correia Afonso, *Jesuit letters and Indian history, 1543–1773*, 2nd edn (Bombay: Oxford University Press, 1969), pp. 1–10, 32–44; Donald F. Lach, *Asia in the making of Europe, volume 1: the century of discovery* (Chicago: University of Chicago Press, 1965), book 1, pp. 314–31; Donald F. Lach and Edwin J. Van Kley, *Asia in the making of Europe, volume 3: a century of advance* (Chicago: University of Chicago Press, 1993), book 1, pp. 367–434.

10 Olga Dror and K. W. Taylor (eds), *Views of seventeenth-century Vietnam: Cristoforo Borri on Cochinchina and Samuel Baron on Tonkin* (Ithaca, NY: Southeast Asia Program Publications, Cornell University Press, 2006), pp. 64–5. Dror reproduces a second, more complete English translation from Awnsham Churchill and John Churchill, (eds), *A collection of voyages and travels, some now first printed from original manuscripts, others now first published in English*, volume 2 (London: Awnsham and John Churchill, 1704), pp. 787–838. She uses the 1732 edition of this collection.

11 Alberts, *Conflict and conversion*, xvi. I have used here the French translation, *Relation nouvelle et curieuse des royaumes de Tunquin et de Lao . . . . Traduite de l'italien du P. Mariny Romain. Par L.P.L.C.C.* (Paris: Chez Gervais Clouzier, 1666).

12 Unless otherwise noted, the information in this paragraph comes from Augustin et Aloys de Backer and Auguste Carayon, *Bibliothèque de la compagnie de Jésus*, new edition par Carlos Sommervogel (Paris: Picard, 1895). On Borri, see vol. 1, cols. 1821–1822; on de Rhodes, see vol. 6, cols 1718–1721; on Cardim, see vol. 2, cols 738–41; and on Marini, see vol. 5, cols 582–4. François Cardim, *Relation de la province du Iapon escrite en portugais . . .* (Paris: Mathurin, Henault, 1645). See also the account by Metello Saccano, *Relation des progrez de la foy au royaume de la Cochinchine des années 1646 & 1647* (Paris: Sebastien Cramoisy, 1653), pp. 8–9, 101.

13 De Rhodes's works relating to Vietnam include: *Relazione de'felici successi della Santa Fede predicata da padre della compagnia di Giesu nel regno di Tunchino* (Rome: Giuseppe Luna, 1650); *Catechismus pro iis, qui volunt suscipere baptismum, in octo dies divisus* (Rome: Typis Sacrae Congregationis de Propaganda Fide, 1651), *Dictionarium annamiticum lusitanum et latinum ope sacrae congregationis de Propaganda Fide in lucem editum* (Rome: Typis & sumptibus eiusdem Sacr. Congreg., 1651); *Histoire du royaume de Tunquin, et des grands progrez que la prédication de l'évangile y a faits en la conversion des infidelles, depuis l'année 1627 jusques à l'année 1646* (Lyon: Jean-Baptiste Devenet, 1651); *Divers voyages et missions du P. Alexandre de Rhodes en la Chine et autres royaumes de l'orient* (Paris: Sebastien Cramoisy, 1653); *La glorieuse mort d'André, catéchiste de la Cochinchine, qui a le premier versé son sang pour la querelle de Jésus-Christ en cette nouvelle église* (Paris: Sebastien Cramoisy, 1653); *Relation des progrez de la foy au royaume de la Cochinchine vers les derniers quartiers du Levant* (Paris: Sebastien Cramoisy, 1652); *Sommaire des divers voyages et missions apostoliques du R. P. Alexandre de Rhodes. . . à la Chine et autres royaumes de l'Orient* (Paris: Florentin Lambert, 1653). De Rhodes also wrote on Catholic martyrs in Japan and on his later missionary work in Persia.

14 De Rhodes, *Histoire du royaume de Tunquin*, p. 263.

15 Cardim, *Relation de la province du Iapon*, p. 76.

16 Joseph P. Tissanier, 'Relation du P. Joseph Tissanier de la Compagnie de Jésus. Son voyage de France au Tonkin; description de ce royaume. Événements mémorables de la mission du Tonkin pendant les années 1658, 1659, 1660', in *Voyages et travaux des missionaires de la compagnie de Jésus publiés par des pères de la même compagnie pour servir de complément aux lettres édifiantes, volume 2: Mission de la Cochinchine et du Tonkin* (Paris: Charles Duniol, 1858), p. 143.

17 Catherine Marin, *Les rôle des missionaires français en Cochinchine au XVIIe & XVIIIe siècles* (Paris: Archives des Missions Étrangères, 1999), p. 53. Marin sees this figure as exaggerated and thinks that the number of converts was probably between 25,000 and 30,000 at the end of the century, decades after de Rhodes wrote. De Rhodes was in Cochinchina twice, from 1624 to 1626, and from 1640 to 1645.

18 Saccano, *Relation du progrés de la Foi*, p. 80.

19 Dror and Taylor, *Views of seventeenth-century Vietnam*, p. 179.

20 Tissanier, 'Relation du P. Joseph Tissanier', pp. 43, 146.

21 De Rhodes, *Glorieuse mort d'André*.

22 Keith P. Luria, *Sacred boundaries: religious co-existence and conflict in early modern France* (Washington, DC: The Catholic University of America Press, 2005), pp. 263–4.

23 Saccano, *Relation du progrés de la Foi*, pp. 6–7.

24 De Rhodes, *Histoire du royaume de Tunquin*, pp. 220, 234–5.
25 Cardim, *Relation de la province du Iapon*, pp. 103, 109. Compare this situation with that described by Eric Dursteler in Chapter 1 in this volume.
26 De Rhodes, *Histoire du royaume de Tunquin*, p. 220. See also Cardim, *Relation de la province du Iapon*, p. 103.
27 De Rhodes, *Histoire du royaume de Tunquin*, pp. 299–300.
28 De Rhodes, *Relation des progrez de la Foy au royaume de la Cochinchine*, p. 41.
29 Saccano, *Relation du progrés de la Foi*, pp. 73–4.
30 De Rhodes, *Relation de progrez*, pp. 77, 120.
31 De Rhodes, *Voyages et missions*, pp. 279–82.
32 Saccano, *Relation du progrés de la Foi*, p. 78. On Marie-Madeleine, see also Phan, *Mission and catechesis*, pp. 47, 60, 63; and Alberts, *Conflict and conversion*, p. 166.
33 De Rhodes, *Voyages et missions*, pp. 91, 169, 212; Saccano, *Relation du progrés de la Foi*, pp. 71–2.
34 Cardim, *Relation de la province du Iapon*, p. 111.
35 Luria, *Sacred boundaries*, p. 196.
36 Alberts, *Conflict and conversion*, p. 167.
37 De Rhodes, *Voyages et missions*, pp. 114–15, 212; De Rhodes, *Histoire du royaume de Tonquin*, pp. 140–2, 164.
38 De Rhodes, *Histoire du royaume de Tunquin*, pp.164, 248; Cardim, *Relation de la province du Iapon*, p. 84; Alberts, *Conflict and conversion*, pp. 127–8, 176. The text is not extant.
39 De Rhodes, *Histoire du royaume de Tunquin*, pp. 299–301.
40 The literature on Catholic-Reformation views on marriage and celibacy is large but for a study that relates them to the work of overseas missionaries, see Merry Wiesner-Hanks, *Christianity and sexuality in the early modern world: regulating desire, reforming practice*, 2nd edn (London: Routledge, 2010), pp. 134–6.
41 De Rhodes, *Histoire du royaume de Tunquin*, pp. 293, 325.
42 For another example of how conversion could disrupt familial strategies, see Hannah Crawforth's contribution (Chapter 3) in this volume.
43 Haruko Nawata Ward has suggested that in Japan women converts found in Christianity an alternative to the norm of patriarchs arranging their marriages; their refusal to submit provoked familial conflicts. Some left their husbands, while others practiced their new faith 'heroically' by remaining with their non-Christian spouses. See *Women religious leaders in Japan's Christian century, 1549–1650* (Farnham: Ashgate, 2009), pp. 5, 15.
44 Saccano, *Relation du progrès de la Foi*, p. 74. For other examples, see Alberts, *Conflict and conversion*, pp. 174–5.
45 De Rhodes, *Histoire du royaume de Tunquin*, pp. 276–9.

46 De Rhodes, *Histoire du royaume de Tunquin*, pp. 306–8.
47 Alberts, *Conflict and conversion*, p. 175.
48 *Relation des missions des evesques françois au royaumes de Siam, de la Cochinchine, de Camboye & du Tonquin &c* (Paris: Charles Angot, 1684), pp. 198, 244; Alberts, *Conflict and conversion*, p. 175. On the role of the Amantes de la Croix in providing Vietnamese Catholic women with an alternative to traditional family life, see Nhung Tuyet Tran, 'Les Amantes de la Croix: an early modern Vietnamese sisterhood', in Gisèle Bousquet and Nora Taylor (eds), *Le Viêtnam au féminin/Viêt Nam: Women's Realities* (Paris: Les Indes Savantes, 2005), pp. 51–66.
49 Moshe Sluhovsky, *Believe not every spirit: possession, mysticism and discernment in early modern Catholicism* (Chicago: University of Chicago Press, 2007), pp. 19–20, 199; Luria, *Sacred boundaries*, pp. 67, 232–45.
50 See the example of sixteenth-century South India, which Ines G. Županov has explored in 'Conversion, illness and possession: Catholic missionary healing in early modern South Asia', in Županov and Caterina Guenzi (eds), *Divins remèdes: médicine et religion en Asie du Sud*, Collection Purushartha, 27 (Paris: École des Hautes Études en Sciences Sociales, 2008), pp. 263–300.
51 Ward, *Women religious leaders*, pp. 14, 109, 159–64, for quote see p. 161.
52 De Rhodes, *Voyages et missions*, pp. 157–8. In this case, her son also suffered from possession.
53 De Rhodes, *Histoire du royaume de Tunquin*, pp. 269–70.
54 De Rhodes, *Voyages et missions*, pp. 163, 170–1.
55 Olga Dror, *Cult, culture and authority: Princess Liễu Hanh in Vietnamese history* (Honolulu: University of Hawai'i Press, 2007); Maurice Durand, *Technique et panthéon des médiums Viétnamiens (Dông)* (Paris: École française d'Extrême-Orient, 1959); Phan, *Mission et catechesis*, pp. 18–19.
56 De Rhodes, *Histoire du royaume de Tunquin*, pp. 77–8; *Voyages et missions*, p. 171.
57 Sluhovsky, *Believe not every spirit*, pp. 61–93, 207–29.
58 De Rhodes, *Voyages et missions*, pp. 171–2.
59 De Rhodes, *Histoire du royaume de Tunquin*, pp. 250–1.
60 De Rhodes, *Voyages et missions*, p. 214; *Relation de progrez*, p. 34.
61 Sluhovsky, *Believe not every spirit*, p. 8.
62 *Ibid.*, p. 16.
63 As Županov puts it: 'Considered in Christianity a mere external envelope of the soul, which was an instrument of damnation or salvation, the body was, especially in missionary situation, the first tangible proof of the failure or success of conversion'; 'Conversion, Illness and Possession', p. 12.
64 See Stuart Clark on visions in his *Vanities of the eye: vision in early modern European culture* (Oxford: Oxford University Press, 2007), pp. 204–35.
65 Luria, *Sacred Boundaries*, pp. 242–3.

10

'I wish to be no other but as he': Persia, masculinity, and conversion in early-seventeenth-century travel writing and drama

Chloë Houston

If the concept of conversion most commonly brings to mind the change from one set of religious beliefs to another, explorations of the subject in the early modern period have demonstrated that it is bound up with various different forms of identity: national, political, and social, for example, as well as religious. Michael C. Questier, in his study of conversion in England in the late sixteenth and early seventeenth centuries, explains that the subject of conversion is 'drawn out of a matrix of political and religious factors'.[1] To pin down a precise notion of what conversion meant in post-Reformation Europe, given the complexity of these religious and political factors, is a difficult task; the questions that surround conversion – what it means to change from one identity to another, and how this is achieved and described – have occupied scholars working on a diverse range of subjects. In the past twenty years, the idea of 'turning Turk' has proved fruitful for those interested in the presentation of different forms of religious and national identity in early modern literature and culture. The study of conversion between Christianity and Islam has occupied scholars interested in how religious identity was constructed in post-Reformation Europe, as well as those looking in particular at the relationship between the two religions.[2]

The function of gender identity in relation to conversion has often been involved in these discussions, particularly because of the associations between religious conversion and sexual temptation in representations of conversion in English literature of the period and on stage. The potential for the elision of the attraction of Christian travellers to Islam and the sexual temptation of Christian Englishmen by Muslims led to an association between religious conversion and unstable gender identity. Jonathan Burton has described how the 'Islamic threat' constituted 'a combined assault on the male Christian body and soul', and Daniel Vitkus has traced the ways in which 'turning Turk' involved the shifting of identities, including sexual ones.³ Conversion thus represents an important point of intersection for thinking about religious and gender identity in the early modern period and the ways in which these identities were represented and related.

This chapter takes as its focus the relationship between gender and conversion in early seventeenth-century travel writing and drama about the travels of the Sherley brothers, Thomas, Anthony, and Robert, in Persia and the Ottoman Empire, focusing on *The travailes of the three English brothers* (1607) by John Day, William Rowley, and George Wilkins, and a pamphlet by Thomas Middleton, *Sir Robert Sherley his entertainment in Cracovia* (1609).⁴ *The travailes* is set in and around Persia, which was during this period a Shi'ite Muslim state. The first Safavid shah, Ismāʿīl I, who ruled from 1501 to 1524, consolidated Persia's status as a Muslim country, introducing Ithnāʿashari or 'Twelver' Shi'ism.⁵ There are two reasons why Persia's identity in early modern Europe makes it particularly relevant for a discussion of gender and conversion in the period. Firstly, Persia, like other Muslim countries at this time, was often associated in European writings with effeminacy, opulence, and decadence.⁶ In addition, some classical authors portrayed pre-Islamic Persia in particular as given to effeminacy. Plato's *Laws* describes how the great Persian king Cyrus's sons were educated by women and eunuchs, and brought up not in 'the traditional Persian discipline', but in a manner that led them to live in 'a riot of unrestrained debauchery'. The descent of Cyrus's enlightened monarchy into oppressive despotism was thus blamed on the replacement of an intelligent king with 'effeminate, undisciplined and dissolute men'.⁷ This is typical of an association between tyranny and effeminacy in classical descriptions of Persia that can be traced in other descriptions of its rulers, such as those of Aeschylus, Herodotus, and Xenophon.

Secondly, Persia was seen as being open to the prospect of conversion from Islam to Christianity; this was especially true during the reign of Shah ʿAbbās I, who governed from 1587 to 1629 CE. In the early 1600s, it was rumoured in Europe that ʿAbbās was considering converting to Christianity, and that he might bring the whole of Persia with him. One pamphlet, printed in France in 1606, even suggested that the shah had already deserted his Islamic faith and had ordered his subjects to accept Christian baptism. A number of English writers, including Anthony Nixon, whose 1607 pamphlet *The three English brothers* is the main source for *Travailes*, recorded the shah's interest in Christianity in a manner that made clear their expectations; Nixon wrote that 'Abbās 'lends such attentive eare' to his Christian visitors that 'he may in time bee brought to become a Christian'.[8] This interest in Persia's potential for conversion, and its reporting in contemporary travel writing, had an effect on the way in which Persia was portrayed on the Renaissance stage. Furthermore, early modern European interest in the possible religious conversion of Persia and its people marks a moment at which contemporary anxieties about religious and gender identities converge.

When writing about Persia, the authors considered here endeavoured to represent it as a place which could be converted to English and/or Christian habits, and where Englishmen themselves would not be under threat of conversion to Islam. Their motivation for this was a desire to promote closer Anglo-Persian relations, and to garner support for the activities of the Sherley brothers, who travelled between Persia and Europe in an attempt to find European support for Shah 'Abbās. Texts about the Sherleys attempted to anticipate and prevent any unease about the perceived threat of emasculation associated with conversion to Islam, and thus to diffuse potential anxieties about the threats of religious conversion to travellers' masculinity. It is worth noting here that religious conversion does not actually take place in any of the sources considered in this chapter; rather it hovers, sometimes suggested and sometimes unspoken, signifying a foreign threat to Englishness and Christianity which is ever present.

CONVERSION ON THE SEVENTEENTH-CENTURY STAGE

The prospect of religious conversion, for English travellers in the Mediterranean and beyond, was a real one. Conversion from Christianity to Islam was relatively common in the early modern period, and conversions were made freely as well as by force; Nabil Matar notes that thousands of Christians converted to Islam, and contends that the Ottoman Empire offered opportunities and attractions to Christians in need of employment or advancement.[9] Conversion to Islam is addressed by a variety of texts that deal with travel to and from Islamic countries; it is particularly prevalent in dramatic literature, where aspects of the performative nature of the theatre and the dramatic functions of the conversion ritual coalesce. On the Renaissance stage, as Daniel Vitkus explores in his chapter in this collection, conversion is often presented as a risk that travellers face, and may not be able to withstand, despite the fact that to turn Turk was, in Jonathan Burton's words, 'to turn from Christian virtue'.[10]

A number of 'Turk plays' from the late sixteenth and early seventeenth centuries displayed anxiety that travellers to Muslim countries might not only be seduced by the temptations of Islam, but even emasculated. Vitkus has read such plays – including Thomas Kyd's *Soliman and Perseda* (1592), Thomas Heywood's *Fair maid of the west part I* (c.1597–1610), Richard Daborne's *A Christian turn'd Turk* (1612), and Philip Massinger's *The renegado* (1623) – as being engrossed with questions of conversion and apostasy, with Islam functioning as a 'religion of temptation' which is 'erotically alluring'.[11] Frequently, in such plays, Muslim women (often contrasted with chaste Christian women) seduce Christian men and the temptations of Islam prove irresistible. Often these temptations prove threatening to the gender identity of the convert. *A Christian turn'd Turk*, for example, tells the story of the well-known pirate John Ward, who converts to Islam in order to marry a Turkish woman, Voada. In the contemporary pamphlets on which Daborne's play is based, there is no record of Ward having undergone a circumcision ceremony as part of his religious conversion.[12] In the play, however, at the moment at which conversion is enacted, the threat of castration (for which the practice of adult circumcision was often confused) is obvious. Bernadette Andrea draws attention to the performance of Ward's 'spectacular circumcision' after he has 'embraced Islam for what the play depicts as the lure of a Muslim woman'.[13]

Other Turk plays also represented Islam as threatening to seduce Christian men from their faith and challenge their masculinity, even when conversion is threatened but does not take place. In *The renegado*, Gazet, the servant of the Venetian merchant Vitelli, knows that turning Turk may cause him to 'lose / A collop of that part my Doll enjoined me / To bring home as she left it' (1. 139–40).[14] Nonetheless, his comic desire to become a eunuch means that he risks just that. Gazet's anxiety over losing his 'collop' draws on the commonplace association of circumcision and emasculation, but also hints at the related fear that he may be unable to procreate: the word 'collop' could also mean 'offspring'.[15] Thus Gazet's fear of physical loss relates not only to his foreskin but also to his future children, and his report of Doll's desire for him to remain intact suggests that she wishes to protect not only his penis but also his capacity for fathering English, Protestant children.[16] Although it was often treated as a source of comedy rather than a serious risk, the threat of emasculation and the danger of the Muslim seductress were clearly associated with conversion to Islam in the minds of early-seventeenth-century audiences.[17] The function of comedy here is perhaps to diffuse potential anxiety about the vulnerability of masculinity in such circumstances. Indeed, the possible malleability of their masculine identity is presented as something to which not only Christian men are subject. Asambeg, the viceroy of Tunis and a Muslim, becomes infatuated with the 'fair Christian virgin' Paulina, whom he wishes to marry (1.1.115). In his attempted seduction, he charges Paulina thus:

> There is something in you
> That can work miracles [. . .]
> Dispose and alter sexes: to my wrong,
> In spite of nature, I will be your nurse,
> Your woman, your physician and your fool. (*The renegado*, 2.5.149–53)

Asambeg's masculinity, the play suggests, may be refashioned through his desire for a woman whose influence 'robs me of the fierceness I was born with' and causes him to 'tremble at her softness' (2.5.107, 109), despite her open dislike of him. The play suggests that the boundary between male and female, like the boundary between Christian and Turk, is porous, despite the seeming rigidity of such oppositions. Proximity to Muslims raises the prospect of conversion for both Vitelli and Paulina, a conversion which, as Jane Hwang Degenhardt has noted, 'implies a transgression from which there seems to be no return'.[18]

SIR ROBERT SHERLEY HIS ENTERTAINMENT IN CRACOVIA

Writers about travel between Persia and Europe in the early modern period were obliged to negotiate the perceived risks associated with proximity to Islam and the possibility of conversion. One such body of writing concerns the Sherley brothers; Anthony and Robert Sherley first travelled to Persia via Venice in 1598. The Sherleys' reasons for being in Persia were to promote English interests and evaluate the potential for trade with Europe, and a number of writings documented their travels and experiences.[19] In 1599, Anthony returned to Europe as the representative of Shah ʿAbbās I, on an ambassadorial visit to a series of European courts.[20] Robert, the younger brother, remained in Persia, also returning to Europe as ʿAbbās's ambassador in 1609.[21] Both Anthony and Robert, Protestant by birth, are believed to have converted to Catholicism whilst in Persia, and knowledge of their conversion had probably reached England by the early 1600s.[22]

During this period, English relations with and perceptions of Persia were undergoing a change. James I took a different approach from that of Elizabeth to the Ottoman Turks, the long-term enemies of the Safavids.[23] In 1601, he wrote to ʿAbbās to praise his military successes against the Ottomans and hint at future help from England in these efforts.[24] As Matthew Dimmock has argued, England's peace with Spain, made in 1604, and the commitment to opposition of the Turk as the mutual enemy of Christendom enabled James to demonstrate his distance from Elizabeth's position.[25] The possibility of a closer relationship between England and Persia, including stronger diplomatic and mercantile ties, thus arose.[26] Travel writings from the period often seek to support such opportunities, and it is within this context that Thomas Middleton's pamphlet *Sir Robert Sherley his entertainment in Cracovia* (1609) must be read.

The bulk of this pamphlet, as Vitkus explains, is a translation of a Latin poem by Andrew Leech, a Scottish Jesuit then living in Poland. It is likely that Leech met Robert during the latter's visit to Cracow during the winter of 1608/9. Leech's poem, *Encomia nominis & negocii D. Roberti Sherlaeii*, has been described by Vitkus as 'an unusually anxious panegyric because it betrays so much concern about Sherley's exotic status', particularly with regard to his divided loyalties between England and Persia.[27] Middleton's translation changes Leech's original considerably, cutting and altering some sections and adding others. These changes tend to portray the Persians in a positive light, and specifically as masculine, virile soldiers, and not wholly Muslim. His additions, for example, include an excerpt from the Greek author Strabo, which describes the Persians as virtuous pagans (rather than Muslims), and praises their 'martial discipline and virility', two characteristics which an early modern reader might have taken as signs of masculinity.[28] This is just one example of how Middleton alters the Latin text in order to make it more suitable for an English audience; he also tones down Leech's suggestion that England was an unsuitable country for so great a spirit as Robert Sherley.[29] By presenting the Persians as martial, virile, and not entirely Muslim, Middleton's pamphlet develops an image of Persia as familiar and unthreatening for the English audience.

Middleton's pamphlet, as Vitkus points out, also endeavours to smooth over the fact that Robert Sherley was by now a Catholic.[30] As well as the material from Strabo, it includes a hint that the Persian shah is even inclined to Christianity, with 'the Persian himself confessing and worshipping Christ' (p. 674, ll. 89–90). Middleton attempts to diffuse Sherley's 'transgressive hybridity' by adding a defence of travel, which he describes as 'the golden mine that enriches the poorest country and fills the barrenest with abundant plenty' (p. 673, ll. 49–50). *Sir Robert Sherley* also obliquely recognises the risk of emasculation associated with conversion to Islam in its attempt to diffuse any anxiety caused by this perceived threat. The 'honoured Englishman' Robert is portrayed as 'that son of mine to me that am his mother', England, who addresses him as 'O thou my darling'; the emphasis on the mother–son relationship stresses Robert's masculine status (p. 675, l. 211, ll. 253–4; p. 676, l. 260). It is possible that Robert's identity as a Catholic convert is another factor that could threaten this status. The Sherleys' Catholicism was not only controversial in terms of its capacity to bring disfavour from a Protestant audience; given that anti-Catholic polemic often depicted its objects as feminine, Robert's Catholic identity could potentially also suggest feminine qualities.

In a gesture that points to the complicated relationships between religious and gender identities in the period, Middleton attempts to represent both Robert and his Persian subjects as both Christian (or potentially so) and masculine. Not only is the Persians' Muslim identity minimised, but their virility and masculinity continues to be actively emphasised. Thus, the Persians are excellent soldiers, 'their cities full of renowned and worthy captains' (p. 675, l. 208). They are sexually profligate, with Persian men taking many wives and producing many children, 'so much do they detest sterility and barrenness' (p. 676, l. 335). Given that sexual prowess and performance were, according to Anthony Fletcher, 'the most telling test of manhood' during this period, the Persians' sexual profligacy may be read as a direct signifier of their masculinity.[31] Indeed, their production of many children and their martial valour are both features that may have been read as suggesting extreme manliness. Alexandra Shepard's study of the meanings of manhood in early modern England describes a 'sliding scale of manhood, conceived in gendered terms', topped by 'the lusty, valiant men' who had, according to conduct books of the time, strong sexual appetites. At the other end of the scale were effeminate men who lacked courage and were unlikely to beget many children.[32] It is clear where Middleton's Persians would be located on such a scale; their bravery and manly fortitude 'shames many other Christian countries and may justly upbraid them of effeminacy and laziness' (p. 676, 344–5). The accusation of effeminacy is thus reversed, and any fear that association with Muslim allies may risk either religious conversion or emasculation laid to rest. These gendered notions of masculinity are explored in greater length in *The travailes of the three English brothers* (1607).

THE TRAVAILES OF THE THREE ENGLISH BROTHERS

The travailes of the three English brothers was written and first performed in 1607. The play was based on a contemporary pamphlet by Anthony Nixon, *The three English brothers*, which related the experiences of Thomas, Anthony, and Robert Sherley in their travels to and from Persia and the Ottoman Empire in the late 1590s and early 1600s.[33] In 1606, while Anthony and Robert were both abroad, their brother Thomas came back to England and it is likely that he encouraged the production of the play as well as commissioning Nixon's pamphlet soon after his return.[34] Thomas Sherley was keen to further his brothers' interests in promoting trade opportunities and closer Anglo-Persian relations; *Travailes* was thus produced and supported by those who had an interest in encouraging the image of Persia as a friendly, accessible place (particularly in contrast to its neighbour, the Ottoman Empire).[35]

The play presents Persia as open to English influences and receptive to English travellers; in doing so, it suggests both that Persia is itself ripe for conversion to Christianity and that it is a place where English Christians are safe from the threat of Muslim conversion. The three English brothers enact a fantasy of how Christians can withstand the threats and enticements of a foreign religion and culture, with Thomas remaining obdurate when faced with torture and the temptation to convert to Islam, and Anthony and Robert providing such impressive examples of English Christianity that they lead Shah 'Abbās to hint at the prospect of his own religious conversion. *Travailes* raises the possibility of religious conversion and transforms it into a successful English conquest, in which the brothers represent a powerful, masculine, Christian Englishness, and notions of gender identity are repeatedly implicated in the play's imagining of how the English might convert the Persians to their faith and habits.

In the opening scene of the play, Anthony and Robert are introduced to the 'Sophy' (Shah 'Abbās) by the Governor of Qazvin, and engage in conversation with him, before the Persians, and then the Christians, enact battle scenes. The Sophy is immediately impressed by Anthony, and expresses his deep admiration and desire to emulate the Englishman:

> What powers do wrap me in amazement thus?
> Methinks this Christian's more than mortal.
> Sure he conceals himself! Within my thoughts
> Never was man so deeply registered.
> But God or Christian, or whate'er he be,
> I wish to be none other but as he.[36]

Here Anthony, as an Englishman and a Christian, is situated in a category that is beyond mortality as conceived by the Sophy. The latter's statement that 'Within my thoughts / Never was man so deeply registered' suggests that Anthony is both a man and something more than a man; so impressive as a man that he must be a god. The performance of masculinity in this play involves the juxtaposition of different national, religious, and gender identities, and so, as in this instance, masculinity is conceived and performed through a series of oppositions and through the impressions made by one category of characters (for example, an English Christian man) on another (a Persian Muslim man). Just as Bruce R. Smith has described the world of *Othello* as one 'where masculinity is achieved in opposition to racial others', so the world of *Travailes* is one in which masculinity is defined and enacted alongside religious and national difference.[37]

The question of social status is also pertinent here. As a dramatisation of an encounter between a monarch and unknown travellers, we might expect the play to emphasise the Sophy's power and status, and indeed the meeting between the two groups involves all the Englishmen save Anthony kissing the Sophy's foot.[38] In his first speech to 'Abbās, Anthony praises his host's wars (from which the shah has just returned) as 'manly, stout and honourable' (l. 55). (Anthony Sherley's own relation of his travels was to describe 'Abbās as 'man-like' in appearance, and to praise his virtue and strength.[39]) As the scene progresses, however, the roles are to some degree reversed. The Sophy seems entirely captivated by Anthony, or 'graced' by him in the words of the Persian noblemen

Halibeck and Calimath, who comment: 'He'll make him his heir next' (l. 119, l. 153). The Sophy speaks several times of 'adoring' Anthony, and of entertaining him with 'arms of love and adoration' (l. 89, l. 127, l. 148); he describes the pleasure of submitting to Anthony's 'embrace', and 'feast[ing]' upon his 'tongue', as 'I delight to hear thee speak' (l. 150, l. 156). Impressed by the Christians' military prowess, the Sophy even doubts Anthony's mortality: 'your honours / And your qualities of war are more than human' (l. 123–4). The scene ends with the two men walking out hand in hand, as the shah exclaims: 'For thy sake do I love all Christians [. . .] Walk in our hand, thou hast possessed our heart' (l. 190, l. 192). The potential disruption that may be caused by the close relationship between Anthony and the Sophy is hinted at in the reactions of Halibeck and Calimath, suggesting the possibility that the Sophy's favour for Anthony may extend to placing him next in line to the throne and disrupting the dominant system of primogeniture.

Anthony, meanwhile, though entirely respectful to the Sophy, makes it clear that he will not transgress his own boundaries by raising his sword against a fellow Christian (l. 147). Other than this, he is willing to put his 'force and power' in the service of the shah, who appoints him general of his army against the Turks (l. 145, l. 152). Anthony then expresses to the Sophy his conviction that their religion should be one and the same, due to their fundamental similarity:

> All that makes up this earthly edifice
> By which we are called men is all alike.
> Each may be the other's anatomy; [. . .]
> One workman made us all, and all offend
> That maker, all taste of interdicted sin. [. . .]
> We live and die, suffer calamities,
> Are underlings to sickness, fire, famine, sword.
> We are all punished by the same hand and rod,
> Our sins are all alike; why not our God? (i. 164–6, 170–1, 177–80)

Anthony's desire for religious unity is met by the Sophy's repeated yearning to emulate the 'brave Englishman', and his belief that Anthony has the power to turn Turks into Persians: 'A camp of spirits equal to thyself / Would turn all Turkey into Persia' (l. 188, ll. 154–5). In fact the play offers not only the prospect of a conversion of Turks into Persians, but, later, that of Persians into Englishmen. In the following scene, Anthony offers to do the Sophy 'manly service' in his wars, and the Sophy entreats him to stay and do so, in an exchange which furthers the image of Anthony as masculine and powerful (scene ii, l. 234).

The closeness of the relationship between Anthony and the Sophy, heightened by Anthony's insistence on their fundamental sameness, calls into question the firmness of boundaries around sexual identities, and, by implication, religious and national identities. Prior to the performance of *The travailes*, contemporary English sources that described the Sherleys' reception at the shah's court stated that, soon after this first meeting, 'Abbās came to the Sherleys and 'embraced Sir Anthony and his brother, kissing them both three or four times over, and taking Sir Anthony by the hand, swearing a great oath that he should be his sworn brother, and so did he call him always',[40] and that 'once a day at the least he ['Abbās] would send for him [Anthony] to confer, and compliment with him; yea, sometimes he must be sent for to come to his bed-chamber at midnight, accompanied with his brother, for that purpose'.[41] As Sanjay Subrahmanyam notes, these sources seek to indicate that Anthony had great 'personal charm'; as they were written by members of the Sherleys' retinue, this was clearly for reasons of propaganda, but for the contemporary reader, the midnight visits to the bed-chamber and enthusiastic kissing could also be interpreted as suggesting a homoerotic potential to the relationship.[42]

Due to what Alan Bray has called the 'uncertainty in masculine friendship', such potential was always present, and references to night-time meetings and physical closeness between the two men suggest the possibility that the boundaries between friendship and sexual intimacy might be blurred. If 'the outline of the "sodomite" . . . [was] never very far from the flower-strewn world of masculine friendship' and 'could never wholly be distinguished from it', then the similarity and closeness between Antony and the Sophy hints at the possibility of sexual activity between the two men.[43] The public kiss in particular, Bray has argued, 'carried the same meaning as the equally public fact of being a powerful man's bedfellow'.[44] Although kissing and bed-sharing do not automatically suggest sexual activity, the public display of intimacy between the two men points to their closeness and mutual influence, which is demonstrated on stage in their hand-holding and loving language. Anthony's avowal that 'All that makes up this earthly edifice / By which we are called men is all alike' calls attention to the sameness of the two men's bodies and the fact that those bodies are male. In insisting upon their sameness, Anthony breaks down the differences between them that might be presumed to exist, most notably of religion and nationality. The potential eroticism of the friendship between the Sophy and Anthony disrupts the notion that they are fundamentally different from one another in any meaningful way.

By the end of the play, English and Persian identities have been brought closer still through the marriage of Robert to the Sophy's niece. In the final scene, Robert persuades the Sophy to grant him religious freedoms that would have been a fantasy indeed for an English man living in a Muslim country: the shah agrees that Robert's child may be baptised a Christian, that he may build a church for Christian worship, and found a school for the education of Christian children. The Sophy even suggests that he should be the child's sponsor: 'Baptize thy child, ourself will aid in it; / Ourself will answer for't, a godfather' (scene xiii, ll. 172–3). The scene ends with the two men embracing:

> In the best embrace of our endearèd love
> We do enclose thee [. . .] Thou shalt not lack
> Our love's plentitude. (ll. 196–7, ll. 199–200)

Any perceived threat that the Sherley brothers may have been presumed to have faced as travellers in Islamic lands has been averted, and the prospect of the Sophy's own conversion to Christianity (a necessary precursor of acting as godparent to a Christian child) strongly hinted at. The linking of the prospect of the Sophy's conversion and the provision made for Robert's children, recalling the earlier aside that the Sophy would make Anthony his heir, hint at the ways in which encounters between peoples of different cultures, and specifically the act of religious conversion, could precede the disruption of long-standing traditions such as primogeniture. In this instance, the Sophy's willingness to associate himself with Christianity and to make new provisions for Christians living in Persia hints at potential benefits for Christians travelling in Muslim lands. At the end of the play, far from being threatened by a feminised or emasculating foreign power, Anthony and Robert have successfully asserted their English and Christian identities and have won a partnership with Persia which is seen as mutually beneficial. *The travailes* thus dramatises the hopes of many Christian travellers to and commentators on Persia, who speculated that Shah ʿAbbās, due to his interest in Christianity and tolerance of Christian minorities, might be persuaded to convert from Islam to Christianity, and to bring the whole of Persia with him. The prospect of a powerful Christian force and ally in the East that such speculations raised was an enticing one, and useful to those who, like the Sherley brothers, sought to promote Anglo-Persian relations.[45]

Alongside the mutually admiring relationship that develops between Anthony, Robert, and the Sophy is placed the more antagonistic interaction between Thomas and the 'Great Turk', the Ottoman sultan Mehmet III. Captured by the Turkish army, Thomas is imprisoned and tortured, and is seen being kept in stocks and raised on a rack whilst being interrogated in scene xii. The Great Turk himself demands to know of Thomas his 'descent / And promise of the ransom that's assigned thee' (scene xii, ll. 60–1), but Thomas successfully refuses the temptations and threats with which this request is made. The Turk addresses Thomas as 'Christian', and Thomas repeatedly refers to his faith, and his (Christ-like) 'patience' which enables him to withstand the pain of his torture (l. 87). As he is 'wrench[ed]' (l. 100) on the stage, the Great Turk offers Thomas the chance to save his life through conversion to Islam:

> [. . .] wilt thou forsake thy faith,
> Become as we are, and to Mahomet
> Our holy prophet, and his Alcoran
> Give thy devotion?   (ll. 108–111)

Thomas's reply demonstrates his strength in the face of direst temptation:

> First shall the sun melt from his restless seat
> Ere that our name shall turn *apostata*;
> Thy kingdoms be unpeopled, and thy nations
> Become as free for beasts as now for men;
> Thyself (as sometimes were thy ancestors)
> Fed in a cage and dragged at conqueror's heels. (ll. 113–18)

Recalling the image of the humiliated Bajazeth in Marlowe's *Tamburlaine Part I*, Thomas elaborates on an opposition between himself and the Turk in which Thomas represents 'Roman spirit' (l. 94) and the Turk, inevitably, 'Turkish tyranny' (l. 97). This binary opposition asserts Thomas's Christianity and his masculinity: 'I am the same through all that made me man / Scorn pagan's threats to die a Christian' (ll. 98–99). The Turk, in turn, is impressed both by Thomas's physical courage and his faith: 'We stand amazèd at thy constancy. [. . .] Thy strength of faith hath bred a wonder in us' (l. 107, l. 122). Thus a potential conversion scene, in which the vulnerable traveller is induced to give up his faith, is transformed into a graphic articulation of the physical and spiritual strength of the English Christian. Thomas's physical strength is tried as he is racked onstage, but is equal to the task; the potential threat of conversion – and emasculation – is reversed into a triumphant assertion of masculine Englishness.

The travailes of the three English brothers also explores the relationship between gender and conversion in its presentation of women. Initially, the two female Persian characters in the play adhere to a well-worn early modern stereotype of Islamic women: that they are sexually rapacious. Dalibra, the maid to the Sophy's niece (who is referred to in the dramatis personae only as 'Niece'), describes the English visitors as 'a dish worth eating', if they are 'as pleasant in taste as they are fair to the eye' (scene iii, ll.5–6). When her mistress asks, 'A cannibal, Dalibra? Wouldst eat men?', the maid replies, 'Why not, madam? Fine men cannot choose but be fine meat' (ll. 7–9), and the Niece responds, 'Ay but they are a filling meat' (l. 10). The women then evaluate Persian and English men in terms of their sexual capacities; Dalibra comments that the 'strangers' can not only speak better than her own countrymen, but could 'do as well if it came once to execution' (ll. 24–5), whilst the Niece comments of her Persian suitor, Halibeck, that he 'could do little and he could not commend himself' (l. 60).

Their innuendo-laden exchange suggests that the Persian women view the English travellers largely in terms of their sexual potential, but when they meet Robert Sherley, their response mirrors that of the Sophy immediately before. The Niece, declaring that 'All Persia sings / The English brothers are co-mates for kings' (ll. 94–5), bids Robert farewell with a half-uttered wish that he might be her suitor: 'Were thy religion. . .' (l. 109). Robert's behaviour is that of the ideal courtly suitor, comparing the Niece's beauty to the sun and claiming his one goal to be 'honoured fame' (l. 77–9, l. 85). The play's fantasy of how Persian women might respond to English men is heightened when, in a reversal that turns the potential threat of conversion on its head, the Sophy's niece converts to Christianity in order to marry Robert. Her conversion is not simply one of convenience; her openness to Christianity is shown as genuine through her switch to a Christian lexis, as she refers to 'the holy angels' and 'heaven' in her defence of Robert to the Sophy (scene xi, l. 213, l. 228). The play thus presents Persia as a potentially welcoming and tolerant place, in which male English travellers can expect to practise their own faith and retain their masculinity. It is also a place in which social rank is recognised and described in ways that may be familiar to an English audience. So, for example, 'honour' or 'honourable' are words used both by Anthony to describe the Persians and by the Sophy to describe Anthony; in establishing social rank, they point to the presence of a gentry class and a recognition of the high ranking of the English travellers within that class.[46] Thus *The travailes of the three English brothers* puts forward a particular performance of masculinity and Englishness in which social, gender, national, and religious identities are amalgamated. Its performance of such identities supports the contention by Bruce R. Smith that masculinity itself – and, by extension, other forms of identity – is 'a matter of contingency, of circumstances, of performance'.[47] In this Persia, the performances of Englishmen are exempla of martial prowess, Christian fortitude, and masculine appeal to Persian men and women alike.

If writings that supported the Sherley brothers' efforts to build closer relationships between Europe and Persia were to convince their audiences that Persia was safe and welcoming to English travellers, then they were obliged to diffuse any potential anxieties surrounding the threat of conversion. In doing so they promoted a fantasy of Englishmen as supremely masculine and supremely impressive to their Islamic hosts. In reality, it was Anthony and Robert, and not Shah 'Abbās, who were converts from their original faith, a fact which the literature related to their travels glosses over, perhaps for obvious reasons. We are familiar with the image of the English Protestant male who is vulnerable in terms of both his religious and gender identity when faced with an Islamic threat.[48] In contrast, the idea of conversion as understood by these writings suggests that it was not only a matter of changing religious belief but could also involve the remaking of other forms of identity, including masculinity. Texts such as *Sir Robert Sherley* and *The travailes* endeavoured to present images of Persia that made it clear that conversion – in relation to either religion or gender identity – was no threat to English men.

Such texts also suggest an overlap between national, religious, and gender identity which obliges us to examine our notions of how these identities were conceived and performed in the early modern period, and to consider the ways in which the intersections between gender and conversion call into question the permeability of the boundaries between different faiths and genders. The presentation of the Sherley brothers, for example, as impervious to the threat of religious conversion involves portraying them both as consistently masculine – as in Thomas's assertion that 'I am the same through all that made me man' – and glossing over their own ambiguous religious identities. In resisting the notion that proximity to other faiths might compromise religious identity, such material points to the close relationship between masculinity, national identity, and religious identity in the early modern period. Such identities were placed centre stage by travel; in experiencing, relating, and dramatising the phenomenon of cross-cultural encounter, English travellers, readers, and audiences were faced with the ways in which boundaries between different identities, as well as those between different lands, could be permeated.

NOTES

1 Michael C. Questier, *Conversion, politics and religion in England, 1580–1625* (Cambridge: Cambridge University Press, 1996), p. 2.

2 For the concept of 'turning Turk', see: Nabil Matar, '"Turning Turk": conversion to Islam in English Renaissance thought', *Durham University Journal*, 86 (1994), 33–42; *Islam in Britain, 1558–1685* (Cambridge: Cambridge University Press, 1998); *Turks, Moors and Englishmen in the age of discovery* (New York: Columbia University Press, 1999); Lois Potter, 'Pirates and "turning Turk" in Renaissance drama', in Jean-Pierre Maquerlot and Michele Willems (eds), *Travel and drama in Shakespeare's time* (Cambridge: Cambridge University Press, 1996), pp. 130–34; Jonathan Burton, 'English anxiety and the Muslim power of conversion: five perspectives on "turning Turk" in early modern texts', *Journal of Early Modern Cultural Studies*, 2 (2002), 35–67; *Traffic and turning: Islam and English drama, 1579–1624* (Newark: University of Delaware Press, 2005); Daniel Vitkus, *Turning Turk: English theater and the multicultural Mediterranean, 1570–1630* (New York: Palgrave Macmillan, 2003); Gerald MacLean, 'On turning Turk, or trying to: national identity in Robert Daborne's *Christian turn'd Turk*', *Explorations in Renaissance Culture*, 29 (2003), 225–52.

3 Burton, *Traffic and turning*, p. 98; Vitkus, *Turning Turk*, p. 107. See also Barbara Fuchs, 'Faithless empires: renegadoes, and the English nation', *English Literary History*, 67 (2000), 45–69; Bindu Malieckal, '"Wanton irreligious madness": conversion and castration in Massinger's *The renegado*', *Essays in Arts and Sciences*, 31 (2002), 25–43. Bernadette Andrea has noted how scholarship on the trope of turning Turk has contributed to 'the effacement of women's agency in literary and cultural studies of early modern England and the Islamic world'. *Women and Islam in early modern English literature* (Cambridge: Cambridge University Press, 2007), p. 3.

4 On this pamphlet see Daniel J. Vitkus, introduction to *Sir Robert Sherley his entertainment in Cracovia*, ed. Jerzy Limon and Daniel J. Vitkus, in *Thomas Middleton: the collected works*, gen. eds Gary Taylor and John Lavagnino (Oxford: Clarendon Press, 2007), p. 670.

5 On Persia under the Safavid dynasty, see Roger Savory, *Iran under the Safavids* (Cambridge: Cambridge University Press, 1980); Peter Jackson and Laurence Lockhart (eds), *The Cambridge history of Iran: volume 6: the Timurid and Safavid periods* (Cambridge: Cambridge University Press, 1986), especially chapter 7; Gene R. Garthwaite, *The Persians* (Oxford: Blackwell, 2005), chapter 6. For the origins of Shi'ism, its emergence as state religion under the Safavids, and its significance in Persia/Iran, see Said Amir Arjomand, *The shadow of God and the hidden Imam: religion, political order, and societal change in Shi'ite Iran from the beginning to 1890* (Chicago: University of Chicago Press, 1984), Part 2; and I. P. Petrushevsky, *Islam in Iran*, trans. Hubert Evans (London: Athlone, 1985), pp. 30–3.

6 See for example Alain Grosrichard, *The sultan's court: European fantasies of the East*, trans. Liz Heron (London: Verso, 1998); Margaret Meserve, *Empires of Islam in Renaissance historical thought* (Cambridge, MA: Harvard University Press, 2008), pp. 98–9. On the representation of a pre-Islamic Persian court as given to feminine decadence, see Chloë Houston, 'Persia and kingship in William Cartwright's *The royall slave* (1636)', *Studies in English Literature 1500–1900*, 54 (2014), 455–73.

7 Plato, *Laws*, Book III, quoted in Josef Wiesehöfer, *Ancient Persia: from 550 BC to 650 AD*, trans. Azizeh Azodi (London: I.B.Tauris, 1996), p. 79.

8 *La nouvelle conversion du roy de Perse* (Paris, 1606); Anthony Nixon, *The three English brothers* (London, 1607), K4^v. On the prospect of 'Abbās's and Persia's conversion to Christianity, see Chloë Houston, 'Turning Persia: the prospect of conversion in Safavid Iran', in Lieke Stelling, Harald Hendrix, and Todd Richardson (eds), *The turn of the soul: representations of religious conversion in early modern art and literature* (Leiden: Brill, 2012), pp. 85–107.

9 Matar, *Islam in Britain*, pp. 15–16. Whilst Christian to Muslim conversion was more common in this period, and has in consequence been more widely studied, Muslim to Christian conversion was by no means a rare phenomenon; see, for example, Matthew Dimmock, *New Turkes: dramatizing Islam and the Ottomans in early modern England* (Aldershot: Ashgate, 2005), pp. 104–6; and Nabil Matar, *Europe through Arab eyes, 1578–1727* (New York: Columbia University Press, 2009), pp. 44, 192–3.

10 Burton, *Traffic and turning*, p. 16.
11 Vitkus, *Turning Turk*, p. 108.
12 Vitkus, *Three Turk plays*, pp. 235–6.
13 Andrea, *Women and Islam*, p. 7.

14 Philip Massinger, *The renegado*, in *Three Turk plays from early modern England*, ed. Daniel J. Vitkus (New York: Columbia University Press, 2000).
15 "collop, n.1" OED Online, Oxford University Press, consulted 9 October 2014.
16 For this point and for sharing her investigations on the word 'collop', I am grateful to Helen Smith.
17 See also Malieckal, '"Wanton irreligious madness"'.
18 Jane Hwang Degenhardt, 'Catholic prophylactics and Islam's sexual threat: preventing and undoing sexual defilement in *The renegado*', *Journal for Early Modern Cultural Studies*, 9 (2009), 62–92.
19 D. W. Davies, *Elizabethans errant: the strange fortunes of Sir Thomas Sherley and his three sons* (Ithaca, NY: Cornell University Press, 1967), pp. 77–84. See chapters 5, 6 and 9 for the Sherleys' time in Persia. See also Franz Babinger, *Sherleiana* (Berlin, Gedruckt In Der Reichsdruckerei, 1932); and Boies Penrose, *The Sherleian odyssey* (Taunton: Wessex, 1938).
20 Niels Steensgaard, *The Asian trade revolution of the seventeenth century: the East India companies and the decline of the caravan trade* (Chicago: University of Chicago Press, 1975), pp. 213–14.
21 Davies, *Elizabethans errant*, pp. 236, 240, 259, 272.
22 Anthony Parr (ed.), *Three Renaissance travel plays: the travels of the three English brothers, the sea voyage, the Antipodes* (Manchester: Manchester University Press, 1995), p. 10.
23 James I and VI, *His maiesties poetical excercises at vacant hours* (London, 1603), H2^r–L4^v, discussed in Dimmock, *New Turkes*, p. 199.
24 Franklin L. Baumer, 'England, the Turk, and the common corps of Christendom', *American Historical Review*, 50 (1944), 37, n. 59.
25 Dimmock, *New Turkes*, p. 200.
26 On the long-held English interest in trade with Persia and the Orient, see Davies, *Elizabethans errant*, p. 82.
27 Vitkus, Introduction to *Sir Robert Sherley*, p. 670.
28 Alexandra Shepard, *Meanings of manhood in early modern England* (Oxford: Oxford University Press, 2003), p. 59.
29 Vitkus, Introduction to *Sir Robert Sherley*, p. 670.
30 *Ibid.*, p. 671.
31 Anthony Fletcher, *Gender, sex and subordination in England 1500–1800* (New Haven, CT: Yale University Press, 1995), p. 93. See also Shepard, *Meanings of manhood*, pp. 120–1.
32 Shepard, *Meanings of manhood*, p. 59–60.
33 On the Sherleys' travel to Persia, see Davies, *Elizabethans errant*; Babinger, *Sherleiana*; Penrose, *The Sherleian odyssey*; Parr (ed.), *Three Renaissance travel plays*, Introduction; Anthony Parr, 'Foreign relations in Jacobean England: the Sherley brothers and the "voyage of Persia"', in Jean-Pierre

Maquerlot and Michèle Willems (eds), *Travel and drama in Shakespeare's time* (Cambridge: Cambridge University Press, 1996), pp. 14–31; Vasco Resende, '"Un homme d'inventions et inconstant": les fidélités politiques d'Anthony Sherley, entre l'ambassade safavide et la diplomatie européenne", in Dejanirah Couto and Rui Manuel Loureiro (eds), *Revisiting Hormuz: Portuguese interactions in the Persian Gulf region in the early modern period* (Wiesbaden: Harrassowitz Verlag, 2008), pp. 235–60. On the relationship between the play and Nixon's pamphlet, see Parr (ed.), *Three Renaissance travel plays*, Introduction, pp. 7–9.

34 Parr (ed.), *Three Renaissance Travel Plays*, Introduction, p. 8.

35 On positive portrayals of Persia in early modern travel writing, and the contrasting of Persia and the Ottoman Empire, see Chloë Houston, '"Thou glorious kingdome, thou chiefe of empires": Persia in seventeenth-century travel literature', *Studies in Travel Writing*, 13 (2009), 141–52; Jane Grogan, 'The not-forgotten empire: images of Persia in English Renaissance writing', *Literature Compass*, 7 (9), 912–21.

36 *The travels of the three English brothers* in Parr (ed.), *Three Renaissance Travel Plays*, scene i, ll. 74–9. All further references will be to this edition and will be given in parentheses in the text.

37 Bruce R. Smith, *Shakespeare and masculinity* (Oxford: Oxford University Press, 2000), p. 118.

38 Anthony is permitted to kiss the Sophy's hand; this preferential treatment is recorded in travel writings recording the Sherleys' visit to Persia, including Nixon's pamphlet. *The three English brothers*, H1r.

39 Anthony Sherley, *Sir Anthony Sherley his relation of his travels into Persia* (London, 1613), p. 29.

40 George Manwaring, *A true discourse of Sir Anthony Sherley's travel into Persia*, ed. E. Denison Ross in *Sir Anthony Sherley and his Persian adventure* [1933] (London: RoutledgeCurzon, 2005), p. 206.

41 William Parry, *A new and large discourse on the travels of Sir Anthony Sherley knight, by sea, and ouer land, to the Persian Empire*, ed. E. Denison Ross in *Sir Anthony Sherley and his Persian adventure*, pp. 206, 118–19.

42 Sanjay Subrahmanyam, *Three ways to be alien: travails and encounters in the early modern world* (Waltham, MA: Brandeis University Press, 2011), p. 98. Edward Denison Ross, author of a biography of Anthony, suggests that he 'must have possessed an almost hypnotic power in personal intercourse'. *Sir Anthony Sherley and his Persian adventure*, p. 81.

43 Alan Bray, *The friend* (Chicago: University of Chicago Press, 2003), p. 201.

44 Alan Bray, 'Homosexuality and the signs of male friendship in Elizabethan England', *History Workshop*, 29 (1990), 4.

45 On the prospect of 'Abbās' conversion to Christianity and its discussion in the early seventeenth century, see Houston, 'Turning Persia'.

46 Bruce R. Smith discusses the use of 'honour' to denote social rank amongst men in *Shakespeare and masculinity*, p. 43.
47 *Ibid.*, p. 4.
48 Jonathan Burton, 'English anxiety and the Muslim power of conversion: five perspectives on "Turning Turk" in early modern texts', *Journal of Early Modern Cultural Studies*, 2 (2002), 40.

11

Turning tricks: erotic commodification, cross-cultural conversion, and the bed-trick on the English stage, 1580–1630

Daniel Vitkus

This chapter concentrates on a particular strain of theatrical trickery: deception by means of substitution. In various permutations, this structure is repeated over and over in the drama of early modern England – and perhaps in all drama. But I will focus my discussion here on three particular strains of deception in English Renaissance drama: erotic or sexual trickery, commercial trickery, and trickery involving religious or racial identity. I want to show that these three forms of deception are often connected or elided because they refer to historically specific anxieties that co-existed in late-sixteenth- and early-seventeenth-century English society.

Early modern theatre in London, especially after the rise of citizen comedy in the 1590s, revelled in situations that involved commercial, erotic, and religious deceit. The chart below indicates a set of related concerns that are repeated so frequently in the culture of early modern England that they form a noticeable pattern, almost a set of archetypes:

trick: verbal promise: commodity-object: trickster/dupe

erotic (love-trick or seduction): vow: hymen: whore/cuckold
commercial (exchange-trick): contract: coin: usurer/bankrupt
religious (conversion-trick): profession of faith: foreskin: renegade or heretic

These three categories are interwoven and entangled in early modern discourse because they operate by the same fundamental structural principle: all three depend upon a dupe or gull who mistakes exchange value for use value – who accepts the object of exchange as a substitute for something more authentic. The foundational form of this trick is the collective delusion that Marx called commodity fetishism, which accepts exchange value as the measure of all things and ignores the reality of use value.[1] That mistake is the primal ruse of emergent capitalism, and it was profoundly disturbing for early modern society in England. This fundamental economic disruption reverberated through various cultural productions, bringing together (and often eliding) economic, erotic, and religious or racial concerns: women are bought and sold as commodities exchanged between men; sexuality becomes radically economised; religious conversion is up for sale; and commercial intercourse between people of different races and religions is repeatedly figured in erotic or sexualised terms.

With very few exceptions, Christian ideology in the early modern period defined any sincere and voluntary conversion that turned away from 'the true religion' (whether Protestant or Catholic) as a conversion effected by means of a trick or misapprehension. Willing conversion to another religion or sect was characterised, from the perspective of those still adhering to the religion that the convert had abandoned, not as an authentic or heartfelt act of piety, but as either a choice prioritising material gain over spiritual righteousness or a foolish choice resulting from a trick or deception. Often quite rightly, conversion was perceived as a course of action carried out by those who sought power, patronage, status, wealth, safety, or financial security. Powerful princes, such as Christian II of Denmark or Henry IV of France, were high-profile examples of interfaith conversions undertaken for reasons of political gain.[2] When a Christian converted to Islam, this was nearly always described as a betrayal motivated by avarice, lust, or a combination of both. An English captivity narrative from 1622, *The famous and wonderful recovery of a ship of Bristol*, claimed that many Christian captives in North Africa converted to Islam because they were tortured or threatened with violence, but also laments the fact that many became Muslims without any compulsion: 'Others again, I must confess, who never knew any god but their own sensual lusts and pleasures, thought that any religion would serve their turns and so for preferment or wealth very voluntarily renounced their faith and became renegadoes, in despite of any counsel which seemed to intercept them.'[3]

If it was not force or gain that moved a convert, then a shift to a different religion could otherwise be defined as a mistake on the part of an ignorant dupe seduced by evil counselors. Protestants claimed that

Catholic believers were misguided, seduced by alluring, sensual images, and tricked by false teachers who led them into damnable 'superstition'. Catholic authors railed against reformers such as Luther and Calvin, who they saw as theological seducers, tricking good Christians and diverting them with tempting words onto the path of heresy. The English Jesuit Robert Parsons wrote a series of tracts that characterised the Protestant movement as a sect led by false prophets and built on error. In *A treatise of three conversions of England* (1604), Parsons set out to refute the claims of John Foxe in *Actes and monuments* and to discredit Foxe's account of the rise of a purified and reformed church before, during, and after the reign of Henry VIII. For Parsons, the English Reformation was, from the start, led by deceivers and charlatans who stood to gain by religious change and so coerced many well-intentioned English souls into choosing the new Protestant heresy. According to Parsons, 'when K. Henry first seemed to favour the ghospell. [...] it was not for God, but for reveng & to enjoy the spoyle of the Church', and the Protestant movement 'had noe other beginning in England, but upon affection of men and women'.[4] In the final summation of his attack, Parsons repeatedly invokes an image of entanglement to describe how the Protestant martyrologist allegedly confuses both himself and his readers: 'He findeth himself extremely intangled, nor cannot tell ... which way to turne his head, but is forced to double hither and thither, to go forth and backe, say and unsay, and to cast a hundred shadowes of wrangling gloses upon the whole matter, thereby to obscure the same to the eyes and eares of his Reader' (629). Parson's Foxe is a kind of con artist who 'playeth fast and loose' (639) in order to trick his readers so that they will continue to see conversion from the 'true' Roman church to the 'false' English Protestant church as justifiable.

Whether they made a sincere conversion, sold out for gain, or were tricked into 'turning', converts were located by their former co-religionists on the receiving end of a swindle, accused of accepting a false substitute in the place of true faith. This way of talking about conversion was intertwined with the commercial discourses of the day. Discussions about religious identity and the condition of the soul were linked to the economic processes that were taking place in western Europe, in the sphere of cross-cultural trade, and abroad in the newly established overseas empires. In all of this, the economic took on a primary role in the dialectical relationship with cultural production. Capitalism, as it emerged in early modern England and beyond, was experienced as a game of fast and loose: a magical (and deeply sinful) means to produce something from nothing.[5] In the early modern era it was the new system of credit, debt, investment, and interest, along with the increasing commodification of all things (including those people who were treated as things) that produced a new class structure and destabilised the old order.[6] Investment and profit-taking from international commerce, after the spatial crisis and the maritime turn of the sixteenth century, were particularly exciting and disturbing.[7] 'Usury' was the term that early modern people often used to describe not only the setting of high interest rates by creditors but all sorts of new speculative financial mechanisms that were designed to generate profit without providing a concrete good or service.[8]

A complex figurative language was employed to comment on the new behaviours and experiences of a society that began during the 1570s to intensify its connections to the global trade matrix.[9] The 1570s were also the decade in which the first permanent playhouses and officially licensed theatre companies were established in London. Some of these theatre companies, including Shakespeare's, were (along with the Levant Company and the East India Company) the earliest joint-stock enterprises in the history of England.[10] The growth of overseas trade brought English subjects into much more frequent contact with people who were designated as 'Mahometans' (i.e. 'Muslims'), 'Turks', and 'Moors', and so it is not surprising that we see many exotic, dark-skinned characters appear on the Elizabethan and early Stuart stage, and that those characters are associated with the new commercial transactions and cross-cultural exchanges that were taking place in the Levant, Africa, and Asia.[11] In a post-Reformation context that saw the decentring and splintering of Christendom, accompanied by the expansion of long-distance trade and a flood of newly gathered ethnographic and geographic knowledge, the sense of exposure to other cultures and religions brought with it a fear that English Protestants would be tempted, seduced, or tricked into conversions of one kind or another. This sense of potential transformation and transgression suffused the London theatre and was taken up by its playwrights.[12]

Obviously, early modern playwrights and playgoers did not employ a Marxist terminology to describe their apprehensions about the economic changes that were taking place around them, but in their descriptions of the disturbing innovations brought on by proto-capitalism, they conveyed an awareness that traditional values and patronage economies were giving way to a new set of values and a new economic structure that they condemned as immoral, unnatural, and sinful. Lacking a modern economic discourse, and without the disciplinary categories that separate 'literature' and 'economics' today, early modern writers commonly used poetic forms of expression to address the economic crisis of their time, which affected everything from wages and land tenure to the marriage market.[13] London's early modern theatre was obsessed with economic issues and featured many plays that dramatised economic transactions, typically of a highly erotic nature – gender and sexuality were closely associated with economic transactions and forms of exchange.

In the romantic comedies of the Elizabethan period, love, sex, and marriage were often presented in terms of patriarchal market forces, with women as commodities, and virgin brides or well-endowed widows as counters of exchange between men.[14] Later, city comedies became a genre that exhibited an especially intensive awareness of commerciality and of fraudulent market transactions. The comedies of Ben Jonson and Thomas Middleton are typical in this regard: in Jonson's *Bartholomew fair*, *The Alchemist*, *Epicoene*, and other plays, the marketplace (including the marriage market) is a corrupt place in which the sharpest dealers prosper and women are commodities to be obtained by hook or by crook. In Middleton's *A chaste maid in Cheapside*, marriage and extra-marital sex are financial arrangements akin to illegal dealing in fresh meat during Lent. In dramatic plots that turn on trickery and deceit, sex, marriage, and reproduction were relentlessly commodified: the figurative language that compared the female body to a commercial good for sale is ever present; prostitutes, bawds, and their customers appear with increasing frequency after the 1590s.[15]

In both comic and tragic drama we find one erotic plot device that is repeated promiscuously – the so-called 'bed-trick'. This is a particular form of deception by means of substitution, related to earlier dramatic devices such as the exchanged beloved, the substitute bride (or groom), and the boy-bride or female-groom. But the bed-trick differs from these since it involves a sexual act between the substituted figure and the character who is subjected to this sexual trickery. The bed-trick is a ruse whereby one character expects to have sex with a particular person, but another character, or body, is substituted instead.

The bed-trick is an ancient plot device found in classical, biblical, folkloric, and medieval romance texts. It occurs in many tales told and written beyond Europe and the Judeo-Christian tradition. It also appears frequently in the 'nouvelle' or 'nouvelles' written by Boccaccio and others during the Renaissance, but does not begin to appear in plays on the London stage until the late 1590s. After that period, and until the closing of the London stage in 1642, the bed-trick became extremely common. As Stuart Clark has pointed out, this was a time of 'radical doubts about the reliability of the senses', a period when thinkers like Montaigne and Descartes 'encouraged the modern-sounding notion that human subjects "make" the objects they perceive, fashioning them out of the qualities that belong intrinsically to perception, not the objects themselves'.[16] Clark's study focuses on scepticism about visual perception, but perhaps the plausibility (or at least, enjoyability) of the bed-trick for early modern playgoers derives from this sense that, in the darkness, imagination can make a bush seem a bear, or one lover's body seem to be another. The bed-trick also relies on the idea that masculine desire could make the fantasy of a specific person's sexual body override the reality that it was someone else. And the prosthetic nature of the sexed body would also function to make the bed-trick a more credible (albeit still playful and fictional) plot device on stage.[17]

According to one scholar's count, there are '52 bed-tricks in 44 plays' written between 1594 and 1641, including five by Middleton and four by Shakespeare.[18] The same scholar, Marliss Desens, tries to account for the delayed arrival of the bed-trick on the London stage when she claims that 'the drama became concerned with exploring love and desire from a less idealized perspective'.[19] If Desens' claim is valid, then what accounts for this turn from Elizabethan optimism and idealism to Jacobean and Caroline disillusionment and cynicism regarding love and marriage? Increasing anxiety about power relations between genders was tied to heightened alarm about social and economic changes produced by the greater economic instability and openness that characterised early capitalism.[20] Perhaps the arrival and proliferation of the bed-trick can be connected to the emergence of capitalism as a system founded on a basic structure of deception by means of substitution in an increasingly aggressive commodity exchange market. The bed-trick undermines and exposes the complex transactions and arrangements of legal contract and erotic intrigue, substituting the bare act of intercourse in the dark, of sex performed without any visual element, emphasising lust and touch (usually ranked as the lowest of the senses in the early modern sensorium). This act takes place, of course, not on stage, but in the mind's eye of the playgoer, invoked by the verbal descriptions delivered by the actors.

As time went on, the bed-trick was handled by playwrights with increasing complexity, but also with a growing satirical intensity and disturbing physical and emotional violence. After all, the non-consensual bed-trick is a form of rape. The later plays adopt a more direct treatment of sexuality, and each author demonstrates their ingenuity by giving the conventional bed-trick a new twist. This playfulness and innovation were clearly intended to please and entertain playgoers by surprising them with a witty new handling of what had become a conventional (and potentially hackneyed) plot device. At the same time, the adaptation of the bed-trick from prose fiction to theatrical performance allowed the playwrights who employed the bed-trick to draw on the instability of gender identity and sexual desire that characterised the early modern stage with its all-male acting companies, cross-dressing, and bawdy wordplay.

Perhaps the best known of the bed-tricks from English Renaissance drama are those that take place in Shakespeare's *Measure for Measure* (1604) and *All's Well That Ends Well* (1605). In both of these plays, a jilted but virtuous woman is reunited with her husband by consummating their marriage contract without the husband knowing that he is doing so. These problem comedies use the device to bring on comic closure, but in a way that retains an uneasy feeling about marriage as a trick – or even a punishment. After having duped her husband Bertram into sleeping with her against his will, Helena makes the following comment:

> HELENA: But O, strange men,
> That can such sweet use make of what they hate,
> When saucy trusting of the cozened thoughts
> Defiles the pitchy night; so lust doth play
> With that it loathes, for that which is away.[21]

This passage points to the substitution of the imagined 'whore' for the legitimate spouse, of the woman as exchangeable and interchangeable object rather than as a valued life-long partner in a traditional monogamous marriage. In their specific verbal register, these lines also suggest that, thanks to the bed-trick, Bertram's misogyny and disgust have been converted, by means of his 'lust', to a 'sweet use', suggesting a kind of loathsome commercial transaction, one that involves the immoral 'cozening' of the dupe who trusts in the immediate sweetness of the loaned coins and eagerly 'doth play' with borrowed filthy lucre while repressing 'that which is away'. This sense of a timely repayment, and commercial language in general, pervades the play as a whole. The Widow's reassurances to Helena, spoken just before the passage quoted above, are a clear example of this persistent economic theme emphasising credit, 'surety' (4.4.3), and 'recompense' (4.4.18): 'You never had a servant to whose trust/Your business was more welcome' (4.4.15–16). Furthermore, the double sense of blackness, the sexual act committed under cover of a darkness that is 'defiled' further, becoming a 'pitchy' trap, invokes a certain kind of sinful blackness which will transliterate into the figure of the demonised or blackface Moor in later plays.

The bed-trick was not used simply to save marriages when virtuous women were married to bad husbands like Bertram in *All's Well* or Angelo in *Measure for Measure* (following Mariana's principle that 'best men are molded out of faults' [5.1.440]). The bed-trick could also be used, for instance, to test a wife's fidelity, to entrap a person in an unwanted marriage, or for more aggressive or lustful purposes. In the case of the anonymous play *The True Trojans* (c.1620–25), the bed-trick is used by a male character to trick a woman into sleeping with his friend, a deception that subordinates heterosexual love to homosocial bonding. The play's main plot involves Caesar's invasion and conquest of Britain, and it features an erotic subplot involving two Roman soldiers, Hirildus and Eulinus. Landora loves Hirildus, but he does not return her affection. At the same time, Hirildus's best friend Eulinus desires Landora. As a demonstration of their merging of identity in true friendship, Hirildus suggests to his close friend Eulinus that he replace Hirildus in a bed-trick. After this is accomplished, it becomes a sign of their homoeroticised friendship as the substitution creates an exchangeability that is described as a merging of two persons into one:

> HIRILDUS: Why Landora loves you not, but me in you.
> EULINUS: But I in you enjoy Landora's love.
> HIRILDUS: But she enjoys not your love, 'cause unknown.
> EULINUS: No matter, I in you, or you in me,
> So that I still possess my dearest dear. (F1^v)

The bed-trick in *The True Trojans* uses the woman (no women actually appear on stage) as a counter in a transaction that is purely 'between men', an exchange of the sort that Eve Kosofsky Sedgwick describes in *Between*

Men.[22] In *The True Trojans*, the absence of women and the intensity of male homosocial desire eventually leads to open aggression between Hirildus and Eulinus when, as part of a funeral masque, the two perform a mock fight that becomes real when Eulinus gets carried away and slays Hirildus. Following these events, Eulinus learns that Landora has committed suicide, taking poison after hearing of Hirildus's death. When Eulinus hears about Landora's death, he becomes mad with grief, and in a long speech reminiscent of Bottom's Pyramus, Eulinus rants, rages, and stabs himself several times. It is a clumsy piece of work, but it shows how a play written by a male author for an all-male audience with no female characters and featuring as its main characters only male warriors could, however ineptly, convey a hysterical form of deadly anxiety about the instability of masculine identity in relation to heterosexual desire. It is also a play that shows the native British defenders of liberty against the Roman Empire crying, 'To armes, to armes, to armes: Wee'll fight and dye' (H4ʳ) at the end of the scene that immediately precedes Eulinus's suicide and his declaration that 'My violent passion must haue sudden vent' (H4ᵛ). Thus, this university drama associates the external threat of Roman (read Roman Catholic) invaders with the mortal threat supposedly posed by women to life, reason, and a stable male identity and essence.[23]

William Davenant's 1628 tragedy *Albovine* imitates the lurid violence of Thomas Middleton's *The Witch* (1615). Among other similarities, these two plays feature a powerful woman who contrives a bed-trick in order to blackmail another man into helping her murder her husband. In *Albovine*, the queen, Rhodolinda, arranges a bed-trick in which she seeks revenge against her husband by substituting herself for the wife of another noble, Paradine. When Paradine playfully pulls his bed-mate from behind the curtains the next morning, he is devastated to discover that it is Rhodolinda and that he has passed a night of sexual pleasure with the wrong woman:

> PARADINE to RHODOLINDA:
> O horror! gape, rugged Earth! Suck me in
> Like some old Pyramid, whose ponderous limmes
> Haue been thy burden since the Flood, and now
> Their owne foundation sinke. Could you make
> No choice to quench your rauenous lust, but me?[24]

Here, an imagistic slippage describes Paradine's shame and associates the woman's sexual body with both gaping earth and collapsing pyramid. These images of natural disaster and this attitude of misogynistic fear reinforce the overall message of the play: 'Davenant exploits the widely held Renaissance fantasy that unless a woman's sexuality is carefully restrained, she becomes destructive to men and to the patriarchal society they have created.'[25] In the face of Paradine's horrified reaction, the queen responds by threatening to 'call my owne adultery / Thy fowle rape' (G3^r) and to accuse Paradine before the court unless he will agree to help Rhodolinda murder Albovine. The substitution of the lustful, murderous queen for Paradine's chaste and lawful wife Valdaura transforms Paradine from a rational, honourable warrior to a volatile murderer and avenger. Later, when the king is dying, Paradine confesses that he has 'by a dark mistake ... whor'd your queen', and he informs Albovine that the 'blacke adulterous Queene betray'd / Me to her lust by wicked Arts' (L3^r). Believing, mistakenly, that Albovine has 'made [Paradine's] wife a blacke adulteresse', Paradine watches the king die. Later, after he murders his wife, Paradine discovers that she was true and this drives him to take revenge on Rhodolinda. In the final, murderous scene of the play, the queen enters and asks Paradine if Albovine is dead. Informed that he is, she is ecstatic. And when Paradine seems to respond with enthusiasm to her request for more murders, Rhodolinda grows amorous, expressing herself in terms that reiterate the theme of rape and violent sexual desire:

> RHODOLINDA: Dear *Paradine*, I sure shall rauish thee,
> My appetite is grown so fierce. Let me
> Begin with thy moyst lip–
> PARADINE: Let's to't like monkeys, or the reeking goat.
>   *Pulls her to kiss him in the chair.*
> RHODOLINDA: Oh! Oh! Oh! Helpe! helpe!
>   *Both are bloody about their mouths.*
> PARADINE: Cease your loud clamour, Royal Whore!
> RHODOLINDA: Thou didst eate my lips.
> PARADINE: Thy flesh is sowre, musty; more tainted then
> A carrion in a phlegmatick ditch; for else,
> Like th'Anthropophagus, I had devour'd thee up. (M1^v)

Davenant's tragedy represents chaste marriage as a fragile state: once Paradine's chastity is violated, he degenerates rapidly. This emphasis on the bed-trick as an aggressive erotic trap occurs frequently in the drama of the 1620s and after. In these early Stuart plays, the bed-trick and other lurid scandals (often located within a corrupt court) are devices that concentrate and intensify fears about changing gender relations. The increasingly visible role of women in the urban marketplace and the shift towards companionate marriage unsettled conservative values and the juridical tradition of matrimony as coverture. In the theatre, what the dominant culture considered to be healthy, consensual sexuality – institutionalised and idealised in a loving, mutually desired marital contract – is still seen in the conventionally happy endings that concluded many comedies, but pat comic closure was less satisfying to audiences after the 1590s. In the forms of drama that were most fashionable on the London stage during the early seventeenth century – problem comedy, tragicomedy, and tragedy – erotic relations ranged from uneasy and uncomfortable (Pandarus wishing his diseases on the audience at the end of Shakespeare's *Troilus and Cressida*) to the shock, horror, mutilation, and high body counts that marked the conclusion of many tragedies.[26]

Erotic stage tricks played upon patriarchal anxieties about control, order, and legitimacy – including not only the fear of female promiscuity or of damnable, adulterous sin, but also the fear of cuckoldry that is so pervasive in early modern drama. As marriage became increasingly a part of the emerging system of social mobility under the sign of the bourgeois commodity, it was repeatedly figured as an economic swindle. Clever male characters succeed in substituting themselves for other men in order to gain the wealth, dowry, and property that the woman as marriage-object embodies and conveys. The bed-trick is just one of a variety of erotic ruses that mark the drama of this time. The disruption of traditional patriarchal power structures that defined family and inheritance, and the response of the legal and religious system to that disruption, along with concerns about the abuse carried out by vestigial institutions like the Court of Wards – all of these issues were explored through theatrical representations.[27]

In early modern England, anxiety about shifting marital and domestic roles merged with contemporary concerns about novel forms of commercial intercourse with Jews, Muslims, and other foreigners, and the risks of extensive contact with people of other faiths in the context of post-Reformation religious strife and Turkish expansion. To demonstrate this tendency in the theatre to project anxieties onto foreign bodies, I want to turn now to a particular form of sexual substitution that began to appear in English Renaissance drama in the early seventeenth century – the substitution of a Moor for an expected bed partner.[28] In these cases, the figurative language of 'black adultery' became literalised and embodied when boy-actors put on blackface to play the role of the Moorish domestic or slave. This occurs in several plays, including John Fletcher's *Monsieur Thomas* (1615), in which Thomas, disguised as his twin sister Dorothea, arrives at her friend Mary's house late at night in hopes of sharing her bed. After Thomas's sister succeeds in alerting Mary to Thomas's intentions, Mary substitutes her Moorish servant. But Thomas does not carry out his intended rape when he sees the Moor, whom he takes for a devil. He reacts first with horror and fear, but when he realises the women have arranged a bed-trick, he becomes angry and beats the Moorish maidservant before departing in a rage.

In Massinger's *The Parliament of Love* (1624), the audience only finds out at the end of the play that a wife has used a bed-trick to regain the sexual attention of her philandering husband. At the beginning, the virtuous Bellisant's guardian requests that she entertain a female Moor as her servant. Bellisant pretends to accept the unwelcome advances of the lustful Clarindor but substitutes her Moorish servant. In the play's last act, at the Parliament of Love convened by King Charles, Clarindor is punished for his dishonourable behaviour, and Bellisant is allowed to choose Clarindor's punishment. When she asks that Clarindor be forced to wed the Moor, Bellisant's guardian reveals that the Moor is really Clarindor's wife in disguise, and Bellisant confirms that that the Moor is the wife 'long by him with violence cast off'.[29] Clarindor then willingly accepts his estranged wife.

In Richard Brome's comedy *The Novella* (1632), a character named Victoria arrives in Venice disguised as a new courtesan offering her virginity for sale, but at the very high cost of 2000 ducats. She invites many men to her house but has set such a high price on her maidenhead that these customers are discouraged. One elderly suitor, Pantaloni, is so insistent, however, that she agrees to meet him in bed, but then substitutes her Moorish servant. As in *Monsieur Thomas*, this bed-trick remains unconsummated because the deceived man wants to see his bedmate in the light of day before proceeding. In the end, Victoria claims that the bed-trick could never have been completed anyway because the servant was in fact a boy-eunuch disguised as a Moorish woman. Brome attempts to preserve the virtue and chastity of Victoria, even though she impersonates a courtesan, by doubly displacing the threat of illicit sex onto the eunuch beneath the blackface make-up worn by the 'Moor'.

For the audience, knowing the full identity of the substitute lover (a boy-actor playing a eunuch disguised as a female Moor) exacerbates the already intense sense of thwarted heterosexual desire. A trick that would substitute one sexual partner for another becomes a swindle that substitutes instead a castrated body (or pre-adolescent body) for one that was, at least potentially, a sexually available one. Furthermore, the play takes a conventional generational conflict between money-minded fathers and young lovers whose desires go against their parents' wishes and pushes the conflict between young love and old money into a more disturbing dramatic space where sex and money are intertwined – that of Venice, the commercial city inhabited by 20,000 courtesans. (Victoria is the 'novella' of the title because she is posing as the new whore in town.) Victoria turns out to be a virtuous virgin who has come to Venice from Rome in this courtesan disguise to seek out her beloved Fabritio, Pantaloni's son. In the end the lovers are reunited and wed, but the play clearly indicates that commercial priorities rule Venetian society and define its handling of sex and marriage. In order to preserve his large inheritance, Fabritio has to outwit his wealthy father, who has plans for him to marry a different woman – Fabritio's dilemma at the outset is that he is unwilling to give up his inheritance in order to marry the woman he loves. In the comic conclusion, he gets both the gold and the girl.

In a later comedy set in London, *The English Moor* (1637), Brome revisited his queering of the bed-trick in *The Novella*. At the play's outset, an old usurer, Mandeville Quicksands, is about to marry a much younger woman, the beautiful Millicent (who loves Theophilus), in a forced marriage. In this later play, the mock Moor turns out to be a white woman in blackface (the 'English Moor' of the play's title). Or rather, two separate white women: first, Millicent agrees to take on the disguise of a Moorish maid-servant in order to remain in Quicksands' house while pretending to have fled elsewhere. Later, the disguise is adopted by Phyllis, a woman who had previously been seduced and abandoned, then told to turn whore, by Nathaniel, a lecherous 'wencher'. Although at first he is unaware that she is really Millicent, Nathaniel initially tries to seduce Quicksands' Moorish servant, offering 'to clap your Barbary buttock / In all her bravery, and get a snatch / In an odd corner, or the dark tonight' (4.723).[30] Millicent, whose disguise is verbal as well as cosmetic, replies in a mock African accent, 'O no, de fine white Zentilmanna / Cannot-a love-a the black-a thing-a' (4.726). Later, believing that the mock Moor is still Millicent in disguise, Nathaniel gets the Moor into bed, only to discover (when they are caught *in flagrante delicto* and exposed) that she is now Phyllis. In the end, Nathaniel is forced to marry the woman he had seduced and jilted. Quicksands, whose marriage to Millicent is eventually annulled because it was never consummated, is thwarted in the end, but not until after he experiences a sexual excitement produced by the 'defacement' of Millicent's white skin, for it is his idea to apply black face-paint to Millicent. He promises to reward her if she will take on a disguise of his choosing:

Millicent	Come to the point. What's the disguise, I pray you?
Quicksands	First know, my sweet, it was the quaint device
	Of a Venetian merchant, which I learnt
	In my young factorship.
Millicent	That of the moor?
	The blackamoor you spake of? Would you make
	An negro of me? (3.427–32)

Here, in this pivotal scene, Quicksands, in a state of erotic excitation, applies the cosmetic covering to Millicent's face himself, and in doing so enacts a sexualised fetishisation of the black body. Quicksands acquired his propensity for black flesh while he was a merchant (or 'factor') in Venice, where Moors and white Europeans, Christians and Muslims, met to trade, and where African servants and slaves were also numerous. Quicksands' *modus operandi*, as a merchant-usurer who uses his gains from investment in long-distance trade to buy out the land held by the traditional landowning class, makes him an avatar of the proto-capitalist type that was displacing the old aristocratic class and its traditional feudal economy. He is connected both to the international trade with the East and to the reinvestment of commercial profits in loans to those who have mortgaged their land to him, including Theophilus and three young gallants, secondary characters in the play who complain of being 'cozened' (1.75) by Quicksands' financial trickery.

In *The Novella* and in *The English Moor*, the substitution of the fetishised Moor for the legitimate object of desire corresponds to an economic transaction whereby a valuable commodity is replaced with something empty, false, and valueless that takes on an exchange value in spite of its vacant use value. Millicent complains when Quicksands produces a 'box of black painting' (3.433) and is about to apply it to her face, asking him, 'Would you blot out / Heaven's workmanship?' (3.434). Ironically, the name 'Millicent' derives from the Old French *Melisende*, which comes, in turn, from the Germanic *amal* 'work' and *swinth* 'strength' – but for Brome's audience, the name would suggest 'thousand' plus 'hundred' and a notion of quantifiable exchange value. Her racialised transformation from white to 'negro' and back again gives her value for the miser Quicksands who would hoard her and keep her from sexual circulation by devaluing her in the eyes of those who are threatened by black alterity.

Eunuchs, Moors, and Muslims appear with great frequency in the drama of Jacobean and Caroline England, and the titillating spectacle of English (or Christian) characters risking contact with Moors and facing the dangers of 'going native' became a common theme in adventure (or voyage) plays such as Thomas Heywood's *The Fair Maid of the West, Part II* (printed in 1631, but probably composed much earlier).[31] This play provides yet another twist on the substitute Moor bed-trick. In Heywood's travel play, Mullisheg, the sultan of Fez, orders his renegade client Goodlack to woo Bess Bridges, the play's virtuous heroine, in the hope that she can be persuaded to sleep with the sultan. Meanwhile, Tota, the sultan's wife, orders another English character, Roughman, to help her gain revenge on her promiscuous husband by arranging for Bess's husband to sleep with Tota. Instead, Goodlack deceives both Mullisheg and Tota by telling them that they will be having sex with Bess and her husband – when in fact, under cover of darkness, they have intercourse with each other. After this encounter, they both sing the praises of their sexual partners, with comic dramatic irony intended to amuse the audience:

> TOTA: Were I again to match, I'd marry one
> Of this brave nation, if a gentleman,
> Before the greatest monarch of the world,
> They are such sweet and loving bedfellows.
> MULLISHEG: Venetian ladies, nor the Persian girls,
> The French, the Spanish, nor the Turkish dames,
> Ethiope, nor Greece can kiss with half the art
> These English can, nor entertain their friends
> Wi' th' tenth part of that ample willingness
> Within these arms.[32]

Part of the joke here is a new racist twist on the old bed-trick: these 'blackamoors' are unable to distinguish identity in the dark because their skin colour supposedly merges with the darkness around them in the bedroom. The racist association of black identity with base passion and hyper-sexuality takes on a different tenor at this moment when the notion of a superior English virility is displaced onto the voluptuousness of Tota and Mullisheg's mistaking passion. Sexual desire is again a disturbingly unstable force – not fixed in a genuine knowledge of one's actual bedmate, but rather driven by a fantasy about the sexual powers of exoticised others.

In each of these plays we encounter the Moor as placeholder, a degraded substitute and readily exchangeable commodity, the monstrous and demonised version of what women could become in the economic system of bourgeois marriage. This kind of image can also be gendered as masculine monstrosity, and we see this in plays such as *Titus Andronicus* (Aaron), *The Merchant of Venice* (Morocco) and *Othello*, plays in which the audience is asked to imagine with horror a sexual encounter between a Moor and a white woman; Othello and Desdemona are described as 'making the beast with two backs' on their wedding night and additional images of animality are employed by Iago and others. In substituting Othello the Moor for Roderigo the Venetian, the play shows a father and a daughter, Brabantio and Desdemona, tricked by Othello's piteous travelling tales, but as a convert to Christianity, Othello's erotic and religious faith is in doubt: Iago's tricks turn Othello into an erotic dupe, a paranoid who imagines himself a cuckold and then relapses into 'Turkish' violence.[33] The delayed sexual consummation of Othello and Desdemona's union becomes, in the tragic final act, a kind of murder-rape, a necrophiliac substitution of a paranoid fantasy for the reality of a virtuous and lawful wife.

While Othello's transformation to a 'Turkish' identity is figurative and does not involve a religious conversion to Islam, in Robert Daborne's *A Christian turn'd Turk* (1612), the conversion of the title character, the play's piratical protagonist John Ward, takes place on stage. In Daborne's play, the renegade Ward is duped by a group of Turks who convince him to undergo religious conversion. The dangerous slipperiness of commercial, sexual, and religious intercourse with Turkish or Moorish partners is presented as a trick whereby Christian men are tempted by material wealth and by physical beauty or pleasure. The characters who work to convert Ward include some who are themselves converts and renegades. Their motives are entirely material and economic: they are not concerned for the welfare of Ward's soul. Rather, they hope to gain by forging stronger ties of obligation with a corsair commander who can capture Christian vessels and bring home rich booty to fill their coffers in Tunis. They approach Ward with an offer of 'profit' and preferment if he will turn Turk. At first he refuses, and so the captain of the janissaries, Crosman, sends in his beautiful sister, Voada, the woman that Ward loves, to entrap him by falsely declaring that she loves him: 'Know then I love, / But not the man whose daily orisons / Invoke confusion on me, whose religion speaks me an infidel', she tells Ward.[34] Moved by his desire for Voada, Ward announces that he will convert to Islam immediately. In fact Voada has no feelings for him, but she hopes to gain financially from their marriage; in an aside to the audience, she says, "I have my ends. / Howe'er thou [Ward] sink, thy wealth shall bear me high' (7.175–6). At the end of their exchange, Ward rationalises his decision by asserting, 'One good I enjoy outweighs all ills whatever / Can be objected' (7.185–6) and then calculating that he now possesses three things more important than the benefit of remaining a Christian:

> To sum my happiness:
> That god on earth, to whom all men stand bare,
> Gold, that doth usher greatness, lackeys me. [...]
> Beauty, command and riches – these are the three
> The world pursues, and these follow me. (7.186–94).

The marriage precedes immediately the conversion ritual, which is staged as a solemn dumb show, and the play's Chorus expresses a sense of horror but assures the audience that Ward's 'black deeds will have black ends' (8.28), foreshadowing his tragic death.

Ward is required to undergo circumcision as part of the conversion ritual. The other pirates, Dansiker and Sares, comment on his turning Turk:

> DANSIKER: Ward turned Turk? It is not possible.
> SARES: I saw him Turk to the circumcision.
> Marry, therein I heard he played the Jew with 'em,
> Made 'em come to the cutting of an ape's tail. (9.1-4)

Ward's circumcision is figured as a deception by substitution, but his conversion to Islam is an act whose dire consequences Ward cannot escape. In that regard, he is the victim of trickery on the part of Voada and the Tunisian Muslims, who lead him into the trap of conversion and then destroy him. In the scene that follows, Ward's fellow pirates mock his conversion in bawdy terms that sexualise his new religious identity, joking about how his circumcision will prevent him from consummating his marriage. When Ward loses his wealth and Voada rejects him, the superficiality and venality of his conversion is exposed. He can only redeem himself by a death through suicide, like that of Othello.

By looking at erotic trickery, at dangerous or dubious economic transactions, and at religious or racial instability in these plays, we begin to glimpse a broad pattern, one in which the fundamental anxieties and instabilities produced by new economic practices in early modern England were projected into stage actions involving rape, theft, swindle, and racial or religious infidelity. In the last few examples, we see, in particular, how the English engagement with foreign cultures, peoples, and commodities, through the rapid expansion of overseas trade, was brought home to the stage in the form of a theatre in which playgoers were warned by these tricks perpetrated by alien peoples who could turn Christians and English subjects to Turks.

The bed-tricks involving a substitute Moor are primal scenes in which the conjugal bed becomes the site of an invasive, foreign monstrosity – the erotic, commercial, and racial fears of English culture are dramatised and encapsulated there. In these emblematic moments, the uncanny Moor returns to invade the domestic scene, disrupting ethno-normative desire and provoking the patriarchal violence that was always prepared to enforce its regime. These stage Moors are figures of exchange and human trafficking whose presence indicates the English engagement with difference. This engagement was, in part, a result of emergent capitalism and the new outward thrust of long-distance venturing that began in the late sixteenth century. This new commerce was exciting and profitable for some, but its ideological and cultural implications include the kind of violent anxieties that are figured in the bed-trick. Capitalism tied the domestic economy ever more tightly to a dependence on foreign peoples and commodities; in doing so capitalism brought the dark spectre of difference home to haunt English culture.

NOTES

1 On commodity fetishism in the literature of early modern England, see David Hawkes, *Idols of the marketplace: idolatry and commodity fetishism in English literature, 1580–1680* (New York: Palgrave Macmillan, 2001). The classic discussion of the commodity form under capitalism is set forth at

the beginning of Marx's *Capital*, in chapters 2 and 3. *Capital: a critique of political economy*, ed. Friedrich Engels, trans. Samuel Moore and Edward Aveling, 1887, https://www.marxists.org/archive/marx/works/1867-c1/.

2 On the conversions of Christian II and Henry IV, see Federico Zuliani, 'The conversion of Christian II of Denmark in Roman Catholic diplomatic literature, 1530–1532' in Lieke Stelling, Harald Hendrix and Todd Richardson (eds), *The turn of the soul: representations of religious conversion in early modern art and literature* (Leiden: Brill, 2012), pp. 39–58; and Michael Wolfe, *The conversion of Henri IV: politics, power, and religious belief in early modern France* (Cambridge, MA: Harvard University Press, 1993).

3 Daniel Vitkus (ed.), *Piracy, slavery and redemption: Barbary captivity narratives from early modern England* (New York: Columbia University Press, 2001), p. 105.

4 Robert Parsons, *A treatise of three conversions of England* (Saint-Omer, 1603), pp. 561, 567.

5 See the early chapters of Marx, *Capital*, vol. 1, on commodity fetishism and the origins of capitalism during the early modern period. For a useful account of how capitalism began, see Ellen Meiksins Wood, *The origin of capitalism: a longer view* (London: Verso, 2000). Still helpful and informative is R. H. Tawney, *Religion and the rise of capitalism, a historical study* (New York: Harcourt, Brace & Co, 1926); to qualify Wood's emphasis on the agrarian economic revolution as the foundation of capitalism, see Robert Brenner's account of the role that international commerce played in the rise of the capitalist classes, *Merchants and revolution: commercial change, political conflict, and London's overseas traders, 1550–1653* (Princeton: Princeton University Press, 1993).

6 See Amanda Bailey, *Of bondage: debt, property, and personhood in early modern England* (Philadelphia: University of Pennsylvania Press, 2013).

7 On the spatial crisis and maritime turn, see Antonis Balasopoulos, '"Suffer a sea change": spatial crisis, maritime modernity, and the politics of Utopia', *Cultural critique*, 63 (2006), 123–56; and Steven Mentz, 'Towards a blue cultural studies: the sea, maritime culture, and early modern English literature', *Literature Compass*, 6.5 (2009): 997–1013.

8 On usury and early modern objections to it, see Benjamin Nelson, *The idea of usury: from tribal brotherhood to universal otherhood*, 2nd edn (Chicago: University of Chicago Press, 1969); David Hawkes, *The culture of usury in Renaissance England* (New York: Palgrave Macmillan, 2010); and Lloyd Edward Kermode, 'Introduction' to *Three Renaissance usury plays: the three ladies of London, Englishmen for my money, The hog hath lost his pearl* (Manchester: Manchester University Press, 2009), pp. 1–28.

9 For recent scholarship on the impact of early globalisation on culture and literature in England, see Stephen Deng and Barbara Sebek (eds), *Global*

traffic: discourses and practices of trade in English literature and culture from 1550 to 1700 (New York: Palgrave Macmillan, 2008) and Jyotsna Singh (ed.), *A companion to the global Renaissance: English literature and culture in the era of expansion* (Oxford: Wiley-Blackwell, 2009).

10 On the early joint-stock corporations, see Philip J. Stern, *The company-state: corporate sovereignty and the early modern foundations of the British Empire in India* (Oxford: Oxford University Press, 2012); on the English East India Company and European trade in the Indian Ocean region, consult Holden Furber, *Rival empires of trade in the Orient, 1600–1800* (Minneapolis: University of Minnesota Press, 1976); K. N. Chaudhuri, *The trading world of Asia and the English East India Company, 1660–1760* (Cambridge: Cambridge University Press, 2006); Michael N. Pearson, *Trade, circulation, and flow in the Indian Ocean world* (New York: Palgrave Macmillan, 2015); and Om Prakash, *Bullion for goods: European and Indian merchants in the Indian Ocean trade, 1500–1800* (New Delhi: Manohar, 2004).

11 See Kim Hall, *Things of darkness: economies of race and gender in early modern England* (Ithaca, NY: Cornell University Press, 1995); Emily C. Bartels, *Speaking of the Moor: from 'Alcazar' to 'Othello'* (Philadelphia: Pennsylvania University Press, 2008); Virginia Mason Vaughan, *Performing blackness on English stages, 1500–1800* (Cambridge: Cambridge University Press, 2005); Ian Smith, 'White skin, black masks: racial cross-dressing on the early modern stage', *Renaissance drama*, 32 (2003), 33–67.

12 Recent scholarship on representations of religious conversion on the English Renaissance stage includes Jane Hwang Degenhardt, *Islamic conversion and Christian resistance on the early modern stage* (Edinburgh: Edinburgh University Press, 2010); some of the essays in Stelling, et al. (eds), *The turn of the soul*; and Tamara Atkins, *The drama of reform: theology and theatricality, 1461–1553* (Turnhout: Brepols, 2013).

13 On the Tudor and early Stuart economic crisis, see A. L. Beier, *Masterless men: the vagrancy problem in England, 1560–1640* (London: Methuen, 1985); Steve Hindle, *The state and social change in early modern England* (New York: Palgrave Macmillan, 2002); Paul Slack, *Poverty and policy in Tudor and Stuart England* (London and New York: Longman, 1988); and Keith Wrightson, *Earthly necessities: economic lives in early modern Britain* (New Haven, CT: Yale University Press, 2000).

14 See Amy Louise Erickson, *Women and property in early modern England* (New York: Routledge, 1993).

15 See Anne M. Haselkorn, *Prostitution in Elizabethan and Jacobean comedy* (Troy, NY: Whitston, 1983); and David Mann, *Shakespeare's women: performance and conception* (Cambridge: Cambridge University Press, 2008). Mann claims that after the late 1590s, prostitution 'featured in nearly a quarter of the adult repertory' (p. 167).

16 Stuart Clark, *Vanities of the eye: vision in early modern European culture* (Oxford: Oxford University Press, 2007), p. 4.
17 See Will Fisher, *Materializing gender in early modern English literature and culture* (Cambridge: Cambridge University Press, 2006), esp. introduction.
18 Marliss C. Desens, *The bed-trick in English Renaissance drama* (Newark: University of Delaware Press, 1994), p. 59.
19 *Ibid.*, p. 85. On the bed-trick as a literary plot device during the early modern period, see also Janet Adelman, 'Bed tricks: on marriage as the end of comedy in *All's Well that Ends Well* and *Measure for Measure*', in Norman N. Holland, Sidney Homan, and Bernard J. Paris (eds), *Shakespeare's personality* (Berkeley: University of California Press, 1989), pp. 151–74; William R. Bowden, 'The bed-trick, 1603–1642: its mechanics, ethics, and effects', *Shakespeare Studies*, 5 (1969), 112–23; and Wendy Doniger, *The bedtrick: tales of sex and masquerade* (Chicago: University of Chicago Press, 2000).
20 See Lisa Jardine, *Still harping on daughters: women and drama in the age of Shakespeare*, 2nd edn (London: Harvester Wheatsheaf, 1989); and Lorna Hutson, *The usurer's daughter: male friendship and fictions of women in 16th Century England* (New York: Routledge, 1997).
21 William Shakespeare, *All's well that ends well*, in *The Norton Shakespeare*, 2nd edn, ed. Stephen Greenblatt, et al. (New York: W. W. Norton, 2008), 4.4.21–25.
22 Eve Kosofsky Sedgwick, *Between men: English literature and male homosocial desire* (New York: Columbia University Press, 1985).
23 See John E. Curran, *Roman invasions: British history, Protestant anti-Romanism and the historical imagination in England, 1530–1660* (Newark: University of Delaware Press, 2002), for a reading of the play as a topical drama conveying 'Protestant Anti-Romanism'.
24 William Davenant, *The tragedy of Albovine, king of the Lombards* (London, 1629), G3r.
25 Desens, *Bed-trick*, p. 132.
26 On this connection between dramatic form and erotic content, see Judith Haber, *Desire and dramatic form in early modern England* (Cambridge: Cambridge University Press, 2009).
27 On marriage, family and gender relations in early modern England, see Susan Dwyer Amussen, *An ordered society: gender and class in early modern England* (Oxford: Oxford University Press, 1988); Anthony Fletcher, *Gender, sex, and subordination in England, 1500–1800* (New Haven, CT: Yale University Press, 1995); Ralph Houlbrooke, *The English family, 1450–1700* (London: Longman, 1984); and Lawrence Stone, *The family, sex and marriage in England 1500–1800* (London: Weidenfeld & Nicolson, 1977).
28 For a discussion of how, through the bed-trick, Black or Moorish women functioned as replacements for privileged white women, see Louise

Denmead, 'The discovery of blackness in the early modern bed-trick', in James D. Fleming (ed.), *The invention of discovery, 1500–1700* (Aldershot: Ashgate, 2011), pp. 153–66.

29 *The parliament of love* in Philip Massinger, *The plays and poems of Philip Massinger*, vol. 3, ed. Philip Edwards and Colin Gibson (Oxford: Oxford University Press, 1976), 5.1.470.

30 In preparing this chapter, I have consulted the useful online edition of Brome's plays edited by Richard Cave. Richard Brome, *The English Moor*, Modern Text, edited by Mark Steggle, *Richard Brome Online*. http://www.hrionline.ac.uk/brome.

31 On how English adventure plays explored the limits of Christian contact with non-Christians, see Daniel Vitkus, 'Adventuring heroes in the Mediterranean: mapping the boundaries of Anglo-Islamic exchange on the early modern stage', *Journal of Medieval and Early Modern Studies*, 37 (2007), 75–95.

32 Thomas Heywood, *The fair maid of the west, parts I and II*, ed. Robert K. Turner, Jr. (Lincoln: University of Nebraska Press, 1967), 3.1.5–8, 13–18.

33 See Daniel Vitkus, 'Turning Turk in *Othello*: the conversion and damnation of the Moor' *Shakespeare Quarterly*, 48 (1997), 145–76; Benedict Robinson, *Islam and early modern English literature: the politics of Romance from Spenser to Milton* (New York: Palgrave, 2007), pp. 71–81; Jonathan Burton, *Traffic and turning: Islam and English drama, 1579–1624* (Newark: University of Delaware Press, 2005), pp. 246–56; and chapter 4 of Dennis Britton, *Becoming Christian: race, reformation, and early modern English Romance* (New York: Fordham University Press, 2014).

34 Robert Daborne, *A Christian turned Turk*, in *Three Turk plays from early modern England*, ed. Daniel Vitkus (New York: Columbia University Press, 2000), 7.119–22.

12

Whatever happened to Dinah the Black? And other questions about gender, race, and the visibility of Protestant saints

Kathleen Lynch

Who was Dinah the Black? That is the first question to be asked, of course. Might she be the first black woman in seventeenth-century London with a recoverable trajectory of experience? That is the claim that Imtiaz Habib stakes for her.[1] Is she thereby another cultural other – this one female – to add to our stock of adult trophy converts to Christianity in the English capital? With her name carrying echoes of the Genesis daughter of Jacob (and therefore of a possibly culpable curiosity, resulting in rape), does she serve as a cautionary tale about feminine cross-cultural initiatives? Or is she an otherwise indistinguishable serving maid? Should we think of her as one among the thousands who are summoned into the historical record by an opportunity to join the self-described visible saints, a completely ordinary convert to the experiential religion developing among English Protestants? Whether in terms of gender, race, or religion, these questions all trouble the division of the one from the many, the singular from the representative, the ordinary from the extraordinary. My goal in this chapter is not to argue any one case, but to keep the prospect of the recovery of an individual life in productive tension with the cultural implications of Dinah's noted presence as a witness to the transformation of Sarah Wight, a young, fasting girl, into a spiritual medium.[2]

Dinah is an improbable witness, not only for being the least of the least privileged (whether measured by economic status, gender, or race) but for seemingly being in the wrong place: a singular member of a mid-century London gathered church rather than an indistinguishable product of a large-scale missionary conversion. Because Dinah crosses so many categories, she can help us probe the interrelations of gender, race, and religion. We may also trace the ways cross-cultural conversionary enterprises shaped – and were shaped by – the internal practices by which the English godly came to identify themselves as such.

CAN A VISUALISATION OF DINAH RENDER HER VISIBLE AS A SUBJECT?

As a name, Dinah the Black does not so much give us a visual image of a black woman as it encourages us to understand her as being visibly marked as different. The descriptor draws on cultural associations of beauty and virtue with whiteness and the religious association of sin with blackness. The name also invites visualisation. Developments in the early modern visual arts highlight the ways artists played with the polarities of light and dark when creating images of black people. As representational subjects, blacks were hardly ever front and centre. They were most often marginal figures, faces in a crowd, filling out a scene, and setting off its white-skinned protagonists. They were silent, subservient witnesses to the main event.[3] We might be tempted to think of Dinah in this way, except that witnessing was so crucial to the credibility of nascent godly communities, such as the one that brought Sarah Wight's experiences to light as a model of female spirituality.

Given the self-conscious care that Civil War religious separatists took to develop methodologies of credible witnessing, it is reasonable to ask if a gathering of young godly women in a domestic space is a place where we could find an example of a black woman who reverses the paradoxical norm that Kim Hall identified for black women – that of being 'both highly visible as symbols and invisible as subjects'.[4] Have we found an early modern black female subject among the godly communities that were just then in the process of creating themselves as new subjects in touch with their own interior lives and individual consciences?

Can we visualise that kind of godly self? One compelling contemporary image of a black girl that seems to fit Dinah's profile is an etching by Wenceslaus Hollar, signed and dated 1645, within two years of the sighting of Dinah the Black in Sarah Wight's home (Figure 12.1). If not our Dinah, is this a counterpart? Can we recover, with some sense of lived experience, a historical agent through this representation? And what might we then know of her – those eyes meeting ours with a demure but direct gaze, that hint of a smile: is it confident or trusting, knowing, or knowing how to please? The dress is fine and speaks to the

Figure 12.1 Wenceslaus Hollar (1607–77). Portrait of a young African woman (1645). Folger Shakespeare Library Shelfmark: Art vol. b. 35, no. 46.

wealth of the mistress and the labour and trade invested in linens and lace while it also hints at the ruptures of acculturation. That we know that Hollar's patrons, the Arundells, brought an African page from Italy in the 1630s suggests that this and related etchings of an Amerindian and a Turk were done from the life.[5] But equally, the stark contrasts of black and white speak to Hollar's mastery of a technical challenge. This is as much a display of virtuosity as it is a portrait. As later copied and circulated in other contexts, the image is as available to stereotyping as it is to individualisation. Hall described herself as 'haunted' by the search for an intimate, personalised representation of an early modern black female subject. Fifteen years on, the quandary she identified remains. How can we query the body as self-evidently carrying markers of racial difference while simultaneously searching for evidence of non-white historical agents?

The gathered churches of those converting to experiential modes of Protestantism would seem to be a place where we could take up these questions. For all kinds of ordinary people hoped to slough off the social orders of class, gender, and (here, perhaps) race for new godly identities. The promise of experiential religion was precisely to transcend those constricting limitations. *Exceeding riches of grace* is a report of Sarah Wight's providential preservation and transformation into a spiritual oracle through months of fasting. Wight's was a sensational experience, edited for publication by the Independent clergyman Henry Jessey, who fashioned himself the 'Recorder'. The book was first published in the summer of 1647, just after the fifteen-year-old Wight made her first appearance back in public, at services at All Hallows Church. Wight's extraordinary experiences of grace remained a touchstone for the English godly through multiple editions in the next two decades. *Exceeding riches of grace* was a landmark celebration of women as models for devotion. In the years following the downfall of Archbishop Laud and the disestablishment of the Church of England, the self-professed visible saints might still be rallied around the transformation of a young girl, 'an empty nothing creature', into a prophetess. Jessey's listing of dozens of witnesses is part of his rhetoric of authenticity. The list is a mixed set, including doctors, ministers, a contingent of the Welsh saints, wives of army officers, an alderman, and Huguenot refugees.[6] The social standing and reliability of Sarah's mother and her own maid are highlighted throughout.

The brief and indirect appearances of Dinah the Black among these English converts to experiential religion highlight a combustible moment in English religious history when two conversionary movements came into uneasy contact. In Civil War English society, conversion was not so much concerned with movements between the Catholic and Protestant churches – though Catholicism remained a perceived threat to the English nation. Rather, conversion was more likely to be

261

understood as a purifying process within Protestantism, a breaking away from devotional conventions that may have been properly adhered to, but were understood by the experientialists to be hollow. For them, conversion was understood to take place individual by individual, by means of divine revelation. Self-identified saints exulted that they were reconstituting a visible church, even as they countered charges that their devotion was merely performative.

Simultaneously, the goal of cross-cultural conversions, such as those already underway in New England and elsewhere, was the wholesale transformation of a godless society. Conversion in this sense picked up on the universalist agendas of Paul and other early Christians. The language of interior motivation may have been adduced, but missionary conversions were subject to widespread scepticism. Visible signs of conversion, including changed dress and daily habits, were denounced as unreliable markers of personal belief by their detractors. The intersection of these two movements infused at least some parts of English society with a sense of millenarianism, which also raised hopes for the conversion of the Jews. Henry Jessey was a leader among these groups, who developed highly self-regulating methodologies for reporting. The establishment of godly networks, the appeal to credible witnesses, and the accuracy of transcription were all critical to the formation of elect communities of visible saints.

These are the circumstances in which Dinah the Black was rendered not so much visible as *visualisable* in her difference. To what ends? It is not my design to settle the indeterminacies of Dinah the Black's case, but rather to underscore how open a question it was – and how consequential a question it was – that Dinah be understood as either an extraordinary and singular convert or a perfectly ordinary model, an every(wo)man of the English gathered churches.

IS DINAH AN ORDINARY OR AN EXTRAORDINARY WITNESS?

Prominent among the millenarians, Jessey was alert to the signs of providentialism by which the saints could prepare for the thousand-year rule of Christ on earth. The presence of Dinah the Black among the saints at All Hallows is one small sign of his congregation's readiness for the time when 'All nations shall call him blessed' (Psalms 72:17). Leaving aside the question of timing for the coming of Christ's rule on earth, the publication of *Exceeding riches of grace* promotes the idea that Sarah Wight is herself an extraordinary conduit of divine grace. The radically religious had a delicate line to walk. They celebrated the extraordinary receptivity of grace of certain members of their congregations, while they also assured most other members of the congregation that conversion and election would most likely come in the ordinary course of life.

Exceeding riches of grace celebrates women's devotional ministrations to each other. Over the course of several months (and without breaking her prophetic fast), Sarah Wight comforted other young women who also suffered from bouts of despair and visited her bedside. Some are identified only by their station: most are maids, some are gentlewomen, one is a pregnant wife. None are named outright, although 'Mrs. A', with whom Sarah has an early conference, is plausibly Anna Trapnell, who would become notorious for her public prophesying a few years later. What Sarah Wight could safely do in her mother's home would not be tolerated in the anterooms of Whitehall.

The last of the young women to consult Sarah for spiritual comfort is 'another maid that was not born in England' (122). This could be 'Dinah the Black'. In many respects, the conference with Dinah follows a pattern that was established early on. The maid confesses her sense that she is outside the circle of those who will be saved, and Sarah provides encouragement not to despair. 'I am sore assaulted by Satan', confesses this maid. Sarah has a ready assurance that 'though you are stung by the old Serpent, yet healing is in Christ for such as you'. But this response glosses over the question: who is 'such' as this maid? With this conferee, Sarah's comforts shade over into areas not touched upon in her earlier conferences. When the maid worries that Christ's mercy is not for her, Wight answers, 'he doth not this to me onely, nor to one Nation onely, for, many Nations must be blessed in him' (123–4).[7] Wight's allusion to cultural difference is amplified by her observation that the soul is 'black in itself, and uncomely' and exhortation to remember that God led the Israelites 'that had been bond-slaves in Egypt' through the wilderness and into Canaan (123). This is the conventional discourse of godly discipline, but does it also speak to the condition of a young black woman in seventeenth-century London?

Without specifying that this maid is a non-native speaker, Jessey makes it clear in his report that he had a hard time understanding her speech (122). Was she speaking heavily accented English or a creole language? Always careful to highlight the accuracy of his own transcriptions of eyewitnessed events, Jessey worries about the reliability of his editorial work here. But he concludes the episode by commenting that he had a follow-up conversation with this young woman, and that she told him that she had received 'some support and refreshing to her, since that conference'. Jessey's report of the episode ends with his editorial conclusion: 'The Lord alone be exalted for it, who works all our works for us, and in us. For what have we, (any of us) that we have not received: And where then is boasting? It is excluded' (125).

This is a quote from Romans 3:27, as the marginal reference specifies. Paul is warning against a presumption of righteousness. Salvation is available only through faith, not deeds. As with so much else about the references to Dinah, however, one senses the struggle to contain as ordinary the very real possibility that Jessey and his associates might well be boasting about a trophy convert. Jessey's report occludes rather than addresses the question of Dinah's presence in the narrative. One longs to know this young woman's back-story. Any detail would individualise her. But, as Habib reminds us, blacks were an 'un-legalized entity' in early modern England.[8] There is scant documentation of their lives. In later editions, the reference to Dinah was amended to 'Dinah the Blackmore'. Can we take Blackmore to register race or culture in a more precise way? As an elaboration, the designation 'more' would seem to offer further information. But information of what category: geographical, cultural, religious? As Michael Neill, Emily Bartels, and others have noted, seventeenth-century English categories of race did not map neatly onto geographies or cultures.[9] 'Moor' was a particularly indeterminate term. As Bartels argues, the term is not only uncodified but uncodifiable, necessarily contingent on the immediate circumstances of its articulation.

IS BAPTISM THE CONDITION OF DINAH'S CREDIBILITY AS A WITNESS?

Probably not. Any uncertainty about Dinah's status vis-à-vis baptism may be resolved by a simple declarative sentence in a later publication of Jessey's, *A Storehouse of provision, to further resolution in severall cases of conscience* (1650): 'Thus also Dinah Massah a Blackmore, was lately Baptized, or dipped (for so the word is in English:) The third Moneth calld May, 23. Day, 1649'.[10] This is plausibly the same Dinah who was earlier noted by Jessey as a credible witness. If so, Dinah's credibility – marking her full acceptance into a Christian community – precedes baptism. As a non-native convert, this makes Dinah even more distinctive in a culture preoccupied with regulating the grounds for social credit. A larger point – occluded by a homogenised view of seventeenth-century English Protestantism – is that the status of adult baptism as the entry point into Christian communion was even more fraught for sectarians than it was for members of the established church. In both cases, the need to create authenticating ceremonies of welcome for non-native converts exposed unresolved tensions around the function of baptism within a reformed society.

Though baptism was one of the two sacraments maintained by the Protestant Reformation, its theological underpinnings were altered in ways that may not have been as fully controversial as those of the Eucharist, but that nonetheless complicated the significance of a popular symbolic and social welcome into the community. In the Church of England, baptism could no longer be considered necessary for salvation. It could not have the same sacramental efficacy as it did in the Catholic Church. God could save whomever he chose to save, and his predetermination could not be overturned by human action or inaction. So baptism could no longer be seen as a necessary cleansing of original sin, nor as a prerequisite for salvation. One consequence of this return of baptism to the realm of the sign was that it troubled the understanding the English had of themselves as an elect nation. Some worried about the status of their children, if baptism was no longer efficacious in salvation. The godly, like Jessey, rather saw opportunity to assemble a church of visible saints that far transcended national boundaries. The political nation barely registered as an element in their identification with the Israelites.

Whatever one's attitude to sacramental efficacy, however, baptism was widely regarded as an appropriately public welcome for a non-native convert. It provided an opportunity for the convert to demonstrate volition and readiness. Dissemination in print helped promote trophy conversions. But the ceremony itself had to be improvised, as Matthew Dimmock has emphasised in his study of the baptism of strangers in early modern London.[11] To take one well-known incident, the minister Meredith Hanmer baptised a Turk at the Hospital Church of St. Katherine's in 1586. 'Now one silly Turk is won', Hanmer notes in the sermon he printed afterwards.[12] Nevertheless, this one is given some individual weight. His story is told: of having been captured and enslaved by the Spanish after one battle, and freed and inspired by Sir Francis Drake and the ship captain, William Hawkins, after another. Chinano, by name, he had been born in Nigroponte. He had never converted to the Spanish faith because they were violent people and they worshipped idols. On these points, Hanmer cites the Spanish Dominican friar, Bartolomé de las Casas, (1474/84–1566) who chronicled Spanish atrocities against the indigenous people of the New World.

Besides, the Spanish worshipped idols. Hanmer is careful to address the processes by which the convert's voluntary embrace of Christianity was achieved. He was catechised through an interpreter; he publicly affirmed several doctrinal principles in church; and he was baptised William by his own choice.

Hanmer is making up the ceremony as he goes. But nevertheless, this is the quintessential English Protestant conversion narrative as it was written against the grain of Spanish precedent. It happens individually, by choice, according to a process of instruction and public affirmation. In writing about this case, Dimmock has exposed the triangulated dynamics among religious cultures, so that this baptism not only represents a victory over Muslims but one over competing Catholic claims to the 'true religion'.[13]

Three-quarters of a century later – nearly contemporary with Dinah the Black's appearance in *Exceeding riches of grace* – the French Protestants in London were promoting their version of this narrative. This time, the minister Jean Despagne set up the baptism of another Turk with distinctions between two biblical brothers, Ishmael and Isaac, the two sons of Abraham.[14] The pseudo-history was rehearsed of nations being descended from these two brothers: one having the aspect of the flesh; the other of the spirit. But then, attention was turned more to the individual, with divisions understood not so much between Christian and Mohamet or Jew as between Christian and Christian. Here, too, Protestant conventions and standards are contrasted with Catholic ones.

Despagne notes the potential disappointment in a single convert. But he attests that:

> the smallnesse of the number of those who are converted, doth not hinder the Angels in Heaven from rejoicing. If God should at this present create a new star, but that one only, would it not ravish us all with admiration? How much more is a Soul considerable which God hath taken out of the bottom of Hell to place it in the Kingdom of Heaven? A long time it is since God hath called whole Nations, and hath opened wide unto them the great gates of Heaven.[15]

The question of national interests does not look quite the same from the perspective of a Huguenot refugee. But it is equally important for this community to be transparent and public about their embrace of a Turk. This convert's original name is not given; he is referred to only as 'the Proselyte' (10). Neither are we told what brought him into contact with the French Huguenots in London. But his godparents are named, and he takes the name of his godfather for his baptismal name (24).[16]

There are no female analogies to these trophy converts in London. Only royal women, perceived to be bargaining chips in a political alliance, would receive anything like that individualising attention in public. One thinks of Pocahontas-turned-Rebecca Rolfe and the sensation she caused on her trip to London in 1616. But Pocahontas was never expected to deliver a first-person statement of volitional conversion, in public. It was sufficient for her husband to attest to 'her desire to be taught and instructed in the knowledge of God, her capablenesse of understanding, her aptnesse and willingness to receive anie good impression, and also the spirituall, besides her owne incitements stirring me up hereunto'.[17]

Far down the socio-economic chain, the closest analogy to Dinah may be 'Marye Phyllis A Blackamore' who got much more than the conventional line in the registers of St. Botolph Aldgate, where her baptism in 1597 was recorded. Mary was noted as 'beinge aboute Twentye yeres of age and dwelling with millicen porter sempster'. Probably because of the unusual nature of this baptism (it is the first such baptism in this parish's records), the case is described at length. We are told that she has been in England for twelve or thirteen years, that her first master was 'one Mr. Barber of Marke Lane a widower', that her father was 'Phyllis of Morisco a blackasmore [sic] being both a basket maker and shovel maker', that her mistress dwelled in the liberties of east Smithfield, and that being 'desyrous to become a christian', Mary 'made suit . . . to have sonme [sic] conversation with the curat' of St. Botolph.[18]

This is a goldmine of information – and of individuation, not to mention volition – compared to our lack of information about Dinah. The record of Mary Phyllis's conversion within parish records again highlights baptism as the public welcome of the cultural other into a Christian community. It also supports Dimmock's argument that ministers had to improvise services and manners of record-keeping for individuals who presented themselves in different circumstances for different reasons.[19] The various contextualising and individualising details in these cases alert us to doctrinal unease with such religious crossings. These ministers may protest too much in their carefully delineated and rationalised sermons and records. Dennis Britton has argued that it was precisely through its reconceptualisation of baptism that Protestant theology contributed to the development of race as a category of identity. As theologians looked for scriptural precedent for a covenant between God and an elect nation, Genesis 17:7 became a key text. There God assured the Israelites that his covenant with them 'and thy seed after thee in their generations' was an everlasting covenant. It established a typology of Jewish circumcision and Christian baptism that also strengthened an understanding of race as a matter of genealogy and lineage. Such a divine assurance of exclusionary favour would be undermined by expansion to other racial lineages.

Questions like these troubled religious polemics, social practices, and cultural productions alike. They were pushed to the extreme with ministers like Jessey, who strongly resisted the Presbyterian model for a renewed national church once Laud had been overthrown. As Achsah Guibbory has argued, the religious radicals of the Civil War years began to abandon 'such dreams of a nation' in favour of 'the more universalist and anti-establishment aspects of the Hebrew Bible'.[20]

Given the centrality of baptism to the welcome of a non-native to early modern Christianity, it remains a curious fact that Dinah's first appearance in the documentary record is not a baptism. Her second most definitely is, however. This disruption in sequence speaks to the evolving practices of the dissenters as well as the different public stances dissenting leaders were willing to risk at diverse moments of political crisis and opportunity. For Jessey's group, specifically, the counter-intuitive sequence speaks to the deeply divisive role of adult baptism for those identifying as Baptists. *A Storehouse of provision* advances an argument for the baptism of adult members of London separatist congregations through the surrogation of cross-cultural converts. In other words, Jessey is backing into an argument for adult baptism for those converting to an experiential religion from a merely dutiful Christian practice. Anabaptists, as they were called by their detractors, were among the most reviled of the religious reformers, not only for the exclusionary theology behind the practice of adult baptism, but also for the violence with which Anabaptists had been associated in the sixteenth-century Munster uprising, one that ended with a massacre and resonated throughout the European Reformations. Even within Jessey's seminal gathered church, adult baptism was a highly divisive issue. Jessey himself had become convinced of its merits and was baptised in

1645 by Hansard Knollys, but for the rest of his life he maintained his own church as an 'open communion'. He did not impose adult baptism as a condition of membership in his church.

Even so, Jessey advances a strong argument for baptism by identifying it as the necessary and sufficient 'ordinance' or ceremony for the conversion of adult non-Europeans as well as one with specific scriptural precedent. Furthermore, he advocates for the cleansing powers of full immersion. He offers an etymological argument from the Greek – 'Bapto, which signifieth to dip' – and amplifies it with printed marginalia. 'What Resemblance of the Buriall, or Resurrection of Christ is in (sprinkling)?' (*Storehouse*, 125). In reference to the case of a Portuguese Jew converted by the Dutch, Jessey notes with approval:

> Hence when he was Baptized, he would not have it by Sprinkling, or powring on of water: But by going into the water, and Dipping into it. As when the (e) Eunuch the Aethiopion, or (f) Blackmore baptized, Philip and the Blackmore went into the water, and there (g) he dipped him. [126; the parenthetical letters are keyed to marginal notes]

These passages immediately precede the announcement of Dinah's baptism. Insisting on the need for full immersion in the cleansing waters of baptism, Jessey at the same time powerfully evokes the proverbial challenge of washing an Ethiopian white. Jessey lets the case of the Dutch baptism of a Portuguese Jewish convert do all the work of persuasion. The unadorned, seemingly incidental mention of Dinah the Black's baptism follows. But it is the next report that makes plain that adult baptism for a non-native convert was being leveraged as a spur for greater acceptance of adult baptism among those who had already been baptised as children. For what follows is a lengthy account of 'Robert S', a member of a London gathered church announcing to his sceptical fellows that he is ready to be baptised as an adult. He is immediately joined by several others. The simplicity and inevitability of adult baptism for a non-native convert has provided an opening for a wider acceptance of adult baptism for an English dissenting congregation.

WHAT'S IN A NAME?

The 1650 report of Dinah's baptism underscores the fact that the name Dinah preceded baptism. That is worth noting as a counter to the assumption that it is only with baptism that a cultural other is given a Christian name. Through a baptismal report, the surname 'Massah' has been recorded, however. Though this detail promises to summon this individual more fully into the historical record, I want to keep alive the possibility that we could have here yet another Dinah – or perhaps it is any Dinah, that Dinah is the name by which any black woman might be summoned in mid-seventeenth-century London. The name Dinah Massah provides no useful clues to a geographical or cultural background for this woman. Her background has not mattered for her congregation. No previous belief system is acknowledged. Her adopted name is a compound of Old Testament references. Massah was a place on the Israelites' exodus from slavery at which they threatened to return to Egypt rather than go on without water. Moses smote a rock with his rod there and produced a flood of saving waters. This certainly confirms Jessey's strong investment in the typology of cleansing waters. A seeker after seals and signs, he elsewhere flirted with the healing powers of oils and waters.

This Exodus surname only heightens the scriptural origin of Dinah's proper name. In Genesis Dinah was the daughter of Jacob by Leah. She plays a minor role in the history of the Israelites. After Jacob pitches a tent in Canaan on land purchased from Hamor, 'Dinah . . . went out to see the daughters of the land. And when Shechem the son of Hamor the Hivite, prince of the country, saw her, he took her, and lay with her, and defiled her' (King James Version, Genesis 34:1–2).[21] In the next verse, we are told that Shechem's soul subsequently 'clave unto Dinah' and that marriage negotiations ensued. But for the rest of the episode, narrative focus turns to the anger and drive for vengeance pursued by Jacob's sons, Simeon and Levi. Hamor's request for a marriage between his son and Jacob's daughter is cast in the language of reconciliation and integration: 'And ye shall dwell with us: and the land shall be before you: dwell and trade ye therein, and get you possessions therein' (Genesis 34:10). Hamor and Shechem and all the men of the city even acceded to the demands of Jacob's sons that they be circumcised. But Jacob's sons were acting in bad faith, for several days later, when the men 'were sore', Simeon and Levi came into the city, slaughtered them, spoiled the city, and seized captive all their wives, children, and goods.[22]

Dinah's point of view has been all but lost in the long tradition of biblical commentary on the brothers' rejection of miscegenation. Are we to understand Dinah to be culpable for going 'out' to see the daughters of the land? Some commentaries add the allure of foreign goods as a motive. 'Seize' and 'violate' are among the possible translations of Shechem's act, and while most insist on its violent nature, the more neutral 'lie with' is also available as an option. The English Hebraist and religious exile, Henry Ainsworth, used that term in his translation of Genesis.[23] A running header in the printed volume also brought out a different interpretation: 'Dinah's Ravishment' turns away from honour codes to at least allow for a sense of encounter with the divine, familiar from both classical and scriptural sources. Paul's conversion, the archetypical conversion experience of the New Testament, has something of ravishment about it, as Paul is struck by light with such force that he falls to the ground. Again, the question of volition at the heart of conversion is beset with internal contradictions. As much as it seems within reach, the utter lack of control over one's election remains a block, and the line between sexual violation and divine ravishment horrifyingly thin.

While we might like to credit Dinah as a pioneer in assimilation and accommodation of cultural difference – and it is at least possible that such was the impulse behind the bestowal of this name on Jessey's 'Dinah the Black' – it is equally likely that the name would have carried the shame of sexual defilement. Whatever exchange value Jacob's daughter had was not cashed in. She is never mentioned again, though some commentators have declared her to be Job's otherwise unnamed wife. For Genesis Dinah, there is no clear answer to the question Jeffrey Shoulson asks of Ruth and Namaan as models of conversion: which Christian communities picked up on which models and what did they make of those models?[24] Possibly Jessey had some interest in developing Dinah as a model of a foreign woman integrated into the Christian community. Possibly he saw rape as an apt metaphor for enforced servitude, weighing that servitude heavily towards slavery, whether or not it was precisely the legal condition of the Dinah he knew. If so, Jessey did not underscore that interpretation with any marginal Scriptural citations. And however he would have translated the verses from Genesis is lost to history. His own Bible translation, in collaboration with John Owen and John Row, Professor of Hebrew at Aberdeen, was reportedly almost complete by 1659, but had no chance of publication under the restored monarchy.[25] We are left with the scriptural name, Dinah, that raises the possibility of the establishment of one cross-cultural community of belief out of cultural difference even as it resonates with the laying of violent hands on women's bodies.

The doubled indebtedness of the name to the Old Testament could also be said to doubly activate what Shoulson calls 'the paradoxical tensions between alienation and familiarization, particularization and universalization' in the quandary of how to translate Biblical names.[26] Doubled, too, are the ruptures in Dinah's identity, so crucial to conversion to an experiential religion. For the seventeenth-century Protestant experientialists, the religious affiliation most deeply forged was with their Israelite precursors. Whoever this woman was, and whatever identity she has left behind, the name Dinah becomes even less solid a marker of acculturated English identity in its allusiveness to biblical typologies.

WHAT WAS DINAH'S ROLE IN JESSEY'S VISION OF A GLOBAL PROTESTANTISM?

Jessey may have lost faith in the established church, but he still understood his congregation's experience as having relevance on a much larger stage. The reportorial networks on which he depended extended throughout the diaspora of English religious dissent and among missionary clerics of other nations. Around the time Jessey was presenting Dinah the Black as just one of the London saints, he was actively tracking down other reports of God's wonders around the world. The claims of the Spanish missionaries in the New World were well known. Jessey might have made it his business to follow the astonishing number of converts the Jesuits were reporting with their missions in Annam and elsewhere (as discussed in Keith Luria's chapter in this volume). The same year he reported Dinah's baptism in London, he edited *Of the conversion of five thousand and nine hundred East-Indians* (1650). The work celebrates Protestant missions. It is based on letters from Caspar Sibelius detailing the successful mass conversions that the Dutch minister Robert Junius had effected in Formosa. Jessey painstakingly describes what we might think of as a forensic chain of custody of the letters. As with *Exceeding riches of grace*, personal recommendations are crucial to the grounds of credibility. Lest any doubt lingers about the authenticity of the number of converts, Jessey prints a portion of his translation alongside a column with the original Latin. As if that were proof! But at least the pathways and agencies by which texts have been transmitted across times and languages are made available for scrutiny.

The astonishing success of the Dutch mass conversions is prefaced with an assurance that 'to be an instrument of saving one soule (snatch'd out of the jawes of that infernell Wolfe) farre exceeds all other gaines'.[27] But Jessey knew that while the winning of one barbarian soul may be news in a western European capital, the winning of souls abroad was a numbers game. Sibelius touts the advanced methods of the Protestants over their Catholic counterparts. Junius learned the 'barbarous language and rude Idiomes of those Heathen', and catechised for a full twelve years in their tongue. Eventually he made 'great and laudable progresse both of men and women, young and old, chiefe ones, middle sort, and meane ones' (5). Soon, five thousand, nine hundred converts were baptised, practising Christians. Six hundred of them learned to read and write. Some joined Junius in translating the Psalms.

To spur on the English godly with this example of Dutch Protestant missionary gains, Jessey supplemented the printed report from the East Indies with summaries of the progress of English missions in the 'West Indies', or New England.[28] He drew on the letters that retrospectively became known as the Eliot Tracts. He did not miss an opportunity to argue that the fulfilment of God's providential contract with his people was at hand. In the year 1630 before the birth of Christ, he noted, for instance, 'Israel with 70 souls went down into Egypt', and in the year 1630 after the birth of Christ 'a great number of our English Brethren were forced hence [to New England] by the Contrivers and Promoters of Destructive Designes, for Introduction of great Evills, both in Church and State' (13–14).

None of these missionary efforts focused on individual women or women as a group. Women from these cultures seemed not to be credited with the kind of cultural memory and religious agency that is described by Dursteler and Graizbord elsewhere in this volume. The goal of the English conversions of Amerindians was to turn male tribal leaders. Patriarchal systems on both sides are assumed and activated. Whole communities, including family units, would follow. More importantly, these wholesale turnings of non-Christian natives were understood – at least by Jessey – as the overtures to the much anticipated conversion of the Jews. Indeed, Jessey soon began advocating for the re-admission of the Jews to England. He was a leader among the party that John Coffey characterises as the 'radical tolerationists'.[29] Jessey looked towards the gathering of the Jewish tribes as a biblical promise to be fulfilled. For that would be the last, greatest sign of the coming Fifth Monarchy.[30]

Characteristically, Jessey took it upon himself to record the series of meetings at Whitehall where merchants, lawyers, and ministers debated the question, which Cromwell had reduced to two parts: whether it was lawful to readmit the Jews and, if so, on what terms.[31] As Eliane Glaser has noted, the prevailing interests at the Whitehall Conferences were 'millenarianism and mercantilism'.[32] Jessey was cheerleader for the millenarian party. We get a sense of the multiple conversations taking place when Jessey writes in answer to merchants' concerns that English interests would suffer: 'It might tend to the benefit of very many in our Nation, even in outward things, besides the hopes of their conversion; which time (it is hoped) is now at hand, even at the door. [This last was spoken of at a more private meeting]'.[33]

Jessey may have fervently advocated for the return of the Jews, and his interests may have intersected at some points with those of Menasseh ben Israel, who petitioned Cromwell for readmission on behalf of the Jews of Amsterdam. Both looked towards the gathering of the Jewish tribes as a biblical promise to be fulfilled. But like most Englishmen, Jessey was little concerned with living Jews. As Achsah Guibbory has written, the English claims to being God's chosen and to inheriting the promises of a biblical Israel, did not easily accommodate the social integration of living Jews. Many tolerationists were in favour of different kinds of 'Judaism', but not of Jews living among them. That is unless the Jews were willing to convert. In his relentless way, Jessey quoted the psalms in his translation of *A Description and explanation of 268 places in Jerusalem . . . as it flourished in the time of Jesus Christ* (1654): 'All kings shall worship him, all Nations shall serve him; Men shall be blessed in him. Psal 72, 4, 11, 17'.

This quick survey of missionary efforts around the world is blinkered by Jessey's biases and selective networks. For that very reason, it is a valuable witness of a particular historical moment and an equally valuable reminder of the interconnectedness of these missionary enterprises. Several quandaries are raised again and again: the one versus the many; the question of choice versus the imposition of violence. Each church works out its own methods against the perceived failures of other churches. We are used to seeing those issues divided differently or having different applications depending on the context – conversion as a large-scale, probably coerced event for natives abroad and conversion as a singular, deeply interiorised voluntary event for English men and women. Dinah the Black interrupts those dualities. She appears in the wrong place, as it were, in the domesticated sphere of English devotion rather than as the exotic, sexualised trophy of conquest.

So, what *did* happen to Dinah Black?

Dinah's name is gone from the list of credible witnesses in the 1652 edition of *Exceeding Riches of grace*. Anna Trapnell and the bookseller Hannah Allen's names were also removed at that time. Others were added. One could speculate about the reasons behind Jessey's continued cultivation of his lists of witnesses. For instance, the book no longer carried Hannah Allen's imprint. She had died, and rights had been assigned to new booksellers.[34] One could also note that there were inevitably uneasy alliances among those named as witnesses. The reach of a network does not in itself establish grounds of communal identity or belief. To take the case of a prominent woman witness added to the list, Robert Boyle's sister, Lady Ranelagh, was developing a political theory of government as a contractual agreement through the less formal means of letter writing from the Civil War through the Restoration. When she moved to London in 1643, an exile from war-torn Ireland, she also broadened the network of her influential friends, from the family alliances established by her father, the Earl of Cork, through the Great Tew monarchists with whom some of her siblings were in sympathy, and on to the Hartlib circle with its parliamentarian leanings. Clearly, she crossed paths with Jessey, as well. There were as many ideological gaps separating these contacts as there were common grounds. It remained an intractable problem to find the appropriate legal grounds for the political contract and the spheres of influence to be given over to religious freedom within and by those political contracts. If Ranelagh's correspondents – as diverse as Elizabeth of Bohemia, Edward Hyde, and Samuel Hartlib – could not be drawn into a grand alliance, why should we think that her appearance at Sarah Wight's home was in itself evidence of essential agreement with Jessey's presentation of Wight's case as providential?[35] Still, the fact that Jessey is advancing women's credit all along the social scale, from a young black maid to an aristocratic lady, is one of the ways he obfuscates ideological differences to opportunistically advance his own agenda. It is also confirmation of the power accrued by women in many dissenting circles.

There is one further tantalising reference to a Dinah Black in the historical record. By virtue of a 1667 appearance of Dinah Black in a case before the Bristol Court of Aldermen, Habib thinks we can recover the trajectory of one black woman's experience in England (and that is the claim with which I opened this paper).[36] The original court records are lost, but in a later summary, there is mention of a Dinah Black who had been baptised and wished to continue to live as a Christian, but whose mistress had apparently sold her to be conveyed to the plantations. Black was freed by the court to earn her living until the case was heard at the next Quarter Sessions, but there is no further word about the case in the court records.

Because there were close connections between the Broadmeath Baptist Church in Bristol and Jessey's in London, it is conceivable that this is the same woman noted among the separatists in London in 1647. When Bristol was captured by the royalists during the Civil War, most of the dissenters moved to London as a group and worshipped with Jessey, but not before a founding member of the congregation, Dorothy Hazzard, led a group of two hundred women and girls to defy the royalist siege at a city gate.[37] Further, the Broadmeath Church had a member by the name of Dorothy Smith, the name of Dinah Black's mistress in the Bristol records. The Broadmeath Church at Bristol also had another notable black member, a 'Blackymore maide named Francis (a servant to one that lived upon the Back of Bristoll)'. Francis left an exhortatory testament to the church, which was recorded in the Church Book, and she was buried with great respect in 1640.[38]

It is conceivable and perhaps even plausible that Broadmeath Dinah is the same woman who visited Sarah Wight for spiritual counsel. But I would argue that we do not need this Dinah Black to be Jessey's Dinah Massah for the two experiences to resonate deeply. For again, what identity adheres in the name Dinah? What is in the name of a convert from another culture, a convert who was more than likely given a Christian name by sponsors rather than choosing her own name, a convert whose surname is an ambiguous ethnic designator, a convert whose past life is rendered irrelevant by conversion? Access to an individualised experience remains an elusive object of study whether we are dealing with a historical serving maid or the trope of Dinah.

Further, the extant paraphrase cannot clarify if Dinah was being subjected to enslavement or indenture, even though the legal status of blacks in England, always vulnerable, was in the process of being sharply redefined as chattel.[39] Here, too, however, Dinah Black marks the categories of race and separatist religion as overlapping constructions of cultural difference. In Bristol after the Restoration, the Conventicle Acts were imposed with special harshness against Quakers, and Baptists were also caught up in the persecutions. Not for nothing did these religious dissenters cast themselves as the Israelites fighting off the shackles of slavery

GENDER, RACE, AND THE VISIBILITY OF PROTESTANT SAINTS

in Egypt. While many dissenters emigrated, deportation was also a steady threat for those who would not come back into the fold of established religion. For the most part, Nonconformists were being harassed and imprisoned (as had been John Bunyan in Bedford and, for that matter, Henry Jessey in London). But in Bristol, in 1665, the authorities decided to deport to Barbados six men and three women who were indicted for having taken part in Nonconformist services, and had been twice before convicted of the same crime.[40] If Dinah Black was saved from being sold into slavery – at least temporarily – so were at least some of the Nonconformists saved from their deportation to Barbados. In this case, several crew members of the ship the *Mary Fortune* of Bristol would not carry away Englishmen without their consent. Moreover, they claimed that there was a similar law in Barbados that people could not be brought there except voluntarily, and so the crew had put these men ashore.[41]

We can certainly argue that Dinah Massah was being forced into a racialised category of selfhood. Despite – and even through – global conversionary enterprises, that racialised category of selfhood would prevail for centuries to follow, as indeed it mostly prevailed even as Henry Jessey welcomed a single young black woman servant into his fold of London saints in 1647 and promoted her as a person of credit. But that racialised category of selfhood had not entirely prevailed for Dinah, not in 1647, and not in 1667. That is the point I am emphasising with this case study. Dinah Massah sufficiently disrupted the polarising categories of race and religion to throw off balance the English conception of itself as an elect nation, and she did so from an entirely vulnerable and singular position within English society. By virtue of her servitude, she upended social hierarchies. By virtue of her blackness, she challenged easy divisions based on national identity. By virtue of her presumably devout – or at least uncontested – demeanor, she exemplified in a wholly unexpected way, the visible saints of mid-century English Protestantism. As a rallying point for a network of millenarian hopefuls around the world, Henry Jessey registered a young woman convert's black skin colour – a visible mark of difference – only to register an even stronger scriptural promise of universal membership in the visible church.

NOTES

1 Imtiaz Habib, *Black lives in the English archives, 1500–1677: imprints of the invisible* (Aldershot: Ashgate, 2008), p. 210. In addition to the members

of the York seminar on 'Gender and Conversion', I am grateful to Habib for conversations about Dinah and to seminar participants in Queen's University Belfast, The International John Bunyan Society, and the Folger Shakespeare Library, where I read versions of this essay.

2 Henry Jessey, *The exceeding riches of grace* (London, 1647).
3 For developments in the visual arts, see the exhibition catalogue edited by Joaneath Spicer, *Revealing the African presence in Renaissance Europe* (Baltimore: The Walters Art Museum, 2012).
4 Kim Hall, 'Object into object: some thoughts on the presence of black women in early modern culture', in Peter Erickson and Clark Hulse (eds), *Early modern visual culture: representation, race, and empire in Renaissance England* (Philadelphia: University of Pennsylvania Press, 2000), p. 348.
5 Hollar etchings of a Turk and an Amerindian also date from 1645. Those both include the phrase 'ad viuum' with Hollar's signature.
6 Barbara Ritter Dailey, 'The visitation of Sarah Wight: holy carnival and the revolution of the saints in civil war London', *Church History*, 55 (1986), 452–4. On *Exceeding riches*, see also my *Protestant autobiography in the seventeenth-century anglophone world* (Oxford: Oxford University Press, 2012), pp. 73–119.
7 Genesis 21 is referenced in the printed margin, with God's promise to Hagar and Ishmael: 'And also of the son of the bondwoman will I make a nation, because he is thy seed'.
8 Habib, *Black lives*, p. 6.
9 Emily C. Bartels, *Speaking of the Moor from 'Alcazar' to 'Othello'* (Philadelphia: University of Pennsylvania Press, 2008), p. 5; Michael Neill, '"Mulattos," "Blacks," and "Indian Moors": *Othello* and early modern constructions of human difference', *Shakespeare Quarterly*, 49 (1998), 61–74.
10 Henry Jessey, *A Storehouse of provision* (London, 1650), p. 126.
11 Matthew Dimmock, 'Converting and not converting "strangers" in early modern London', *Journal of Early Modern History*, 17 (2013), 457–78.
12 Meredith Hanmer, *The baptizing of a Turke. A sermon preached at the hospitall of Saint Katherin* [sic], ([London, 1586]), p. 5.
13 Matthew Dimmock, *New Turkes: dramatizing Islam in early modern England* (Aldershot: Ashgate, 2005).
14 John Despagne, *The joyfull convert . . . preached at the baptizing of a Turke* (London, 1658).
15 *Ibid.*, 9–10.
16 His godmother, the Lady Mayerne, was daughter to the Huguenot court physician, Sir Theodore Turquet de Mayerne. Her mother is one of the named witnesses in *Exceeding riches of grace*.
17 Ralph Hamor, *A true discourse of the present estate of Virginia* (London, 1615), pp. 65–6.

18 Habib, *Black lives*, pp. 324–5.
19 Dimmock, 'Converting', p. 474.
20 Achsah Guibbory, *Christian identity: Jews & Israel in seventeenth-century England* (Oxford: Oxford University Press, 2010), pp. 119–20.
21 Dinah does not figure in Michele Osherow, *Biblical women's voices in early modern England* (Aldershot: Ashgate, 2009), for Dinah has no voice. Also absent from Phyllis Trible, *Texts of terror: literary-feminist readings of biblical narratives* (Philadelphia: Fortress Press, 1984), Dinah's story still resonates with Trible's reading of the rape and dismemberment of the concubine from Bethlehem. I am grateful to Osherow and Kevin Killeen for discussion on Genesis Dinah.
22 Walter Brueggemann, *Genesis: interpretation. A Bible commentary* (Westminster: John Knox Press, 2010), pp. 278 and, on the singular mention of defilement, 275.
23 Henry Ainsworth, *Annotations upon the First Book of Moses, called Genesis* ([Amsterdam], 1616). Ainsworth translates Gen. 34:2–3 as 'And Shechem the son of Hamor, the Evite, prince of the land, saw her: and he took her, & lay with her, and humbled her. And his sowl clave unto Dinah the daughter of Jakob: & he loved the damsel, & spake to the hart of the damsel' (AA3r).
24 Jeffrey S. Shoulson, *Fictions of conversion: Jews, Christians, and cultures of change in early modern England* (Philadelphia: University of Pennsylvania Press, 2013).
25 *Oxford Dictionary of National Biography*, s.v. Jessey [Jacie], Henry.
26 Shoulson, *Fictions of conversion*, p. 98.
27 Caspar Sibelius, *Of the conversion of five thousand and nine hundred East-Indians*, trans. Henry Jessey (London, 1650), p. 4.
28 Jessey's spirit of collecting disparate pieces of evidence is given material form in the volume at Dr. Williams's Library in which the Sibelius tract is bound (564.B.10). The volume also includes three Eliot tracts (*Clear sunshine of the gospel*, *A further discovery of the present state of the Indians in New-England*, and *Tears of repentance*) and four expositions of the scriptural books of Daniel and Revelations.
29 John Coffey, 'The toleration controversy during the English revolution', in Christopher Durston and Judith Maltby (eds), *Religion in revolutionary England* (Manchester: Manchester University Press, 2006), pp. 43–4.
30 On the Quakers as relentless proselytisers of Jews, see Guibbory, *Christian identity*, pp. 243–51.
31 [Henry Jessey], *A narrative of the late proceeds at Whitehall, concerning the Jews* (London, 1656).
32 Eliane Glaser, *Judaism without Jews: philosemitism and Christian polemic in early modern England* (Houndmills Basingstoke: Palgrave Macmillan, 2007), p. 114.

33 *Narrative of the late proceeds*, p. 9.
34 On Allen, see Maureen Bell, 'Hannah Allen and the development of a Puritan publishing business, 1646–1651', *Publishing History*, 26 (1989), 5–66.
35 See Ruth Connolly, 'A Proselytising Protestant commonwealth: the religious and political ideals of Katherine Jones, Viscountess Ranelagh (1614–1691)', *Seventeenth Century*, 20 (2008), 244–64.
36 Habib, *Black lives*, p. 210.
37 Ann Hughes, *Gender and the English Revolution* (London: Routledge, 2012), pp. 74–5.
38 Roger Hayden, *Records of a Church of Christ in Bristol, 1640–1687*, ed. Bristol Record Society (Bristol: University of Bristol, 1974), pp. 9, 101–2; see also Anne Dunan-Page on the mixed genres of manuscript Church books, including that of Broadmeath: 'Writing "things ecclesiastical": the literary acts of the gathered churches', *Etudes Epistémè*, 21 (2012). www.etudes-episteme.org/2e/?-21-2012-.
39 On patterns of emigration from Bristol in the Restoration, see David Harris Sacks, *The widening gate: Bristol and the Atlantic economy, 1450–1700* (Berkeley: University of California Press, 1991), pp. 282–303.
40 John Latimer, *The annals of Bristol in the seventeenth century* (Bristol: William George's Sons, 1900), p. 335.
41 *Ibid.*, quoting *State papers colonial*, 7 January 1665 [6].

Afterword

Matthew Dimmock

~

Over the course of its introduction and twelve chapters this volume has consistently challenged a traditionally narrow scholarly approach to conversion in the post-Reformation world, opening up manifold contexts and revealing the complex interplay of conversion with gendered ideologies and affiliations. It is a timely as well as an important intervention, for such matters are arguably more prominent today, in the early twenty-first century, than they have been at any time since the period with which this volume is primarily concerned. The convert is once again a conspicuously divisive and ambivalent figure around whom competing narratives coalesce, and conversion a process that produces and enacts difference.

As I have suggested, it was not always thus. Of course people never entirely stopped believing in and converting between belief systems, but Enlightenment legacies and the apparently benign faiths of the later European empires gently pushed the exemplary transition between faiths to the periphery (although associated anxieties resurfaced in the repeated horrors of 'turning native'). In the twentieth-century Cold War clash of political ideologies prominent religious conversions did take place, but when they were narrated at all they were conspicuously presented as a personal, inward matter of little wider import. Such actions were also largely the preserve of men. One prominent example is that of Harry St. John Bridger Philby (later Sheikh Abdullah), English agent in the Arabian Peninsula, and his 1930 conversion to the Wahhabi Islam of the new Saudi state he later came to serve. For him conversion came as a sort of return, for he felt 'like some disembodied spirit restored by accident or miracle to its proper environment'.¹ Although his new faith may have altered the terms in which his contemporaries viewed him (he expected 'a good deal of comment and criticism'), it was no bar to further employment by the Saudis, the British, or the Americans, nor to standing as a British MP.² In the Cold War one might politically defect, but not, it seems, politically convert.

This 'post-religious' emphasis on the political was mirrored in the academy. It is surprising now how little either of the two founding works of post-colonial and oriental studies, Edward Said's *Orientalism* (1978) and Alain Grosrichard's *Structure du sérail: la fiction du despotisme Asiatique dans l'Occident classique* (1979), have to say about religion – and both are silent about converts or conversion.³ It is in the new geo-political circumstances that developed in the aftermath of the collapse of the Soviet Union, and in particular the new prominence of a widely perceived antagonism between Islam and 'the West', that conversion has once again taken a central role.⁴ The much vaunted 'religious turn' in early modern studies has also followed in its wake, generating new perspectives on the complexities of post-Reformation devotional worlds and their interaction, work that – as this volume demonstrates – is finding in conversion a means to better understand these worlds and our own.⁵

The popular stages and printing presses of sixteenth- and seventeenth-century England were more interested in luridly reconstructing the erotically motivated conversion of anti-heroes like John Ward (Issouf Reis, Captain Wardiyya) to Islam, or – as Chloë Houston outlines in this volume – in the stoic masculine resistance to conversion of men like Thomas Sherley, than in converts from other faiths to Anglican Protestantism. But there were many such converts: men and women like Marye Phyllis, a 'blackamore' from Morisco (possibly Morocco); or 'Chinano' (later William), a Turk from Nigroponte; or Yehuda (later Nathaniel) Menda, a Jew from Barbary – all accommodated into the body of the Anglican church through a malleable ritual that required only their public profession of faith and their acceptance by and into a parish congregation.⁶ Their gendered and ethnic identities were – at least officially – reshaped in their becoming English, just as their personal narratives were reshaped to make them millenarian beacons affirming England's godly destiny and lighting the way for their compatriots to follow. For instance, Chinano's 'Turkish' masculinity, one repeatedly associated by writers and dramatists with excessive lust and sodomy, seems to have been reformed, if not erased, in his public baptism; it was certainly no obstacle to his subsequent Christian marriage to one Mary Newbye.[7] Knowing what motivated these converts, their experience of conversion, and what happened to them afterwards is often impossible, as a number of contributors to this volume acknowledge, and was likely to have been considered irrelevant to the process anyway; any trace of individual subjectivity or authentic belief in these accounts and/or records serves only to further their exemplary purpose.

The dominant narratives of conversion in twenty-first-century Britain are not so different. They invariably concern conversion to, rather than from, Islam, a ritual undergone by an estimated five thousand Britons a year, the majority of them women, a fact that returns us to the exemplary character and wider influence of women's conversions, explored by Helen Smith and Claire Canavan in Chapter 5.[8] This specific convert community finds itself trapped in a conspicuous liminality. Although comprising women from a wide range of socio-economic and ethnic backgrounds, the mainstream media tends to shape their stories into a few core essentialising narratives: the working class convert who finds religion as an escape from poverty, abuse, and/or addiction; conversion for the purposes of marriage; and (less prominent because it is less easily explained) conversion as a consequence of a professional middle-class crisis and subsequent search for meaning.[9] The 'trophy' convert (a role discussed in Chapter 12 by Kathleen Lynch) in each of these examples is also invariably white, despite the preponderance of Afro-Caribbean women in this convert community, whose own voices are silenced.[10] Each narrative purports to privilege authentic experience even as they contort it to fit a recognisable pattern. As in the early modern contexts explored by Eric Dursteler in this volume, such narratives serve to connect the anxious energies associated with female conversion, particularly to Islam, with attendant fears of 'fifth column' terrorism.[11]

These recognisable trajectories demystify and fall back on gendered assumptions about the shifting expectations of women between the two monolithic blocs of 'Islam' and 'the West'. There is little room for nuance, particularly since this specific group of converts is also burdened with the expectation, in certain quarters, that they are best placed to act as an intellectual and maternal 'bridge' between Muslim and non-Muslim communities, that as Western Muslims familiar with both contexts they represent the geopolitical frontier. It is such individuals who bear, in Tariq Ramadan's words, a 'heavy responsibility', for they are expected to 'bring about the avoidance of a breakdown and the emergence of a path to fair dialogue and reconciliation'.[12] It is they who 'will play a decisive role in the evolution of Islam worldwide'.[13]

High-minded rhetoric aside, the reality for such converts is often very different. They describe being made to feel uncomfortable, if not inferior, about their cultural backgrounds, and female exclusion from some institutional structures 'such as mosques and Islamic organisations' means they struggle to be accepted or to find a voice within 'heritage Muslim' communities.[14] Conversely, many talk of rejection by their non-Muslim families and the particular betrayal of kin and nation associated with female conversion as well as the intrusive combination of suspicion and fascination they face in public dealings.[15] The fractured, multiple identities such women are forced to assume suggest that, as in earlier periods, recognising the complex entanglement of gender with conversion is fundamental to any understanding of the way ideologies compete, cleave, and cohere on the global stage.

Although it is an undoubtedly timely reflection on such issues, this volume is not the first reappraisal of conversion in the post-Reformation era, a period which Eric Dursteler calls 'the age of the renegade'. As early as the seventeenth century, dramatists and writers had begun projecting back to earlier periods – especially the mid-sixteenth-century peak of Ottoman–Habsburg rivalry in the Mediterranean – using the convert and conversion to delineate the forces involved. The most celebrated example comes a little later, and usefully functions as a kind of afterword to the period covered by this volume: Mozart's early opera *Die Entführung aus dem Serail* (*The abduction from the seraglio*), with a libretto by Gottlieb Stephanie the Younger, first performed in Vienna in 1782. Mozart and Stephanie were, above all, seeking a box-office success, and decided upon a thorough adaptation of Christoph Friedrich Bretzner's original libretto *Belmont und Constanze, oder Die Entführung aus dem Serail* (1780) because the comic oriental theme was all the rage in late-eighteenth-century Viennese and wider European theatres and salons.[16] The subject is fairly conventional: set in the mid-sixteenth century in and around Pasha Selim's palace on the Turkish coast, *Die Entführung* features an attempt by the Spanish nobleman Belmonte and his servant Pedrillo to rescue his beloved Konstanze and her English maid (Pedrillo's love) Blonde, who have fallen under Selim's control having been captured by Muslim pirates.

The opera presents different models of masculinity and femininity in power and under duress in this Ottoman environment. Belmonte is honourable, absolutely committed to his beloved (although anxious about her chastity), and stoical in the face of death. Konstanze is defined by her fidelity and her chastity, determined to maintain her vows to Belmonte in the face of Selim's repeated attempts to woo her, and the underlying threat of violence that accompanies such wooing. Pedrillo and Blonde, the two non-elite Christian figures, are resourceful, adaptable, and able to thrive despite their capture and captivity. Blonde is given by Selim to his steward Osmin, the most popular character in *Die Entführung*. He is, by contrast, a caricature of excessive Ottoman masculinity. His repeated threats of violence – 'Erst geköpft, dann gehangen, dann gespießt auf heiße Stangen, dann verbrannt, dann gebunden, und getaucht, zuletzt geschunden' ('First beheaded, then hanged, then spitted on hot skewers, then burned, then bound, and drowned, and finally skinned') – are intended to recall the extreme bombast of earlier stage Turks, and yet he is denied the enactment of his violent fantasies; here such threats are empty, and Osmin is rendered ridiculous by the comic music of the 'Turkish refrain' that accompanies him on stage.[17] His model of masculinity is shown to be outmoded, his bombast misplaced.

It is the enigmatic Pasha Selim, placed at the heart of the opera, who is its most curious creation. We learn early on that he is a renegade when Pedrillo reassures Belmonte that Konstanze has remained faithful. Belmonte need not worry, for 'Der Bassa ist ein Renegat und hat noch so viel Delikatesse, keine seiner Weiber zu seiner Liebe zu zwingen' ('the Pasha is a renegade and still has sufficient delicacy not to force any of his women into loving him').[18] The suggestion that enough of Selim's Christian nobility remains to prevent him forcing Konstanze to his will is a provocative one, and jars with the presumably disapproving reference to 'his women' – those contained in the enclosed harem space that so fascinated Christian writers, and around which the architecture of *Die Entführung* is constructed.[19] The dedication of such spaces to the confinement of women, and their endless elaboration in later 'Western' writing, connects in obvious ways to the exploration of convent enclosures and rituals of claustration, discussed by Elizabeth Lehfeldt and Saundra Weddle in Chapters 6 and 7, respectively. Despite the stage directions indicating the presence of 'Turkish women' an audience never hears from them, and the harem is defined by the caging of Konstanze whose life is lived under the threat of coercion and conversion. In this respect, as in others, the harem is implicitly an extension of Selim and a manifestation of his power, and for Pedrillo (as well as for Mozart's audiences) his renegade status places him somewhere between Christian and Muslim models of masculinity, and denies the totalising transformation suggested by the Pauline paradigm of conversion.

We only learn more about the circumstances of Selim's conversion at the opera's climax, when he has caught Belmonte and Pedrillo and learns that Belmonte is the son of his arch-enemy Lostados, the Commandant of Oran, a man who had forced Selim to leave his 'Vaterland' (Fatherland), whose greed took away his beloved, and who tore from him 'Ehrenstellen, Vermögen, um alles' ('honourable standing, fortune, everything').[20] Selim is thus at the elite end of the hundreds of thousands of men and women who converted in the period concerning this volume and for whom, as Dursteler remarks in his chapter, conversions 'seem rarely to have been all-encompassing, transformative metamorphoses; rather, they were often acts of desperation or aspiration, religious indifference, or ignorance'.[21] Selim's repeated references to fathers and sons here should remind us of Hannah Crawforth's reflections on family and generation in Chapter 3, for despite, or perhaps because of, his conversion, *Die Entführung* leads us (and Belmonte) to expect exemplary violence in continuation of the explicitly masculine cycle of vengeance initiated by Belmonte's father. Everything an audience knew about the staged 'Turk' pointed to the same end.

Such expectations are, however, disappointed. Instead of punishment, Selim resolves – to Osmin's astonishment – to set all the Christians free, resolving that 'es wäre ein weit größeres Vergnügen eine erlittene Ungerechtigkeit durch Wohltaten zu vergelten, als laster mit lastern tilgen' ('it is a far greater pleasure to repay injustice with a good deed than to repay one depravity with another').[22] Rather than the effeminacy, lust, sodomy, and violence associated with the performance of Islamic conversion in earlier periods, as considered in different ways in the chapters by Chloë Houston (Chapter 10) and Daniel Vitkus (Chapter 11), here we have calm, rational benevolence, as though Selim were an Enlightenment interloper in the sixteenth-century world of the opera. He is content to reverse the traditional Christian association of barbarity and Islam, affirming instead that Belmonte's father is the 'Barbar' or barbarian. Selim had been a renegade in Bretzner's original libretto, but there the plot is neatly resolved when Belmonte is revealed to be his long-lost son. Mozart and Stephanie innovated in denying an easy resolution that erased religious and cultural difference in favour of a celebration of paternal bonds. Instead, they sought to turn an audience's preconceptions upside down, in ways that resonate with other Enlightenment depictions of noble 'Orientals'.[23]

One element that connects many of the chapters in this innovative volume is a concern with the nature and form of what emerges out of the act of conversion. This matter is considered from a variety of angles, but is epitomised in the convert's voice, a primary concern of Kathleen Lynch's fascinating chapter, but also engaged by Hannah Crawforth, Eric Dursteler, David Graizbord, Jane Hatter, Keith Luria, and Abigail Shinn. To what extent are such voices gendered and/or transformed? How are they informed and constrained by the demands of narrative? Can they be authentically recovered? In (re)creating Pasha Selim, Mozart and Stephanie grappled with the challenge of how to operatically stage such a voice. Their response indicates – as this volume's chapters reveal – the ambivalence generated by conversion. The Singspiel form required the integration of dialogue and music, but whereas every other major character in the opera is given prominent moments of song, Selim only speaks his lines. This denies an audience easy access to any sort of interiority, and Selim has none of the moments of introspection given to others – the very structure of *Die Entführung* renders him unknowable. The opera's moments of song also allow its major characters to explicitly perform their assigned gender roles: the jealous lover; the bombastic Turk seeking vengeance; the plucky heroine; the melancholy harem prisoner longing for her beloved. Although an audience is given different accounts of him, Selim's lack of a singing voice makes him indeterminate, which in turn allows him to defy category and convention.

In the character of Pasha Selim in their *Die Entführung aus dem Serail*, Mozart and Stephanie sought to draw upon and scrutinise the suppositions and stereotypes that remained from the earlier age of the renegade. In doing so, they reframed the interrelation of Islam and Christianity, and in Selim's convert voice they provoked a reconsideration of faith and gender for their contemporaries. In a less spectacular, but no less valid fashion, this important volume has done the same.

NOTES

1 Harry St. John Bridger Philby, *Arabian days: an autobiography* (London: Robert Hale, 1948), p. 281. Philby (1885–1960) was also father of that

notorious 'convert', the double agent for the Soviet Union, Harold Adrian Russel 'Kim' Philby (1912-88).

2 *Ibid.*, p. 281. Philby did, however, lose his deposit as an anti-war candidate in the Hythe by-election of July 1939.

3 Edward Said, *Orientalism* (London: Vintage, 1978); Alain Grosrichard, *Structure du sérail: la fiction du despotisme Asiatique dans l'Occident classique* (Paris: Editions du Seuil, 1979), published in English as *The sultan's court: European fantasies of the East*, trans. Liz Heron (London: Verso, 1998).

4 Bernard Lewis – against whom Edward Said was famously opposed – was instrumental in this historiographical shift, exemplified in a popular context by his widely read book *The Middle East and the West* (New York: Harper & Row, 1964). Lewis was in turn a strong influence on Samuel P. Huntington's controversial but influential *The clash of civilizations and the remaking of the world order* (New York: Simon & Shuster, 1996) – Lewis had used the title phrase in a 1990 article – but Huntington's article and subsequent book remains the most prominent statement of this position.

5 See Ken Jackson and Arthur F. Marotti, 'The turn to religion in early modern English studies', *Criticism*, 46 (2004), 167–90.

6 Thomas Sherley is discussed in this volume by Chlöe Houston; Mary Phyllis by Kathleen Lynch. The latter and the others mentioned here are considered in further detail in Matthew Dimmock, 'Converting and not converting "strangers" in London in 1586', *Journal of Early Modern History*, 17 (2013), 457–78. The difficulty of pinpointing the North African origins of these converts is an indication of how indistinct this region was in the early modern English imagination.

7 These associations are drawn most vividly in William Lithgow's account of his travels, *A most delectable, and true discourse, of an admired and painefull peregrination* (London, 1614), and are explored further by Chlöe Houston in this volume. The details of Chinano's marriage are discussed in Dimmock, 'Converting', 477–8.

8 Yasmin Suleiman [project leader], *Narratives of conversion to Islam in Britain: female perspectives* (Cambridge: Prince Alwaleed Bin Talal Centre for Islamic Studies, University of Cambridge, 2013). See also a recent *Guardian* article on this topic, Veronique Mistiaen, 'Converting to Islam: British women on prayer, peace and prejudice' (11 October 2013). See: http://www.theguardian.com/world/2013/oct/11/islam-converts-british-women-prejudice.

9 Suleiman, *Narratives of conversion*, pp. 84–6.

10 *Ibid.*, p. 85.

11 See also Eric Dursteler, *Renegade women: gender, identity and boundaries in the early modern Mediterranean* (Baltimore: Johns Hopkins University Press, 2011).

12 Tariq Ramadan, *Western Muslims and the future of Islam* (Oxford: Oxford University Press, 2003), p. 226. Humayan Ansari adopts a similar, if less portentous, line in his '*The infidel within*': *Muslims in Britain since 1800* (London: Hurst & Company, 2004), pp. 389–406.
13 Ramadan, *Western Muslims*, p. 225.
14 Suleiman, *Narratives of conversion*, p. 81.
15 *Ibid.*, p. 84.
16 Discussed and contextualised further throughout Thomas Bauman's *W.A. Mozart: die entfuhrung aus dem serail* (Cambridge: Cambridge University Press, 1987). As Bauman notes, Mozart's great innovation was not necessarily his incorporation of 'Turkish' music – this pastiche of Turkish instrumentation with its crashing symbols, tambourines, and bass drums was already a part of a European tradition – but rather the way this musical style takes on a dramatic function in the opera, conveying something of the nature of its 'Turkish' characters.
17 On earlier stage Turks see Jonathan Burton, *Traffic and turning: Islam and English drama, 1579–1624* (Newark: University of Delaware Press, 2005); Matthew Dimmock, *New Turkes: dramatizing Islam and the Ottomans in early modern England* (Aldershot: Ashgate, 2005); and Daniel Vitkus, *Turning Turk: English theater and the multicultural Mediterranean, 1570–1630* (New York: Palgrave Macmillan, 2003).
18 Wolfgang Amadeus Mozart and Gottlieb Stephanie the Younger, *Die entführung aus dem serail* ed. Gerhard Croll (Kassell: Bärenreiter-Verlag, 2014), p. 409.
19 A slightly earlier example of a comic opera that is similarly preoccupied with the harem is Dibdin and Bickerstaffe's *The sultan, or a peep into the seraglio* (1775).
20 *Die entführung aus dem serail*, p. 497.
21 Chapter 1, this volume, p. 23.
22 *Die entführung aus dem serail*, p. 503.
23 Examples abound in Ros Ballaster's *Fabulous orients: fictions of the East in England, 1662–1785* (Oxford: Oxford University Press, 2005).

Bibliography

MANUSCRIPTS

Archivio di stato di Venezia
Capi del consiglio dei X, lettere di rettori, b. 281.
Provveditori sopra monasteri, b. 1.
San Sepolcro, b. 1.
Santa Lucia, b. 3.
Santa Maria delle Vergini, b. 43.
Santa Marta, b. 2.
Santa Marta, b. 7. Senato deliberazioni Costantinopoli, b. 6.
Senato deliberazioni Costantinopoli, b. 8.
Senato deliberazioni Costantinopoli, b. 10.
Senato dispacci Costantinopoli, b. 32.
Senato dispacci Costantinopoli, b. 33.
V Savii alla mercanzia, Risposte, reg. 142.

Archivio Storico del Patriarcato di Venezia
Liber diversorum E.

Archivo Histórico Nacional, Madrid
Clero, leg. 7761.
Clero, leg. 7810.
Clero, leg. 7847.
Clero, leg. 7907.
Clero, leg. 7910.
Inquisición de Toledo, legajo 137, expediente 15 (1791–1792).
Inquisición de Toledo, legajo 159, expediente 11 (1790–1791).
Inquisición de Toledo, legajo 187, expediente 4 (1687–1688).

Biblioteca del Museo Correr, Venezia
Cicogna 2570.
Correr 317.
Gradenigo-Dolfin 56, *Memorie lasciate da Francesco Amadi della sua familia*.

Bibliothek der Ludwig-Maximilians-Universität, Munich
Mss. 8° 326.

Bodleian Library, Oxford
MS Auct. D. 4. 2.
MS Bodl. 22.
MS Douce 5.
MS Douce 313.
MS Douce 49.
MS Eng. poet. e.4.
MS Rawl. poet. 84.
MS Rawl. poet. 153.

Darlington Carmelite Convent, County Durham (Lierre archive)
L13.7.

Državni Arhiv u Dubrovniku
Lettere di Levante b. 38, 5 February 1593.

Hampshire Record Office
Register of Bishop Richard Fox, vol. 2.

Lambeth Palace Library
MS. 446.

Real Biblioteca del Monasterio de San Lorenzo de El Escorial, Madrid
Ms. V. II. 14.

Yale
Osborn MS b421

PRINTED PRIMARY SOURCES

Acosta, J. De, *De procuranda indorum salute*, ed. L. Pareña, 2 vols (Madrid: CSIC, 1984–87).
Ainsworth, Henry, *Annotations upon the First Book of Moses, called Genesis* ([Amsterdam: Giles Thorp], 1616).

Andrade, Antonio de, *Libro de la guia de la virtud, y de la imitación de Nuestra Señora: segunda parte* (Madrid: por Francisco Maroto, 1644).
Augustine, *The confessions*, trans. Henry Chadwick (Oxford: Oxford University Press, 2008).
Bastwick, John, *The utter routing of the whole army of all the Independents* (London: John Macock for Michael Spark, 1646).
Baxter, Richard, *A breviate of the life of Margaret, the daughter of Francis Charlton . . . and wife of Richard Baxter* (London: for B. Simmons, 1683).
The Bible: authorized King James Version with Apocrypha, ed. Robert Carroll and Stephen Prickett (Oxford: Oxford University Press, 1997).
Bible, *Douay-Rheims and Latin Vulgate Online*, 2001–2013. http://www.drbo.org.
Blount, Henry, *A Voyage into the Levant . . . The second edition* (London: I. L. for Andrew Crooke, 1636).
Boccaccio, Giovanni, *The decameron containing an hundred pleasant nouels* (London: Isaac Jaggard, 1620).
Boccaccio, Giovanni, *The Decameron*, trans. J. M. Rigg, 2 vols (London: The Navarre Society, 1903). http://www.brown.edu/Departments/Italian_Studies/dweb/texts/.
Boccaccio, Giovanni, *Decameron*, ed. Vittore Branca (Turin: Einaudi, 1992). http://www.brown.edu/Departments/Italian_Studies/dweb/texts/.
Bouchareb, Ahmed, *Al-Maghariba fi al-Burtugal khilala al-Qarn as-Sadis Ashar* (Rabat: Manshurat Kulliyat al-Adab, 1996).
Brabantina, Charlotte, Duchess of Tremoille, *The conuersion of a most noble lady of Fraunce*, anon. trans. (London: Thomas Purfoot for Nathaniel Butter, 1608).
Bramston, John, *The autobiography of Sir John Bramston*, ed. Lord Braybrooke (London: Camden Society, 1845).
Brome, Richard, *The English Moor*, ed. Mark Steggle, *Richard Brome Online*. http://www.hrionline.ac.uk/brome.
Burgess, Anthony, *A treatise of original sin* (London: [Abraham Miller for Thomas Underhill], 1658).
Burroughs, Jeremiah, *An exposition of the prophesie of Hosea* (London: for R. Dawlman, 1652).
Burton, Robert, *The anatomy of melancholy*, ed. Nicolas K. Kiessling, Thomas C. Faulkner, and Rhonda L. Blair, 3 vols (Oxford: Clarendon Press, 1990).
Cabezón, Antonio de, *Obras de musica para tecla arpa y vihuela*, ed. Hernando de Cabezón (Madrid: Francisco Sanchez, 1570).
Cardim, François, *Relation de la province du Iapon escrite en portugais . . .* (Paris: Mathurin, Henault, 1645).
Cawdry, Robert, *A table alphabeticall, conteyning and teaching the true writing, and understanding of hard usuall English wordes* (London: James Roberts for Edmund Weaver, 1604).

Cecil, William, *Certaine precepts, or directions, for the well ordering of a mans life: left by a father of eminent note and place in this kingdome* (London: Thomas Creede for Richard Meighen and Thomas Jones, 1615).

Cleveland, John, J. *Cleaveland revived . . . with some other exquisite remains* (London: for Nathaniel Brook, 1659).

Constituciones de la congregacion de San Benito de la Observancia, que tuvo principio en el Real Monasterio de San Benito de Valladolid (Madrid: por Luis Sánchez, 1612).

Constituciones generales para todas las monjas, y religiosas sujetas a la obediencia de la orden de N.P.S. Francisco (Madrid: En la Imprenta Real, 1642).

Corner, Flaminio, *Notizie storiche delle chiese e monasteri di Venezia, e di Torcello* (Padua: Giovanni Manfrè, 1758).

Covarrubias, Sebastián de, *Tesoro de la lengua Castellana o Española* (Madrid: Luis Sanchez, 1611). http://fondosdigitales.us.es/fondos/libros/765/1083/tesoro-de-la-lengua-castellana-o-espanola.

Daborne, Robert, *A Christian turn'd Turke: or, the tragical liues and deaths of the two famous pyrates, Ward and Dansiker* (London: William Barrenger, 1612).

Davenant, William, *The tragedy of Albovine, king of the Lombards* (London: for R. M., 1629).

Despagne, John, *The joyfull convert . . . preached at the baptizing of a Turke* (London: I Leach, 1658).

Le dictionnaire de l'Académie françoise, dédié au Roy (Paris: Veuve de Jean Baptiste Coignard, 1694).

Gerard, John, *The autobiography of a hunted priest* (Chicago: Thomas More Press, 1988).

Gouge, William, *Of domesticall dvties eight treatises* (London: John Haviland for William Bladen, 1622).

The great eclipse of the sun, or Charles his waine over-clouded ([London]: G.B., 1644).

Grimani, Antonio, *Costitutioni dell'illustrissimo et reverendissimo Monsignor Antonio Grimani Vescovo di Torcello* (Venice: Giovanni Battista Meietti, 1592).

Hamor, Ralph, *A true discourse of the present estate of Virginia* (London: John Beale for William Welby, 1615).

Hanmer, Meredith, *The baptizing of a Turke. A sermon preached at the hospitall of Saint Katherin* [sic], ([London]: Robert Walde-grave, [1586?]).

Herrick, Robert, *The complete poetry of Robert Herrick*, ed. J. Max Patrick (New York: New York University Press, 1963).

Heywood, Thomas, *The fair maid of the west, parts I and II*, ed. Robert K. Turner, Jr. (Lincoln: University of Nebraska Press, 1967).

Hoby, Edward, *A letter to Mr. T. H.* (London: F[elix] K[ingston] for Edward Blount and William Barret, 1609).

Hoby, Margaret, *The private life of an Elizabethan lady: the diary of Lady Margaret Hoby, 1599–1605*, ed. Joanna Moody (Stroud: Sutton Publishing, 1998).

Hohndorff, Andreas, *Calendarium sanctorum & historiarum* (Frankfurt: Nicolaum Basseum, 1587).

Homza, Lu Ann (ed. and trans.), *The Spanish Inquisition, 1478–1614: an anthology of sources* (Indianapolis, IN: Hackett Publishing, 2006).

James I and VI, *[Basilikon Doron] or his majesties instructions to his dearest sonne, Henry the prince* (Edinburgh: Robert Waldegrave, 1603).

James I and VI, *His maiesties poeticall excercises at vacant houres* (Edinburgh: Robert Waldegrave, 1603).

Jessey, Henry, *The exceeding riches of grace* (London: Matthew Simmons for Henry Overton and Hannah Allen, 1647).

Jessey, Henry, *A Storehouse of provision* (London: Charles Sumptner for T[homas] Brewster and G[regory] Moule, 1650).

Jessey, Henry, *A narrative of the late proceeds at Whitehall, concerning the Jews* (London: for L. Chapman, 1656).

Josquin des Prez, *New Josquin Edition*, ed. William Elders, et al., 30 vols (Utrecht: Koninklijke vereniging voor nederlandse muziekgeschiedenis, 1987–).

Kermode, Lloyd Edward (ed.), *Three Renaissance usury plays: the three ladies of London, Englishmen for my money, The hog hath lost his pearl* (Manchester: Manchester University Press, 2009).

Liber usualis, ed. by the Benedictines of Solesmes, (Tournai: Desclee Company, 1961).

Lithgow, William, *A most delectable, and true discourse, of an admired and painefull peregrination* (London: Nicholas Okes, 1614).

Luther, Martin, *D. Martin Luthers sämtliche Werke*, ed. E. L. Enders, 26 vols, 2nd edn (Erlangen and Frankfurt: Heyder and Zimmer, 1862–85).

Massinger, Philip, *The plays and poems of Philip Massinger*, ed. Philip Edwards and Colin Gibson, 5 vols (Oxford: Oxford University Press, 1976).

Massinger, Philip, *The renegado*, in *Three Turk plays from early modern England*, ed. Daniel J. Vitkus (New York: Columbia University Press, 2000).

Mayne, Jasper, *The citye match a comoedye. Presented to the king and queene at White-hall* (Oxford: Leonard Lichfield, 1639).

Middleton, Thomas, *Sir Robert Sherley his entertainment in Cracovia*, ed. Jerzy Limon and Daniel J. Vitkus, in *Thomas Middleton: the collected works*, gen. eds Gary Taylor and John Lavagnino (Oxford: Clarendon Press, 2007), pp. 670–8.

Miège, Guy, *A new dictionary French and English, with another English and French* (London: Thomas Dawks for Thomas Basset, 1677).

Minsheu, John, *Ductor in linguas: the guide into tongues* (London: William Stansby and Eliot's Court Press, 1617).

More, Henry, *Historia missionis Anglicanae Societas Jesu* (Audomari [i.e. St Omer]: Thomæ Geubels, 1660).

More, Henry, *The Elizabethan Jesuits: 'Historia Missionis Anglicanae Societas Jesu' (1660) of Henry More*, ed. and trans. Francis Edwards (London: Phillimore, 1981).

A mothers teares over hir seduced sonne (London: s.n., 1627).

Mozart, Wolfgang Amadeus and Gottlieb Stephanie the Younger, *Die entführung aus dem serail* ed. Gerhard Croll (Kassell: Bärenreiter-Verlag, 2014).

Nashe, Thomas, *Christs teares over Jerusalem* (London: James Roberts, 1593).

Niccolini, Giustina, *The chronicle of Le Murate*, ed. and trans. Saundra Weddle (Toronto: CRRS, 2011).

Nixon, Anthony, *The three English brothers* (London: [Adam Islip?], 1607; repr. Amsterdam: Theatrum Orbis Terrarvm, 1970).

La nouvelle conversion du roy de Perse. Avec la deffette de deux cents mil Turcs après sa conversion (Paris: François Hyby, 1606).

Osborne, Francis, *Advice to a son; or, directions for your better conduct* (Oxford: Henry Hall for Thomas Robinson, 1656 [i.e. 1655]).

Palmes, William, *The life of Mrs Dorothy Lawson, of St. Antony's near Newcastle-on-Tyne*, ed. and with an introduction by G. Bouchier Richardson (London: Charles Dolman, 1855).

Parr, Anthony (ed.), *Three Renaissance travel plays: the travels of the three English brothers, the sea voyage, the Antipodes* (Manchester: Manchester University Press, 1995).

Parsons, Robert, *A treatise of three conversions of England* ([Saint-Omer: François Bellet], 1603[-1604]).

Politi, Adriano, *Dittionario toscano: compendio del vocabolario della Crusca* (Rome: Gio. Angelo Ruffinelli, 1614).

Priuli, Girolama, *I diarii di Girolamo Priuli*, ed. Roberto Cessi, *Rerum italicarum scriptores* 24: 12–14 (Bologna: Zanichelli, 1938–41).

Priuli, Lorenzo, *Ordini et avvertimenti che si devono osservare ne' monasteri di monache di Venetia* (Venice: s.n., 1591).

Purchas, Samuel, *Pvrchas his pilgrims ... The Second Part* (London: William Stansby for Henry Fetherstone, 1625).

R., D. S., *Cronichetta dell'origine, principio e fondatione del Monastero, Chiesa, e Madonna detta de' Miracoli di Venetia* (Venezia: Baba, 1664).

Ralegh, Walter, *The poems of Sir Walter Ralegh*, ed. Agnes C. Latham (London: Routledge & Kegan Paul, 1929).

Relation des missions des evesques françois au royaumes de Siam, de la Cochinchine, de Camboye & du Tonquin &C (Paris: Charles Angot, 1684).

Relation nouvelle et curieuse des royaumes de Tunquin et de Lao . . .. Traduite de l'italien du P. Mariny Romain. Par L.P.L.C.C. (Paris: Chez Gervais Clouzier, 1666).

Renaissance music in facsimile, ed. Howard Mayer Brown, et al., 50 vols (New York: Garland Publishing, 1986–88).

'The Rewle of sustris menouresses enclosid', in R. W. Chambers and W. W. Seton (eds), *A fifteenth century courtesy book and two fifteenth-century Franciscan Rules* (London: K. Paul, Trench, Trübner & Co, 1914), pp. 81–119.

Rhodes, Alexandre de, *Relazione de'felici successi delli Santa Fede predicata da padre della compagnia di Giesu nel regno di Tunchino* (Rome: Giuseppe Luna, 1650).

Rhodes, Alexandre de, *Catechismus pro iis, qui volunt suscipere baptismum, in octo dies divisus* (Rome: Typis Sacrae Congregationis de Propaganda Fide, 1651).

Rhodes, Alexandre de, *Dictionarium annamiticum lusitanum et latinum ope sacrae congregationis de Propaganda Fide in lucem editum* (Rome: Typis & sumptibus eiusdem Sacr. Congreg., 1651).

Rhodes, Alexandre de, *Histoire du royaume de Tunquin, et des grands progrez que la prédication de l'évangile y a faits en la conversion des infidelles, depuis l'année 1627 jusques à l'année 1646*, trans. Henry Albi (Lyon: Jean-Baptiste Devenet, 1651).

Rhodes, Alexandre de, *Relation des progrez de la foy au royaume de la Cochinchine vers les derniers quartiers du Levant . . .* (Paris: Sebastien Cramoisy, 1652).

Rhodes, Alexandre de, *Divers voyages et missions du P. Alexandre de Rhodes en la Chine et autres royaumes de l'orient . . .* (Paris: Sebastien Cramoisy, 1653).

Rhodes, Alexandre de, *La glorieuse mort d'André, catéchiste de la Cochinchine, qui a le premier versé son sang pour la querelle de Jésus-Christ en cette nouvelle église* (Paris: Sebastien Cramoisy, 1653).

Rhodes, Alexandre de, *Sommaire des divers voyages et missions apostoliques du R. P. Alexandre de Rhodes. . . àla Chine et autres royaumes de l'Orient . . .* (Paris: Florentin Lambert, 1653).

Rhodes, Alexandre de, *Les voyages et missions du P. Alexandre de Rhodes de la compagnie de Jésus en la Chine et autres Royaumes de l'Orient, Nouvelle édition par un père de la même compagnie* (Paris: Julien, Lanier et Cie, 1854).

Ricci, Matteo, *De Christiana expeditione apud Sinas suscepta ab Societate Iesu ex Mattaei Riccii eiusdem societatis commentariis libri V*, ed. Nicolas Trigault (Augsburg: Christoph. Mangium, 1615)

The Roman martyrologe ([St Omer: English College Press, 1627]).

Saccano, Metello, *Relation des progrez de la foy au royaume de la Cochinchine des années 1646 & 1647* (Paris: Sebastien Cramoisy, 1653).

Sanudo, Marin, *Venice, città excelentissima: selections from the Renaissance diaries of Marin Sanudo*, ed. Patricia Labalme and Laura Sanguineti White, trans. Linda L. Carroll (Baltimore: Johns Hopkins Press, 2008).

Secundus tomus novi operis musici, sex, quinque et quatuor vocum. . . (Nuremberg: H. Grapheus, 1538).

Shakespeare, William, *The Norton Shakespeare*, 2nd edn, ed. Stephen Greenblatt, et al. (New York: W. W. Norton, 2008).

Sherley, Anthony, *Sir Anthony Sherley his relation of his travels into Persia* (London: [Nicholas Okes] for Nathaniel Butter, 1613).

Sibelius, Caspar, *Of the conversion of five thousand and nine hundred East-Indians*, trans. Henry Jessey (London: John Hammond, 1650).

Southwell, Anne, *The Southwell-Sibthorpe commonplace book: Folger MS V.b.198*, ed. Jean Klene (Tempe, Ariz: Medieval & Renaissance Texts and Studies, 1997).

Southwell, Robert, *Mary Magdalen's funeral teares* (London: John Wolfe for Gabriel Cawood, 1591).

Southwell, Robert, *A short rule of good life. Newly set forth according to the authours direction before his death* (London: Father Garnett's second press, 1597?).

Southwell, Robert, *A short rule of good life. To direct the deuout Christian in a regular and orderly course* (St Omer: C. Boscard for John Heigham, 1622).

Southwell, Robert, *Two letters and short rules of good life*, ed. Nancy Pollard Brown (Charlottesville: University Press of Virginia for the Folger Shakespeare Library, 1973).

Southwell, Robert, *Robert Southwell: collected poems*, ed. Anne Sweeney and Peter Davidson (Manchester: Fyfield Books for Carcanet Press, 2007).

The spirituall experiences of sundry beleevers (London: Robert Ibbitson, 1653).

Taylor, Thomas, *The pilgrims profession. . . . To which (by his consent) also is added, a short relation of the life and death of the said gentle-woman* (London: I. Dawson for Io: Bartlet, 1622).

Tetzel, Gabriel, *The travels of Leo of Rozmital through Germany, Flanders, England, France, Spain, Portugal, and Italy, 1465–1467*, ed. and trans. Malcolm Letts (Cambridge: Cambridge University Press, 1957).

Thurgood, Rose, 'A Lecture of Repentance', in Naomi Baker (ed.), *Scripture women: Rose Thurgood, 'A lecture of repentance' & Cicely Johnson, 'Fanatical reveries'* (Nottingham: Trent Editions, 2005), pp. 1–27.

Tissanier, Joseph P., 'Relation du P. Joseph Tissanier de la Compagnie de Jésus. Son voyage de France au Tonkin; description de ce royaume. Événements mémorables de la mission du Tonkin pendant les années 1658, 1659, 1660', in *Voyages et travaux des missionaires de la compagnie de Jésus publiés par des pères de la même compagnie pour servir de complément aux lettres édifiantes, volume 2: Mission de la Cochinchine et du Tonkin* (Paris: Charles Duniol, 1858), pp. 63–202.

Trapnell, Anna, *A legacy for saints* (London: T. Brewster, 1654).

Turner, Jane, *Choice experiences of the kind dealings of God before, in, and after conversion* (London: Henry Hills, 1653).

Valderrábano, Enríquez de, *Libro de musica de vihuela intitulado Silva* (Valladolid: Francisco Fernández, 1547).

Vitkus, Daniel (ed.), *Three Turk plays from early modern England*, ed. Daniel Vitkus (New York: Columbia University Press, 2000).

Vitkus, Daniel (ed.), *Piracy, slavery and redemption: Barbary captivity narratives from early modern England* (New York: Columbia University Press, 2001).

Vives, Juan Luis, *The education of a Christian woman: a sixteenth-century manual*, ed. and trans. Charles Fantazzi (Chicago: Chicago University Press, 2000).

Voragine, Jacobus de, *The golden legend: readings on the saints*, trans. William Granger Ryan, 2 vols (Princeton: Princeton University Press, 1993).

Wadsworth, James, *The English Spanish pilgrime. Or, a new discoverie of Spanish popery, and jesuiticall strategems, &c.* (London: Thomas Cotes for Michael Sparke, 1629).

Walker, Anthony, *Eureka, eureka . . . . At the funeral of that most excellent lady . . . Mary, Countess Dowager of Warwick* (London: for Nathaniel Ranew, 1678).

Wright, Abraham (compiler), *Parnassus biceps. Or severall choice pieces of poetry* (London: for George Eversden, 1656).

Wright, Abraham, *Parnassus biceps, or, severall choice pieces of poetry* (1656), facsimile edn with introduction and indexes by Peter Beal (Aldershot: Scolar Press, 1990).

Recordings

Eternal music of the Sistine Chapel, performed by De Labyrintho, dir. by Walter Testolin, 2008 (Berlin Classics: B0012RW6EI).

Harmonia caelestis: 16th-century motets for voice and lute, Duo Mignarda (2010).

Josquin: Missa de beata Virgine et motets à la Vierge, performed by A Sei Voci (Astrée 8560, 1995).

Musica gregoriana, perf. Polifónica Turolense (Classic Records Gold, 2014).

PRINTED SECONDARY SOURCES

Adelman, Janet, 'Bed tricks: on marriage as the end of comedy in *All's Well that Ends Well* and *Measure for Measure*', in Norman N. Holland, Sidney Homan, and Bernard J. Paris (eds), *Shakespeare's personality* (Berkeley: University of California Press, 1989), pp. 151–74.

Afonso, John Correia, *Jesuit letters and Indian history, 1543–1773*, 2nd edn (Bombay: Oxford University Press, 1969).

Ahlgren, Gillian T. W., *Teresa of Avila and the politics of sanctity* (Ithaca, NY: Cornell University Press, 1996).

Ahlgren, Gillian T. W., 'Francisca de los Apóstoles: a visionary voice for reform in sixteenth-century Toledo', in Mary E. Giles (ed.), *Women in the Inquisition: Spain and the New World* (Baltimore: Johns Hopkins University Press, 1999), pp. 119–33.

Ahmed, Sara, *Queer phenomenology: orientations, objects, others* (Durham, NC: Duke University Press, 2006).

Albèri, Eugenio (ed.), *Relazioni degli ambasciatori veneti al senato durante il secolo decimosesto*, series 3, vol. 3 (Florence: Società editrice fiorentina, 1855).

Alberts, Tara, *Conflict and conversion: Catholicism in Southeast Asia* (Oxford: Oxford University Press, 2013).

Algeo, John and Thomas Pyles, *The origins and development of the English language*, 6th edn (Boston: Wadsworth, Cengage Learning, 2005).

Allegra, Luciano, 'All'origini del mito della Jewish momie. Ruoli economici e ideali domestici delle ebree italiane nell'età moderna', in Claire E. Honess and Verina R. Jones (eds), *Donne delle minoranze. Le ebree e le protestanti d'Italia* (Turin: Claudiana, 1999), pp. 211–21.

Allegra, Luciano, 'Modelli di conversione', *Quaderni storici*, 78 (1991), 901–15.

Allegra, Luciano, 'Conversioni dal ghetto di Torino', *Dimensioni e problemi della ricerca storica* 2 (1996), 187–202.

Al-Misri, Ahmad ibn Naqib, *Reliance of the traveller*, ed. and trans. Nuh Ha Mim Keller (Evanston, IL: Sunna Books, 1994).

Amussen, Susan Dwyer, *An ordered society: gender and class in early modern England* (Oxford: Oxford University Press, 1988).

Andrea, Bernadette, *Women and Islam in early modern English literature* (Cambridge: Cambridge University Press, 2007).

Ansari, Humayan, *'The infidel within': Muslims in Britain since 1800* (London: Hurst & Company, 2004).

Arjomand, Said Amir, *The shadow of God and the hidden Imam: religion, political order, and societal change in Shi'ite Iran from the beginning to 1890* (Chicago: University of Chicago Press, 1984).

Atkins, Tamara, *The drama of reform: theology and theatricality, 1461–1553* (Turnhout: Brepols, 2013).

Babinger, Franz, *Sherleiana* (Berlin, Gedruckt In Der Reichsdruckerei, 1932).

Backer, Augustin and Aloys de and Auguste Carayon, *Bibliothèque de la compagnie de Jésus*, nouvelle edition par Carlos Sommervogel (Paris: Picard, 1895).

Baer, Marc, 'Islamic conversion narratives of women: social change and gendered religious hierarchy in early modern Ottoman Istanbul', *Gender & History*, 16 (2004), 425–58.

Baer, Marc, *Honored by the glory of Islam: conversion and conquest in Ottoman Europe* (Oxford: Oxford University Press, 2008).

Baernstein, P. Renèe, 'In widow's habit: women between convent and family in sixteenth-century Milan', *Sixteenth Century Journal*, 25 (1994), 787–807.

Baernstein, P. Reneé, *A convent tale: a century of sisterhood in Spanish Milan* (New York: Routledge, 2002).

Bailey, Amanda, *Of bondage: debt, property, and personhood in early modern England* (Philadelphia: University of Pennsylvania Press, 2013).

Balasopoulos, Antonis, '"Suffer a sea change": spatial crisis, maritime modernity, and the politics of Utopia', *Cultural Critique*, 63 (2006), 123–56.

Ballaster, Ros, *Fabulous orients: fictions of the East in England, 1662–1785* (Oxford: Oxford University Press, 2005).

Balsera, Viviana Díaz, 'Celebrating the rise of a new sun: the Tlaxcalans conquer Jerusalem in 1539', *Estudios de cultura Náhuatl*, 39 (2008), 311–30.

Baltasar, María Dolores Pérez, *Mujeres marginadas: las casas de recogidas en Madrid* (Madrid: Gráficas Lormo, 1984).

Bartels, Emily C., *Speaking of the Moor from 'Alcazar' to 'Othello'* (Philadelphia: University of Pennsylvania Press, 2008).

Batnitzky, Laora, *How Judaism became a religion: an introduction to modern Jewish thought* (Princeton: Princeton University Press, 2011).

Bauman, Thomas, W.A. *Mozart: die entfuhrung aus dem serail* (Cambridge: Cambridge University Press, 1987).

Baumer, Franklin L., 'England, the Turk, and the common corps of Christendom', *American Historical Review*, 50 (1944), 26–48.

Beier, A. L., *Masterless men: the vagrancy problem in England, 1560–1640* (London: Methuen, 1985).

Bekkaoui, Khalid, *White women captives in North Africa: narratives of enslavement, 1735–1830* (London: Palgrave Macmillan, 2011).

Bell, Maureen, 'Hannah Allen and the development of a Puritan publishing business, 1646–1651', *Publishing History*, 26 (1989), 5–66.

Bennassar, Bartolomé, 'Conversion ou reniement? Modalités d'une adhésion ambigué des chrétiens à l'Islam (XVIe–XVIIe siècles)', *Annales, ESC*, 6 (1988), 1349–66.

Bennassar, Bartolomé, 'Conversions, esclavage et commerce des femmes dans les peninsules iberique, italienne ou balkanique aux XVIe et XVIIe siècles', *Dimensioni e problemi della ricerca storica*, 2 (1996), 101–9.

Bennassar, Bartolomé and Lucile Bennassar, *Les chrétiens d'Allah: l'histoire extraordinaire des renégats, XVIe–XVIIe siècles* (Paris: Perrin, 1989), trans. José Luis Gil Aristu as *Los cristianos de Alá* (Madrid: Nerea, 1989).

Bernos, Marcel, 'Conversion ou apostasie? Comment les chrétiens voyaient ceux qui quittaient leur eglise pour l' "eglise adverse"', *Seventeenth-Century French Studies*, 18 (1996), 33–48.

Blume, Clemens, '*Inviolata*, der älteste Marien-tropus im brevier. Geschichte des textes und der melodie', *Die Kirchen musik*, 9 (1908), 41–8.

Boies Penrose, *The Sherleian odyssey* (Taunton: Wessex, 1938).

Bono, Salvatore, 'Pascià e Raìs algerini di origine italiana', in R. H. Raniero (ed.), *Algeria e Italia* (Milan: Marzorati, 1982), pp. 199–222.

Bono, Salvatore, *Un altro Mediterraneo: una storia comune fra scontri e integrazioni* (Rome: Salerno Editrice, 2008).

Bori, Pier Cesare, *The golden calf and the origins of the anti-Jewish controversy*, trans. David Ward (Atlanta: Scholars Press, 1990).

Bowden, William R., 'The bed-trick, 1603–1642: its mechanics, ethics, and effects', *Shakespeare Studies*, 5 (1969), 112–23.

Braudel, Fernand, *La Méditerranée et le Monde Méditerranéen à l'epoque de Philippe II*, 3 vols (Paris: Armand Colin, 1949).

Bray, Alan, 'Homosexuality and the signs of male friendship in Elizabethan England', *History Workshop*, 29 (1990), 1–19.

Bray, Alan, *The friend* (Chicago: University of Chicago Press, 2003).

Brenner, Robert, *Merchants and revolution: commercial change, political conflict, and London's overseas traders, 1550–1653* (Princeton: Princeton University Press, 1993).

Britton, Dennis, *Becoming Christian: race, reformation, and early modern English Romance* (New York: Fordham University Press, 2014).

Brook, Xanthe, *The Lady Lever art gallery: catalogue of embroideries* (Stroud: Alan Sutton, 1992).

Brooks, Douglas (ed.), *Printing and parenting in early modern England* (Farnham: Ashgate, 2003).

Brooks, Mary M., *English embroideries of the sixteenth and seventeenth centuries in the collection of the Ashmolean Museum* (Oxford and London: Ashmolean Museum, in association with Jonathan Horne Publications, 2004).

Brown, Horatio Forbes, *Studies in the history of Venice*, vol. 2 (London: John Murray, 1907).

Brown, Nancy Pollard, 'Southwell, Robert (1561–1595)', *Oxford Dictionary of National Biography* (Oxford: Oxford University Press, 2004).

Brown, Patricia Fortini, 'Behind the walls: the material culture of Venetian elites', in John Jeffries Martin and Dennis Romano (eds), *Venice reconsidered: the history and civilization of an Italian city-state, 1297–1797* (Baltimore: Johns Hopkins University Press, 2002), pp. 295–338.

Brown, Sylvia, 'The reproductive word: gender and textuality in the writings of John Bunyan', *Bunyan Studies*, 11 (2003/2004), 23–46.

Brown, Sylvia (ed.), *Women, gender and radical religion in early modern Europe* (Leiden: Brill, 2007).

Brueggemann, Walter, *Genesis: interpretation. A Bible commentary* (Westminster: John Knox Press, 2010).

Burkhart, Louise M., 'The destruction of Jerusalem as colonial Nahuatl historical drama', in Susan Schroeder (ed.), *The conquest all over again: Nahuas and*

Zapotecs thinking, writing, and painting Spanish colonialism (Eastbourne: Sussex Academic Press, 2010), pp. 74–100.

Burton, Jonathan, 'English anxiety and the Muslim power of conversion: five perspectives on "turning Turk" in early modern texts', *Journal of Early Modern Cultural Studies*, 2 (2002), 35–67.

Burton, Jonathan, *Traffic and turning: Islam and English drama, 1579–1624* (Newark: University of Delaware Press, 2005).

Butler, Judith, *Gender trouble: feminism and the subversion of identity* (London: Routledge, 1990).

Bynum, Caroline Walker, *Holy fast and holy feast: the religious significance of food to medieval women* (Berkeley: University of California Press, 1987).

Cadden, Joan, *Meanings of sex difference in the Middle Ages: medicine, science, and culture* (Cambridge: Cambridge University Press, 1993).

Calabresi, Bianca F.-C., '"you sow, Ile read": letters and literacies in early modern samplers', in Heidi Brayman Hackel and Catherine Kelly (eds), *Reading women: literacy, authorship, and culture in the Atlantic World, 1500–1800* (Philadelphia: University of Pennsylvania Press, 2008), pp. 79–104.

Caldwell, Patricia, *The Puritan conversion narrative: the beginnings of American expression* (Cambridge: Cambridge University Press, 1983).

Cambers, Andrew, *Godly reading: print, manuscript and Puritanism in England, 1580–1720* (Cambridge: Cambridge University Press, 2011).

Casanova, Cesarina, 'Il buon matrimonio di Anna Maria alias Cremesina, neofita lughese', in Claire E. Honess and Verina R. Jones (eds), *Donne delle minoranze. Le ebree e le protestanti d'Italia* (Turin: Claudiana, 1999), pp. 201–10.

Cassia, Paul Sant, 'Religion, politics and ethnicity in Cyprus during the Turkocratia (1571–1878)', *Archives Européennes de sociologie*, 27 (1986), 3–28.

Cavillac, Michell, *Pícaros y mercaderes en el Guzman de Alfarache: reformismo burgués y mentalidad aristocrática en la España del siglo de oro*, trans. Juan M. Azpitarte (Granada: Universidad de Granada, 1994).

Ceriana, Matteo, 'La chiesa e il monastero del Santo Sepolcro di Venezia ai tempi di Chiara Bugni', in Reinhold C. Mueller and Gabriella Zarri (eds), *La vita e i sermoni di Chiara Bugni Clarissa Veneziana (1471–1514) Temi e testi* 89 (Rome: Edizioni di Storia e Letteratura, 2011), pp. 31–61.

Charlton, Kenneth, *Women, religion and education in early modern England* (London: Routledge, 1999).

Chaudhuri, K. N., *The trading world of Asia and the English East India Company, 1660–1760* (Cambridge: Cambridge University Press, 2006).

Chojnacka, Monica, 'Women, charity and community in early modern Venice: the Casa delle Zitelle', *Renaissance Quarterly*, 51 (1998), 68–91.

Chojnacka, Monica, *Working women of early modern Venice* (Baltimore: Johns Hopkins University Press, 2001).

Chojnacki, Stanley, 'Dowries and kinsmen in early Renaissance Venice', *Journal of Interdisciplinary History*, 5 (1975), 571–600.

Chojnacki, Stanley, 'Getting back the dowry', in *Women and men in Renaissance Venice: twelve essays on patrician society* (Baltimore: Johns Hopkins University Press, 2000), pp. 95–114.

Cicogna, Emmanuele Antonio, *Delle inscrizioni Veneziane raccolte ed illustrate da Emmanuele Antonio Cicogna*, v. 6 (Venice: Tipografia Andreola, 1853).

Clark, Stuart, *Vanities of the eye: vision in early modern European culture* (Oxford: Oxford University Press, 2007).

Clissold, Stephen, 'Christian renegades and Barbary Corsairs', *History Today*, 26 (1976), 508–15.

Coffey, John, 'The toleration controversy during the English revolution', in Christopher Durston and Judith Maltby (eds), *Religion in revolutionary England* (Manchester: Manchester University Press, 2006), pp. 42–68.

Coleman, Simon, 'Continuous conversion? The rhetoric, practice, and rhetorical practice of charismatic Protestant conversion', in Andrew Buckser and Stephen D. Glazier (eds), *The anthropology of religious conversion* (Lanham, MD: Rowman and Littlefield, 2003), pp. 15–28.

Connolly, Ruth, 'A Proselytising Protestant commonwealth: the religious and political ideals of Katherine Jones, Viscountess Ranelagh (1614–1691)', *Seventeenth Century*, 20 (2008), 244–64.

Cooper, Alix, *Inventing the indigenous: local knowledge and natural history in early modern Europe* (Cambridge: Cambridge University Press, 2007).

Cooper, Tracy E., *Palladio's Venice: architecture and society in a Renaissance republic* (New Haven, CT: Yale University Press, 2005).

Crawford, Patricia, 'The construction and experience of maternity in seventeenth-century England', in Valerie Fildes (ed.), *Women as mothers in pre-industrial England* (London: Routledge, 1990), pp. 3–38.

Crawford, Patricia, *Women and religion in England, 1500–1720* (London: Routledge, 1993).

Cressy, David, 'Purification, thanksgiving and the churching of women in post-Reformation England', *Past and Present*, 141 (1993), 106–46.

Crocker, Richard L., *The early medieval sequence* (Berkeley: University of California Press, 1977).

Crouzet-Pavan, Elizabeth, 'An ecological understanding of the myth of Venice', in John Jeffries Martin and Dennis Romano (eds), *Venice reconsidered: the history and civilization of an Italian city-state* (Baltimore: Johns Hopkins University Press, 2002), pp. 39–64.

Curran, John E., *Roman invasions: British history, Protestant anti-Romanism and the historical imagination in England, 1530–1660* (Newark: University of Delaware Press, 2002).

Dailey, Barbara Ritter, 'The visitation of Sarah Wight: holy carnival and the revolution of the saints in civil war London', *Church History*, 55 (1986), 438–55.

Dakhlia, Jocelyne and Wolfgang Kaiser (eds), *Les Musulmans dans l'histoire de l'Europe: tome 2 – passages et contacts en Méditerranée* (Paris: Albin Michel, 2013).

Dakhlia, Jocelyne, 'Turcs de profession? Réinscriptions lignagères et redéfinitions sexuelles des convertis dans les cours maghrébines (XVIᵉ–XIXᵉ siècles)', in Mercedes García-Arenal (ed.), *Conversion islamiques: Identités religieuses en Islam méditerranéen?* (Paris: Maisonneuve et Larose, 2001), pp. 151–71.

Damrosch, Leopold, *God's plot and man's stories* (Chicago and London: University of Chicago Press, 1985).

Daniel, Norman, *Islam and the West: the making of an image*, rev. edn (Oxford: Oneworld, 1993).

Davies, D. W., *Elizabethans errant: the strange fortunes of Sir Thomas Sherley and his three sons* (Ithaca, NY: Cornell University Press, 1967).

Davis, Natalie Zemon, *Society and culture in early modern France* (Stanford: Stanford University Press, 1975).

Davis, Natalie Zemon, 'Women on top: symbolic sexual inversion and political disorder in early modern Europe', in Barbara A. Babcock (ed.), *The reversible world: symbolic inversion in art and society* (Ithaca, NY: Cornell University Press, 1978), pp. 147–90.

Davis, Natalie Zemon, *Fiction in the archives: pardon tales and their tellers in sixteenth-century France* (Stanford: Stanford University Press, 1987).

Davis, Robert C., *Holy war and human bondage: tales of Christian-Muslim slavery in the early-modern Mediterranean* (Santa Barbara, CA: ABC–CLIO, 2009).

Degenhardt, Jane Hwang, 'Catholic prophylactics and Islam's sexual threat: preventing and undoing sexual defilement in *The renegado*', *Journal for Early Modern Cultural Studies*, 9 (2009), 62–92.

Degenhardt, Jane Hwang, *Islamic conversion and Christian resistance on the early modern stage* (Edinburgh: Edinburgh University Press, 2010).

Deng, Stephen and Barbara Sebek (eds), *Global traffic: discourses and practices of trade in English literature and culture from 1550 to 1700* (New York: Palgrave Macmillan, 2008).

Denmead, Louise, 'The discovery of blackness in the early modern bed-trick', in James D. Fleming (ed.), *The invention of discovery, 1500–1700* (Aldershot: Ashgate, 2011), pp. 153–66.

Desens, Marliss C., *The bed-trick in English Renaissance drama* (Newark: University of Delaware Press, 1994).

Devlin, Christopher, *The life of Robert Southwell, poet and martyr* (London: Longmans, Green & Co., 1956).

Diefendorf, Barbara B., *From penitence to charity: pious women and the Catholic Reformation in Europe* (Oxford: Oxford University Press, 2004).

Dimmock, Matthew, *New Turkes: dramatizing Islam and the Ottomans in early modern England* (Aldershot: Ashgate, 2005).

Dimmock, Matthew, 'Converting and not converting "strangers" in early modern London', *Journal of Early Modern History*, special issue, 'Conversion Narratives in the Early Modern World', ed. Peter Mazur and Abigail Shinn, 17 (2013), 457–78.

Djebli, Moktar, 'Takiyya', in H. A. R. Gibbs, et al. (eds), *Encyclopedia of Islam*, 2nd edn, 12 vols (Leiden: Brill, 1960–2004), 10.134–36.

Dolan, Frances, *Whores of Babylon: Catholicism, gender, and seventeenth-century print culture* (Ithaca, NY: Cornell University Press, 1999).

Doniger, Wendy, *The bedtrick: tales of sex and masquerade* (Chicago: University of Chicago Press, 2000).

Dowd, Michelle and Julia Eckerle, *Genre and women's life writing in early modern England* (Aldershot: Ashgate, 2007).

Dowd, Michelle M. and Julie A. Eckerle 'The Devotional Writings of Dorothy Calthorpe', *ANQ: A Quarterly Journal of Short Articles, Notes and Reviews*, 24 (2011), 89–98.

Dror, Olga, *Cult, culture and authority: Princess Lieu Hanh in Vietnamese history* (Honolulu: University of Hawai'i Press, 2007).

Dror, Olga and K. W. Taylor (eds), *Views of seventeenth-century Vietnam: Cristoforo Borri on Cochinchina and Samuel Baron on Tonkin* (Ithaca, NY: Southeast Asia Program Publications, Cornell University Press, 2006).

Duffy, Eamon, *The stripping of the altars: traditional religion in England. c. 1400–c. 1580*, 2nd edn (New Haven, CT: Yale University Press, 2005).

Dunan-Page, Anne, 'Writing "things ecclesiastical": the literary acts of the gathered churches', *Etudes Epistémè*, 21 (2012). www.etudes-episteme.org/2e/?-21-2012-.

Durand, Maurice, *Technique et panthéon des médiums Viétnamiens (Dông)* (Paris: École française d'Extrême-Orient, 1959).

Dursteler, Eric R., *Venetians in Constantinople: nation, identity, and coexistence in the early modern Mediterranean* (Baltimore: Johns Hopkins University Press, 2006).

Dursteler, Eric R., 'Defending virtue and preserving reputation: gender and institutional honor on the early modern Dalmatian Frontier', *Journal of Early Modern History*, 15 (2011), 367–84.

Dursteler, Eric R., *Renegade women: gender, identity and boundaries in the early modern Mediterranean* (Baltimore: Johns Hopkins University Press, 2011).

Eales, Jacqueline, *Women in early modern England, 1500–1700* (London: UCL Press, 1998).

Edwards, John, *The Spanish Inquisition* (Charleston: Tempus, 1999).

Ellington, Donna Spivey, 'Impassioned mother or passive icon: the Virgin's role in late medieval and early modern Passion sermons', *Renaissance Quarterly*, 48 (1995), 227–61.

Erickson, Amy Louise, *Women and property in early modern England* (New York: Routledge, 1993).
Esdaile, Katharine A., 'Gunpowder plot in needlework: Dame Dorothy Selby, "Whose arte disclos'd that plot"', *Country Life* (18 June 1943), 1094–6.
Esposito, John L., *What everyone needs to know about Islam*, 2nd edn (Oxford: Oxford University Press, 2011).
Evangelisti, Silvia, *Nuns: a history of convent life, 1450–1700* (Oxford: Oxford University Press, 2007).
Fisher, Alexander, *Music, piety and propaganda: the soundscape of Counter-Reformation Bavaria* (Oxford: Oxford University Press, 2014).
Fisher, Will, *Materializing gender in early modern English literature and culture* (Cambridge: Cambridge University Press, 2006).
Fletcher, Anthony, *Gender, sex and subordination in England 1500–1800* (New Haven, CT: Yale University Press, 1995).
Foa, Anna, 'Le donne nella storia degli ebrei in Italia', in Claire E. Honess and Verina R. Jones (eds), *Donne delle minoranze. Le ebree e le protestanti d'Italia* (Turin: Claudiana, 1999), pp. 11–30.
Foa, Anna, 'The Marrano's kitchen: external stimuli, internal response, and the formation of the Marrano persona', in Elliott Horowitz and Moises Orfali (eds), *The Mediterranean and the Jews: society, culture, and economy in early modern times* (Ramat Gan: Bar-Ilan University Press, 2002), pp. 13–25.
Forest, Alain, *Les missionnaires français au Tonkin et Siam, XVIIe–XVII siècles: analyse comparée d'un relatif succès et d'un total échec*, 3 vols (Paris: Éditions l'Harmattan, 1998).
Fournel-Guérin, Jacqueline, 'La femme morisque en Aragon', in Louis Cardillac (ed.), *Les morisques et leur temps* (Paris: Éditions du Centre national de la recherche scientifique, 1983), pp. 523–38.
Franz, Adolph, *Die kirchlichen Benediktionen im Mittelalter*, 2 vols (Freiburg im Breisgau: Herder, 1909).
Frye, Susan, *Pens and needles: women's textualities in early modern England* (Philadelphia: University of Pennsylvania Press, 2010).
Fuchs, Barbara, 'Faithless empires: renegadoes, and the English nation', *English Literary History*, 67 (2000), 45–69.
Furber, Holden, *Rival empires of trade in the Orient, 1600–1800* (Minneapolis: University of Minnesota Press, 1976).
García-Arenal, Mercedes, 'Les conversions d'Européens à l'Islam dans l'histoire: esquisse générale', *Social Compass*, 46 (1999).
García-Arenal, Mercedes (ed.), *Entre el Islam y Occidente. Los judíos magrebíes en la Edad Moderna* (Madrid: Casa de Velázquez, 2003).
García-Arenal, Mercedes and Miguel Ángel de Bunes, *Los españoles y el Norte de África. Siglos XV–XVIII* (Madrid: Editorial MAPFRE, 1992).

García-Arenal, Mercedes and Gerard Weigers, *A man of three worlds: Samuel Pallache, a Moroccan Jew in Catholic and Protestant Europe*, trans. Martin Beagles (Baltimore: Johns Hopkins University Press, 2003).
Garthwaite, Gene R., *The Persians* (Oxford: Blackwell, 2005).
Gélis, Jacques, *History of childbirth: fertility, pregnancy, and birth in early modern Europe*, trans. Rosemary Morris (Cambridge: Polity Press, 1991).
Gilchrist, Roberta, *Gender and material culture: the archaeology of religious women* (London: Routledge, 1993).
Gilman, Sander, *The Jew's body* (London: Routledge, 1991).
Ginio, Eyal, 'Childhood, mental capacity and conversion to Islam in the Ottoman state', *Byzantine and Modern Greek Studies*, 25 (2001), 90–119.
Ginzburg, Carlo, 'The inquisitor as anthropologist', in *Clues, myths, and historical method*, trans. John Tedeschi and Anne C. Tedeschi (Baltimore: Johns Hopkins University Press, 1986), pp. 141–48.
Ginzburg, Carlo, *The night battles: witchcraft and agrarian cults in the sixteenth and seventeenth centuries*, trans. John Tedeschi and Anne C. Tedeschi (Baltimore: Johns Hopkins University Press, 1992).
Glaser, Eliane, *Judaism without Jews: philosemitism and Christian polemic in early modern England* (Houndmills Basingstoke: Palgrave Macmillan, 2007).
Goldberg, Alicia Gojman and Luis Manuel Martínez Escutia, 'La funcion del Edicto de Fe en el proceso inquisitorial'. http://biblio.juridicas.unam.mx/libros/2/700/19.pdf.
Göllner, Marie Louise, '*Praeter rerum seriem*: its history and sources', in Wolfgang Osthoff, Frank Heidlberger, and Reinhard Wiesend (eds), *Von Isaac bis Bach—studien zur älteren deutschen musikgeschichte: festschrift Martin Just zum 60. Geburtstag* (Kassel: Bärenreiter, 1991), pp. 41–51.
Goodblatt, Morris S., *Jewish life in Turkey in the XVIth century: as reflected in the legal writings of Samuel De Medina* (New York: The Jewish Theological Seminary of America, 1952).
Goy, Richard John, *Building Renaissance Venice: patrons, architects and builders, c. 1430–1500* (New Haven, CT: Yale University Press, 2006).
Graizbord, David, *Souls in dispute: converso identities in Iberia and the Jewish diaspora, 1580–1700* (Philadelphia: University of Pennsylvania Press, 2004).
Graizbord, David, 'A historical contextualization of Sephardi apostates and self-styled missionaries of the seventeenth century', *Jewish History*, 19 (2005), 287–313.
Greenblatt, Stephen, *Renaissance self-fashioning: from More to Shakespeare* (Chicago: University of Chicago Press, 1980).
Greene, Molly, *A shared world: Christians and Muslims in the early modern Mediterranean* (Princeton: Princeton University Press, 2000).
Grogan, Jane, 'The not-forgotten empire: images of Persia in English Renaissance writing', *Literature Compass*, 7 (9), 912–21.

Grosrichard, Alain, *Structure du sérail: la fiction du despotisme Asiatique dans l'Occident classique* (Paris: Editions du Seuil, 1979), published in English as *The sultan's court: European fantasies of the East*, trans. Liz Heron (London: Verso, 1998).

Grosz, Elizabeth, *Space, time, and perversion: essays on the politics of bodies* (London: Routledge, 2005).

Guibbory, Achsah, *Christian identity: Jews & Israel in seventeenth-century England* (Oxford: Oxford University Press, 2010).

Haber, Judith, *Desire and dramatic form in early modern England* (Cambridge: Cambridge University Press, 2009).

Habib, Imtiaz, *Black lives in the English archives, 1500–1677: imprints of the invisible* (Aldershot: Ashgate, 2008).

Hall, Kim, *Things of darkness: economies of race and gender in early modern England* (Ithaca, NY: Cornell University Press, 1995).

Hall, Kim, 'Object into object: some thoughts on the presence of black women in early modern culture', in Peter Erickson and Clark Hulse (eds), *Early modern visual culture: representation, race, and empire in Renaissance England* (Philadelphia: University of Pennsylvania Press, 2000), pp. 346–77.

Hallett, Nicky (ed.), *Lives of spirit: English Carmelite self-writing of the early modern period* (Aldershot: Ashgate, 2007).

Hallett, Nicky, *The senses in religious communities, 1600–1800: early modern 'convents of pleasure'* (Farnham: Ashgate, 2013).

Hamling, Tara, *Decorating the Godly household: religious art in post-Reformation Britain* (New Haven, CT: Yale University Press, 2011).

Haselkorn, Anne M., *Prostitution in Elizabethan and Jacobean comedy* (Troy, NY: Whitston, 1983).

Hawkes, David, *Idols of the marketplace: idolatry and commodity fetishism in English literature, 1580–1680* (New York: Palgrave Macmillan, 2001).

Hawkes, David, *The culture of usury in Renaissance England* (New York: Palgrave Macmillan, 2010).

Hawthorne, Sîan, 'Religion and gender', in Peter B. Clarke (ed.), *The Oxford handbook of the sociology of religion* (Oxford: Oxford University Press, 2009), pp. 134–51.

Hayden, Roger, *Records of a Church of Christ in Bristol, 1640–1687*, ed. Bristol Record Society (Bristol: University of Bristol, 1974).

Heal, Bridget, *The cult of the Virgin Mary in early modern Germany: Protestant and Catholic piety, 1500–1648* (Cambridge: Cambridge University Press, 2007).

Heller, Jennifer, *The mother's legacy in early modern England* (Aldershot: Ashgate, 2011).

Hennecke, Edgar, *New Testament Apocrypha*, ed. Wilhelm Schneemelcher, trans. R McL. Wilson, 2 vols (Philadelphia: Westminster Press, 1963).

Hernández, Luis Alberto Anya, 'La invasión de 1618 en Lanzarote y sus repercusiones socio-económicas', in Francisco Morales Padrón (ed.), *VI coloquio de historia Canario-Americana*, 6 Tomo 3 (Las Palmas: Cabildo Insular de Gran Canaria, 1987), pp. 192–223.

Heyberger, Bernard, 'Frontières confessionnelles et conversions chez les chrétiens orientaux (XVII–XVIII siècles)', in Mercedes García-Arenal (ed.), *Conversions islamiques: Identités religieuses en Islam méditerranéen* (Paris: Maisonneuve–Larose, 2001), pp. 245–58.

Hiley, David, *Western plainchant: a handbook* (Oxford: Clarendon Press, 1993).

Hills, Helen (ed.), *Architecture and the politics of gender in early modern Europe* (Aldershot: Ashgate, 2003).

Hills, Helen, *Invisible city: the architecture of devotion in seventeenth century Neapolitan convents* (Oxford: Oxford University Press, 2004).

Hindle, Steve, *The state and social change in early modern England* (New York: Palgrave Macmillan, 2002).

Hindmarsh, D. Bruce, *The evangelical conversion narrative: spiritual autobiography in early modern England* (Oxford: Oxford University Press, 2005).

Hinds, Hilary, *God's Englishwomen: seventeenth-century radical sectarian writing and feminist criticism* (Manchester: Manchester University Press, 1996).

Hirst, Julie, '"Mother of love": spiritual maternity in the works of Jane Lead (1624–1704)', in Sylvia Brown (ed.), *Women, gender and radical religion in early modern Europe* (Leiden: Brill, 2007), pp.161–87.

Hobby, Elaine, *Virtue of necessity: English women's writing 1649–88* (London: Virago Press, 1988).

Hodges, Laura, *Chaucer and clothing: clerical and academic costume in the general prologue to the Canterbury Tales*, Chaucer Studies, 34 (Woodbridge: Boydell and Brewer, 2005).

Holroyd, Sophie, '"Rich embrodered churchstuffe": the vestments of Helena Wintour', in Ronald Corthell, et al. (eds), *Catholic culture in early modern England* (Notre Dame, IN: University of Notre Dame Press, 2007), 73–116.

Hotchin, Julie, 'The nun's crown', *Early modern women: an interdisciplinary journal*, 4 (2009), 187–94.

Houlbrooke, Ralph, *The English family, 1450–1700* (London: Longman, 1984).

Houston, Chloë, '"Thou glorious kingdome, thou chiefe of empires": Persia in seventeenth-century travel literature', *Studies in Travel Writing*, 13 (2009), 141–52.

Houston, Chloë, 'Turning Persia: the prospect of conversion in Safavid Iran', in Lieke Stelling, Harald Hendrix, and Todd Richardson (eds), *The turn of the soul: representations of religious conversion in early modern art and literature* (Leiden: Brill, 2012), pp. 85–108.

Houston, Chloë, 'Persia and kingship in William Cartwright's *The royall slave* (1636)', *Studies in English Literature 1500–1900*, 54 (2014), 455–73.

Hughes, Ann, *Gender and the English Revolution* (London: Routledge, 2012).
Hughey, Ruth and Philip Hereford, 'Elizabeth Grymeston and her *Miscellanea*', *The Library*, Fourth Series, 15 (1934), 61–91.
Huntington, Samuel P., *The clash of civilizations and the remaking of the world order* (New York: Simon & Shuster, 1996).
Huse, Norbert, *The art of Renaissance Venice: architecture, sculpture, and painting, 1460–1590* (Chicago: University of Chicago Press, 1993).
Hutson, Lorna, *The usurer's daughter: male friendship and fictions of women in 16th Century England* (New York: Routledge, 1997).
Jackson, Ken and Arthur F. Marotti, 'The turn to religion in early modern English studies', *Criticism*, 46 (2004), 167–90.
Jackson, Peter and Laurence Lockhart (eds), *The Cambridge history of Iran: volume 6: the Timurid and Safavid periods* (Cambridge: Cambridge University Press, 1986).
Janelle, Pierre, *Robert Southwell the writer: a study in religious inspiration* (London: Sheed & Ward, 1935).
Janin-Thivos, Michèle, 'Entre développement des affaires et convictions personnelles: la conversion des marchands étrangers devant l'Inquisition portugaise à l'époque moderne', in Albrecht Burkardt (ed.), *Commerce, voyage et expérience religieuse, XVIe–XVIIe siècles* (Rennes: Presses Universitaires de Rennes, 2007), pp. 275–86.
Jardine, Lisa, *Still harping on daughters: women and drama in the age of Shakespeare*, 2nd edn (London: Harvester Wheatsheaf, 1989).
Jennings, Ronald C., *Christians and Muslims in Ottoman Cyprus and the Mediterranean world, 1571–1640* (New York: New York University Press, 1993).
Kagan, Richard L. and Abigail Dyer, *Inquisitorial inquiries: brief lives of secret Jews and other heretics* (Baltimore: Johns Hopkins University Press, 2004).
Kaiser, Walter (ed.), *Le commerce des captifs, les intermédiaires dans l'échange et le rachat des prisonniers en Méditerranée xv–xviii siècles* (Rome: École française de Rome, 2008).
Kamen, Henry, 'Toleration and dissent in sixteenth-century Spain: the alternative tradition', *The Sixteenth Century Journal*, 19 (1988), 3–23.
Kaminsky, Amy Katz (ed.), *Water lilies / Flores de agua, an anthology of Spanish women writers from the fifteenth through the nineteenth century* (Minneapolis: University of Minnesota Press, 1996).
Karant-Nunn, Susan C., 'Continuity and change: some effects of the Reformation on the women of Zwickau', *Sixteenth Century Journal*, 12 (1982), 17–42.
Karant-Nunn, Susan, *The reformation of ritual: an interpretation of early modern Germany* (London: Routledge, 1997).
Kelly-Gadol, Joan, 'Did women have a Renaissance?' in Renate Bridenthal and Claudia Koon (eds), *Becoming visible: women in European history* (Boston: Houghton Mifflin, 1987), pp. 137–64.

Kessler-Harris, Alice, 'What is gender history now?', in David Cannadine (ed.), *What is history now?* (New York: Palgrave Macmillan, 2004), pp. 95–112.

King, Catherine E., *Renaissance women patrons: wives and widows in Italy c. 1300–1550* (Manchester: Manchester University Press, 1998).

King, Helen, 'The mathematics of sex: one to two, or two to one?', *Studies in Medieval and Renaissance History*, special issue on 'Sexuality and Culture in Medieval and Renaissance Europe', 3rd series, II (2005), 47–58.

Kraemer, Ross S., 'The conversion of women to ascetic forms of Christianity', *Signs*, 6 (1980), 298–307.

Kreitzer, Beth, *Reforming Mary: changing images of the Virgin Mary in Lutheran sermons of the sixteenth century* (Oxford: Oxford University Press, 2004).

Krstić, Tijana, 'Illuminated by the light of Islam and the glory of the Ottoman sultanate: self-narratives of conversion to Islam in the age of confessionalization', *Comparative Studies in Society and History*, 51 (2009), 35–63.

Krstić, Tijana, *Contested conversions to Islam: narratives of religious change in the early modern Ottoman Empire* (Stanford: Stanford University Press, 2011).

Kuchar, Gary, 'Gender and Recusant melancholia in Robert Southwell's *Mary Magdalene's funeral tears*', in Ronald Corthell, et al. (eds), *Catholic culture in early modern England* (Notre Dame, IN: University of Notre Dame Press, 2007), pp. 135–157.

Lach, Donald F and Edwin J. Van Kley (eds), *Asia in the making of Europe*, 3 vols (Chicago: University of Chicago Press, 1993).

Laiou, Sophia, 'Christian women in an Ottoman world: interpersonal and family cases brought before the Shari'a courts during the seventeenth and eighteenth centuries (cases involving the Greek community)', in Amila Buturović and İrvin Cemil Schick (eds), *Women in the Ottoman Balkans: gender, culture, and history* (London: I.B.Tauris, 2007), pp. 243–71.

Lamb, Mary Ellen, 'Inventing the early modern woman reader through the world of goods: Lyly's gentlewoman reader and Katherine Stubbes', in Heidi Brayman Hackel and Catherine Kelly (eds), *Reading women: literacy, authorship, and culture in the Atlantic World, 1500–1800* (Philadelphia: University of Pennsylvania Press, 2008), pp. 15–35.

Lanham, Richard, *A handlist of rhetorical terms*, 2nd edn (Berkeley & Los Angeles: University of California Press, 1991).

Laqueur, Thomas, *Making sex: the body and gender from the Greeks to Freud* (Cambridge, MA: Harvard University Press, 1990).

Latham, Agnes, 'Sir Walter Ralegh's *Instructions to his son*', in Herbert Davis and Helen Gardner (eds), *Elizabethan and Jacobean studies (presented to Frank Percy Wilson in honour of his seventieth birthday)* (Oxford: Oxford University Press, 1959), pp. 199–218.

Latimer, John, *The annals of Bristol in the seventeenth century* (Bristol: William George's Sons, 1900).

Laven, Mary, *The virgins of Venice: broken vows and cloistered lives in the Renaissance convent* (New York: Viking, 2002).
Lavrín, Asunción, *Brides of Christ: conventual life in Colonial Mexico* (Stanford: Stanford University Press, 2008).
Le Bras, Gabriel, *Histoire de l'eglise depuis les origines jusqu'a nos jours* (Paris: Bloud & Gray, 1964).
Lehfeldt, Elizabeth A., *Religious women in Golden Age Spain: the permeable cloister* (Aldershot: Ashgate, 2005).
Leone, Massimo, *Saints and signs: a semiotic reading of conversion in early modern Catholicism* (Berlin: Walter de Gruyter, 2010).
Levey, Santina M., *Of houshold stuff: the 1601 inventories of Bess of Hardwick* (London: The National Trust, 2001).
Levy, Allison Mary (ed.), *Widowhood and visual culture in early modern Europe* (Aldershot: Ashgate, 2003).
Lewis, Bernard, *The Middle East and the West* (New York: Harper & Row, 1964).
Lewis, Bernard, *Islam and the West* (Oxford: Oxford University Press, 1993).
Lewis, Laura A., 'The "weakness" of women and the feminization of the Indian in colonial Mexico', *Colonial Latin America Review*, 5 (1996), 73–94.
Lieu, Judith, 'The "attraction of women" in/to early Judaism and Christianity: gender and the politics of conversion', *Journal for the Study of the New Testament*, 72 (1998), 5–22.
Lofland, John and Norman Skonovd, 'Conversion motifs', *Journal for the Scientific Study of Religion*, 20 (1981), 373–85.
Longfellow, Erica, *Women and religious writing in early modern England* (Cambridge: Cambridge University Press, 2004).
Loomie, A. J., 'Wadsworth, James [*pseud.* Diego de Vadesfoote] (b.1604)', *ODNB*.
Lowe, K. J. P., 'Secular brides and convent brides: wedding ceremonies in Italy during the Renaissance and Counter-Reformation', in Trevor Dean and Lowe (eds), *Marriage in Italy, 1300–1650* (Cambridge: Cambridge University Press, 1998), pp. 41–65.
Lowe, K. J. P., *Nuns' chronicles and convent culture in Renaissance and Counter-Reformation Italy* (Cambridge: Cambridge University Press, 2004).
Luria, Keith P., *Sacred boundaries: religious co-existence and conflict in early modern France* (Washington, DC: The Catholic University of America Press, 2005).
Lynch, Kathleen, *Protestant autobiography in the seventeenth-century Anglophone world* (Oxford: Oxford University Press, 2012).
Maccoby, Hyam (ed.), *Judaism on trial: Jewish-Christian disputations in the middle ages* (London: The Littman Library of Jewish Civilization, 1993).
McDowell, Nicholas, *The English radical imagination: culture, religion, and revolution, 1630–1660* (Oxford: Clarendon Press, 2003).

McIver, Katherine A., *Women, art, and architecture in northern Italy, 1520–1580: negotiating power* (Aldershot: Ashgate, 2006).

Mack, Phyllis, *Visionary women: ecstatic prophecy in seventeenth-century England* (Berkeley and Los Angeles: University of California Press, 1992).

McLaughlin, Mary Martin, 'Creating and recreating communities of women: the case of Corpus Domini, Ferrara', 1406–1452', *Signs*, 14 (1989), 293–321.

MacLean, Gerald, 'On turning Turk, or trying to: national identity in Robert Daborne's *Christian turn'd Turk*', *Explorations in Renaissance Culture*, 29 (2003), 225–52.

Macray, William Dunn, *Annals of the Bodleian Library, Oxford; with a notice of the earlier library of the University*, 2nd edn (Oxford: Oxford University Press, 1890).

McSheffrey, Shannon, *Gender and heresy: women and men in Lollard communities, 1420–1530* (Philadelphia: University of Pennsylvania Press, 1995).

Malieckal, Bindu, '"Wanton irreligious madness": conversion and castration in Massinger's *The renegado*', *Essays in Arts and Sciences*, 31 (2002), 25–43.

Mann, David, *Shakespeare's women: performance and conception* (Cambridge: Cambridge University Press, 2008).

Mannheim, Karl, *Ideology and utopia: an introduction to the sociology of knowledge*, trans. Louis Wirth and Eward Shils (New York: Harcourt, Brace & World, 1936).

Marin, Catherine, *Les rôle des missionaires français en Cochinchine au XVIIe & XVIIIe siècles* (Paris: Archives des Missions Étrangères, 1999).

Marina, Areli, 'From the myth to the margins: the patriarch's piazza at San Pietro di Castello in Venice', *Renaissance Quarterly*, 64 (2011), 353–429.

Martz, Louis L., *The poetry of meditation: a study in English religious literature of the seventeenth century* (New Haven, CT: Yale University Press, 1954).

Masters, Bruce, *Christians and Jews in the Ottoman Arab world* (Cambridge: Cambridge University Press, 2001).

Marx, Karl, *Capital: a critique of political economy*, ed. Friedrich Engels, trans. Samuel Moore and Edward Aveling, 1887, https://www.marxists.org/archive/marx/works/1867-c1/.

Matar, Nabil, '"Turning Turk": conversion to Islam in English Renaissance thought', *Durham University Journal*, 86 (1994), 33–42.

Matar, Nabil, *Islam in Britain, 1558–1685* (Cambridge: Cambridge University Press, 1998).

Matar, Nabil, *Turks, Moors and Englishmen in the age of discovery* (New York: Columbia University Press, 1999).

Matar, Nabil, *Europe through Arab eyes, 1578–1727* (New York: Columbia University Press, 2009).

Mazur, Peter and Abigail Shinn (eds), 'Introduction: conversion narratives in the early modern world', *Journal of Early Modern History*, 17 (2013), 427–36.

Mazur, Peter, *Improbable lives: conversion to Catholicism in early modern Italy*, forthcoming.

Meisel, Anthony C. and M. L. deMastro (eds), *The Rule of Saint Benedict* (New York: Image, 1975).

Melammed, Renée Levine, *Heretics or daughters of Israel? The crypto-Jewish women of Castile* (Oxford: Oxford University Press, 1999).

Melammed, Renée Levine, 'Crypto-Jewish women facing the Spanish Inquisition: transmitting religious practices, beliefs, and attitudes', in Mark D. Meyerson and Edward D. English (eds), *Christians, Muslims, and Jews in medieval and early modern Spain: interaction and cultural change* (Notre Dame, IN: University of Notre Dame Press, 2000), pp. 197–219.

Mendelson, Sara and Patricia Crawford, *Women in early modern England 1550–1720* (Oxford: Clarendon Press, 1998).

Mentz, Steven, 'Towards a blue cultural studies: the sea, maritime culture, and early modern English literature', *Literature Compass*, 6.5 (2009), 997–1013.

Meserve, Margaret, *Empires of Islam in Renaissance historical thought* (Cambridge, MA: Harvard University Press, 2008).

Meyerson, Mark D., 'Aragonese and Catalan Jewish converts at the time of the expulsion', *Jewish History*, 6 (1992), 131–49.

Miller, Alan S. and John P. Hoffman, 'Risk and religion: an explanation of gender differences in religiosity', *Journal for the Scientific Study of Religion*, 34 (1995), 63–75.

Miller, Naomi J. and Naomi Yavneh, 'Early modern children as subjects: gender matters', in Miller and Yavneh (eds), *Gender and early modern constructions of childhood* (Farnham: Ashgate, 2011), pp. 1–14.

Mills, Kenneth and Anthony Grafton (eds), *Conversions: old worlds and new* (Rochester: University of Rochester Press, 2003).

Milner, Matthew, *The senses and the English Reformation* (Farnham: Ashgate, 2011).

Minkov, Anton, *Conversion to Islam in the Balkans: Kisve Bahası petitions and Ottoman social life, 1670–1730* (Leiden: Brill, 2004).

Mistiaen, Veronique, 'Converting to Islam: British women on prayer, peace and prejudice' (11 October 2013). http://www.theguardian.com/world/2013/oct/11/islam-converts-british-women-prejudice.

Molekamp, Femke, *Women and the Bible in early modern England: religious reading and writing* (Oxford: Oxford University Press, 2013).

Molho, Anthony, 'Review of *The corrupting sea*', *Journal of World History*, 13 (2002), 486–92.

Monson, Craig, *Disembodied voices: music and culture in an early modern Italian convent* (Berkeley: University of California Press, 1995).

Morgan, David (ed.), *Religion and material culture: the matter of belief* (London: Routledge, 2010).

Morgan, Sue, 'Rethinking religion in gender history: historiographical and methodological reflections', in Ursula King and Tina Beattie (eds), *Gender, religion and diversity: cross-cultural perspectives* (London: Continuum, 2005), pp. 113-24.

Moroni, Gaetano, *Dizionario di erudizione storcico-ecclesiastica da S. Pietro sino ai Nostri Tempi*, 103 vols (Venice: Tipografia Emilia, 1840-61).

Morrall, Andrew and Melinda Watt (eds), *English embroidery from the Metropolitan Museum of Art, 1580-1700: 'twixt art and nature* (New Haven, CT: Yale University Press, 2008; Published for The Bard Center for Studies in the Decorative Arts, Design, and Culture, New York).

Morrall, Andrew, 'Representations of Adam and Eve in late sixteenth and seventeenth century English embroidery', in Celeste Brusati, Karl A. E. Enenkel, and Walter S. Melion (eds), *The authority of the word: reflecting on image and text in northern Europe, 1400-1700* (Leiden: Brill, 2012), pp. 313-53.

Murray, Molly, *The poetics of conversion in early modern English literature: verse and change from Donne to Dryden* (Cambridge: Cambridge University Press, 2009).

Musacchio, Jacqueline, *The art and ritual of childbirth in Renaissance Italy* (New Haven, CT: Yale University Press, 1999).

Neill, Michael, '"Mulattos," "Blacks," and "Indian Moors": *Othello* and early modern constructions of human difference', *Shakespeare Quarterly*, 49 (1998), 61-74.

Nelson, Benjamin, *The idea of usury: from tribal brotherhood to universal otherhood*, 2nd edn (Chicago: University of Chicago Press, 1969).

Ng, Su Fang, *Literature and the politics of family in seventeenth-century England* (Cambridge: Cambridge University Press, 2007).

Niebrzydowski, Sue, '*Asperges me, Domine, hyssopo*: male voices, female interpretation and the medieval English purification of women after childbirth ceremony', *Early Music*, 39 (2011), 327-33.

Nocentelli, Carmen, *Empires of love: Europe, Asia, and the making of early modern identity* (Philadelphia: University of Pennsylvania Press, 2013).

North, Marcy, *The anonymous Renaissance: cultures of discretion in Tudor-Stuart England* (Chicago: Chicago University Press, 2003).

Oliva, Marilyn, *The convent and the community in late medieval England* (Woodbridge: Boydell & Brewer, 1998).

Oliva, Marilyn, 'Nuns at home: the domesticity of sacred space', in Maryanne Kowaleski and P. J. P. Goldberg (eds), *Medieval domesticity: home, housing and household in medieval England* (Cambridge: Cambridge University Press, 2009), pp. 145-61.

Ortega, Stephen, '"Pleading for help": gender relations and cross-cultural logic in the early modern Mediterranean', *Gender and History*, 20 (2008), 332-48.

Osherow, Michele, *Biblical women's voices in early modern England* (Aldershot: Ashgate, 2009).

Osherow, Michele, 'Mary Sidney's embroidered psalms', *Renaissance Studies*, 29 (2015), 650–70.

Oualdi, M' hamed, 'D' Europe et d'Orient, les approches de l'esclavage des chrétiens en terres d'Islam', *Annales. Histoires et sciences sociales*, 63 (2008), 829–43.

Page, William (ed.), *A History of the County of Buckingham: Volume 1* (London: A. Constable, 1905). British History Online, http://www.british-history.ac.uk/vch/bucks/vol1/pp357-360.

Page, William and J. Horace Round (eds), *A History of the County of Essex: Volume 2* (London: Victoria County History, 1907). British History Online, http://www.british-history.ac.uk/vch/essex/vol2/pp123-125.

Parker, Patricia, *Literary fat ladies: rhetoric, gender, property* (London: Methuen, 1987).

Parker, Rozsika, *The subversive stitch: embroidery and the making of the feminine* (London: Routledge, 1989).

Parr, Anthony, 'Foreign relations in Jacobean England: the Sherley brothers and the "voyage of Persia"', in Jean-Pierre Maquerlot and Michèle Willems (eds), *Travel and drama in Shakespeare's time* (Cambridge: Cambridge University Press, 1996), pp. 14–31.

Parry, Graham, *Trophies of time: English antiquarians of the seventeenth century* (Oxford: Oxford University Press, 1995).

Pearson, Michael N., *Trade, circulation, and flow in the Indian ocean world* (New York: Palgrave Macmillan, 2015).

Pedani, Maria Pia, 'Monasteri agostiniane a Venezia', *Archivio Veneto*, V:125 (1985), 35–78.

Pedani, Maria Pia, 'Veneziani a Costantinopoli alla fine del XVI secolo', *Quaderni di studi arabi*, supplement to 5 (1997), 67–84.

Peirce, Leslie P., *The imperial harem: women and sovereignty in the Ottoman Empire* (Oxford: Oxford University Press, 1993).

Pender, Patricia, *Early modern women's writing and the rhetoric of modesty* (Basingstoke: Palgrave Macmillan, 2012).

Perry, Mary Elizabeth, *Gender and disorder in early modern Seville* (Princeton: Princeton University Press, 1990).

Perry, Mary Elizabeth, 'Behind the veil: Moriscas and the politics of resistance and survival', in Magdalena S. Sanchez and Alain Saint-Saens (eds), *Spanish women in the Golden Age: images and realities* (Westport, CT: Greenwood Press, 1996), pp. 37–53.

Perry, Mary Elizabeth, 'Moriscas and the limits of assimilation', in Mark D. Meyerson and Edward D. English (eds), *Christians, Muslims, and Jews in medieval and early modern Spain: interaction and cultural change* (Notre Dame, IN: University of Notre Dame Press, 2000), p. 274–89.

Perry, Mary Elizabeth, *The handless maiden: Moriscos and the politics of religion in early modern Spain* (Princeton: Princeton University Press, 2005).
Peters, Christine, *Patterns of piety: women, gender and religion in late medieval and Reformation England* (Cambridge: Cambridge University Press, 2003).
Peters, Christine, *Women in early modern Britain, 1450–1640* (New York: Palgrave Macmillan, 2004).
Petrushevsky, I. P., *Islam in Iran*, trans. Hubert Evans (London: Athlone, 1985).
Phan, Peter C., *Missions and catechists: Alexandre de Rhodes and inculturation in seventeenth-century Vietnam* (Maryknoll, NY: Orbis Books, 2005).
Philby, Harry St. John Bridger, *Arabian days: an autobiography* (London: Robert Hale, 1948).
Pilarz, Scott, *Robert Southwell and the mission of literature, 1561–1595: writing reconciliation* (Aldershot: Ashgate, 2004).
Pollard, Alfred W., *A short-title catalogue of books printed in England, Scotland, and Ireland, and of English books printed abroad, 1475–1640*, 2nd edn, revised and enlarged by Katharine F. Panzer, 3 vols (London: Bibliographical Society, 1976–91).
Potter, Lois, 'Pirates and "turning Turk" in Renaissance drama', in Jean-Pierre Maquerlot and Michele Willems (eds), *Travel and drama in Shakespeare's time* (Cambridge: Cambridge University Press, 1996), pp. 124–40.
Povero, Chiara, *Missioni in terra di frontiera: la Controriforma nelle Valli del Pinerolese. Secoli XVI–XVIII* (Rome: Istituto Storico dei Cappuccini, 2006).
Prakash, Om, *Bullion for goods: European and Indian merchants in the Indian Ocean trade, 1500–1800* (New Delhi: Manohar, 2004).
Price, Paola Malpezzi, *Moderata fonte: women and life in sixteenth-century Venice* (Cranbury, NJ: Associated University Presses, 2003).
Pullan, Brian, 'A ship with two rudders: Righetto Marrano and the Venetian Inquisition', *The Historical Journal*, 20 (1977), 25–58.
Pullan, Brian, *The Jews of Europe and the Inquisition of Venice, 1550–1670* (Oxford: Basil Blackwell, 1983).
Pullan, Brian, 'La nuova filantropia nella Venezia cinquecentesca', in Bernard Aikema and Dulcia Meijers (eds), *Nel regno dei poveri: arte e storia dei grandi ospedali veneziani in età moderna 1474–1797* (Venice: Arsenale, 1989), pp. 17–34.
Pullan, Brian, 'Wage earners and the Venetian economy, 1550–1630', in Pullan (ed.), *Crisis and change in the Venetian economy in the sixteenth and seventeenth centuries* (London and New York: Routledge, 2013), pp. 146–74.
Purcell, Nicholas, 'The boundless sea of unlikeness? On defining the Mediterranean', *Mediterranean Historical Review*, 18 (2003), 9–29.
Purkiss, Diane, 'Producing the voice, consuming the body: women prophets of the seventeenth century', in Isobel Grundy and Susan Wiseman (eds), *Women, writing, history 1640–1740* (London: B. T. Batsford, 1992), pp. 139–58.

Purkiss, Diane, *Literature, gender, and politics during the English Civil War* (Cambridge: Cambridge University Press, 2005).

Questier, Michael C., *Conversion, politics and religion in England, 1580–1625* (Cambridge: Cambridge University Press, 1996).

Ramadan, Tariq, *Western Muslims and the future of Islam* (Oxford: Oxford University Press, 2003).

Rambo, Lewis R., *Understanding religious conversion* (New Haven, CT: Yale University Press, 1993).

Rambo, Lewis R., 'Theories of conversion: understanding and interpreting religious change', *Social Compass*, 46 (1999), 259–71.

Rapley, Elizabeth, *A social history of the cloister* (Montreal: McGill-Queen's University Press, 2001).

Resende, Vasco, '"Un homme d'inventions et inconstant": les fidélités politiques d'Anthony Sherley, entre l'ambassade safavide et la diplomatie européenne', in Dejanirah Couto and Rui Manuel Loureiro (eds), *Revisiting Hormuz: Portuguese interactions in the Persian Gulf region in the early modern period* (Wiesbaden: Harrassowitz Verlag, 2008), pp. 235–60.

Rice, Stephen, 'Resonances of Josquin in later *Inviolata* settings', in Katelijne Schiltz and Bonnie J. Blackburn (eds), *Canons and canonic techniques, 14th–16th centuries: theory, practice, and reception history* (Leuven: Peeters, 2007), pp. 197–220.

Rieder, Paula, *On the purification of women: churching in northern France, 1100–1500* (New York: Palgrave Macmillan, 2006).

Robert Mantran, *Istanbul au siècle de Soliman le Magnifique* (Paris: Hachette, 1994).

Robinson, Benedict, *Islam and early modern English literature: the politics of Romance from Spenser to Milton* (New York: Palgrave, 2007).

Rocca, Giancarlo (ed.), *La sostanza dell'effimero: gli abiti degli ordini religiosi in Occidente* (Rome: Edizioni Paoline, 2000).

Roelker, Nancy, 'The appeal of Calvinism to French noblewomen in the sixteenth century', *Journal of Interdisciplinary History*, 2 (1972), 391–418.

Romano, Dennis, *Patricians and popolani: the social foundations of the Venetian Renaissance state* (Baltimore: Johns Hopkins University Press, 1987).

Roper, Lyndal, *Holy household: women and morals in Renaissance Augsburg* (Oxford: Oxford University Press, 1989).

Ross, E. Denison *Sir Anthony Sherley and his Persian adventure* [1933] (London: RoutledgeCurzon, 2005).

Rostenberg, Leona, *The minority press and the English crown: a study in repression, 1558–1625* (Nieuwkoop: B. De Graaf, 1971).

Rothman, Ella-Natalie, 'Between Venice and Istanbul: trans-imperial subjects and cultural mediation in the early modern Mediterranean' (Ph.D. dissertation, University of Michigan, 2006).

Rothman, E. Natalie, 'Becoming Venetian: conversion and transformation in the seventeenth-century Mediterranean', *Mediterranean Historical Review*, 21 (2006), 39–75.

Rothman, E. Natalie, *Brokering empire: trans-imperial subjects between Venice and Istanbul* (Ithaca, NY: Cornell University Press, 2011).

Rubin, Gayle, 'The traffic in women: notes on the "political economy" of sex', in Rayna Reiter (ed.), *Toward an anthropology of women* (New York: Monthly Review Press, 1975), pp. 157–210.

Ryrie, Alec, 'Sleep, waking and dreaming in Protestant piety', in Jessica Martin and Ryrie (eds), *Private and domestic devotion in early modern Britain* (Farnham: Ashgate, 2012), pp. 73–92.

Sacks, David Harris, *The widening gate: Bristol and the Atlantic economy, 1450–1700* (Berkeley: University of California Press, 1991).

Said, Edward, *Orientalism* (London: Vintage, 1978).

Saint-Saëns, Alain and Magdalena Sánchez (eds), *Portraits of Spanish women in the Golden Age: images and realities* (Westport, CT: Greenwood Press, 1996).

Salih, Sarah, *Versions of virginity in late medieval England* (Woodbridge: Boydell & Brewer, 2001).

Salisbury, Joyce E., *Perpetua's passion: the death and memory of a young Roman woman* (New York: Routledge, 1997).

Samuel, Edgar R., 'The trade of the New Christians of Portugal in the seventeenth century', in R. D. Barnett and W. M. Schwab (eds), *The Sephardi heritage, vol. II. The Western Sephardim* (Grendon: Gibraltar Books, 1989), pp. 100–14.

Saraiva, António José, *The Marrano factory: the Portuguese Inquisition and its New Christians 1536–1765*, trans. and augmented by H. P. Salomon and I. S. D. Sassoon (New York: Brill, 2001).

Savory, Roger, *Iran under the Safavids* (Cambridge: Cambridge University Press, 1980).

Scaraffia, Lucetta, *Rinnegati: per una storia dell'identità occidentale* (Rome-Bari: Laterza, 1993).

Scott, James C., *Weapons of the weak: everyday forms of peasant resistance* (New Haven, CT: Yale University Press, 1985).

Scott, Joan W., 'Gender: a useful category of analysis', *American Historical Review*, 91 (1986), 1053–75.

Scott, Joan Wallach, *Gender and the politics of history* (New York: Columbia University Press, 1999).

Scribner, Robert, 'The impact of the Reformation on daily life', in Lyndal Roper (ed.), *Religion and culture in Germany (1400–1800)* (Leiden: Brill, 2001), pp. 275–301.

Sedgwick, Eve Kosofky, *Between men: English literature and male homosocial desire* (New York: Columbia University Press, 1985).

Selby, Dorothy, '"Whose arte disclos'd that plot"', *Country Life* 93 (1943), 1094–6.

Shatzmiller, Maya, 'Marriage, family, and the faith: women's conversion to Islam', *Journal of Family History*, 21 (1996), 235–66.

Shell, Alison, *Catholicism, controversy and the English literary imagination* (Cambridge: Cambridge University Press, 1999).

Shepard, Alexandra, *Meanings of manhood in early modern England* (Oxford: Oxford University Press, 2003).

Shorr, Dorothy C., 'The iconographical development of the presentation in the Temple', *The Art Bulletin*, 28 (1946), 17–32.

Shoulson, Jeffrey S., *Fictions of conversion: Jews, Christians, and cultures of change in early modern England* (Philadelphia: University of Pennsylvania Press, 2013).

Siebenhüner, Kim, 'Conversion, mobility and the Roman Inquisition in Italy around 1600', *Past & Present*, 200 (2008), 5–35.

Sieber, Dominik, *Jesuitische Missionierung, priesterliche Liebe, sakramentale magie: Volkskulturen in Luzern, 1563–1614* (Schwabe: Basel, 2005).

Singh, Jyotsna (ed.), *A companion to the global Renaissance: English literature and culture in the era of expansion* (Oxford: Wiley-Blackwell, 2009).

Skendi, Stavro, 'Crypto-Christianity in the Balkan area under the Ottomans', *Slavic Review*, 26 (1967), 227–46.

Slack, Paul, *Poverty and policy in Tudor and Stuart England* (London and New York: Longman, 1988).

Sluhovsky, Moshe, *Believe not every spirit: possession, mysticism and discernment in early modern Catholicism* (Chicago: University of Chicago Press, 2007).

Smith, Bruce R., *Shakespeare and masculinity* (Oxford: Oxford University Press, 2000).

Smith, Helen, '"Wilt thou not read me, Atheist?": the Bible and conversion', in Kevin Killeen, Helen Smith, and Rachel Willie (eds), *The Oxford Handbook of the Bible in Early Modern England* (Oxford: Oxford University Press, 2015), pp. 350–64.

Smith, Ian, 'White skin, black masks: racial cross-dressing on the early modern stage', *Renaissance drama*, 32 (2003), 33–67.

Smith, Nigel, *Perfection proclaimed: language and literature in English radical religion 1640–1660* (Oxford: Clarendon Press, 1989).

Smith, Nigel, *Literature and revolution in England 1640–1660* (New Haven, CT: Yale University Press, 1994).

Snook, Edith, *Women, reading, and the cultural politics of early modern England* (Aldershot: Ashgate, 2005).

Sperling, Jutta, *Convents and the body politic in late Renaissance Venice* (Chicago: University of Chicago Press, 1999).

Spicer, Joaneath (ed.), *Revealing the African presence in Renaissance Europe* (Baltimore: The Walters Art Museum, 2012).

Spufford, Margaret, 'First steps in literacy: the reading and writing experiences of the humblest seventeenth-century spiritual autobiographers', *Social History*, 4 (1979), 407-35.

Stachniewski, John, *The persecutory imagination: English Puritanism and the literature of religious despair* (Oxford: Clarendon Press, 1991).

Stallybrass, Peter, 'Naming, renaming and unnaming in the Shakespearean quartos and folio', in Andrew Murphy (ed.), *The Renaissance text: theory, editing, textuality* (Manchester: Manchester University Press, 2000), pp. 108-134.

Stark, Rodney, *The rise of Christianity* (New York: HarperCollins, 1996).

Steensgaard, Niels, *The Asian trade revolution of the seventeenth century: the East India companies and the decline of the caravan trade* (Chicago: University of Chicago Press, 1975).

Stern, Philip J., *The company-state: corporate sovereignty and the early modern foundations of the British Empire in India* (Oxford: Oxford University Press, 2012).

Stone, Lawrence, *The family, sex and marriage in England 1500-1800* (London: Weidenfeld & Nicolson, 1977).

Strasser, Ulrike, *State of virginity: gender, religion and politics in an early modern Catholic state* (Ann Arbor: University of Michigan Press, 2004).

Streete, Gail Corrington, *Redeemed bodies: women martyrs in early Christianity* (Louisville, KY: Westminster John Knox press, 2009).

Strocchia, Sharon, 'Naming a nun: spiritual exemplars and corporate identity in Florentine convents', in William J. Connell (ed.), *Society and individual in Renaissance Florence* (Berkeley: University of California Press, 2002), pp. 215-40.

Strocchia, Sharon, *Nuns and nunneries in Renaissance Florence* (Baltimore: Johns Hopkins University Press, 2009).

Subrahmanyam, Sanjay, *Mughals and Franks* (Oxford: Oxford University Press, 2005).

Subrahmanyam, Sanjay, *Three ways to be alien: travails and encounters in the early modern world* (Waltham, MA: Brandeis University Press, 2011).

Suleiman, Yasmin, *Narratives of conversion to Islam in Britain: female perspectives* (Cambridge: Prince Alwaleed Bin Talal Centre for Islamic Studies, University of Cambridge, 2013).

Sweeney, Anne, *Robert Southwell: snow in Arcadia: redrawing the English lyric landscape, 1586-95* (Manchester: Manchester University Press, 2006).

Taglia, Kathryn, 'Delivering a Christian identity: midwives in northern French synodal legislation, c. 1200-1500', in Peter Biller and Joseph Ziegler (eds), *Religion and medicine in the Middle Ages* (York: York Medieval Press, 2001), pp. 77-90.

Tassini, Giuseppe, 'Iscrizioni dell'ex chiesa e monastero del S. Sepolcro in Venezia', *Archivio Veneto*, 17, 18 (1879), 274.

Tawney, R. H., *Religion and the rise of capitalism, a historical study* (New York: Harcourt, Brace & Co, 1926).

Taylor, Bruce, 'The enemy within and without: an anatomy of fear on the Spanish Mediterranean littoral', in William G. Naphy and Penny Roberts (eds), *Fear in early modern society* (Manchester: Manchester University Press, 1997), pp. 78–99.

Teter, Magdalena, 'Jewish conversions to Catholicism in the Polish-Lithuania commonwealth of the seventeenth and eighteenth centuries', *Jewish History*, 17 (2003), 257–83.

Thomas, Keith, 'Women and the Civil War sects' *Past & Present*, 13 (1958), 42–62.

Thompson, Jr., Edward H., 'Beneath the status characteristic: gender variations in religiousness', *Journal for the Scientific Study of Religion*, 30 (1991), 381–94.

Topping, Eva C., 'Patriarchal prejudice and pride in Greek Christianity: some notes on origins', *Journal of Modern Greek Studies*, 1 (1983), 7–17.

Tran, Nhung Tuyet, 'Les Amantes de la Croix: an early modern Vietnamese sisterhood', in Gisèle Bousquet and Nora Taylor (eds), *Le Viêtnam au féminin/Việt Nam: Women's Realities* (Paris: Les Indes Savantes, 2005), pp. 51–66.

Travitsky, Betty S., *Subordination and authorship in early modern England: the case of Elizabeth Cavendish Egerton and her "loose papers"* (Tempe, AZ: Arizona Center for Medieval and Renaissance Studies, 1999).

Trible, Phyllis, *Texts of terror: literary-feminist readings of biblical narratives* (Philadelphia: Fortress Press, 1984).

Tucker, Judith E., 'Rescued from obscurity: contributions and challenges in writing the history of gender in the Middle East and North Africa', in Teresa A. Meade and Merry E. Wiesner-Hanks (eds), *A companion to gender history* (Malden: Blackwell, 2004), pp. 393–412.

Tueller, James B., 'The assimilating Morisco: four families in Valladolid', *Mediterranean Studies*, 7 (1998), 167–77.

Tuttle, Leslie, 'French Jesuits and Indian dreams in seventeenth-century New France', in Ann Marie Plane and Leslie Tuttle (eds), *Dreams, dreamers and visions: the early modern Atlantic world* (Philadelphia: University of Pennsylvania Press, 2013), pp. 166–84.

Urban, Marsha, *Seventeenth-century mother's advice books* (New York & Basingstoke: Palgrave Macmillan, 2006).

Valone, Carolyn, 'Roman matrons as patrons: various views of the cloister wall', in Craig Monson (ed.), *The crannied wall: women, religion and the arts in early modern Europe* (Ann Arbor: University of Michigan Press, 1992), pp. 49–72.

Vaughan, Virginia Mason, *Performing blackness on English stages, 1500–1800* (Cambridge: Cambridge University Press, 2005).

Vaus, David de and Ian McAllister, 'Gender differences in religion: a test of the structural location theory', *American Sociological Review*, 52 (1987), 472–81.

Veinstein, Gilles, 'Sur les conversions à l'Islam dans le Balkans Ottomans avant le XIXe Siecle', *Dimensioni e problemi della ricerca storica* 2 (1996), 153–68.

Villanueva, Joaquín Pérez, Bartolomé Escandell Bonet, and Angel Alcalá (eds), *Historia de la Inquisición en España y América*, 3 vols (Madrid: Biblioteca de Autores Cristianos, 1984–1993).

Vine, Angus, *In defiance of time: antiquarian writing in early modern England* (Oxford: Oxford University Press, 2010).

Vitkus, Daniel, 'Turning Turk in *Othello*: the conversion and damnation of the Moor' *Shakespeare Quarterly*, 48 (1997),145–76.

Vitkus, Daniel J., 'Early modern orientalism: representations of Islam in sixteenth- and seventeenth-century Europe', in David R. Blanks and Michael Frassetto (eds), *Western views of Islam in medieval and early modern Europe: perception of other* (New York: St. Martin's Press, 1999), pp. 207–30.

Vitkus, Daniel, *Turning Turk: English theater and the multicultural Mediterranean, 1570–1630* (New York: Palgrave Macmillan, 2003).

Vitkus, Daniel, 'Adventuring heroes in the Mediterranean: mapping the boundaries of Anglo-Islamic exchange on the early modern stage', *Journal of Medieval and Early Modern Studies*, 37 (2007), 75–95.

Wagner, Peter *Einführung in die gregorianische melodien: ein handbuch der choralwissenshaft*, 2 vols (Fribourg: Universitätsbuchhandlung, 1895).

Wall, Wendy, *The imprint of gender: authorship and publication in the Renaissance* (Ithaca, NY: Cornell University Press, 1993).

Walsham, Alexandra, *Charitable hatred: tolerance and intolerance in England, 1500–1700* (Manchester: Manchester University Press, 2006).

Walter, Tony and Grace Davie, 'The religiosity of women in the modern West', *British Journal of Sociology*, 49 (1998), 640–60.

Ward, Haruko Nawata, *Women religious leaders in Japan's Christian century, 1549–1650* (Farnham: Ashgate, 2009).

Warren, Nancy Bradley, *Spiritual economies: female monasticism in later medieval England* (Philadelphia: University of Pennsylvania Press, 2001).

Warren, Nancy Bradley, 'The ritual for the ordination of nuns' in Miri Rubin, ed. *Medieval Christianity in practice* (Princeton: Princeton University Press, 2009), pp. 318–23.

Watkins, Owen C., *The Puritan experience* (London: Routledge & Kegan Paul, 1972).

Weaver, Elissa, *Convent theater in early modern Italy* (Cambridge: Cambridge University Press, 2002).

Weber, Alison, *Teresa of Avila and the rhetoric of femininity* (Princeton: Princeton University Press, 1996).

Weiss, Gillian, 'Commerce, conversion and French religious identity in the early modern Mediterranean', in Keith Cameron, Mark Greengrass, and Penny Roberts (eds), *The adventure of religious pluralism in early modern France* (Oxford: Peter Lang, 2000), pp. 275–88.

Weiss, Gillian, *Captives and corsairs: France and slavery in the early modern Mediterranean* (Stanford, CA: Stanford University Press, 2011).

White, Michelle, *Henrietta Maria and the English Civil Wars* (Aldershot: Ashgate, 2006).

Wiesehöfer, Josef, *Ancient Persia: from 550 BC to 650 AD*, trans. Azizeh Azodi (London: I.B.Tauris, 1996).

Wiesner, Merry E., 'Luther and women: the death of two Marys', in J. Obelkevich and Lyndal Roper (eds), *Disciplines of faith: studies in religion, politics and patriarchy* (London: Routledge & Kegan Paul, 1987), pp. 295–308.

Wiesner, Merry E., 'Women's response to the Reformation', in R. Po-chia Hsia (ed.), *The German people and the Reformation* (Ithaca, NY: Cornell University Press, 1988), pp. 148–72.

Wiesner, Merry E., *Gender, church and state in early modern Germany* (London: Longman, 1998).

Wiesner-Hanks, Merry E., *Women and gender in early modern Europe*, 3rd edn (Cambridge: Cambridge University Press, 2008).

Wiesner-Hanks, Merry E., *Christianity and sexuality in the early modern world: regulating desire, reforming practice*, 2nd edn (London: Routledge, 2010).

Wilke, Carsten Lorenz, 'Un Judaïsme clandestin dans la France du XVIIe siècle: un rite au rythem de l'imprimerie', in Esther Benbassa (ed.), *Transmission et passages en monde juif* (Paris: Publisud, 1996), pp. 281–311.

Wilson, Adrian, 'The ceremony of childbirth and its interpretation', in Valerie Fildes and Dorothy McLaren (eds), *Women as mothers in pre-industrial society* (London: Routledge, 1990), pp. 68–107.

Wolfe, Michael, *The conversion of Henri IV: politics, power, and religious belief in early modern France* (Cambridge, MA: Harvard University Press, 1993).

Wood, Ellen Meiksins, *The origin of capitalism: a longer view* (London: Verso, 2000).

Woodberry, J. Dudley, 'Conversion in Islam', in H. Newton Malony and Samuel Southard (eds), *Handbook of religious conversion* (Birmingham, AL: Religious Education Press, 1992), pp. 22–40.

Wrightson, Keith, *Earthly necessities: economic lives in early modern Britain* (New Haven, CT: Yale University Press, 2000).

Wyhe, Cordula van (ed.), *Female monasticism in early modern Europe: an interdisciplinary view* (Farnham & Burlington, VT: Ashgate, 2008).

Yardley, Anne Bagnall, *Performing piety: musical culture in medieval English nunneries* (New York: Palgrave Macmillan, 2006).

Yerushalmi, Yosef, 'Professing Jews in post-expulsion Spain and Portugal', in Saul Leiberman (ed.), *Salo Wittmayer Baron Jubilee Volume*, 3 vols (New York: Columbia University Press, 1974).

Zanovello, Giovanni, '"In the Church and in the Chapel": music and devotional spaces in the Florentine church of Santissima Annunziata', *Journal of the American Musicological Society*, 67 (2014), 379–428.

Zarri, Gabriella, 'Living saints: a typology of female sanctity in the early sixteenth century', in Daniel Bornstein and Roberto Rusconi (eds), *Women and religion in medieval and renaissance Italy*, trans. Margery J. Schneider (Chicago: University of Chicago Press, 1996), pp. 219–303.

Zilfi, Madeline C., 'Muslim women in the early modern era', in Suraiya N. Faroqhi (ed.), *The Cambridge history of Turkey, vol. 3: the later Ottoman Empire, 1603-1839* (Cambridge: Cambridge University Press, 2006), pp. 226–55.

Zuliani, Federico, 'The conversion of Christian II of Denmark in Roman Catholic diplomatic literature, 1530-1532' in Lieke Stelling, Harald Hendrix and Todd Richardson (eds), *The turn of the soul: representations of religious conversion in early modern art and literature* (Leiden: Brill, 2012), pp. 39–58.

Županov, Ines G., 'Conversion, illness and possession: Catholic missionary healing in early modern South Asia' in Županov and Caterina Guenzi (eds), *Divins remèdes: médicine et religion en Asie du Sud*, Collection Purushartha, 27 (Paris: École des Hautes Études en Sciences Sociales, 2008), pp. 263–300.

Index

'Abbās I, Shah of Persia 217–18, 221, 223, 224, 226, 227, 230
accounts *see* mission accounts
advice letter 65, 67–9, 70–2
affect 5–6, 11, 66, 71, 107, 110, 114, 120–1, 132, 183, 186, 242
Alexander VI, Pope 151, 166 n. 27
Algiers 22, 30
alumbradas 54
amazons 202, 205
ambassadors 21, 154, 221
Amerindians 260, 273
Anabaptists 171, 268
ancestors, veneration of 197, 207
Andrew, Saint 152
angels 69, 116, 172, 205, 229, 266
angels, cult of the 132
Anglo-Persian relations 216–18, 220–1, 223, 227–8
Anne, mother of Mary 173
anonymity 10, 70, 83, 84–5, 98, 109, 114, 144, 179, 180, 183, 184, 243
Anti-Jewish tropes 43–4
apocalypse 81, 262, 273–4
apostasy 3, 23, 25, 111, 219, 228
architecture 9, 11, 136–7, 138, 144–6, 148, 150–1, 153, 155–62, 162 n. 1, 285
  as statement of identity 160, 162
  see also space
archives 8, 22, 157, 171, 179
Armada, Spanish 114–15
audience 10, 12, 13, 53, 68, 73, 75, 198, 220, 221–2, 230, 241–2, 244, 246, 247, 248, 250, 251, 252, 285–6, 287

Augustine, Saint 7, 23, 112
Augustinian order 153–4, 155, 157, 158, 160
authenticity 5, 24, 237, 261, 265, 272, 283, 287
Avila, Teresa de 54

Balkans 23, 27–8, 29, 30
baptism 26, 42, 43, 49, 51, 56, 177, 197, 201, 202, 204, 206, 218, 227, 264–70, 272, 275–6, 283
  adult 268–9
  avoidance of 25
  by catechists 200
  as cure for possession 206–7, 208
  of dead infants 205
  during childbirth 170
  forced 42, 285
  mass 199, 272–3, 274
  serial 45, 50
Baptists 268, 276–7
'Barebones' parliament 81
Bede 2
bed-trick 13, 240–8, 250, 253
bells 154
Benedictine Order 3, 133, 136, 171
  England 128
  Italy 136, 146, 158
  Spain 134
Bible 3, 82, 86, 87, 89, 91, 92, 96, 106, 112, 113, 118, 147, 187, 268, 270–1
  Abraham and Isaac 116, 118
  Book of Genesis 258, 268
  Book of Rachel 87
  Deuteronomy 87

INDEX

Ethiopian, the 269
Gospel of John 175–6
Gospel of Luke 172–3
Gospel of Matthew 86
Ishmael and Isaac 266
Psalms 91, 262, 273, 274
Romans 264
Samson 118
woman at Canaan 87, 90
woman of Samaria 112
blackface 243, 247, 248
Boccaccio, Giovanni 1, 8, 9, 241
bodies 6, 8–9, 63, 66, 68, 71, 73, 74, 75, 83, 86, 88, 89, 91, 94, 95, 98, 107, 117, 120, 127, 128, 133, 135, 147, 154, 174, 177, 203, 204, 206–9, 211, 215 n. 63, 217, 226, 240, 241, 244–6, 248
   black 249
   black in portraits 259
   racial difference 261
book of hours 176
bride of Christ *see* marriage, mystical
Bristol 276–7
Britain 114, 243, 283
Brome, Richard 247–8, 250
Buddhism 197, 206
bureaucracy 8, 146, 157, 161

Caesar, Julius 243
Calvin, Jean 238
Calvinism 29, 171
Candlemas 169, 170, 171, 172–4, 176, 177, 179, 180, 183, 184
candles 130, 169, 171–3, 177–8, 187, 188
cantus firmus 180, 183–4
capitalism 41, 237, 238–40, 241, 249, 253, 254 n. 5
   see also commerce
Cartwright, William 119, 121
Castile 41, 42, 43, 45, 52, 53, 55
castration 219, 248
catechism 110, 111, 199, 203, 207, 266, 273
catechists
   Vietnam 200, 201, 202, 203, 204, 209
Catholic Reformation 1, 2, 28, 148, 178, 195–6, 200, 205, 210

Catholicism 2, 3, 4, 5, 9, 12, 25, 27, 41, 43, 47, 52, 54, 62–4, 65, 66, 69, 71, 75, 84, 105–6, 109–10, 112, 116, 121, 169, 172, 174, 185, 195–6, 200, 203–4, 211, 237–8, 244, 261, 265, 266, 273
   conversion to 28, 29, 44–5, 51, 54, 55–6, 108, 111, 120–1, 197, 221, 222
   demonology and 209–10
   possession and 205–8
Cecil, Sir Robert 61, 63
Cecil, William 67
celibacy 169, 196, 203–5
   after childbirth 169
Charles I 109, 247
chastity *see* virginity
childbirth 69, 87, 94, 169–71, 173, 177, 180, 184, 187
childhood 68–9, 72, 111
children 3, 23, 25, 26, 27, 28, 30, 31, 43, 48, 65–6, 70–2, 87–92, 93, 96, 110, 111, 113, 122, 170, 219–20, 227, 265, 270
   death of 170
   as proof of masculinity 222–3
Christ 5, 52–3, 68, 73–4, 87, 89, 90–1, 92, 94, 96, 97, 110, 120, 130, 132, 172–4, 186, 228, 262, 263, 269
Christendom 24, 221, 239
Christian II of Denmark 237
Christian Science 27
Christianity 1–2, 3, 4, 5, 7, 10–11, 13, 22, 23–4, 25, 26, 27, 28, 29, 42, 45, 46, 52–3, 54–5, 69, 90, 110, 112, 118, 132, 135, 169, 195–6, 197, 199, 200–4, 206, 207–8, 216–19, 220, 222, 223–4, 227–9, 237–8, 251, 253, 258, 262, 264–5, 266, 267, 268, 271, 273, 276, 285–6, 287
   as global religion 2, 12, 198
churching 9, 12, 169–77, 179–84, 187
circumcision 43, 52, 219, 236, 252–3, 268, 270
Cistercian Order 131, 157
Civil War, the English 81, 87, 89, 98, 259, 261, 268, 275, 276

claustration 29, 135, 137, 138, 285
    perpetual or modest 139
    see also enclosure
clothing 8, 9, 11, 26, 114–15, 127, 130,
    131–2, 133, 134, 135, 140, 142 n.
    36, 173, 177, 259–60
Cluniac Order 157
Cochinchina *see* Vietnam
Cold War 281
collop 219–20
comedy 96, 114, 219–20, 236, 240,
    242, 246, 248, 250, 284–5
commerce 47, 70, 159, 220, 223, 236,
    237, 238–9, 243, 246, 249, 251,
    253, 260, 270
    marriage and 248, 249
    millenarianism and 274
    see also convents, commerce
commodity 236, 239, 246
    child as 70
    Moor as 249, 251
    women as 12–13, 237, 240, 242,
        246, 250
commodity exchange 241
commodity fetishism 237
community 4, 11, 26, 52, 54, 62, 73,
    75, 81–2, 95, 106, 107, 109–10,
    111, 112, 122, 127–9, 132, 135,
    144, 147, 148, 156–7, 176, 180,
    199–200, 264, 265, 267, 271, 273,
    275
    conflict and 152–5, 159, 161
    female 133, 151, 170, 174, 188, 205,
        210, 263, 283
    invisible 157
Conceptionist Order, nuns 130
concubines 28, 201, 204
conduct literature 67, 69, 135, 147,
    223
confessions 2, 3, 7, 10, 43, 106, 109,
    112–13, 114, 171, 185
    personal 26, 46, 91, 95, 97, 111, 134
        199, 208
conformity 44, 50, 54, 63, 67
Confucianism 201
congregation 75, 81–4, 86, 90, 91, 95,
    97–8, 262–3, 268, 269, 270, 272,
    282
conscience 63–4, 121, 122, 259, 264
constancy 110, 162, 202, 228

Constantinople, fall of 158
Conventicle Acts 276
convents 1, 2–3, 9, 11, 54, 127–32,
    134, 136–9, 144–62, 285
    administration 161
    commerce and 138, 150
    cost of construction, 149
    porter 161
    reform of 158, 159, 160–1
    Venetian 139, 144–62
    Vietnam 205
    windows and doors 137–8, 161
    see also enclosure
conversation 52–3, 109, 111, 120, 137,
    139, 140, 224, 264, 267, 274
conversion narrative 7–8, 10, 11, 13,
    28–9, 42, 46, 62, 81–6, 91, 92–3,
    94–5, 97, 117–18, 211, 266,
    282–3
conversion 1–2, 4, 6–7, 10, 11, 21–2,
    23, 28, 32, 64, 69, 74, 82–3, 85–6,
    88, 90, 94, 97, 105–6, 107, 116,
    120–2, 144, 187, 209, 216, 230,
    238, 263, 269
    of ceremonies 9, 171, 271, 272,
        281–2, 283
    of convent buildings 11, 144–62
    cross-cultural 259–60, 262
    forced 131
    as foreign threat 218, 223
    gender and 3, 4, 22–7, 29–31, 48,
        62, 85–6, 89, 108, 110–12, 200,
        217, 229–30, 283–4
    high-profile 200–3, 237
    identity and 216
    intra- and inter-faith 2, 113, 127,
        237, 261–2
    to Islam 4, 218–19, 228, 237, 250,
        251, 281, 283
    of Jews, 42–5, 262, 273–4
    to nun 1, 8, 105, 127–33, 138, 139,
        140
    mass 23, 258, 272–3, 274
    pragmatic 5, 21, 23–4, 237
    race and 267, 269, 276
    serial 5, 22, 45, 110
    sexual temptation 4, 216, 237, 282
    sincere 51, 197, 237
    staged 5–6, 216–17, 218–23, 251–3
    as trick 236–7, 239, 285–7

328

INDEX

volition and 271, 274
see also apostasy; Catholicism; convert; Islam; Judaism; 'turning Turk'
convert, as verb or noun 74
convert, figure of 2, 7, 8, 11, 12, 13, 42–3, 90, 95, 106, 107, 110, 237, 262, 281, 284
  trophy 258, 264, 265, 267, 283
Coptic Orthodox Church 25
copying 71–2, 82–3, 120
Council of Ten 154, 161
Council of Trent 3, 131, 139, 161
counsel 237, 276
Counter Reformation *see* Catholic Reformation
Court of Wards 246
court culture 108, 176, 202–3, 221, 226, 245–6
credibility 10, 13, 51, 53, 241, 259, 262, 264, 272
credit 239, 243, 277
  social 265
  women's 275
Cromwell, Oliver 82, 273–4
crypto-Christians (Crete) 25
crypto-Jews 43, 44, 50
crypto-Muslims 31
cuckoldry 236, 246, 251
Cult of the Mothers 207
Cult of the Princess Liễu Hanh 207
'cultural commuting' 45
Cyrus, Persian king 217

Daborne, Robert 4, 219, 251
dancing 26, 176
Dar al-Harb 27
deathbed 63, 75, 111, 203
debt 239
demons 196–7, 200, 205–10
deportation 277
Descartes, René 241
despair 86, 87, 89, 96, 97, 100 n. 21, 263
despotism, and effeminacy 217
Devil's door 175–6
dialogue 72, 94, 284, 287
difference, production of 7, 9, 262, 281
dilatio 86

disestablishment, Church of England 261
dissenters 268, 269, 272, 275, 276–7
  see also gathered churches
divorce 28
domestic interior 9, 43, 114–18, 136, 259
  see also household religion
Dominican Order 42, 153, 154, 266
Donne, John 63
dowries 22, 131, 133, 138, 140, 148–9, 164 n. 17 and 18, 246
Drake, Francis 265
dreams 87, 90–1, 92, 96, 97, 173–4, 207

East India Company 239
economics 3, 4, 13, 22, 23–4, 25, 29, 30, 50, 146, 148–9, 150, 158–9, 237, 238–40, 253
  gender relations and 241
  marriage and 246, 251
  poetry and 240
  race and 250
ecstatic cults 206
education, women and 25, 43, 53–4, 71, 91, 96, 110, 116, 122, 123 n. 22, 154, 157, 203, 217
Egypt 25
  biblical 263, 270, 273, 276–7
election 81, 90, 97, 159, 262–3, 265, 268, 271, 277
Eliot Tracts, the 273
Elizabeth I 221
embroidery *see* needlework
emotion *see* affect
enclosure 3, 12, 54, 127, 135–40, 144–6, 149, 159, 161, 162, 196, 210, 285
  not observed 137–9
  see also claustration
Enlightenment, the 47, 281, 286–7
Erasmus, Desiderius 54, 96
estate management 111–12, 122, 138, 150
ethnography 52, 239
Eucharist 69, 128, 265
Eugenius IV, Pope 154, 157, 158
eunuchs 30, 217, 219, 247–8, 250, 269

329

Europe 1–3, 10, 27, 41, 45, 46–7, 127, 129, 174, 195–6, 198, 199, 200, 201, 202, 203, 205, 206, 208, 209–10, 211, 216–18, 220–1, 230, 238, 249, 268, 273, 281, 284
European–Asian encounters 4, 195–211, 239
Evangelism 2, 11, 27, 90, 96, 98, 111, 112, 114–15, 116, 119–20, 196, 197, 198, 201, 205
exchange value 236–7, 249–50, 271
excommunication 155
exorcism 172, 200, 206–9
experience, religious 4, 6, 7, 8–9, 10, 23, 24, 31, 32, 69, 106–8, 127–8, 210
experiential religion 81, 82–3, 85, 86–7, 94, 258, 261–2, 268, 272

fabrics 116, 129, 134
  see also needlework
family 10, 22, 27, 30, 31, 43, 62, 63–8, 74–5, 83, 91, 97, 109–11, 112, 118, 129–31, 133, 138–9, 140, 146, 172, 174, 175, 181, 195, 196, 201–2, 207, 246, 273, 275, 286
  conflict with 138, 204, 248, 284
  see also household religion; education, women and
fashion 108, 130, 134, 246
fasting 147, 258, 261, 263
Feast of the Purification of the Virgin see Candlemas
fees, for marriage and churching 181
fertility 84–90, 95, 98, 170
Fifth Monarchy 81, 273
Florence 129, 131, 132
fondatrice 147
Four Palaces Cult see Cult of the Mothers
Fox, Bishop Richard 137
Foxe, John 115, 238
France 22, 25, 27, 31, 47, 51–2, 54, 108–9, 129, 175, 198–9, 205–6, 217, 237, 250
Franciscan Order 133, 134, 137, 151, 157, 158

gambling 92
Garnett, Henry 62, 75, 76, n. 1

gathered churches 7, 11, 13, 81, 82, 83, 86, 88, 89, 95, 98, 258, 261, 262, 268, 269
gender 1, 3–10, 22–3, 29, 31–2, 41–2, 46, 48, 50, 51, 53, 55–6, 61–3, 67, 68–9, 70–2, 75, 80 n. 38, 83–5, 89–95, 97, 98, 107–10, 121–2, 133, 135–6, 187, 210–11, 216–19, 220, 222–4, 229–30, 240–2, 246, 251, 258–9, 261, 281–5, 287
  voice and 287
  see also masculinity; women
genealogy 62, 64
  race and 268
General Tran cult 207
generation 10–11, 23, 26, 43, 46, 61–7, 69–70, 73, 75, 85, 88–90, 92, 94, 95, 98, 239, 248, 268, 286, 287
  see also reproduction
genre 7, 10, 13, 65, 67–8, 70–2, 75, 81, 106, 177, 180, 240, 280 n. 38
Germany 129, 170, 180, 198, 268
Ghent 171, 172
gifts 129, 131, 159
good works 200, 202, 209
gossips' feast 182
grace 13, 82–3, 84, 87–8, 92, 98, 100 n. 21, 261, 263
Great Tew monarchists 275
Grymeston, Elizabeth 69, 72–3
Gunpowder Plot 114–15

habits 9, 11, 13, 127–30, 133–5, 138, 140, 218, 262
  Benedictine 133, 134
  Franciscan 133, 134
habitus 11, 114
Habsburg Empire 284
harem 29, 285–6, 287
Hartlib circle 275
healing 97, 112, 174, 197, 200, 205, 206, 210, 211, 263, 270
hearing 8, 52–3, 82, 88, 105, 112, 133, 157, 133, 188, 201, 202, 218, 225
  see also listeners
Hebrew 116, 271
Henrietta Maria 109
Henry IV of France 237
Henry VIII 238

INDEX

heresy 4, 27, 52, 54, 56, 121, 203, 236, 238
Hexameron 117
Heywood, Thomas 219, 250
Holland 109, 198–9, 269, 272–3
Hollar, Wenceslaus 259–60
'Holy Household' 3
Holy Office *see* Inquisition
Holy Spirit 82, 206, 266
holy water 171, 175, 200, 206, 208
homoeroticism 226, 243
homosociality 225–6, 243–4
hospices 147
hospitals 47, 152, 155, 202
household religion
    Christian 25, 54, 105–7, 110–12, 114, 115, 116–18, 121–2, 136, 201
    Jewish 3, 25, 43–4
    Muslim 25, 26
Huguenots 25, 206, 261, 266–7
humility 71, 84, 128, 130, 133, 135, 139, 144

Iberia 25, 41–6, 48, 54, 56
    see also Portugal; Spain
identities 1–13, 23, 28, 31, 42, 46, 62, 63, 72–3, 82, 84, 93, 95, 106–8, 122, 132, 133–4, 144–5, 188, 216–20, 222–4, 227, 230–1, 238, 242–4, 253, 272–3, 284
    godly 261
    institutional 134–5, 145–6, 151–2, 154, 157–8, 159, 162, 284
    race and 43, 236, 251, 268, 277, 282
    sexual 217, 226
idols 120, 202, 266
Independents 108
indigenous, invention of the 2
individuality 85, 95, 106–7, 134, 197, 158, 262, 264, 266, 267, 276, 283
inheritance 131–2, 246, 248
    see also primogeniture
Inquisition, Spanish 8, 10, 26, 41–7, 49–55
interiority 5, 16 n. 23, 23, 24, 82, 107, 132, 209, 259, 262, 274, 281, 287
Inviolata, integra et casta es Maria (plainchant) 171, 177–87

Ireland 81, 87, 275
Islam 4, 5, 12, 13, 21–3, 25–31, 216–17, 229–30, 239, 246, 266, 281–4
    conversion to Christianity 217–20, 224–5, 227, 229, 237, 251–2, 265, 266
Israelites, identification with 263, 265, 270, 272–4, 276–7
Istanbul 22, 27, 30
Italy 3, 132, 140, 156, 260
    see also convents; Rome; Venice

James VI and I 67, 221
Jerusalem 172, 274
Jessey, Henry 13, 261–4, 268–77
Jesuit College, Rome 63, 110
Jesuits 2, 11, 61–2, 75, 108–9, 121, 195, 197–202, 206–8, 221, 238, 272
    accounts of 196–200, 202, 209
    letters of 198
Jewish law 44
    see also Law of Moses
Josquin *see* Prez, Josquin des
Judaism 3, 4, 7, 10, 22, 25, 27–9, 42–4, 45, 48, 50–6, 246, 252, 268, 269, 273–4, 282
    conversion to Christianity 10
judeoconversos 43
Judíos de señal 43
Junius, Robert 272–3

kadı courts 31
kissing 128, 224, 226
Knox, John 115
Koerbecke, Johann 172–3
Kyd, Thomas 219

language 7, 8, 12, 26, 54, 55, 69, 75, 94, 116, 128, 131, 136, 207, 226, 239, 240, 242–3, 247, 263, 270, 272, 273
Lanzarote 30
Laqueur, Thomas 6
Laud, William, Archbishop 261, 268
Laudianism 121
Law of Grace 52
Law of Moses 52, 54, 172, 173, 187
laypeople 129, 148

INDEX

laywomen 151, 169, 172, 176, 177, 179, 183, 187–8, 196
Lê dynasty 197
League of Cambrai 158–9
Leech, Andrew 221
Leigh, Dorothy 69
Leo X, Pope 159
letters 53, 54, 62, 63, 65, 67–9, 71, 82, 108–10, 154, 198, 272, 273, 275
Levant 27, 45, 239
Levant Company 239
Liber usualis 178
life course
  conversion and 68
  gender and 5, 48, 187
  see also childhood; family; widows
Liot, Carlota 10, 43–5, 47–50, 54–6
listeners, in convents 139
literacy 41, 53–4, 116, 123 n. 22, 273
  see also education
liturgy 177
'living saints' 196
London 61, 174, 236, 258, 265–70, 275–7
  theatre in 239–41, 246
Lucia, Saint, relics of 154–5
Luther, Martin 2–3, 170, 176–7, 238
Lutheranism 169, 171, 187

Madrid 45, 48, 181
Magdalene, Mary 87, 90
manhood *see* masculinity
manuscript circulation 7, 62, 66, 111, 117, 119, 130, 170–1, 177, 179, 185, 186
Marini, Giovanni Filippo 199
maritime turn 239
Marlowe, Christopher 228
marriage 2–3, 22, 27–8, 30, 47, 96, 109, 128, 169, 174, 181, 187, 196, 200–1, 204, 210, 227, 240–3, 245–8, 251–3, 270, 283
  mystical 127, 129–33, 135
  refusal of 204, 214 n. 43
martyrdom 10, 25, 31, 62, 70, 73, 96, 112, 115, 154, 200
Marx, Karl 237, 239
masculinity 4–5, 10, 12, 31, 42, 51, 53, 61–2, 77 n. 10, 83, 89, 92–4, 110, 118, 217–26, 228–31, 241, 244, 251, 282, 284–6
  race and 224, 251
  Mass 121, 138, 173–6, 177, 180, 184, 195, 202
Massah, Dinah *see* Dinah the Black
Massinger, Philip 219, 247
materiality 8–9, 11, 13, 43, 46, 62, 73, 86, 105, 107, 113–22, 127, 131–2, 134, 171, 203, 279
  see also architecture; visual arts
Mediterranean 3, 4, 10, 22–5, 27, 2–32, 218, 284
Mehmet III, Sultan 228
melancholy 76 n. 4, 113, 287
metaphor 61, 64, 66, 69, 70, 73, 94, 96, 110, 117, 133–4, 271
Mexico 129–30, 132
Middleton, Thomas 217, 221–3, 240, 241, 244
midwives 169, 170, 173, 174, 188
millenarians 82, 262, 274–5, 277, 282
miracles 69, 75, 119, 149–50, 173–4, 195–7, 200, 205, 208, 210, 220, 281–2
miscegenation 270
Misericordia 156
misogyny 24, 242, 245
mission accounts 197–9, 205, 272–3
missionaries 2, 4, 8, 12, 27, 195–203, 205–11, 258, 262, 272–3, 274
  see also Jesuits
models *see* patterns
modesty topos 71, 84
Mohammed 228
Monasteries, Dissolution of the 64
monastic complexes, seizure 156
Monica (Mother of Augustine) 112
Montaigne, Michel de 241
Moor, figure of 13, 239, 243, 247–51, 253, 264, 267, 269, 276
Moriscos/as 25–6, 267, 282
Mormonism 27
motets 177–87
mother's legacy (genre) 69–73
motherhood 25, 26, 69–73, 84, 87–92, 94, 96, 98, 110, 169–70, 174, 178–9, 183, 186, 187, 283
  masculine status and 222
Mozart, Wolfgang Amadeus 284–7

Munster uprising 268
music 7, 12, 132, 169, 171–2, 174–88, 284–7, 289 n. 16
see also singing

naming 8, 10, 13, 18, 21, 25, 95, 132, 250, 258, 259, 267, 269–72, 275, 276
Naples 9
narrative 7, 8, 11, 25, 46, 50–1, 83–8, 90, 93–5, 97, 98, 106, 118, 172–3, 211, 237, 264, 266, 270, 281, 282, 283, 287
see also conversion narrative
nationhood 43, 47, 216, 218, 223–4, 226–7, 229–30, 250–1, 261, 263, 265, 266, 268, 272, 274, 277, 284
needlework 9, 107, 113–22
networks 150, 262, 272, 274–5, 277
New Christians 43, 48, 54, 200, 206
New England 262, 273
New World 2, 4, 12, 266, 272
Nguyen dynasty 197
Nixon, Anthony 218, 223
Nonconformists 111, 277
North Africa 22, 45, 237, 239, 288 n. 6
novices 127–9, 132
nun portraits 130, 133
nuns 1, 3, 5, 8–9, 11, 105, 127–40, 146–62, 196, 206, 210
conventual and observant 159
music and 183
Ursuline, possessed 206
wills of 131
see also convents; profession ceremony

occupational identity 21, 83, 116, 283
one-sex model 6
'open reclusion' 138
orientation 49, 117, 120, 121
Orthodox Ottomans 31
Osborne, Francis 67
Ottoman Empire 1, 4, 21, 24–5, 28, 31, 45, 151, 217, 218, 221, 223, 228, 246, 284–5

padroado system 198
paganism 27, 45, 221, 228

pain bénit 175–6
painted cloths 116
paradox 67, 69, 70, 79 n. 35, 84, 144, 209, 259, 272
Parliament of Saints 81
Parsons, Robert 238
partitio 86
paternity 66, 68, 286
patriarchy 3, 4, 66, 71, 106, 107, 118, 122, 136, 176, 240, 245, 246, 253, 273
patronage 51, 110, 121, 138, 146–8, 150, 154–5, 157, 196, 237, 240, 260
patterns (of conversion/devotion) 5, 9, 73, 85–6, 89–90, 97, 196, 211, 259, 262, 263, 271, 283
Paul, Apostle 7, 23, 88, 89–90, 116, 118, 262, 264, 271, 286.
perception 9, 174, 241
performance 5–6, 9, 10, 12, 13, 31, 108, 128, 172, 177, 182–4, 219, 223, 224, 230, 242, 244, 262, 265–6, 284, 286, 287
see also theatre
Persia 12, 217–18, 220–9
Peter, Saint 62, 75, 109
pietà 87
piety 5, 10, 11, 12, 24, 26, 31, 66, 74, 111, 113, 157, 158, 173, 196, 198, 199, 200, 201, 203, 209, 237
pilgrims 110, 137, 154
women 151
piracy 4, 21, 219, 251–2, 284
Pius II, Pope 154
Plato 217
playhouses 5, 239
see also theatre
Pocahontas 267
poems, composed for profession 132
polygyny 201, 222
Portugal 25, 42, 45, 201
possession 12
as evidence for conversion 209
in France 206
in Vietnam 196–7, 205–10
preachers 82–3, 96, 148, 187, 200, 202, 206
pregnancy 22, 69, 87–9, 170, 174, 263

Presbyterianism 108, 268
Presentation of Christ, the 172–3
Prez, Josquin des 180, 182–3, 185–6
primogeniture, disrupted by
    conversion 225, 227
print 2, 7, 11, 13, 62, 67–8, 72, 81, 83,
    86, 105, 108, 114, 117, 119, 121,
    136, 171, 177, 179, 182–3, 185–6,
    198, 217, 250, 265, 269, 271–3,
    275, 282
problem comedy 242, 246
processions 169–77, 179–80, 184
profession ceremony 127–33, 135,
    138–40
promiscuity 246, 250
pronouns 83, 94–5, 97
prophecy 81, 261
prophesy 207, 263
proselytising *see* Evangelism
prostitution 147–8, 240, 247
prostration 128, 133
Protectorate, the 82, 98
Protestantism 1–5, 12, 27, 61, 62, 69,
    75, 81, 83–6, 97, 106–12, 114,
    116–17, 121, 169, 171, 172, 174,
    181, 183, 184–7, 195, 206, 210,
    220–2, 230, 237–9, 258, 261–2,
    265–6, 268, 272–3, 277, 282
Psalters 171–2
public/private divide 5–6, 11–12,
    28–9, 31, 42–4, 53, 96, 107–8,
    111, 113, 122, 135–6, 144, 151,
    155, 158, 160–2, 169, 170, 174–6,
    187, 201, 202, 203, 226, 261, 263,
    265–8, 274, 282–4
purgatory 195, 197, 211
purification *see* churching
Puritanism 82, 85, 112, 114–15
pythonesses 207–10

Quakers 276–7
queer phenomenology 107
Qur'an 26, 228

race 13, 43, 52, 61, 236–7, 239, 243,
    247, 248–9, 250, 258–61, 264,
    267–8, 276, 282–3
    violence and 251, 258, 259, 261,
    263, 264, 268, 276–7
Ralegh, Sir Walter 65–8, 71

rape 204, 242, 245, 247, 251, 253, 258,
    270–1
ravishment 271
    see also rape
reading 2, 7, 8, 12, 13, 44, 73–4, 82,
    87, 96, 106, 110, 111–12, 147,
    195–6, 198–9, 207, 238, 273
    aloud 95, 105, 111–12, 128, 175–6
    gender and 84, 85
recusancy 62–3, 65, 70, 74, 112, 121
Reformation 1–3, 9, 12, 27, 63, 68, 84,
    121, 184, 187, 216, 238, 239, 246,
    265, 268, 281–2, 284
relics 154–5, 173–4, 206
religious turn 282
renegades 22–4, 29–30, 32, 236–7,
    250–1, 284–7
reproduction 13, 81–7, 90, 91, 94,
    96, 98, 107–8, 116, 120, 122,
    169, 171, 181, 219–20, 222, 240,
    261
Restoration, the 275, 276
revelation 7, 68, 107, 262
rhetoric 7, 54, 67, 69, 71, 86, 97, 261
Rhodes, Alexandre de 195, 199,
    201–4, 206–9
ritual 5, 6, 9, 12, 13, 26, 52, 129, 133,
    140, 169–71, 173–7, 183–4, 187,
    206–8, 211, 219, 252, 265, 269,
    282–3, 285
Rome 28, 63

Salome 173
satire 1, 114, 242
Saudi Arabia 281–2
scepticism 210, 241, 262
schism 63–4
scriptures *see* Bible
secret press 62
sectarianism 83, 85, 98, 238, 265
selfhood *see* identity
senses 8–9, 61–2, 82, 121, 133, 229,
    241
separatists 81, 259, 268
    and race 276–7
sermons 42, 44, 53, 54, 97, 105,
    110–12, 130, 134, 177, 187, 202,
    265, 267–8
servants 77 n. 10, 110–11, 113,
    114–15, 116, 219, 229, 263, 284

black 247–9, 258, 260, 271, 275, 276, 277
sexuality 4, 109, 216–17, 222–3, 226, 229, 236–7, 241–51, 253, 271
  economics and 240
shahada 21
Shakespeare, William 224, 239, 241, 242, 246, 251
Sherley brothers 217–18, 220, 223, 226
Shi'ism 217, 232 n. 5
Shinto-Buddhism 206
Sibelius, Caspar 272–3
silkworms 73
sincerity 5–6, 24, 45, 51, 197, 237, 238
singing 128, 171–2, 174–7, 179, 182–4, 287
Sixtus IV, Pope 154
slavery 22, 27, 28, 29–30, 247, 249, 263, 265, 270, 271, 275–7
social status 1, 27, 51–6, 96, 131, 147, 155, 180–1, 224, 230, 237, 239, 241, 246, 258, 261, 263, 277, 283
  see also servants
sodomy 4, 226, 283, 286
soldiers 202, 204, 221–2, 243
soundscape 9, 12, 169, 177–83, 186, 187
  see also music; bells
Southwell, Robert 5, 10, 61–4, 66, 68, 69, 73–5
Soviet Union 282
space 3, 5, 9, 11–12, 29, 31, 43, 114, 120, 128–9, 135, 136, 139–40, 144, 149, 154, 160, 177, 285
  domestic 110, 259, 263
  place and 162
  see also spatial turn
Spain 8, 10, 25–6, 41–56, 110, 114, 131, 132, 136, 139, 221, 250, 265–6, 272, 284
Spanish Match 114
spatial crisis 239
speech acts 6, 7, 91
staggering 105–6, 108
Stephanie, Gottlieb the Younger 284–7
Strabo 221–2

suicide 88, 92, 244, 253
Syrian Christians 29

Taoism 207
taste 8, 82, 225, 229
tears 5, 70–1, 207
temptation 25, 89, 106, 136, 209, 216, 219, 228
Testimony 5, 10, 41–4, 46, 48, 50, 52, 55, 82, 86
theatre 218–19, 236, 239–40, 242, 246, 250, 252, 253, 282, 284, 285–6
  companies 239
Three Palaces Cult *see* Cult of the Mothers
Toledo 44, 45, 48, 53
toleration 67, 198, 227, 229, 273–5
Tonkin *see* Vietnam
Torno 137–8
torture 61, 198, 202, 204, 223, 228, 237
trade *see* commerce
tragedy 96, 244–6
tragicomedy 96, 246
translation 1, 12, 109, 198–9, 221, 271–4
  as conversion 105, 109
Trapnell, Anna 81, 99–100 n. 15, 263, 275
travel 3, 43–5, 48–51, 54, 87, 205, 216, 223, 227, 228–9, 230, 231
  literature 12, 23, 24, 27, 170, 174, 176, 198–9, 217–22, 224, 230, 250–1
tree of life 65, 121
Trent, Council of *see* Council of Trent
trickery 13, 121, 236–8, 240–53
Trinh dynasty 197
Tunis 23, 252
Turk plays 4, 219
turning 1, 69, 97, 105–6, 107, 108, 117, 120, 121, 225, 228, 238, 273
'turning native' 281
'turning Turk' 4, 21, 30, 32, 216–17, 219, 252–3

Unification Church 27
use value 236–7, 249
usury 236–7, 239, 242–3, 248, 249

335

INDEX

Valentinian I, Emperor 27
Valladolid 131, 138, 139, 181
veiling 1, 8, 127–30, 133
Venice 22, 29, 134, 144–62, 181, 185, 220, 247–9
  parishes 146
verse catechism, Chinese 203
versus rapportatus 74
vestition 129
  see also habits; veiling
Vietnam 12, 195–211, 272
violence 21, 25, 42, 73, 89, 113, 118, 204–5, 237, 242, 244, 245, 251, 253, 266, 268, 271, 274, 285–6
virginity 1, 8, 112, 128, 130, 133, 135, 137, 154, 204–5, 220, 240, 247, 248, 285
Virgin Mary 62, 69, 71, 78 n. 20, 87–91, 134, 156, 169, 171–4, 176, 178–9, 200, 203
  as *Hausmutter* 185–7
visible saints 258, 261–2, 265, 277
visions 195
visitation records 129, 134, 137, 139, 187
visual arts 129, 130, 259
  see also materiality

Waldensians 29
widows 28, 43, 49–50, 54, 114, 151–2, 158, 203, 205, 240, 243
  convent foundation and 147–8, 151, 158
Wight, Sarah 13, 81, 258–9, 261–3, 275–6
witnesses 13, 21, 54, 85, 195, 258–9, 261–3, 275
  to nun's conversion 133

women 6, 10, 12, 31, 42, 47, 49–50, 87–9, 95, 113, 116, 169–77, 179, 181, 183–4, 187–8, 237, 240, 243–4, 246, 251, 267, 275, 276
  Afro-Caribbean 283
  conversion and 3, 10, 23–4, 27, 29, 31, 48, 90–1, 106–10, 114, 121–2, 196, 200–4, 273, 283–4
  crypto-Jewish 43
  as miracle workers 196, 210
  as models for devotion 83–4, 258, 261
  Muslim 219, 229, 285
  philanthropy and 147
  political influence 202–3
  possession and 206–10
  recusants 121
  Reformation and 2–3, 9
  religiosity and 24–9, 105–7, 195–6, 259, 263
  religious agency and 9, 107, 112–13, 119, 197, 205, 273, 277
  renegades 23, 29–30
  as spiritual leaders 11, 54, 98, 196, 200–1, 196, 210, 275
  see also Evangelism
  as threat to masculinity 244
  work and 48, 186
  writing and 3, 71–2, 84–5, 98, 106, 117
  unmarried 151
  see also education; nuns
Woodville, Elizabeth 174–6

yellow badge 43

EU authorised representative for GPSR:
Easy Access System Europe, Mustamäe tee 50,
10621 Tallinn, Estonia
gpsr.requests@easproject.com

www.ingramcontent.com/pod-product-compliance
Lightning Source LLC
Chambersburg PA
CBHW071359300426
44114CB00016B/2118